Death and the Afterlife in Ancient Egypt

DEATH AND THE

John H. Taylor

Afterlife in Ancient Egypt

The University of Chicago Press

John H. Taylor is an assistant keeper in the Department of Egyptian Antiquities at the British Museum. He is the author of *Unwrapping a Mummy* and *Egypt and Nubia*.

TO ROXIE WALKER

The University of Chicago Press, Chicago 60637
The British Museum Company Ltd, WC1B 3QQ

First published in 2001 by The British Museum Press
A division of The British Museum Company Ltd
 Published 2001
Printed in Slovenia

10 09 08 07 06 05 04 03 02 01   1 2 3 4 5

ISBN 0-226-79164-5 (paperback)

Designed by Harry Green

HALF-TITLE PAGE Inner coffin of a woman of high status named Henutmehyt. Early 19th Dynasty, about 1250 BC. From Thebes. H. 188 cm. (See fig. 167.)

TITLE PAGE Rituals performed on the day of burial, from the tomb chapel of Nebamun and Ipuky at Thebes, late 18th Dynasty, about 1380 BC. (See fig. 97.)

Cataloging in Publication data are available from the Library of Congress

This book is printed on acid-free paper

Contents

PREFACE

Paintings on the interior of the outer coffin of the priest of Amun Amenemope. Early 22nd Dynasty, about 945–900BC. From Thebes. (See fig. 170.)

We still speak of death as one of the great rites of passage of human existence. Whether we believe that life continues beyond death, or ends at that moment, or whether we admit that we do not know, death is a door through which we must all pass. Every civilisation, ancient and modern, has confronted this issue. A society's attitude to death is one of the factors which enables us both to define its culture and to empathise with its people as individuals, however widely their reactions to death may differ from our own.

Among the peoples of the ancient world, the Egyptians occupy a unique position with regard to their approach to death and the possibility of resurrection, since so much of the evidence that has survived comes from a funerary context. Egyptologists are fortunate in having at their disposal a wealth of evidence which illuminates the thought-processes, theological concepts and attitudes of the ancient Egyptians. Yet in spite of this, we are still some distance from a full understanding of their systems of belief. The surviving texts and images, abundant though they are, all too frequently allude to concepts and narratives that were known to the members of that society, but are not explained for the benefit of a disinterested observer from a quite different culture 3000 years later. It is our duty, then, to tread cautiously as we make our interpretations, taking particular care to avoid straying beyond the limitations of the evidence.

The present book arose in the context of the creation of a new permanent display of the collections of funerary material in the British Museum funded by the Bioanthropology Foundation. It seeks to provide the museum visitor and the general reader with the background information needed to understand the motivating factors and the practicalities of the ancient Egyptians' funerary practices. In the present climate of ultra-specialisation, few, if any, would attempt to write a definitive work on so large a subject – and this has not been my intention. If the chapters which follow serve as a stimulus to the reader to seek further information, they will have achieved their purpose.

It is a pleasure to dedicate this book to Roxie Walker. Thanks to her enthusiasm and dedication, the public display of Egyptian funerary artefacts at the

British Museum has itself been given new life. It is owing in large measure to her generous financial backing and her interest in every aspect of the work that this project has been brought to a successful conclusion. A special word of gratitude is also due to the British Museum Friends, for additional financial support.

For assistance in the preparation of this book, I would also like to thank my colleagues in the Department of Egyptian Antiquities, Vivian Davies, Jeffrey Spencer, Richard Parkinson, Nigel Strudwick and Joyce Filer. Andrew Middleton and Caroline Cartwright of the Department of Scientific Research have shared with me the results of their investigations of ancient timbers, pigments and embalming substances, references to which appear in the text. Kenneth Thomas kindly identified the insect remains illustrated in fig. 53. I wish also to thank the following members of the Department of Conservation, who patiently restored and studied many of the objects illustrated: Rachel Berridge, Karen Birkhölzer, Anne Brodrick, Hayley Bullock, Lorna Butler, Pippa Cruickshank, Vincent Daniels, Jane Foley, Marilyn Hockey, Bridget Leach, Heidi Leseur, Denise Ling, Amelie Mithivier, Jennifer Potter, Monique Pullan, Janet Quinton, Sophie Rowe, Fleur Shearman, David Singleton, Helen Tayler, Wendy Walker, Clare Ward, Fiona Ward and Barbara Wills. Claire Thorne created the admirable reconstructions which appear as figs 73 and 103–6. Thanks are also due to Andrew Boyce for permission to reproduce his drawing of the miniature coffin from Amarna (fig. 166).

Coralie Hepburn and Laura Brockbank ably and patiently edited the text. Finally, a special word of thanks is due to the British Museum's photographers, Lisa Baylis, Christi Graham, Sandra Marshall, Janet Peckham and James Rossiter.

The quotations appearing on pp. 35, 45, 170 and 177 are reproduced from M. Lichtheim, *Ancient Egyptian Literature* (Berkeley, Los Angeles, London), II (1976), 17, 115–6, I (1973), 19, 24. Those on pp. 13, 39–40, 43 and 45 are from R. Parkinson, *Voices from Ancient Egypt* (London, 1991), 133, 134, 142, 145–6. Those on pp. 50–1 and 78 are from C. Andrews, *Egyptian Mummies*, 2nd edn. (London,1998), 12–13. Those on pp. 47 and 215 are from, respectively: M.P. Pearson, *The Archaeology of Death and Burial* (Stroud, 1999), 71, and J. Assmann, 'Death and initiation in the funerary religion of ancient Egypt', in: *Religion and Philosophy in Ancient Egypt* (Yale Egyptological Studies 3, New Haven, 1989), 140.

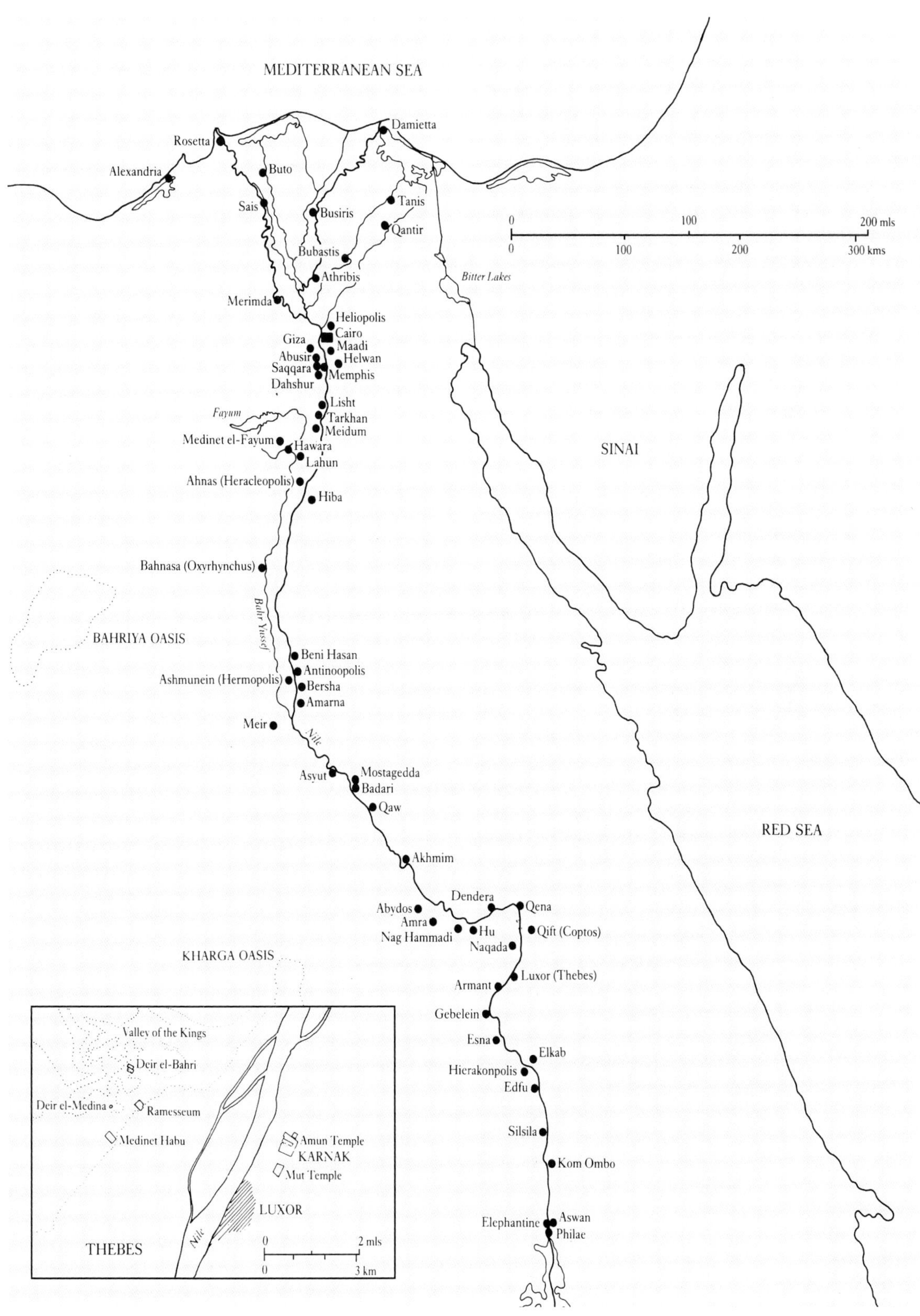
MEDITERRANEAN SEA
Rosetta
Damietta
Alexandria
Buto
Sais
Busiris
Tanis
Qantir
0
100
200 mls
0
100
200
300 kms
Bubastis
Athribis
Bitter Lakes
Merimda
Heliopolis
Cairo
Giza
Maadi
Abusir
Helwan
Saqqara
Memphis
Dahshur
Lisht
Fayum
Tarkhan
Meidum
Medinet el-Fayum
Hawara
Lahun
SINAI
Ahnas (Heracleopolis)
Hiba
Bahnasa (Oxyrhynchus)
Bahr Yussef
BAHRIYA OASIS
Beni Hasan
Antinoopolis
Ashmunein (Hermopolis)
Bersha
Amarna
Meir
Nile
Mostagedda
Asyut
Badari
Qaw
RED SEA
Akhmim
Dendera
Abydos
Qena
Amra
Hu
Qift (Coptos)
Nag Hammadi
Naqada
KHARGA OASIS
Luxor (Thebes)
Armant
Gebelein
Valley of the Kings
Esna
Elkab
Deir el-Bahri
Hierakonpolis
Edfu
Deir el-Medina
Ramesseum
Silsila
Medinet Habu
Amun Temple
KARNAK
Kom Ombo
Mut Temple
LUXOR
Aswan
Elephantine
Philae
Nile
0
2 mls
THEBES
0
3 km

CHAPTER I

Death and Resurrection in Ancient Egyptian Society

1. The sun setting behind the cliffs on the west bank of the Nile, regarded by the Egyptians as the land of the dead.

The civilisation of the ancient Egyptians has fascinated the outside world for more than two thousand years. Their vast technological achievements in raising the pyramids and the myriad temples which stand along the Nile vie for our admiration with the beauty of their painting and sculpture and the extraordinary elegance and complexity of the hieroglyphic script.

The Egyptians' success was founded on the fortunate occupation of a friendly homeland – an environment protected by deserts, sea and turbulent river cataracts, and watered and made endlessly fruitful by the action of the Nile, bringing its annual gift of fertilising silt. Within this world, the Egyptians demonstrated unique organisational talents to create a well-balanced society, in which every man, woman and child knew his place, and confidently expected to enjoy the necessities of life, provided that the king's word was obeyed and the gods contented by offerings in their temples. The stability of their culture over more than four thousand years provided an unrivalled opportunity for the long-term development of strategies to deal with the demands of life and the challenge posed by death. These attitudes were expressed in many ways – in monumental architecture, in sculpture and painting, and in writing. Thanks to the hot, dry climate of Egypt, in which even a scribe's rough memorandum on a scrap of papyrus can survive for millennia without decay, we are able to enter into the minds of the people of the past, to form an understanding of their hopes and fears, and to perceive the ways by which they sought to control their own destinies.

The Egyptians, like the members of other ancient societies, saw their homeland as the centre of the universe. The welfare of Egypt could be assured provided that the cosmos was maintained in order, through performing the will of the gods. If the conditions for perpetuating life on earth could be determined, why should life after death be unattainable? And why should not this new life be an eternal existence, endowed with the best elements of the earthly life and purged of its ills and misfortunes?

It was, then, out of a love of life that the ancient Egyptians derived their firm

belief in a life after death. It is often observed that they appear to have devoted greater efforts and resources to preparing for the afterlife than to creating a convenient environment for the living. Although this impression is partly the result of the history of archaeological investigation in Egypt, there is a degree of truth in it; the houses of the living, even the palaces of the kings, were constructed chiefly of perishable materials such as mud-brick, reeds and wood. The tombs of the dead, for the most part, were made of stone. This reflects the contrast apparent to the minds of the Egyptians, between the transient earthly life, requiring only a temporary dwelling, and the eternal afterlife, for which a permanent setting was needed. The tomb was frequently referred to as the 'house of eternity' and collections of instructions urge the use of stone for its construction. It was, then, a firm belief in an eternal afterlife, rather than an obsession with death itself, which provided the motivation for the building of the pyramids and the spectacular funerary monuments which have drawn visitors to the banks of the Nile from the classical era to the present day.

Attitudes to life and death

In the ancient Egyptians' view of the universe, the continued existence of the world and its inhabitants depended to a large degree on the fulfillment of natural cycles. The rising and setting of the sun, the phases of the moon, the motions of the stars, the annual flooding of the Nile, and the growth and death of plants were perceived as manifestations of potent creative forces and as reassuring signs that the ideal order of familiar things would continue indefinitely. Human life was also viewed as part of the great scheme of creation, and was regarded as cyclical, an experience which, like the endless re-emergence of the sun each dawn, could be expected to repeat itself throughout eternity.

Texts show that the Egyptians perceived an individual human life as a series of changes, beginning at birth and passing via adolescence and maturity to old age and death. Death, however, was regarded not as an end, but merely as a further change, albeit a highly important one, leading forward to another type of existence. Spell 178 of the *Book of the Dead* (see pp. 196–8) describes death as 'the night of going forth to life', emphasising that it was viewed as a transitional state, leading to the afterlife.

Naturally, this conception was the product of many centuries of thought. The relatively sophisticated rationalisation of death which it implies surely did not allay all fears. Hence the Egyptians' attitude to death, as expressed in their writings, was an ambivalent one. From the emotional viewpoint, they feared and abhorred the ending of human life as much as any other society. Tomb inscriptions appeal to the living as 'O you who love life and hate death . . .'. Some texts even deny the occurrence of death: spell 144 in the *Coffin Texts* contains the passages 'You have departed living; you have not departed dead' and 'Rise up to life, for you have not died'. Yet intellectually the Egyptians recognised that death was inevitable; only by passing through it could the afterlife be attained. The majority of funerary texts, therefore, express an acceptance of death, which is usually referred to obliquely or euphemistically. Dying was likened to the arrival of a boat at its harbour; it was the end of one journey but at the same time the beginning of another. The realm of the dead was 'the land that loves silence' or 'the beautiful West'. The west, where the sun set, was regarded as the entrance to the netherworld, and hence as the region of the dead; it was probably for this reason that cemeteries were usually situated on the west bank of the Nile. Death was sometimes rendered more acceptable by emphasising that whereas life is short, the afterlife is eternal:

> As to the time of deeds on earth,
> It is the occurrence of a dream;
> One says: 'Welcome safe and sound,'
> To him who reaches the West.

The two opposing views of death are contrasted in a literary text of the Middle Kingdom, the 'Dialogue between a man tired of life and his *ba*'. In this work, two aspects of the same individual, the physical being and the *ba* (a spiritual entity; see pp. 20–3) deliver different attitudes to death. The *ba* emphasises the painfulness arising from death, which separates a man from his home and deprives him of the light and warmth of the sun. The pessimistic man, on the other hand, welcomes death in a series of poetic similes:

> Death is to me today
> Like a sick man's recovery,
> Like going outside after confinement.
>
> Death is to me today
> Like the scent of myrrh,
> Like sitting under a sail on a windy day.
>
> Death is to me today
> Like a man's longing to see home,
> Having spent many years abroad.

The earliest clear signs of a belief in the survival of death date from the beginning of the fourth millennium BC. During the Badarian and Naqada I–II cultures (*c*. 4400–3200 BC), the corpse was usually laid in an individual pit-grave, which would probably have been covered by a low mound of earth to serve as a protection and a marker. Gifts for the dead were placed with the body (see fig. 2). The essentially practical character of most of the objects provided – ceramic and stone jars of food and drink, maceheads, flint knives and other tools and weapons, cosmetic palettes and personal jewellery – indicate that at this stage the afterlife was regarded as an extension of earthly existence, a state in which the deceased would experience the same needs and require the same comforts as those in life. Already at this formative period it is possible to recognise the fundamental aspects which were to characterise Egyptian funerary practices

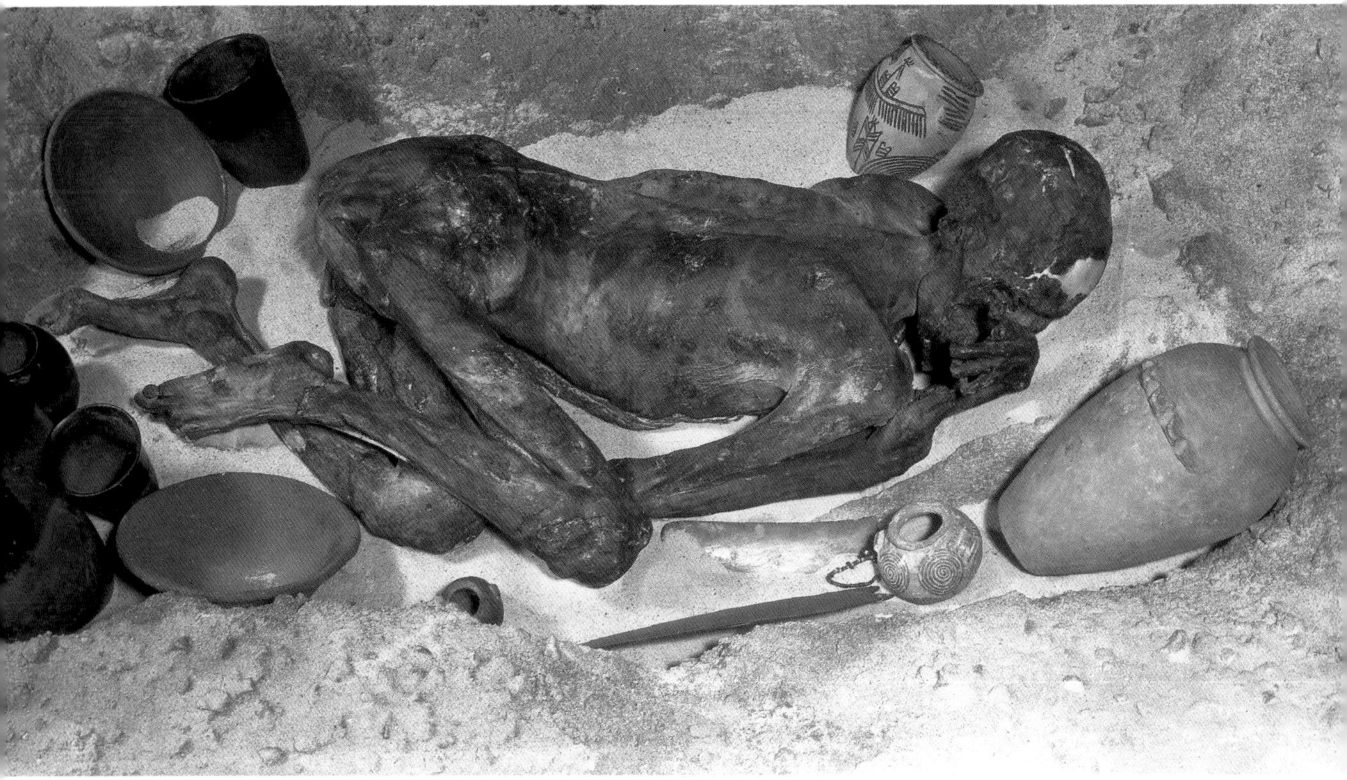

2. Reconstructed burial of an unidentified adult man of the late Predynastic period, about 3400 BC. Around the naturally preserved body are stone and pottery vessels, flint knives, a mudstone palette and beads. From Gebelein. L. of body 163 cm.

3. Sandstone relief showing the Sons of Horus carrying four of the principal modes of human existence, which they present to the deceased Amenemhat. Imsety holds the heart, Hapy the *ba*, Duamutef the *ka* and Qebehsenuef the mummy. The deceased and his wife are depicted again at left. 19th Dynasty, about 1250 BC. From the tomb of Amenemhat (no. 163) at Thebes. 130×42 cm.

throughout the succeeding four millennia. Chief among these were the notions that the deceased required nourishment, and that some form of physical activity was possible (since tools and weapons could not be used without the ability to move, nor could offerings be consumed). Moreover, the provision of objects of amuletic or magical significance, even at this early date, is indicative of a belief that the individual could gain personal access to the supernatural.

The establishment of a unified state with centralised government and a literate bureaucracy, about 3100 BC, coincided with an acceleration in the development of burial practices. Tombs evolved into complex architectural structures, and proper burial ultimately came to involve a series of rituals and the provision of magical texts and images. The underlying notions of posthumous existence evolved throughout many centuries, and the nature of the afterlife came to be formulated within a framework of religious doctrines, texts and practices.

The individual, and personal survival of death

The Egyptians believed that the universe was inhabited by three kinds of beings: the gods, the living and the transfigured dead. Egyptian cosmogonic mythology explains the origins of the principal gods, but does not provide a detailed or coherent account of the creation of humanity. It is clear, however, that man was considered to be a complex being, who could experience immortality in various forms. The Egyptian view of man is evident from many texts, and it is important

to recognise that a simple dualistic division into 'body' and 'soul', as expressed in some other religions, does not reflect the reality of their approach. Writings reveal that the ancient Egyptians perceived man as a composite of physical and non-physical elements. These were termed *kheperu*, 'manifestations', and might be more accurately described as 'aspects' or 'modes' of human existence. The most important of these aspects were the physical body and the heart, and the non-physical entities known as the *ka* and the *ba*. Each of these, together with the name and the shadow, were believed to enshrine some unique quality of the individual. Several texts and artistic representations point to the importance of preserving a range of these aspects in order to survive death. In the tomb of the scribe Amenemhat (18th Dynasty) at Thebes, *ka*, *ba*, corpse (*khat*) and shadow (among others) are mentioned; in a relief from the tomb of another Amenemhat of the following dynasty, the totality of the deceased is represented by his body, his heart, his *ka* and his *ba*, which are shown being presented by divinities to their owner (see fig. 3). Each of these aspects was capable of supporting independently the continued existence of the person after death, but each had to be nurtured and maintained according to its special needs if the afterlife was to be successfully attained. It would not be an exaggeration to say that the whole of the Egyptians' elaborate funerary preparations were devoted to preserving these elements throughout eternity.

The body and the heart

As the most familiar form of human existence, the body was, understandably, held to be of paramount importance. The process of physical development and deterioration which it underwent during the earthly life was regarded as part of a larger cycle of existence, one in which the body would continue to play a part after physical death. Proper disposal of the dead body was a matter of concern to the Egyptians from prehistoric times. As in other pre-literate cultures, it is probable that – initially at least – the manner of its treatment was determined as much by factors of hygiene and control of grief as by notions of preparing for an afterlife. However, by the late fourth millennium BC, the treatment of the body and the deliberate selection of gifts placed in the grave point to developing ideas about human survival beyond death. It is clear that a physical body was considered essential for the deceased's continued existence. Attainment of the afterlife depended on preservation of the body and the ability of the individual members to function, but more importantly the body served as the physical base for the entities known as the *ka* and the *ba*, which required a physical form. Mummification, the preservation of the corpse by artificial methods, arose in response to this need. But ancient Egyptian mummification was not simply the preservation of the body as it had been in life; the aim was to transform the corpse into a new eternal body, a perfect image of the deceased. This body, the *sah*, was not expected to rise up and be physically active after death, since its principal function was to house the *ka* and the *ba*. Only through the survival and union of these aspects of the individual after death could resurrection take place.

The distinction between the earthly body and the transfigured eternal one is apparent in the terminology used. The words *khet* and *iru* ('form' and 'appearance') denoted the body in life. The dead body – either unmummified or embalmed – could be termed *khat*, but specifically appropriate to the embalmed body were the words *tut*, which can mean 'mummy' or, more generally, 'image', and *sah*, denoting a body on which the proper rites of mummification had been performed, fitting it for its special role in the afterlife. The distinctive appearance of the *sah* is well-known from mummies, anthropoid coffins and mummiform statues: the limbs enveloped in brilliant white wrappings, the face and hands of gold, the hair a long tripartite wig, usually coloured blue (see fig. 4). These were attributes which belonged to divinities, and through the processes of mummification they were conferred on the deceased, making him too a divine being. The divine character of this eternal body is emphasised elsewhere in a genre of texts which equate each of the individual parts of the body with a deity:

> My hair is Nun; my face is Ra; my eyes are Hathor; my ears are Wepwawet; my nose is She who presides over her lotus leaf; my lips are Anubis; my molars are Selkis; my incisors are Isis the goddess; my arms are the Ram, the Lord of Mendes . . .

4. Painted wooden figurine representing the mummy of the deceased lying on a bier. The figure forms part of a model of a funerary boat (see fig. 67) and illustrates the idealised appearance of the mummified dead. 12th Dynasty, about 1850 BC. From a tomb at Thebes. L. 18 cm.

The creation of this new, eternal body involved the special treatment of the corpse and involved the use of materials with magical significance. The aims of these treatments, and the procedures used, varied from one period to another, and will be described below, pp. 46–91. Here it should be noted that preservation of the body as in life was not a primary aim.

Special importance was also attached to the heart (see fig. 5), which was regarded as the centre of the individual, both anatomically and emotionally. Medical texts written on papyri show that the heart was believed to be the focal point from which vessels communicated with all parts of the body, and it was the heart, rather than the brain, that was regarded by the Egyptians as the location of the intellect and memory. Here also resided the moral aspect of the individual. Retaining command over one's heart was essential, for not only did it govern the mental processes but it gave control over the bodily faculties in the afterlife. Care was taken to preserve it *in situ* during mummification, and the *Book of the Dead* included several spells to ensure that the deceased should retain his own heart, and that it should not be taken from him or turned against him in the hall of judgement by any of the denizens of the underworld. Spell 26 includes the words:

> I shall have power in my heart, I shall have power in my arms,
> I shall have power in my legs, I shall have power to do whatever
> I desire; my *ba* and my corpse shall not be restrained at the portals
> of the West when I go in or out in peace.

Further magical protection was provided in the tomb via heart amulets and the heart scarab inscribed with appropriate spells from the *Book of the Dead*. Besides ensuring continuity from the living to the resurrected person, the importance of the heart was further manifested in the judgement of the deceased before Osiris, an episode described in detail in spells 30B and 125 of the *Book of the Dead*. Here the symbolic weighing of the heart in the balance against the image of *maat* (the cosmic order) was believed to determine the deceased's worthiness to be admitted into the afterlife (see below, p. 37).

5. Painted wooden pectoral depicting a woman named Mehytkhati in a posture associated with ritual purification. Between her hands she protects her heart, retention of which was regarded as essential if the deceased was to enter the afterlife. 19th Dynasty, about 1250 BC. From Thebes. 10×7.5 cm.

The ka

The most important of the non-physical aspects of man was the *ka*. This word, written with a hieroglyphic symbol representing a pair of upraised human arms, embodied a highly complex notion, which defies direct translation into a single English word or phrase. The nature of the *ka* was multi-faceted and, as the concept changed over time, the Egyptians' use of the term was not consistent.

The relationship of the *ka* with an individual had some of the character of that of a twin or 'double'. It came into existence at a person's birth and was sometimes depicted as an identical copy of the individual. Scenes of the mythological birth of the king show the god Khnum fashioning the child-king and the *ka* simultaneously on a potter's wheel. The *ka* was not a physical counterpart; it had no concrete form, and so it was given substance by representation in the form of a statue which served as its dwelling (see fig. 6). The *ka* also had connotations of reproduction. It is phonetically identical to a common word meaning 'bull', and forms an element of other words of related significance (including 'vagina' and 'to be pregnant'). Through its connection with male potency and the passage of seed from father to child at the moment of conception, the *ka* represented a continuous link with past generations. The Instruction of Ptahhotep expresses this idea in the words: 'He is your son. Your *ka* begot him'. Utterance 600 in the *Pyramid Texts* contains references to the creator god Atum implanting the *ka* within the gods and the king by embracing them. This notion may explain the hieroglyphic sign of the two upraised arms, which perhaps represents the embrace symbolising the contact between one generation and the next.

6. Wooden statue representing the *ka* of King Awibra Hor, from his tomb at Dahshur. The lifesize figure, originally painted and gilded, stands within a shrine and is identified as the ruler's *ka* by the upraised-arms hieroglyph attached to the top of the head. 13th Dynasty, about 1750 BC. H. 170 cm.

The role of the *ka* in funerary beliefs is well attested. Most important is its association with the 'life force' of the individual. It was of course understood that food and drink were essential to life, and the *ka* was intimately connected with sustenance. A fundamental connection between *ka* and food and agriculture is apparent from semantic evidence, since the sound *ka* formed an element of several related words, including 'food' or 'sustenance', 'crops' and 'to plough'. During life, an individual could feed himself, but after death it was no longer possible for the body to receive nourishment. It was by feeding the *ka* that the individual was kept alive. Fulfilling this crucial need was the most important role of the *ka* in the afterlife, for it was the principal mode of existence through which the deceased received nourishment. Tomb inscriptions regularly state that the funerary offerings were 'for the *ka*' of the deceased (see fig. 7). The *ka* could leave the body in the burial chamber, passing into the tomb chapel, where offerings were

7. Nestanebisheru before an offering table in the shape of the *ka* hieroglyph. The chief importance of the *ka* in the cult of the dead lay in the fact that it was the state of existence in which the deceased received sustenance. Food offerings were regularly described as being 'for the *ka*'; here the form of the offering table reflects this. Early 22nd Dynasty, about 930 BC. From the 'Royal Cache' at Deir el-Bahri, Thebes. H. 52 cm.

presented. The *ka* required a physical form to inhabit after death and for this reason the corpse was mummified. To receive nourishment, however, the *ka* needed to leave the body and move to the offering-place. Here, a statue was provided, in which the *ka* resided during the important nourishing process. Statues could be set up in temples as well as in the tomb to enable the person represented to receive a share of the offerings made to the gods. This nourishment did not of course take place in any concrete sense – the *ka* was believed to absorb the life-giving power of food, and this sufficed to keep the individual alive. The *ka* was thus essential for survival in the next world and in order to reach the transfigured state and enter the afterlife the deceased needed to be reunited with his *ka*, which separated from the body at death. Hence the dead were often referred to as 'those who have gone to their *kas*', while the tomb was termed the 'house of the *ka*'.

The ba

The concept of the *ba* (like that of the *ka*) was complex and diverse, and the use of the term changed through time and according to whether it was applied to gods, to the king or to non-royal individuals. As described in texts of the Old Kingdom, the *ba* of a god or of the king encompassed the powers of that entity. It was the vehicle by which they were manifested as individuals, and hence the word is sometimes translated as 'personality' – though this is not an altogether satisfactory interpretation, since even an inanimate thing such as a town or a door had its own *ba*. In these early texts, and in later inscriptions of a non-funerary character, a god or a place could have two or more *bau* (pl.), which embodied the totality of the divine powers or deities associated with them.

But it is in funerary literature from the Middle Kingdom onwards that the concept of the *ba* in relation to the ordinary mortal is most clearly developed. In these texts each individual has his own *ba*-spirit, personified as one of the modes in which he continues to exist after death. Although not a physical being, the *ba* was credited with many human characteristics. It was able to eat, drink, speak and move. The capacity for free and unrestricted movement was in fact the single most important characteristic which the *ba* possessed; it was the means by which the dead were empowered to leave the tomb and to travel. Depictions of the *ba* in tomb-paintings, and on papyri and coffins begin in the New Kingdom and continue to the Roman Period. Doubtless on account of its association with mobility, the form chosen for the representation of the *ba* was that of a bird with a human head, and often with human hands and arms as well (see figs 8–10).

The behaviour of the *ba* is described in many mortuary texts of the New Kingdom and later periods. These sources emphasise its ability to separate from the body at death. While the corpse remained inert in the tomb (which was frequently equated with the netherworld), the *ba* was able to fly away to visit the world of the living, or ascend to the sky to travel with the sun god in his barque. Vignettes from the *Book of the Dead* show the *ba* perched on the façade of the tomb (see fig. 8), and some funerary stelae of the Late Period have a small *ba* figure attached to the top. During these absences from the tomb the *ba* could feed itself, but each night it had to return to the corpse in order to be reunited with its physical 'base' or 'anchor'. Without this periodic contact the deceased would perish. Several spells in the *Book of the Dead* are concerned with the relationship between the *ba* and the corpse, in particular spell 89, 'for letting a *ba* rejoin its corpse in the realm of the dead', which addresses the gods with the words: 'The sacred barque will be joyful and the Great God will proceed in peace when you allow this *ba* of mine to ascend vindicated to the gods . . . May it see my corpse, may it rest on my mummy, which will never be destroyed or perish.' The vignette of this spell shows the *ba* hovering above the mummy, with which it is about to merge (see fig. 10). The papyrus of Nebqed in the Louvre contains a

8. Section of the *Book of the Dead* papyrus of the scribe Any. On the left, Any and his wife Tutu are shown playing the board-game *senet* in the afterlife. To the right they appear again in the form of their *ba*-spirits perched on the façade of the tomb. 19th Dynasty, about 1270 BC. From Thebes. H. 42 cm.

9. Wooden *shabti* figure representing the deceased holding the *ba* in his hand. 18th Dynasty, about 1300 BC. Provenance unknown. H. 30.3 cm.

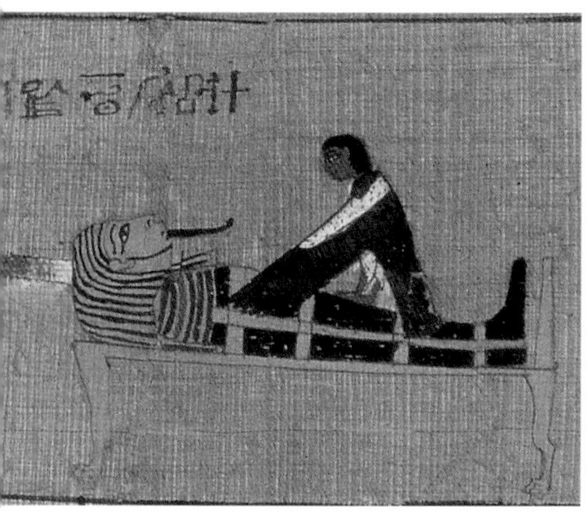

10. The *ba*, depicted as a human-headed bird, rejoins the corpse in the tomb. Vignette from spell 89 of the *Book of the Dead* in the papyrus of the scribe Nakht, late 18th Dynasty, about 1300 BC. From Thebes. H. 35.5 cm.

unique scene in which the *ba* is depicted flying down the shaft of the tomb to the burial chamber in which lies the mummy. This union of *ba* and corpse produced resurrection, just as the uniting of the sun god and Osiris in the underworld each night (see below, p. 29) rejuvenated both gods. On account of this doctrine, it was essential that the corpse should be transformed through mummification into an eternal, perfect body which could be reunited with the *ba*.

The name and the shadow

The preservation of the name (*ren*) was also very important to the survival of death. The name was not simply a means of identifying the owner; it was, just as much as the body, heart, *ba* or *ka*, an essential aspect of his individuality, a medium through which his existence was manifested, distinguishing one person from the multitude. The concept of the name's holding the essence of the being is familiar from many ancient societies besides that of Egypt, and is reflected in the late story in which the goddess Isis obtains influence over the sun god Ra by discovering his secret name. Most ancient Egyptian names embodied a meaning which was believed to have a direct relationship with its owner's wellbeing. Many express the protection or favour of a god or goddess, such as Amenhotep ('Amun is content'). One penalty for the most serious crimes was to have one's name changed from one of good omen to one which would bring misfortune: there are several examples of this practice in the records of the trials of persons implicated in the harem conspiracy against Ramesses III (*c.* 1184–1153 BC), where, for example, the name Ramose ('Ra is the one who gave birth to me') is replaced by 'Ramesedsu ('Ra is the one who hates him').

Since the name was so closely linked with the prosperity of the bearer, survival of death was linked to remembrance of the name. It was necessary for it to be pronounced in the context of the offering ritual (see pp. 94 and 192–3), in order to provide nourishment for the dead. Failing that, funerary texts appealed to anyone who might visit the tomb in future years to pronounce the appropriate formula so as to supply offerings for the dead person; thus, as long as the name was remembered, the dead would continue to live. Many texts emphasise the importance of remembrance as a means of survival after death. The *Instruction of Papyrus Insinger*, a wisdom text of the Graeco-Roman Period, contains the line: 'The renewal of life for the dead is leaving his name on earth behind him.' The Egyptians therefore took great care to ensure that the names of the dead were preserved. They were inscribed prominently on the public parts of the tomb structure, such as the doorways, façade, stelae and funerary cones, and also on coffins, sarcophagi and other objects which were to be sealed up in the burial chamber or storerooms within the tomb. Although these things were not intended to be seen again after the burial, the very presence of the written name on the objects would ensure the owner's survival. The preparation and equipping of a tomb for one's parents, a mark of filial piety, was often recorded as having been done 'in order that his/her name might live'.

Particularly important was the association between the name and the representation of the deceased in the form of a statue or a two-dimensional painted or carved figure. In conceptual terms, name and depiction were complementary, standing in the same relationship to the person depicted. Images of human beings were therefore wherever possible identified by a name, and also often by titles. Placing the name on a statue appropriated the image to the deceased, providing him with a second or substitute body in which to exist and through which to receive offerings. It was also important that the mummy itself should be identified. The name was usually written on the coffin or cartonnage casing, symbolically a substitute for the mummy itself, and often the vehicle for the all-important iconography of the transfigured deceased. In the Graeco-Roman Period, when many mummies were buried without coffins, the name was inscribed on a wooden label attached to the wrappings. This ensured identification after embalming, and delivery to the correct necropolis.

Still more telling is a passage in one of several texts which eulogise the life of the scribe (Papyrus Chester Beatty IV). Here it is stated that although the tomb and the paraphernalia of the mortuary cult may perish, an individual's writings will ensure that his name endures. Obliteration of the written name from any object or monument destroyed its association with the original owner. There are many examples of the intentional destruction of names in tombs and on sarcophagi and statues. This was often done to enable them to be reused for another person (see pp. 180–2), but in some cases the damage appears to have been intended to hinder an individual's prospects of rebirth by destroying one of the modes in which he could exist after death.

The aspect of the individual which had the least clearly defined role was the shadow. It was believed that the shadow, like the *ba*, could be dissociated from the body, so as to move freely and independently. It was occasionally depicted as a silhouette of the deceased emerging from the tomb. Since each body cast a shadow, it was perceived as containing some part of the individuality of the owner. Sometimes, however, the shadow was closely identified with the body itself.

Although the deceased could survive through each of the aspects described above, the ideal was for all of these forms to be perpetuated after death, and to be united. This applied above all to the relationship between the body, the *ba* and the *ka*. To make certain of the union of these aspects after death was the principal purpose of the funerary rituals, and the desired state which would result is expressed in the following text from the *Book of the Dead*: 'may his heart be sweet, may it join his body, his *ba*-spirit to his body . . . Twice purification to his *ka*-spirit, to his *ba*-spirit, to his corpse, to his shade, to his mummy; he shall never perish before the lord of the sacred land'.

Mythologies of rebirth

The desire to survive death is of course a hope common to most human societies, and it is usually placed in a framework of religious belief. In this, ancient Egyptian culture was no exception. Although belief in an afterlife undoubtedly arose before the invention of writing, ways of expressing the belief in mythological terms – and thus rationalising it – developed during the dynastic era. Egyptian writings enable us to trace the evolution of a succession of different concepts of human survival after death. Each major concept was first articulated for the king, and was originally reserved for his use alone, subsequently becoming available to non-royal persons. It was highly characteristic of Egyptian culture, however, that the emergence of a new concept did not necessarily displace that held previously. Different beliefs were maintained side by side for centuries and, although some rationalisation occurred, the divergent doctrines were never fully synthesised.

The earliest written sources for the nature of the Egyptians' beliefs about the afterlife are contained in the *Pyramid Texts* of the late Old Kingdom (see pp. 193–4). This great collection of spells draws on different traditions and contains several divergent views as to the king's afterlife. The earliest concept of the afterlife of the king was that he would ascend to the sky, joining the circumpolar stars, regarded by the Egyptians as eternal since they are always visible from Egypt. While this idea was still prominent in the *Pyramid Texts*, it was later superseded by other myths, centering on the gods Osiris and Ra. Both these gods were endowed with the power of creation, being associated with the cycles of the sun, the Nile and vegetation. Both, too, were perceived as having triumphed over death, and hence offered excellent models for mortals to aspire to. Their respective mythologies thus provided an explanation for the resurrection of man as well as a means of describing the world in which the dead would dwell. In time, these systems of belief became applied not only to the king, but to his subjects as well, giving everyone an equal chance of reaching the afterlife.

Osiris

Osiris is chiefly famous as the central figure of a cycle of myths describing his death and resurrection. He was also, however, an important figure in one of the main Egyptian accounts of creation, associated with the cult centre of Heliopolis. This story describes how from a primeval watery chaos (Nun) there emerged a mound of earth on which appeared the god Atum. Atum created first atmosphere and moisture (the god Shu and the goddess Tefnut), and they in turn produced the god Geb (earth) and the goddess Nut (sky). The offspring of this pair were the gods Osiris and Seth, and the goddesses Isis and Nephthys. The story of Osiris' subsequent murder and resurrection is alluded to countless times in texts and images from the Old Kingdom onward, but the most complete account of the myth is that recorded by the Greek author Plutarch in the second century AD. In Plutarch's version Osiris figures as a king of Egypt in the remote past, who civilised his people, teaching them agriculture and establishing laws. His jealous brother Seth, seeking to destroy Osiris, invited him to a feast, at which a beautiful chest was offered to the guest who would fit perfectly inside it. When Osiris climbed in, Seth's confederates sealed the lid and threw the chest into the Nile, and Osiris was drowned. After a long search, Isis, the sister and wife of Osiris, recovered her husband's body, only for it to fall into the hands of Seth, who cut it into fourteen

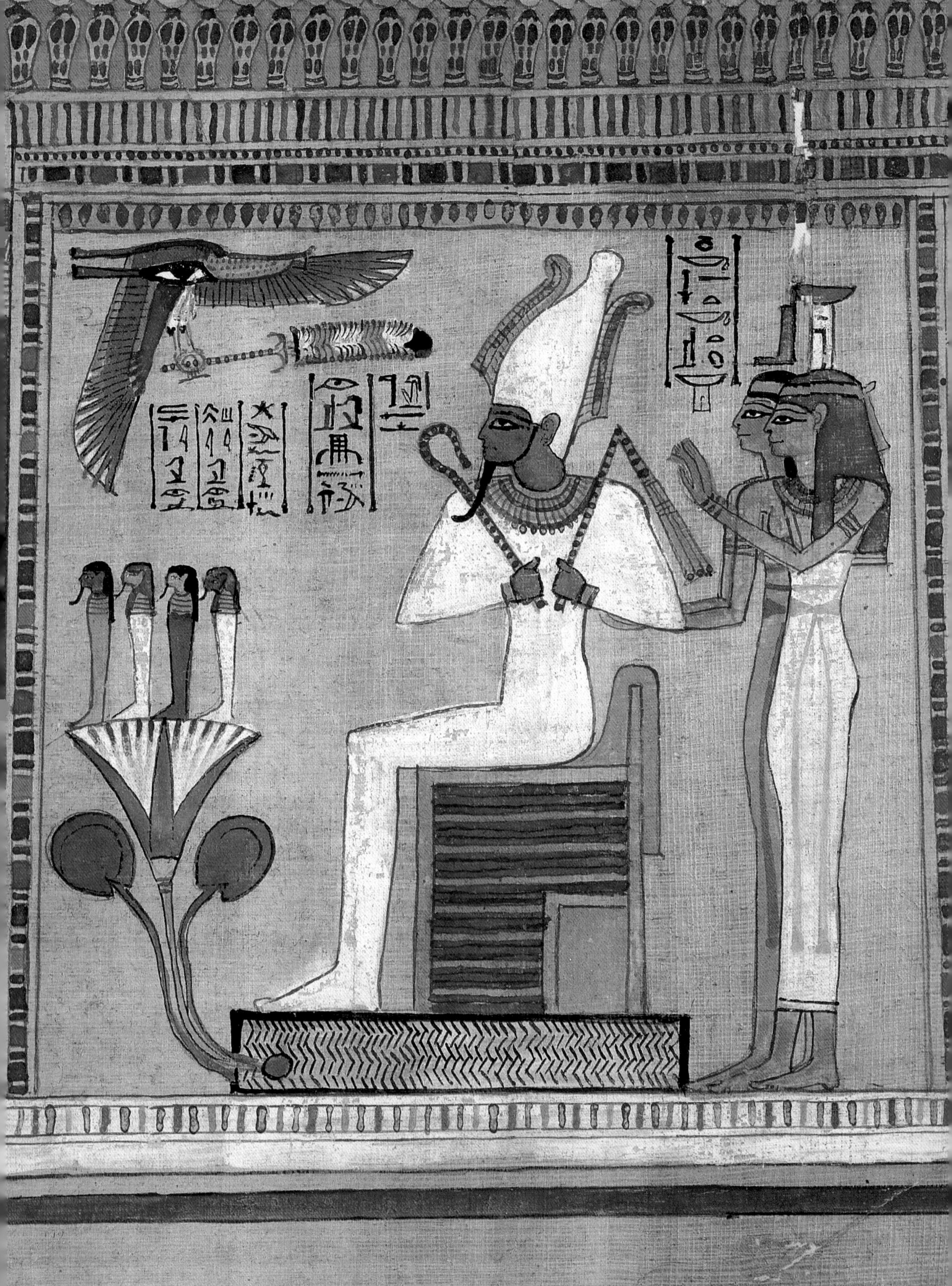

pieces which he scattered throughout Egypt. Isis and Nephthys again searched and retrieved every part of Osiris' body with the exception of the phallus. The jackal-headed Anubis mummified the corpse, and Osiris was resurrected by Isis and Nephthys. Osiris then became the ruler of the realm of the dead, while his son Horus, having successfully challenged the usurper Seth for the kingship of Egypt, avenged his father's murder and assumed his place on the throne.

11. The god Osiris, ruler of the underworld, enthroned under a canopy. He is attended by the goddesses Isis and Nephthys, and before him on a lotus flower stand the four Sons of Horus. The royal sceptres held by Osiris symbolise his kingly status, and the green colour of his skin reflects his associations with the new growth of plants, regarded by the Egyptians as a metaphor for rebirth. From the papyrus of Hunefer, early 19th Dynasty, about 1280 BC. From Thebes. H. of sheet 40 cm.

Plutarch's narrative is a relatively late synthesis made up of elements which originally formed parts of other myths, notably the conflict between Horus and Seth, with its important links with kingship and the royal succession. These earlier myths included episodes which are frequently alluded to in funerary texts and iconography, such as the injuring and restoration of the *wedjat*, the eye of Horus, which later became a powerful protective amulet. According to another element of the myth, Horus and Seth came before a tribunal of the gods which resulted in the vindication of Horus, a scenario which was reflected in the judgement before Osiris which every dead man and woman had to undergo in order to enter the next life (see below, pp. 36–7).

In some of the Old Kingdom *Pyramid Texts* (5th to 6th Dynasties) the dead king is identified with Osiris, and thereby was believed to experience rebirth just as the murdered god had done. In the First Intermediate Period, this path to new life became available to all Egyptians, each of whom could be individually identified with Osiris. From this time onwards the names of the dead were regularly preceded by that of Osiris, so that 'the Osiris N' became synonymous with 'the deceased N', who could then experience resurrection. Many features of the burial ritual and the tomb equipment promote this assimilation. The deceased in his coffin takes the place of the mummified Osiris and is addressed in texts as Osiris; he receives the protection of Nut, Isis, Nephthys and Anubis – all deities who played important roles in the Osirian myth.

The principal centre of the cult of Osiris was at the city of Abydos, traditionally identified as the god's burial-place. This site had been important since the formative years of the Egyptian state (before 3000 BC), when the earliest kings were buried there. The original local deity of Abydos was the jackal-god Khentimentiu, the 'Foremost of the Westerners' (i.e. the dead), but his identity became absorbed by Osiris as the cult of the latter acquired ever greater prominence. This amalgamation resulted in the name Khentimentiu being applied to Osiris as an epithet, which appropriately reflected his later role as ruler over the dead. Osiris' cult-centre at Abydos became a major place of pilgrimage. Those who could make the journey paid at least one visit there during their lifetime, and this formed an element of the ideal funeral ceremonies after death. This journey is shown in tomb paintings, and model boats to convey the dead to Abydos were provided in tombs.

Osiris was represented as a mummiform figure, dressed in a white linen shroud, and provided with royal crook and flail sceptres, and distinctive crowns (see fig. 11). In several images, both two-dimensional and in the round, he also appears with erect phallus (miraculously restored by Isis after the reconstitution of Osiris' body). This signifies the notion that the fertility of the land was also closely linked with the resurrection of the god. Osiris also had links with the inundation of the Nile and the life-cycle of vegetation. In this manner he symbolised the capacity of the earth to bring forth new life. This was another metaphor for resurrection and was manifested in art, Osiris often being depicted with green flesh. By assimilation, the deceased is sometimes also shown thus, particularly on coffins of the Late Period.

The sun god

According to one of the main Egyptian creation myths, the sun god was the creator of the universe and the originator of all life. He is most familiar under

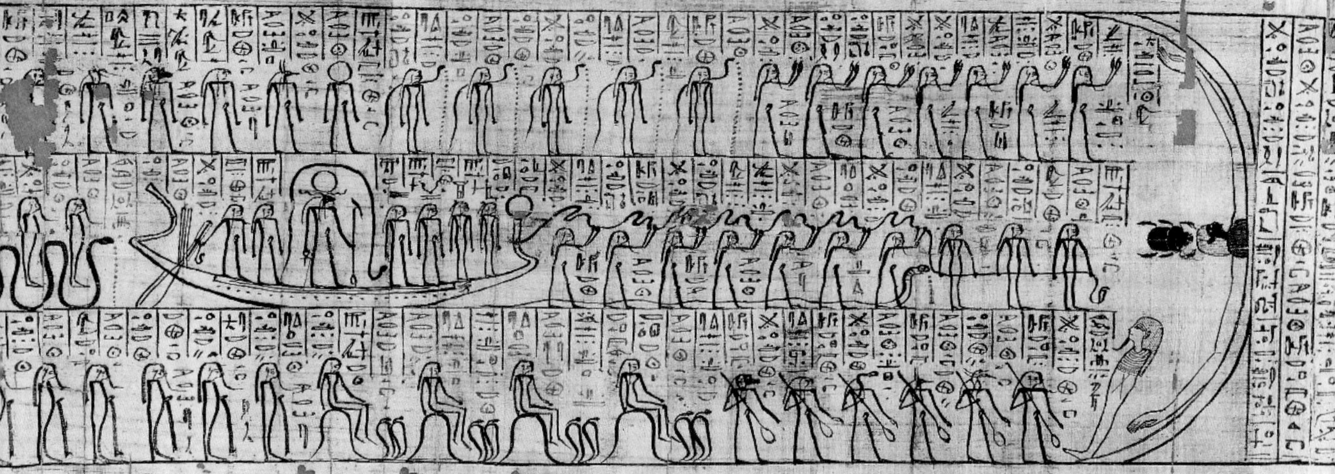

12. Scene from the *Book of Amduat*, which describes and illustrates the nocturnal journey of the sun god through the *Duat* or underworld. The god, in his ram-headed nocturnal form, stands within a barque, which is towed along a waterway towards the eastern horizon. Here, in the guise of the scarab beetle Khepri, he projects the solar disc into the sky, while his corpse (lower right) remains in the underworld. From the papyrus of the priest of Amun Ankhefenkhons. Late 21st or early 22nd Dynasty, about 970–900 BC. From Thebes. H. 20 cm.

the name Ra, essentially the daytime sun, but could also be manifested under many other names and guises. The newly-risen sun at dawn was known as Khepri, represented as a scarab beetle propelling the solar disc into the sky; the evening sun was equated with Atum, the creator god in one of the main cosmogonic myths.

As noted above, the Egyptians saw the act of creation as cyclical. Hence rebirth was brought about by the same god who originally created the universe and life. The endless cycle of sunrise and sunset was perceived as a powerful metaphor for continuous rebirth after death, and the daily journey of the sun became the model for eternal existence. The *Books of the Underworld*, inscribed in the royal tombs of the New Kingdom, describe how each evening the sun was believed to enter the subterranean netherworld, or *Duat* (see fig. 12). Here he travelled by barque during the twelve hours of night along a river which passed through a series of underground caverns, populated by divine beings both amiable and hostile, and also by the dead, who awoke to new life as the sun god's rays shone on them (see below, pp. 33–4). His journey was opposed by the forces of chaos, embodied in a giant serpent named Apep, who had to be combatted and

13. A symbolic depiction of the sunrise. In its complete state, the scene showed two symmetrical images of the Theban priest Amenemope offering to seated gods. In the centre stands Nun (personification of the primeval watery abyss) transferring the barque of the sun at dawn into the arms of the sky goddess Nut. From a fragment of the coffin of Amenemope. End of 21st or beginning of 22nd Dynasty, about 950–900 BC. From Thebes. H. 47.7 cm.

overthrown each night before the eastern horizon was reached. The crucial episode in the journey took place in the fifth hour of the night, when the sun god encountered his own corpse, equated with the mummified Osiris, and the two were united. The sun god's power resurrected Osiris, and the sun god, by merging with his corpse, was himself rejuvenated, releasing the creative forces necessary for the continuation of life. This union served as the model for the joining of *ba* and mummy, by which ordinary mortals were rejuvenated (see above, pp. 21–3). Hence funerary texts emphasise the close association of the deceased with both Osiris and the sun god. This relationship becomes particularly marked in funerary texts and images from the 19th Dynasty onwards.

Each new day therefore was a repetition of the 'first time', the original creation of the universe, and, consistent with this idea, the sun god was himself regarded as emerging from the earth as a newborn child at dawn (see fig. 13). The sun at dawn was Khepri, and hence the scarab became a symbol of regeneration.

Rebirth was thus seen as being dependent on association with the sun god (see fig. 14). In the case of the dead king this association was particularly close. In many of the spells of the *Pyramid Texts* the dead king spends his afterlife travelling

14. The sun god, in the form of a winged solar disc with human arms, holds the sign of life (*ankh*) to the face of the mummy. Above is the sky in the form of the goddess Nut, and beneath the mummy's bier are the four canopic jars. Painting on the foot of the inner coffin of the priest Hor. 25th Dynasty, about 700–680 BC. From Thebes. H. of coffin 180 cm.

with the sun god across the sky, and even at this early period a direct identification of the king with the sun god was made: 'Your body is [King] Pepy, O Ra; your body will be nourished as Pepy, O Ra'. The identification of the king with the god himself was expressed even more forcibly in the later *Books of the Underworld*. From the Middle Kingdom, however, this afterlife with the sun god (like that with Osiris) was accessible to the king's subjects as well, as many passages from the *Coffin Texts* and the *Book of the Dead* show. The dead travelled with Ra in his barque, partaking of his resurrection, and fighting his foes in the underworld. For this reason, the deceased is often represented spearing the Apep serpent on behalf of Ra. In characteristic Egyptian fashion, this concept was held alongside that already mentioned, in which the dead were resurrected by the life-giving rays of the sun as the god passed through the realm of the dead each night.

Achieving immortality: becoming *akh*

The survival of the dead depended, in broad terms, on their entering a new state of existence, in which they were integrated into the cyclical patterns of the universe. Since gods such as Ra and Osiris were immortal and were repeatedly rejuvenated, the deceased, through a close identification with them, could hope to partake of endless rebirths as well. This cyclical eternity, manifested in the world through the motions of sun and the changes of the seasons, was denoted by the word *neheh*. This was differentiated from *djet*, eternity, in which time was viewed as linear, carrying the implication of a static, unchanging existence: this was the continuous afterlife in the tomb, in which the dead were nourished and provisioned for ever by the mortuary cult and by the magical power of texts and images. The dead could survive in both ways as long as the universe endured, and this is reflected in two common but alternative names for the tomb: *hut en neheh* and *per-djet*, both of which can be translated as 'house of eternity'.

Attaining the afterlife depended on the deceased's survival through the various modes of existence discussed above (*ka*, *ba*, body, name, etc.). Proper preparation had therefore to be made. A secure burial place was needed for the body, which ideally should be preserved by mummification to enable the *ba* to be reunited with it. A chapel or offering place was needed, where the rituals to sustain the *ka* could be performed. The deceased also required access to special powers and knowledge to pass safely through hazards and to enjoy a comfortable existence in the netherworld. All these needs were satisfied by a *qerset neferet*, or 'a good [proper] burial', the various elements of which will be examined in the following chapters.

The state of existence which the deceased aimed to reach in the beyond was called *akh*. This word, written with the hieroglyphic sign of a crested ibis, is used to denote the individual dead in the netherworld, and also their state of being. In this context it can be translated as 'transfigured being'. But the term *akh* is also used outside the context of non-royal funerary literature. In secular texts it has connotations of 'effectiveness'; in religious texts it is an attribute of gods who are closely associated with the powers of creation and regeneration. Atum, Ra,

Nut, Osiris, Isis and Horus were all described as *akh* and had the power to confer the status of *akh* on others. The deceased, by becoming *akh*, acquired 'effectiveness' as well as some of the qualities of those gods, not becoming their full equals, but being identified with them and endowed with a creative energy akin to that employed in the creation of the world. This gave them the means to arise from the inertia of death to new life (as the inert state of the primordial chaos was transformed into the ordered, created universe capable of supporting life). *Akh* also had associations with light and luminosity, perhaps also to be understood in the context of the origin of the universe, which is linked in Egyptian thought with the notion of the creation of light. To be *akh*, then, was to be an effective spirit, enjoying the qualities and prerogatives of gods, having the capacity for eternal life and being capable of influencing other beings – as seen in the letters to the dead (see below, pp. 42–3).

Akh is different to the other 'modes' of human existence. Unlike the *ka*, *ba* and name, which are aspects of the individual, *akh* is the state achieved only after death, and after a successful passage through tests and dangers. Not all the dead were imagined as *akhu*. Those who had lived wicked lives were denied the blessed state, and were condemned to a second death, total extinction, after suffering horrifying punishments. To help the deceased to become *akh* was the primary aim of all the funerary preparations, and hence funerary texts were collectively called *sakhu*, 'that which makes [a person] *akh*' (see p. 193).

The realm of the dead

The reaching of the transfigured state, the 'afterlife', was conceived in terms of a 'physical passage', a journey along prescribed paths which the deceased had to take. Burial in the tomb was the prelude to this journey; the procession to the tomb on the day of burial is paraphrased as letting 'the god [the deceased] ascend to his horizon'. The horizon, as the place where the sun rises and sets, was of course endowed with regenerative significance, and denoted the goal of the transfigured dead.

The actual location and topography of the world of the dead, as described in texts of different periods, was subject to numerous variations. The *Pyramid Texts* of the Old Kingdom situate it in the northern sky, and the dead king was to reach it by ascending to the heavens, after which he would live among the gods, accompanying the sun god Ra. The *Coffin Texts*, formulated in the period after the Old Kingdom, present a more developed concept. The celestial realm of the sun god is now complemented by an earth-bound underworld, which was the kingdom of Osiris. In order to reach this realm safely, the dead had to possess special knowledge: the names of the denizens of the underworld, the locations of paths, waterways and gates, and the necessary words and acts to pass these. This information was included in the *Coffin Texts*, into which were incorporated compositions now known as 'guides to the hereafter', which provided the inexperienced deceased with the information required to lead him safely to his destination. One of the

15. Map of the routes to the netherworld from the *Book of Two Ways*, a painting on the floor of the outer coffin of the physician Gua. The diagram and its accompanying text served as a guidebook to inform the deceased about the topography of the hereafter and to equip him with the knowledge to behave correctly when encountering its inhabitants. 12th Dynasty, about 1850 BC. From Deir el-Bersha. L. of coffin 260.5 cm.

earliest of these compositions is the *Book of Two Ways*, inscribed chiefly on coffins of the Middle Kingdom (see fig. 15). This gives precise details of the paths leading to the hereafter, one of which consists of earth, the other of water, and details are included of important features of the region; the deceased must negotiate mounds and fiery lakes, and pass hostile demons whose names he must know in order to pacify them. This text is accompanied by a large graphic element, in effect a 'map', painted on the floor of the coffin, on which the deceased can walk. Funerary literature, images and amulets provided the deceased with special knowledge and magical aid to overcome obstacles to reaching the afterlife safely.

The most detailed sources which actually describe the realm of the dead are the *Books of the Underworld*, composed in the New Kingdom. These describe the nightly journey of the sun god through the subterranean underworld as he makes his way from the western to the eastern horizon. According to the *Book of Amduat* and *Book of Gates*, the underworld was divided into twelve regions, each of which corresponded to one hour in the sun god's journey, and each of which was occupied by the dead. As hour succeeded hour, the sun god's barque, sailing on the underworld river, entered cavern after cavern. As his rays illuminated the cavern they brought new life to the dead, who until that moment had lain inert in their

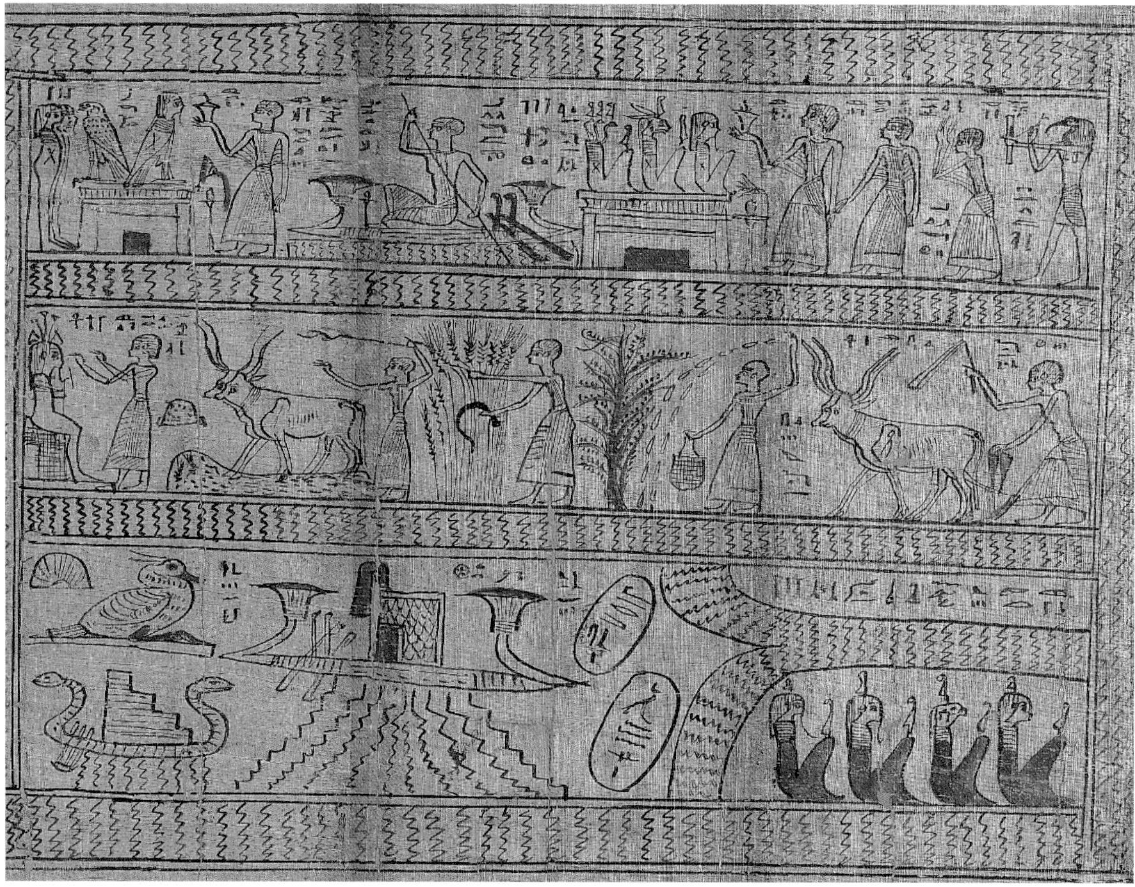

16. Representation of agriculture in the afterlife, the vignette of spell 110 of the *Book of the Dead*. The ideal state of existence, which the dead achieved after becoming *akh*, included an agricultural paradise known as the Field of Reeds. From the papyrus of Kerqun. Ptolemaic Period, 305–30 BC. From Thebes. H. 38.5 cm.

coffins. They would awake, throw off their mummy-wrappings, and enjoy a complete human lifespan during the single hour of the night when they were in the presence of Ra. The dead were judged and rewarded according to their behaviour. The righteous cultivated and received offerings. The wicked received their punishments. At the end of the hour the god sailed on and the great doors slammed shut; the dead would lament his departure and return to their sleep until the next night.

Once they have reached the eternal realm, the transfigured dead are represented either as *ba*s or as humans. They may be depicted in the iconography of the *sah*: white-clad, with golden skin, the iconography in fact familiar from mummies and mummiform coffins. Alternatively, they appear as living beings dressed in the costume of everyday life. In this guise, they are often represented in the *Book of the Dead* in a specific environment called the Field of Reeds or Field of Offerings. This is a kind of 'paradise' reserved for the righteous, which is a reflection of the environment of Egypt, with waterways and cultivated banks. Here the deceased would plough, sow, and harvest abundant crops, which would provide food offerings for eternity (see fig. 16). Even this ideal world could however have unwelcome aspects. Every deceased Egyptian was subject to perform agricultural labour for the gods, and to escape this unpleasant task was one of the main functions of the magical figurines known as *shabtis*, which became increasingly common elements of burial equipment from the Middle Kingdom (see pp. 112–135).

The rationalisation of different concepts of the hereafter had by the New Kingdom produced a vision of the afterlife in which the deceased had a variety of alternative experiences at his disposal. This well-known text from the tomb of Paheri at Elkab introduces us to a number of the important elements of the Egyptian attitude to the afterlife: sustenance, the use of the bodily faculties, freedom of movement and the capacity to exist in a variety of forms:

> You come in, you go out,
> Your heart in joy at the praise of the lord of gods;
> A good burial after revered old age,
> After old age has come.
> You take your place in the lord-of-life [the coffin],
> You come to the earth in the tomb of the West.
> To become indeed a living *ba*,
> It shall thrive on bread, water and air;
> To assume the form of phoenix, swallow,
> Of falcon or heron, as you wish.
> You cross in the ferry without being hindered,
> You fare on the water's flowing flood.
> You come to life a second time,
> Your *ba* shall not forsake your corpse.
> Your *ba* is divine among the spirits [*akhu*],
> The worthy *ba*s converse with you.
> You join them to receive what is given on earth,
> You thrive on water, you breathe air,
> You drink as your heart desires.
> Your eyes are given you to see,
> Your ears to hear what is spoken;
> Your mouth speaks, your feet walk,
> Your hands, your arms have motion.
> Your flesh is firm, your muscles are smooth,
> You delight in all your limbs;
> You count your members: all there, sound,
> There is no fault in what is yours.
> Your heart is yours in very truth,
> You have your own, your former heart.
> You rise to heaven, you open *duat*,
> In any shape that you desire . . .

THE JUDGEMENT OF THE DEAD

To enter the afterlife it was not enough that proper funerary preparations be made. The deceased also had to demonstrate that he was of good character, as

17. The judgement of the dead. On the left, Hunefer is conducted to the balance by the jackal-headed Anubis, who also adjusts the scales. The monster Ammut crouches beneath the balance, so as to swallow the heart should the weighing indicate a life of wickedness. The ibis-headed Thoth records the outcome and, on the right, Hunefer, having been declared *maa-kheru* ('true of voice' or 'justified'), is led by Horus towards Osiris (not shown). From the papyrus of Hunefer. Early 19th Dynasty, about 1280 BC. From Thebes. H. 40 cm.

evidenced by proper conduct during his life on earth. Many tombs contain biographical inscriptions intended to demonstrate that the deceased was of upright character, by emphasising good deeds and the avoidance of evil acts, in general conformity to what were regarded as acceptable standards of behaviour. This was living according to *maat*, conceived by the ancient Egyptians as the basis for all order in the universe. *Maat* was 'what is right' and embraces the notions of truth and justice. It was personified as a goddess. For the universe to continue it was essential that *maat* be maintained; without *maat* chaos would ensue, in which the ideal hierarchy of society would be overturned. A crucial duty of the king was to increase *maat*, and every individual had a responsibility to live according to this principle by following accepted codes of proper behaviour. Doing *maat* brought rewards in the form of a good afterlife: 'She accompanies the person who practises *maat* down into the realm of death. He is placed in a coffin and buried with her; his name shall not be erased from the earth'.

The concept of a judgement of the dead is mentioned as early as the Old Kingdom, when tomb inscriptions refer to a tribunal of the gods, though this is chiefly for obtaining justice for misdemeanours committed on earth, such as damaging a tomb. The idea was developed during the Second Intermediate Period by including a judgement as the culmination of the deceased's passage to the next world. This judgement described at length in spell 125 of the *Book of the Dead* was an inescapable trial through which every deceased had to pass to reach the state of resurrection.

The judgement took place in the Hall of the Two Truths (or Two *Maats*), into which the deceased was conducted by Anubis who had been responsible for his mummification (see fig. 17). The dead man greeted the gods of the judgement hall with the words 'I know you, I know your names'. As in his passage through the gateways of the hereafter, he was again cross-examined to establish that he possessed arcane knowledge. In versions dating to the New Kingdom the judgement is usually presided over by Osiris, accompanied by Isis and Nephthys and the Sons of Horus; in later periods, the place of Osiris is often taken by Ra. Forty-two gods who acted as assessors sat in the hall, and the deceased had to greet each one by name and deny that he had committed a specific misdemeanour while alive. The forty-two 'sins' enumerated in this 'declaration of innocence' included offences against ethics, society and cult practices:

O Far-strider who came forth from Heliopolis, I have done no falsehood.
O Fire-embracer who came forth from Kheraha, I have not robbed.
O Dangerous One who came forth from Rosetjau, I have not killed men.
O Flame which came forth backwards, I have not stolen the god's offerings.
O Blood-eater who came forth from the shambles, I have not killed
a sacred bull.
O Serpent with raised head who came forth from the cavern,
I am not wealthy except with my own property.
O Commander of mankind who came forth from your house,
I have not reviled God.

Having made this declaration, the deceased stood before a balance. His heart was placed on one of the scale pans, to be weighed against the image of *maat* (either personified as a goddess figure wearing an ostrich feather, or the feather alone). The heart, as the seat of the intelligence and memory, contained a record of the deceased's actions in life. The symbolic weighing revealed the nature of the deceased's relationship with *maat*. An even balance signified a life in conformity with *maat*, whereas wrongdoing caused the heart to weigh heavier than the image. During this weighing, the heart was temporarily out of the deceased's control, and there was a fear that it might reveal to the gods of the judgement hall something which would harm its owner's chances of attaining the afterlife. Spell 30B of the *Book of the Dead* would prevent the heart from disclosing anything untoward:

O my heart which I had from my mother!
O my heart which I had from my mother!
O my heart of my different ages!
Do not stand up as a witness against me,
Do not be opposed to me in the tribunal,
Do not be hostile to me in the presence of the Keeper of the Balance.

This spell was inscribed on an amulet called a 'heart-scarab' which was placed on the mummy's breast or within the wrappings (see pp. 205–6). Successful passing of judgement meant that the deceased was declared *maa-kheru* 'true of voice' or justified. His eternal survival was confirmed, and he was assured of perpetual sustenance. He is depicted in jubilant pose, arms upraised, and adorned with feathers symbolising his being in harmony with *maat*. In *Book of the Dead* vignettes he is presented by Horus to Osiris. In the papyrus of Any, the gods declare the verdict:

> The Osiris scribe Any, justified, is righteous. He has committed no crime, nor has he acted against us. Ammut shall not be permitted to prevail over him. Let there be given to him of the bread-offerings which go before Osiris and a permanent grant of land in the Field of Offerings as for the followers of Horus.

Ammut, 'The Devourer (of the Dead)', was a hybrid creature depicted as a composite of animals which had a reputation for ferocity. Her head was that of a crocodile, her front legs those of a lion, and her hindparts those of a hippopotamus. In the vignette of the judgement, she crouches near the balance ready to swallow the hearts of those who the weighing reveals to have lived a life of wickedness. This consumption of the heart of an unrighteous person denied him access to the afterlife.

The world of the dead was a hierarchical society, just as the earthly life had been, but one divided on a somewhat different basis. Besides the gods and the deceased king, it was inhabited by the blessed and the damned. The notion that the afterlife was reserved only for those of good character is clear from the judgement of the dead, in which the hearts of those found to have lived wickedly are swallowed by Ammut. In this tradition, no further details of their fate are revealed. The contemporary *Books of the Underworld*, however, dwell at greater length on the separation of the righteous from the damned. The subterranean world through which the sun god passes each night is occupied by both categories of being. The visitation of the sun god provides the occasion for their fates to be assigned to them. The blessed dead, or *akhu*, who have lived according to the principle of *maat*, are granted new life and offerings; those who have not are termed *mut*, literally 'the dead', the term signifying those who would not experience rebirth. Whereas the *akhu* are said to have adored the sun god, the *mut* are equated with his foes (the forces of chaos who threaten the continuation of the cosmic order). They are condemned to a series of horrifying torments, including decapitation and burning in furnaces, images somewhat reminiscent for us of early Christian notions of hell. These tortures resulted in the total extinction of these negative entities, to whom the afterlife was forever denied.

The possibility of this 'second death' provoked a very real fear, and numerous funerary texts were intended to protect the unwary deceased from this fate. The realm of the dead, indeed, held many perils for those who were unprepared. The integrity of the body had to be preserved, and spells were provided to ensure this, while other spells warded off hunger and thirst. Several passages in the

Coffin Texts allude to the danger of existing in a manner in which the normal functions of life were reversed – walking upside down, and, even worse, eating and drinking one's own excrement and urine.

Death and the dead in ancient Egyptian society

The circumstances of death

Among the varied terminology applied to the act of dying, comforting euphemisms abound. Hence death is described as being 'at rest', or becoming 'weary' or 'weary of heart'. It is likened to sleep (an appropriate prelude to an awakening to new life), departure on a journey, or arrival at a destination. The vast majority of written references to death shun the unpleasant reality of the experience. Artistic depictions of the moment of death are virtually unknown, except in the case of the defeated enemies of the king or the gods.

Examination of human remains from tombs shows that most Egyptians could not expect to live much beyond the age of thirty. As in all ancient societies, certain population-groups such as young children and mothers were particularly vulnerable. The prevalence of disease in ancient Egypt is abundantly evident, both from the medical papyri and the study of mummies, and there can be no doubt that illnesses were responsible for a high proportion of deaths, yet the cause of death of known individuals is rarely mentioned in texts. While some ailments, such as blindness, were interpreted in certain circumstances as punishments from the gods for misdemeanours, many were probably regarded simply as hazards of living, to which everyone was subject.

The immediate cause of death appears to have been less important to the Egyptians than the manner or circumstances in which it occurred. Long life was desired, provided that it was not accompanied by excessive debility. 'A good burial after an honoured old age' is often mentioned as an aspiration, and an ideal lifespan of 110 years is frequently mentioned. What was important was to be able to make proper preparations for one's burial in the traditional manner. There was clearly anxiety lest one should die in circumstances which might hinder this being done, and hence harm the chances of reaching the afterlife. The components desired for a good burial are neatly summarised in a passage from the tale of Sinuhe:

> Return to Egypt!
> For it is today that you have begun to be old, have lost your manhood,
> and have thought of the day of burial,
> the traversing to blessedness.
>
> A night is assigned for you with oils,
> and wrappings from the hands of Tayet.
> A procession shall be made for you on the day of burial,
> with a mummy case of gold,
> a mask of lapis lazuli, a sky over you,

and you on a hearse,
with oxen dragging you,
and chantresses before you.
The dance of the Dead shall be performed at the mouth of your tomb,
and the funeral invocation recited for you;
sacrifice shall be made at the mouth of your tomb-chamber,
with your pillars, built of white stone,
in the midst of the royal children's.

To die in a foreign land was therefore highly undesirable for the ancient Egyptians, not simply on account of suffering death in unfamiliar surroundings, but because to die among foreigners carried the danger that the individual might be denied a proper burial according to Egyptian custom – and this might jeopardise one's chance of reaching the afterlife. Texts lay emphasis on this undesirability of dying outside Egypt. In the tale of Sinuhe, the hero, who has spent many years dwelling abroad, longs for home, declaring: 'What is more important than that my corpse be buried in the land in which I was born.' He is urged by the Egyptian king to return, in terms alluding directly to this matter: 'You shall not die abroad! Not shall Asiatics inter you. You shall not be wrapped in the skin of a ram to serve as your coffin.' Sinuhe gratefully responds: 'Truly good is the kindness that saves me from death. Your *ka* will grant me to reach my end, my body being at home!'

For those who did die beyond the frontiers, an attempt might be made to recover the body for mummification and burial in Egypt. Pepinakht (who lived during the reign of Pepy II, *c.* 2278–2184 BC) records in his tomb inscription at Aswan how he was commanded by the king to rescue the body of Anankhet, who had been killed by the 'sand dwellers' on the Red Sea coast, where he was building a ship to sail to the land of Punt. Another example is contained in the autobiography of Sabni (6th Dynasty), inscribed in his tomb chapel, also at Aswan. Sabni's father Mekhu had died while leading an expedition into Nubia, and Sabni records how he set out with troops and with gifts for the local Nubian ruler, in order to retrieve the body of his father. The body was found, loaded on to a donkey, and brought to Egypt. Sabni proudly records that the king praised him for this act of piety, and dispatched embalmers from the Residence to carry out the mummification of Mekhu (see also p. 76). Not all Egyptians who died abroad were as fortunate as Mekhu, however; some were buried where they died – but not necessarily without Egyptian rites. The records of later foreign expeditions list embalmers among the personnel, to mummify those who died outside Egypt; an expedition to the Wadi Hammamat under Senusret I (*c.* 1965–1920 BC) included thirty embalmers.

Probably the largest numbers of Egyptians who died abroad were soldiers. Garrison troops might be buried locally, as were some of those who were stationed at fortresses in Nubia during the late Middle Kingdom. The majority of those killed in battle were probably buried on the spot. Some might be brought home, but perhaps only under special circumstances. One such group was the approximately sixty battle casualties of the early Middle Kingdom buried at Deir el-Bahri. Their funerary preparation was rudimentary – arrows were found still embedded in some of the bodies – but evidently some trouble had been taken to bring them to Thebes for burial.

Among the many forms in which death came, drowning was regarded as a particularly fortunate fate. Those who drowned in the Nile were thought to be specially honoured by the gods, and in texts from the 30th Dynasty and later they are entitled *hesy*, 'favoured one'. It was apparently believed that the drowned were transmitted immediately to the realm of the dead, and a scene in the *Books of the Underworld* shows the inert bodies of drowned persons being brought ashore by the gods. This notion perhaps owes its origins to the idea that waters were a medium for the renewal of life.

It is apparent from the above that premature death, even in violent circumstances, did not necessarily harm one's chances of reaching the afterlife. Those who were executed for major crimes such as treason, however, were potentially denied the afterlife, as expressed in the phrase 'There is no tomb for the rebel'. Execution by burning was a punishment for serious offences, and since the corpse was destroyed in the process no afterlife was possible for those condemned to suffer this fate. In the trials of persons charged with conspiring to murder Ramesses III (*c.* 1184–1153 BC), a distinction was made between the punishments decreed for those of ordinary status, and those of high rank, the former being executed, but the latter being allowed to commit suicide, apparently as a mark of clemency. The distinction perhaps lay in the notion that execution terminated existence permanently, whereas suicide was still compatible with an afterlife. In the *Dialogue between a man tired of life and his Ba* (cf. p. 13), the man contemplates suicide as a means of release from suffering, and there is no implication that this was viewed as morally wrong.

The status of the dead in Egyptian society

For the ancient Egyptians, the barriers between the world of the living and that of the dead were somewhat fluid. It is abundantly clear from texts that the dead were not excluded from society. The dead were remembered through the funerary monument, and contact was maintained principally through the performance of the mortuary cult. This provided the occasion for the living to visit the burial places of their deceased relatives, to make offerings and to hold communication with the dead. In this way the continuity with the past which was so important to the Egyptians was maintained, while at the same time the integrity of the family unit was reaffirmed. Relatives bore the chief responsibility for maintaining the cult of the dead, a duty which fell above all to the eldest son. Inheritance of family property was linked to this act, but in any case providing for dead parents was regarded as an important filial duty (see p. 171). The dead, indeed, exercised considerable influence over the economy of Egypt, since substantial resources, manpower and material wealth were expended in equipping them for eternity.

Funerary inscriptions often list the special occasions on which the dead hoped to receive offerings in their tombs. These were various festivals in the religious calendar, such as the New Year festival, the monthly and half-monthly festival or the festivals of particular deities. At Thebes, the most important of these occasions was the Beautiful Festival of the Valley, an annual event which took place between inundation and harvest. This centred on the visit of the cult-image of Amun-Ra to the mortuary temples of the New Kingdom rulers on the west bank. This visit took place amid great ceremony, the image being brought out of its sanctuary at Karnak and ferried across the Nile on a barque and then conveyed in a great procession by canal to the mortuary temples of the kings. The culmination of the festival was the god's visit to Deir el-Bahri, where he was installed in the mortuary temple of Hatshepsut. The cultic significance of the event lay in the supposed union which took place between the god Amun and the goddess Hathor, to whom the Deir el-Bahri valley was particularly sacred. In this way the fertility of the land was renewed. The festival also provided the opportunity for a reunion of the living with their dead relatives. The funerary images of the dead followed that of Amun in the procession and this was followed by a feast, in which the deceased was the 'guest of honour', receiving renewed offerings.

Contact with the dead was also maintained in the home. Small sculptured busts of painted limestone or wood have been found in houses of the New Kingdom, particularly at Deir el-Medina, the community which housed the craftsmen who built and decorated the royal tombs in the Valley of the Kings. These busts are exceptional in Egyptian art in representing only a part of the body, the head and shoulders, usually wearing a tripartite wig and a floral collar (see fig. 18). A few bear the name of a particular deceased person, but most are uninscribed and appear to be generic images of unspecified ancestors. These busts were probably installed in small shrines located in the frontal part of the house, functioning as the foci of domestic cults of ancestors. Some busts have been found in cemeteries, indicating that these cults were also maintained at the tomb (see pp. 184–5). A related category of monuments, also well-represented at Deir el-Medina, are small limestone stelae on which are images of specific ancestors who carry the title 'effective spirit of Ra' (*akh iqer en Ra*). This designation makes clear that those represented were the transfigured dead who dwelt in the realms of the sun god and Osiris. They were doubtless also the subjects of the busts.

The dead were believed to be capable of intervening in the world of the living. The most striking illustration of this is the fact that letters were written to the dead. Some of these were written on papyrus, the main epistolary medium used among the living, but the majority were inscribed in hieratic script on the surfaces of pottery bowls. It is likely that these bowls were filled with food and placed in the tomb chapel in the expectation that the spirits of the dead would be attracted by the food-offerings and would then read the letters. Another

18. Limestone busts representing deceased ancestors. Images such as this were set up in household shrines and at tombs, and appear to have acted as the focus for cults maintained by private individuals on behalf of their dead relatives. 19th or 20th Dynasty, about 1295–1070 BC. Probably from Thebes. H. (left) 25.5 cm.

example is inscribed on a stela. Most of the letters date to the Old and Middle Kingdoms, though later examples are known. In most cases the deceased person, addressed as *akh*, was a relative of the writer. The letters outline a variety of problems to which, it would seem, no solution could be found by natural means. The writers were therefore petitioning the dead to help them, or complaining of problems which they attributed to the influence of the dead. The letters show that the *akhu* were believed to be able to intercede in a tribunal in the hereafter. Some suggest that the dead were thought to retain something of their character beyond death, whereas others express a sense of outrage at hostile behaviour attributed to dead relatives.

In a letter written on the back of a funerary stela of the First Intermediate Period, a sick man asks his dead wife to act on his behalf:

> How are you? Is the West taking care (of you) [as you] desire?
> Look, I am your beloved on earth,
> (so) fight for me, intercede for my name!
> I have not garbled a spell before you, while making your name to live upon earth.
> Drive off the illness of my limbs!
> May you appear for me as a blessed one [*akh*] before me,
> that I may see you fighting for me in a dream.
> I shall lay down offerings for you when the sun's light has risen,
> And I shall establish an altar for you.

It is interesting that the inducement for the dead lady's intercession is the assurance of proper funerary offerings. Also unusual is the suggestion here that communication may take place via a dream, a very early instance of this notion, which is better known from later periods.

Much more bitter is the celebrated letter to the dead woman Ankhiry, a rare example of a letter to the dead from the New Kingdom preserved in Papyrus Leiden 371. Here the husband rebukes his dead wife, attributing evil to her although he had treated her well in her lifetime and has performed the proper funerary rites for her:

> What evil thing have I done to you that I should have come into this wretched state in which I am? What have I done to you? What you have done is that you have laid hands on me, although I had done nothing evil to you . . . I made you a married woman when I was a youth. I was with you when I was performing all manner of offices. I was with you, and did not put you away. I did not cause your heart to grieve . . . And when you did sicken of the sickness that you did have, I caused to be brought a master-physician, and he treated you, and he did everything whereof you did say, 'Do it.' . . . And when I arrived in Memphis, I asked leave of Pharaoh, and I came to the place where you were [buried], and I wept exceedingly together with my people in front of my street-quarter, and I gave linen clothes to wrap you, and I caused many clothes to be made, and I left no good thing that it should not be done for you . . . But behold, you do not know good from bad. It shall be decided between you and me . . .

In a passage from the same letter, not cited here, the widower states that he expects to have justice by means of a tribunal of the gods, in which his letter will be used to plead his case. The precise nature of the 'evil' which he attributes to Ankhiry does not emerge, although there is an indication that he was contemplating remarriage and was suffering uneasy emotions.

There is no doubt that the dead were also to be feared. Those who presented the greatest threat to the living were the hostile dead, or *mut*, those who had been denied transfiguration into the blessed state either on account of evil conduct in life or because some other factor had prevented them from entering the hereafter – violent death, or not having been given proper burial. *Mut* could harm the living, and magical texts provide instructions for warding off their influence. The *akhu*, or transfigured dead, could also prove troublesome to those on earth. Magical spells protected houses and their inhabitants, particularly those asleep, from the unwelcome attentions of the spirits of the dead, who were believed to bring illness and bad dreams. In a 'ghost story' preserved on ostraca from the New Kingdom, the *akh* of a long-dead official haunts the Theban necropolis because his tomb has fallen into ruin, and is only appeased when promised a new tomb and mortuary cult to provide offerings for eternity.

Positive and negative views of death: scepticism and counter-scepticism

The Egyptians were fully aware that even the most careful preparations for death could not avert the eventual decay or destruction of the tomb and the cessation of the mortuary cult. The positive, hopeful tone of the mortuary texts is balanced by a genre of literary compositions, mainly dating to the Middle Kingdom, which express scepticism about the worth of making elaborate preparation for the afterlife. This theme was taken up in the Harper's songs, the most famous of which is stated to have been inscribed in the tomb of one of the kings named Intef at Thebes. The general tone of these texts is that tombs fall into ruins, mortuary cults do not endure and no one returns from the realm of the dead to strengthen the hopes of the living. Therefore one should live only for the present, enjoying the pleasures of life to the full.

Those gods who existed aforetime,
who rest in their pyramids,
and the blessed noble dead likewise,
buried in their pyramids.
The builders of chapels, their places are no more.
What has become of them?

I have heard the words of Imhotep and Hordedef,
whose sayings are so told:
what of their places? Their walls have fallen;
their places are no more, like those who never were.
None returns from there to tell their conditions,
to tell their state, to reassure us,
until we attain the place where they have gone . . .
. . . Be not weary-hearted! Follow your heart and happiness!
Make your things on earth! Do not destroy your heart,
until that day of lamentation comes for you!
The Weary-hearted does not hear their lamentation;
mourning cannot save a man from the tomb-pit.

chorus: Make holiday! Do not weary of it!
Look, no one can take his things with him.
Look, no one who has gone there returns again.

A text from a much later period (first century BC) on the stela of Taimhotep presents a pessimistic view of the state of existence in the hereafter. The dead lady, who had been wife of the High priest of Ptah at Memphis, had died young and addresses her husband, urging him to take pleasure in life, for the netherworld is a dark and gloomy place, populated by the inert dead.

The negative view of the afterlife produced an opposing reaction, which is most eloquently expressed in the harper's song from the tomb of Neferhotep:

I have heard those songs that are in the tombs of old,
What they tell in extolling life on earth,
In belittling the land of the dead.
Why is this done to the land of eternity,
The right and just that has no terrors?
Strife is abhorrent to it,
No one girds himself against his fellow;
This land that has no opponent,
All our kinsmen rest in it
Since the time of the first beginning.
Those to be born to millions of millions,
All of them will come to it.

CHAPTER 2

The Eternal Body: Mummification

The function and origins of mummification

The notion of the importance of the corpse is implicit in the practice of inhumation, which began in Egypt perhaps as early as 55,000 BC. We do not know how the Egyptians first conceived the idea of an association between the preservation of the corpse and a life after death, although we can speculate. In many burials of the Predynastic period, the hot, dry sand which formed the filling of the shallow grave quickly and effectively absorbed all fluids from the corpse, leaving skin, hair and finger- and toe-nails very well preserved. It is often supposed that this lifelike appearance, perhaps observed when such bodies were accidentally disinterred during later tomb-making, may have generated a belief that human existence did not end with death, and that survival of the body played a part in the new life. Whether or not this is true, it is clear from later texts that, by the dynastic period, the body was regarded as an important medium through which the individual could continue to exist after death (see pp. 16–17). Its principal importance was as a home or harbour for the *ka* and the *ba*, each of which would be united with the body in the realm of the dead, and so perpetuate the existence of the deceased. It was therefore highly important that it should not decay. Many funerary texts emphasise the importance attached to retaining the integrity of the bodily members. There was a notion of the sanctity of the human body, and a horror of its destruction, particularly by fire. Death by burning was the punishment for some of the most serious offences, and was the fate reserved in the next world for the unrighteous who opposed the sun god, as described and depicted in the *Books of the Underworld* of the New Kingdom; here the evil are seen being decapitated and their bodies burned in fiery furnaces. Since fire consumed the corpse almost completely, nothing remained to serve as a dwelling for the spiritual aspects of the individual. For this reason, cremation was never practised by the ancient Egyptians, and even members of the Roman élite of Egypt were mummified. According to a tradition recorded by Herodotus, the Persian conqueror Cambyses (525–522 BC) had the mummy of King Ahmose II (d. 526 BC) exhumed, abused and finally burned; the story may be apocryphal but the impiety with which the act was regarded is beyond doubt.

A primary aim of proper burial, then, was to protect the corpse from destruction, and as funerary practices evolved greater efforts were devoted to ensuring the security of the body. The culmination of this trend was mummification, the preservation of the corpse by artificial methods. In essence, the process perfected by the Egyptians consisted of extraction of the internal organs, thorough drying of the body, packing, anointing and wrapping in linen. This process is nowadays referred to by the terms embalming or mummification. 'Embalming', derived from the Latin *in balsamum*, means to preserve through the agency of balm; 'mummy' derives from the Persian word *mummia*, 'bitumen'. The word was applied to Egyptian preserved bodies probably on account of their often blackened appearance, which might have suggested that they had been treated with bitumen. The occasional use of bitumen in mummification as early as the New Kingdom is suggested by recent analytical studies, but so far there is no proof that it was widely used until the Late Period – the darkening of the skin of many mummies being a consequence of the use of resin. None the less, the term 'mummy' has become firmly established as a description for an artificially preserved corpse.

19. Body of a woman of the mid-Predynastic period (about 3500 BC), excavated in the cemetery of Hierakonpolis. Human remains from this site show the earliest evidence so far discovered for attempts at artificial preservation of the corpse using linen wrappings and resin. Remains of matting in which the body was wrapped are visible at the top.

It is often supposed that these techniques were adopted because the introduction of deeper graves, wood- or brick-lined burial chambers and coffins, around 3000 BC, frustrated the natural preservative process by insulating the corpse from the dry sand which had so efficiently desiccated earlier bodies. This may have been a consideration, but it cannot be regarded as the only factor involved. Mummification, in fact, was more than an elaborate procedure to prevent or retard decay. It was carried out in a ritual context. By the Old Kingdom, the notion had arisen that the body had to undergo special treatment to equip it for its new role as an eternal image of the deceased. The concept of transforming the corpse is found in many societies both ancient and modern. In the words of Pearson: 'The body is not simply a biological entity but is a carefully crafted artefact, further worked and transformed after the moment of death.' Egyptian mummification provides a classic illustration of this notion.

Ritual treatments of the corpse are already attested in Egypt in prehistoric times, and it was in this context that mummification arose. As early as the second half of the fourth millennium BC, as discoveries at Hierakonpolis show, corpses were being wrapped in hides or linen, and resin and linen padding were being used to create an idealised body (see fig. 19). These practices became more widespread with the passage of time. These treatments clearly influenced later mummification procedures, so that by the 1st Dynasty the use of linen wrappings was well-established. However, other traditions co-existed alongside that of preservation, notably the practice of intentionally dismembering the body. In this process the soft tissues of the corpse were permitted to decompose, after which the bones were placed back together - though not always in their correct anatomical relationship. Bodies treated according to this method have been found in graves of the late Predynastic period at Naqada and Adaima, and in some Old Kingdom tombs at Giza, Meidum and Deshasha, and there are isolated examples of the practice as late as the 6th Dynasty. Such burials are, however, rare at all periods; in the Old Kingdom this treatment seems to have been restricted to persons of high status.

At a remote period of prehistory, dismemberment may have been designed to incapacitate the dead, so as to ward off any harm which they might bring to the living. But other concerns were also operating. The notion of dismemberment of the body occurs repeatedly in religious texts of the dynastic period. Usually it is perceived in a negative light, as a hazard to be avoided in the netherworld. In the myth of Osiris, the concept is to some degree rationalised. The dismemberment of the god's body by Seth – an act repugnant in itself – represents the state of deprivation which death brings about, and the reconstituting of the corpse through mummification becomes a metaphor for the overcoming of death itself. Passages in the *Pyramid Texts* urge the dead king: 'Receive your head, collect your bones, gather your limbs together'. It would therefore be less strange than it may at first appear if mummification in its early stages encompassed the dismemberment and subsequent rejoining of the bodily parts.

It seems then, that the procedures which we call mummification arose in Egypt from multifarious traditions. In the course of the Old Kingdom, dismemberment seems to have been abandoned, and the treatment of the body moved in a different direction. The aim of the process was to transform the corpse into a *sah*, an eternal and perfect image of the deceased, a new body endowed with magical attributes. This necessarily involved the use of parts of the earthly body, but at most periods it was not the intention to preserve the body exactly as it had appeared in life. Indeed, a substantial proportion of the body's substance was removed during the mummification process and either disposed of or buried in separate containers.

Particular attention was focused on the external appearance of the wrapped mummy, creating a perfect image around the 'core' of the original corpse. This ideal image changed through time. In the Old Kingdom, the exterior of the body was modelled in resin-soaked linen or plaster to resemble a statue, and dressed in clothes. From the First Intermediate Period to the Roman era a different iconography was in vogue, the limbs confined within the wrappings and the head covered with an idealised mask. The physical remains inside the wrappings were often poorly preserved. Most mummies of the Old and Middle Kingdoms contain little more than the bones, and – with the exception of the mummies of the royal family – the same is largely true for the New Kingdom. The most striking illustrations of this tendency date from the Roman period, when treatment of the corpse was often extremely crude and careless, yet the external trappings were rich and elaborate. The main exception to this situation is during the Third Intermediate Period, when special efforts were made by the embalmers to restore the integrity of the corpse and to reproduce its appearance in life.

Since the creation of this perfect body was an important element in the transfiguration of the dead, each of the various stages of embalming took place in a ritual context, with accompanying liturgy and ritual acts. Even some of the materials used in mummification had religious as well as preservative functions. Beeswax, with which the body was sometimes coated, had connotations of rebirth, while the molten resin with which many mummies were treated was perhaps regarded as conferring divine status on the deceased.

20. Scenes of mummification painted on the coffin of the priest Djedbastiuefankh from el-Hiba. Below, the corpse (depicted as a silhouette of the naked body) undergoes the preliminary washing. Above is the body laid on a lion-shaped table and attended by embalmers, one of whom represents the jackal-headed god Anubis. The hatched area below the corpse possibly represents the natron used as a drying agent. Late Period, about 600–300 BC. H. of coffin 177 cm.

SOURCES FOR THE PROCEDURES

Ancient Egyptian records are remarkably reticent on the technical procedures of embalming. This reflects both the nature of the surviving sources, which are heavily biased towards formal, religious subjects, and a reluctance to depict the details of a process which, however essential to the survival of death, involved violation of the human body. Many tomb chapels were decorated with scenes of craftsmen preparing equipment for the burial, but mummification is usually represented only in a discreet and formal fashion, the embalmer-god Anubis tending the fully wrapped body, which is provided with a set of canopic jars. It was probably considered inappropriate to depict the details of evisceration and desiccation in the ritually sensitive context of the tomb because of the firm belief that what was represented pictorially could through magic become eternal reality. A few scenes from Theban tombs of the New Kingdom have been interpreted as representations of mummification, but more plausibly depict the manufacture and decoration of anthropoid coffins. However, mummification does appear to be shown in a series of figured scenes on the lids of two coffins of the Late Period from el-Hiba, now in Hildesheim (see fig. 20).

Textual allusions are also scanty, and usually consist of no more than passing references to the duration of the deceased's sojourn in the embalming workshop, and rather formal listings of materials to be used in mummification. More informative are the rare archaeological discoveries of embalmers' tools, and the more numerous caches of embalmers' refuse. The sacerdotal component of mummification is best documented in the *Ritual of Embalming*, a text devised as a manual for those preparing the corpse. It comprises sections describing the practical manipulation, wrapping and anointing of the body, and the prescribed ritual acts and words which accompanied each stage in the process. The principal surviving documents of this text are hieratic papyri of the Roman Period (P. Bulaq 3, Louvre 5158 and a document in Durham). These almost certainly enshrine traditions deriving from a much earlier period; unfortunately, no document preserves the complete text, only the later stages of the ritual surviving. The *Rhind Magical Papyrus*, dating from about 200 BC, also contains some details of embalming procedures, including the positioning of incisions in the skin for subcutaneous packing.

If indigenous sources are relatively unrevealing, the same cannot be said of the writings of the Classical authors Herodotus and Diodorus Siculus. Their accounts of mummification preserve much information which is not found in any other written source, but which can often be confirmed through examination of the mummies themselves.

Herodotus of Halicarnassus, the 'Father of History', visited Egypt in about 450 BC, during the First Persian Period. His account of mummification is the single most important written source on the subject, and, though often quoted, cannot be omitted here:

> There are those who are established in this profession and who practise the craft. When a corpse is carried in to them they show the bearers wooden models of mummies, painted in exact imitation of the real thing. The best method of embalming, so they say, is that which was practised on one whose name I cannot mention in this context [i.e. Osiris]. The second method they demonstrate is somewhat inferior and costs less. The third is cheapest of all. Having indicated the differences, they ask by which method the corpse is to be prepared. And when the bearers have agreed a price and departed, the embalmers, left behind in the workshop, begin embalming.
>
> In the best treatment, first of all they draw out the brains through the nostrils with an iron hook. When they have removed what they can in this way they flush out the remainder with drugs. Next they make an incision in the flank with a sharp obsidian blade, through which they extract all the internal organs. Then they clean out the body cavity, rinsing it with palm wine and pounded spices, all except frankincense, and stitching it up again. And when they have done this they cover the corpse with natron for seventy days, but for no longer, and so mummify it. After the seventy days are up they wash the corpse and wrap it from head to toe in bandages of the finest linen anointed with gum, which the Egyptians use for the most part instead of glue. Finally they hand over the body to the relatives who place it in a wooden coffin in the shape of a man before shutting it up in a burial chamber, propped upright against a wall. This is the most costly method of preparing the dead.

> Those for whom the second and less expensive way has been chosen are treated as follows: the embalmers fill their syringes with cedar oil which they inject into the abdomen, neither cutting the flesh nor extracting the internal organs but introducing the oil through the anus which is then stopped up. Then they mummify the body for the prescribed number of days, at the end of which they allow the oil which had been injected to escape. So great is its strength that it brings away all the internal organs in liquid form. Moreover the natron eats away the flesh, reducing the body to skin and bone. After they have done this the embalmers give back the body without further ado.
>
> The third method of embalming which is practised upon the bodies of the poor is this: the embalmers wash out the abdomen with a purge, mummify the corpse for seventy days, then give it back to be taken away

Diodorus' account agrees with that of Herodotus in many respects, notably the three 'classes' of burial and the evisceration of the corpse. He also supplies a number of interesting details not mentioned by Herodotus, particularly with reference to the embalmers (see pp. 54 and 76).

Much of the data derived from these sources has been confirmed and greatly expanded through the modern examination of mummies. Occasional unwrappings had taken place before the nineteenth century but had yielded little information of lasting value. The Napoleonic Egyptian expedition of 1798–1801 and the publication of the massive *Description de l'Egypte* aroused widespread interest in all things Egyptian during the early nineteenth century. One manifestation of this was the frequent unwrapping of mummies, and although many of these operations were motivated chiefly by morbid curiosity, others were organised along lines of scientific enquiry, resulting in the recovery of detailed information about the procedures involved. The advent of radiography, and, more recently, computerised tomography (CT) scanning, has greatly facilitated the collection of data while having the advantage of being totally non-invasive.

Main features of Egyptian mummification

The methods of mummification evolved through time, from the late fourth millennium BC to the first few centuries AD. Examination of mummies has demonstrated the basic accuracy of Herodotus' statement that different processes were available simultaneously, apparently according to the status or wealth of the individual. The following account describes the procedures which would have been observed in the most elaborate mummification.

Washing

The first stage was the purification of the corpse by washing. This would be done very soon after death since, in the hot climate of Egypt, decomposition began immediately. For this preliminary washing a dilute solution of natron (see below,

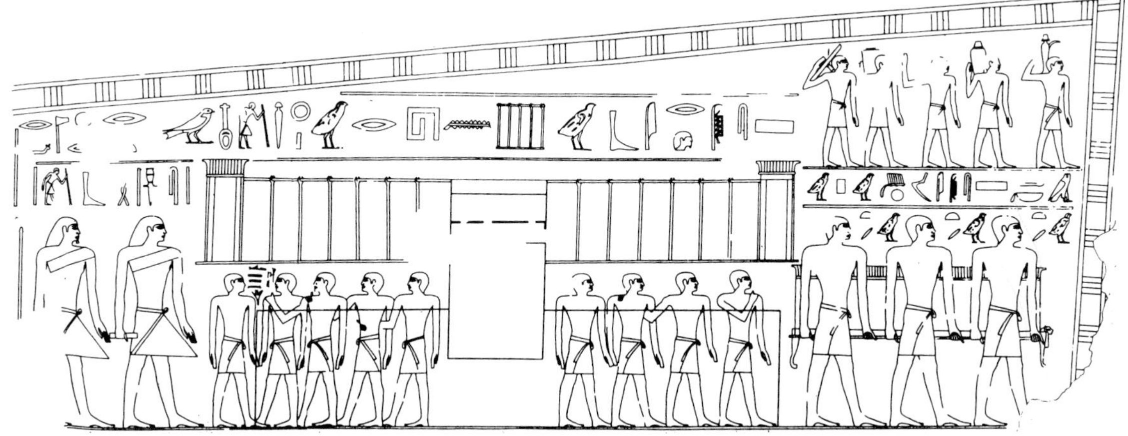

21. The *ibu*, or tent of purification, as depicted in the tomb of Pepiankh at Meir. The *ibu* was a temporary structure erected close to the tomb, in which the corpse underwent a ritual cleansing prior to mummification. On the right, the coffin, mounted on a lion-shaped bier, is carried out by the embalmers. 6th Dynasty, about 2200 BC.

22. Ritual purification of the deceased by the gods Horus and Thoth. The streams of liquid consist of the hieroglyphic signs for life (*ankh*) and dominion (*was*). Painting on the cartonnage mummy-case of Tjentmutengebtiu. Early 22nd Dynasty, about 900 BC. From Thebes. H. 169 cm.

pp. 55–6) in water was probably used. It took place in a temporary structure, probably a tent of reeds and matting, close to the Nile or to a canal. In the Old Kingdom, the structure in which the body of the king was purified was called the *seh-netjer* (divine booth), that for non-royals the *ibu* (short for *ibu en wab*, tent of purification); in later periods, the term *seh-netjer* predominated. Images of the *ibu* in Old Kingdom tombs (see fig. 21) depict it as a tent-like structure with two entrances or ramps communicating with water; emplacements for such a structure have been identified in the valley temples of the pyramids of kings Khafra (*c.* 2558–2532 BC) and Pepy II (*c.* 2278–2184 BC).

Cleansing of the corpse before mummification was doubtless a practical necessity, but the ritual aspects of the washing were perhaps of greater significance. According to Egyptian belief, water held important purifying and life-giving qualities. Each dawn was a repetition of the original birth of the sun god from the watery chaos of Nun (see fig. 13), and his emergence into the sky as a newborn god was preceded by a washing performed by Horus and Thoth. Hence lustration came to be closely associated with rebirth, and this accounts for its incorporation into the funerary rites. A ritual purification was necessary before the dead king could ascend to heaven in the manner of his divine model, the sun god, and private individuals are occasionally depicted in tombs and on coffins, undergoing this lustration (see fig. 22). Here again, Horus and Thoth may be depicted performing the ceremony, and in Papyrus Rhind they are mentioned specifically as cleansing the deceased on his entrance into the necropolis.

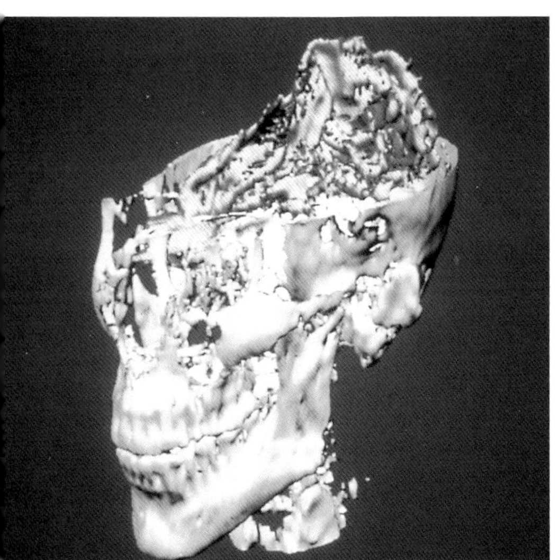

23. Cutaway view of the skull of the mummy of Tjentmutengebtiu (see fig. 22), a three-dimensional image created using a CT-scanner. The brain has been extracted by the embalmers, and the cerebral cavity packed with linen (here artificially coloured purple), inserted via the left nostril. CT images of the roots of the molar teeth demonstrated that Tjentmutengebtiu died aged between nineteen and twenty-three years. Early 22nd Dynasty, about 900 BC. From Thebes.

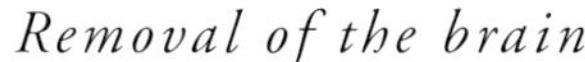

Removal of the brain

The next stages of mummification were carried out in another structure, the *wabet* or *per-nefer* (see below, p. 77). Here, the embalmers set about extracting the internal organs. These were subject to very rapid decomposition and would quickly spread corruption to the entire corpse if they were not removed or treated as soon as possible. The first operation was the extraction of the brain, which, according to Herodotus, was only performed in the most expensive method of embalming. Examination of mummified heads shows that the majority have an artificial perforation through the roof of the nasal cavity (via the ethmoid bone) into the cranium. This was probably made using a small chisel or awl and was an operation requiring great skill. In the majority of examples examined the perforation had been made through the left nostril, and in some cases the adjacent flesh is visibly distorted as a consequence. The perforation sometimes extended to the ethmoid air cells and even to the eye socket, though this is probably an indication of lack of skill by the operative. Once access to the cranium had been gained the iron hook mentioned by Herodotus was inserted into the cranial cavity to break up the brain tissue (assuming that this had not already liquefied through natural processes of decay). The remains would then have been extracted via the nostril and disposed of. The ancient Egyptians apparently did not understand the function of the brain and hence adopted no special measures to preserve it.

As an alternative to extraction via the nose, the embalmers occasionally withdrew the brain through an eye-socket, through a hole made in the cranium, or, in one instance (see below, p. 84), via the *foramen magnum* at the base of the skull. The empty skull cavity was often packed with linen cloth or sawdust, inserted by the same route as that used to remove the brain (see fig. 23). In some cases, molten resin was poured into the skull and allowed to solidify.

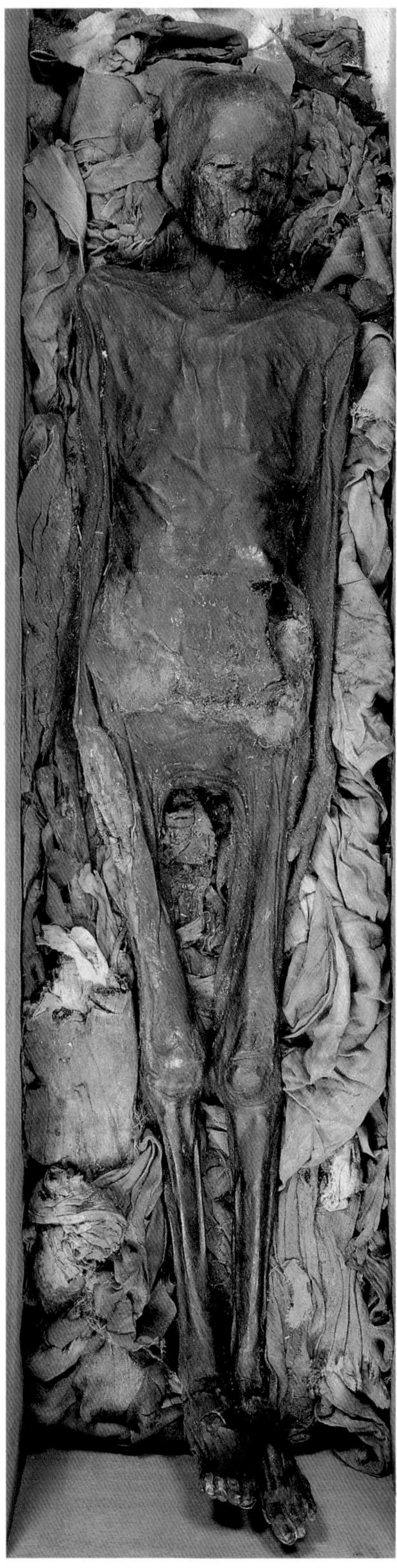

Removal of viscera

The embalmers' next task was the removal of the organs within the body cavity. For this operation, the corpse was laid on its back on a stone table. Actual examples of calcite embalming tables have been found at the Step Pyramid at Saqqara (*c.* 2670 BC), in the tomb of King Horemheb in the Valley of the Kings (*c.* 1295 BC), and at Memphis, where the sacred bulls of Apis were mummified. The sides of the tables were carved in the form of standing lions, and the central surface sloped slightly towards the foot end, to enable the body fluids to drain into a receptacle. For the mummification of persons of lower status a wooden table was used; an example found at Thebes, and used in the embalming of the official Ipy (11th Dynasty), consisted of a wooden board with four wooden battens positioned at intervals to support the corpse.

Using a knife of obsidian or some sharp stone such as flint, the embalmer made a short, straight incision in the left side of the abdomen, and removed the stomach and intestines by hand (see fig. 24). After perforating the diaphragm, he also extracted the lungs and the liver from the thorax. The heart was intentionally left in place since, as the location of the intellect and memory, it would be required to play a major part in the judgement of the deceased before the god Osiris (see Chapter 1), and therefore had to remain under the direct control of its owner. The kidneys were sometimes removed during this stage of mummification, but are often found to have been left *in situ*. The principal organs extracted from the body – the liver, lungs, stomach and intestines – were embalmed separately (see below, pp. 64–76).

Diodorus Siculus, in his account of mummification, records a strange tradition which applied to the evisceration of the corpse. The man who made the incision, to whom Diodorus gives the name *paraschistes* (literally, the 'ripper-up'), immediately ran away, while his colleagues shouted curses and threw stones at him. Diodorus explains: 'They suppose him to be worthy of hatred who applies force to the corpse of a fellow creature, or wounds it, or executes any evil in general upon it.' It is likely that this ritual

24. Unwrapped mummy of an unidentified woman of high status. The incision made on the left side of the abdomen to extract the viscera is clearly visible. The entire corpse has been carefully coated with molten resin, and particular attention was paid by the embalmers to the preservation of the facial features and the finger- and toe-nails. Late Third Intermediate Period, about 700 BC. Probably from Thebes. H. 152 cm.

condemnation (as it surely must have been) was a means of averting by magic any negative consequences which might follow from the performance of an act that was necessary but still fundamentally abhorrent to Egyptian principles of proper conduct.

As an alternative to extracting the viscera through the abdomen, the embalmers sometimes injected a fluid into the rectum, as stated by Herodotus. The 'oil of cedar' which he mentions (in fact, probably juniper oil) would not, however, dissolve the organs in the manner suggested, and some uncertainty hangs over the identification of the substance used. It is possible that the true intention of the embalmers was to preserve the organs *in situ*, rather than to remove them in liquid form, since in several mummies treated in this manner substantial remains of the internal organs were found to be present.

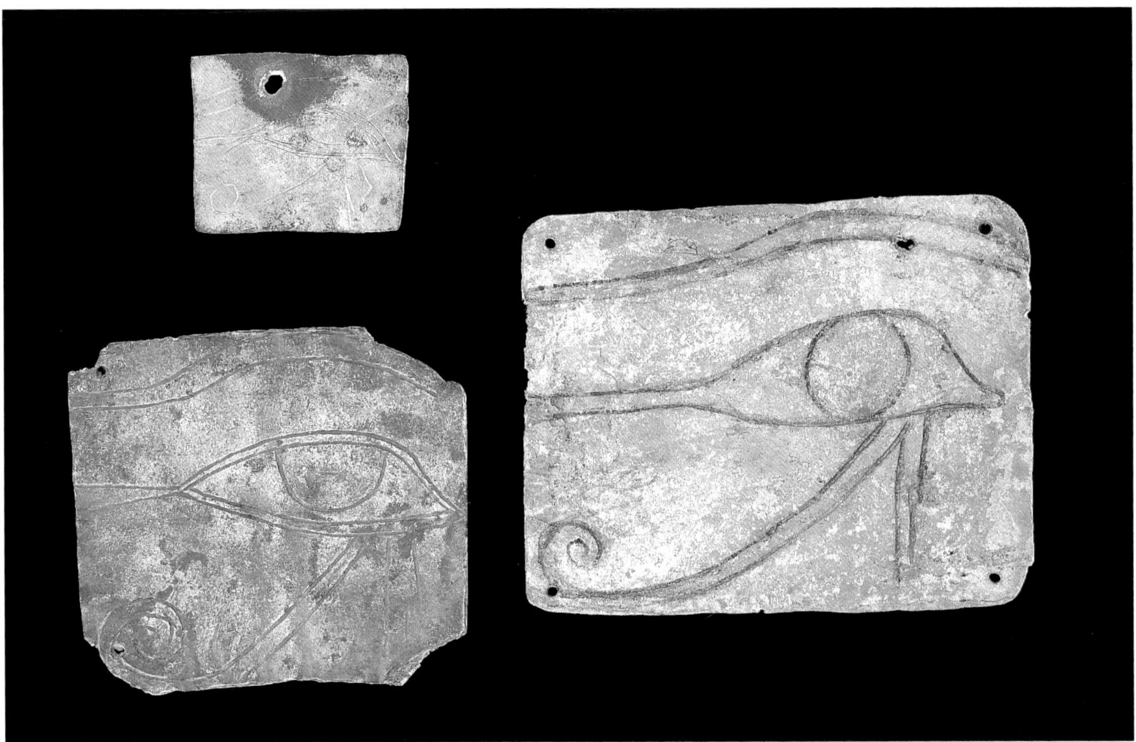

25. When the embalmers had completed the mummification of a corpse a rectangular plaque of metal or wax was often placed over the evisceration-wound. Like many others, these examples of white metal (perhaps tin) bear the image of the *wedjat* eye which represents the eye of the god Horus. Probably Third Intermediate Period, about 1069–664 BC. Provenance unknown. Dimensions of largest specimen 8×6.4 cm.

After the removal of the contents of the thorax and abdomen, the interior of the body was cleansed with water and – according to Herodotus – with palm wine. This was done in preparation for the desiccation of the body.

Drying the body; the use of natron

The lengthiest part of the process was the dehydration of the body. Removal of all fluid effectively prevented the growth of bacteria which might lead to decay. Occasionally this was accomplished simply by air-drying, but in the majority of cases of authentic mummification a chemical process was employed. As an alternative to the desert sand which had preserved the bodies of predynastic Egyptians, another natural substance was used as a drying agent. This was natron – a compound of sodium salts which occurs in a natural state at several locations within Egypt, chiefly in the Wadi Natrun in the Libyan Desert, north-west of Cairo. This was the site of an ancient branch of the Nile, now occupied by a series of salt lakes. Natron occurs in solution in the waters and as an encrusted deposit on the bottom of the lakes and on the ground around their shores. Textual sources confirm that both these sources – and doubtless others besides – were exploited by the ancient Egyptians.

Natron had a number of uses in ancient Egypt, but it is best known as a drying agent for the embalming of corpses. It effectively drew moisture from the body, and may have been valued particularly for its effectiveness in breaking down the fatty tissues. Scientific analyses of embalmers' salts from various periods has indicated that the chemical composition of natron was variable. In many samples the predominant constituents are sodium carbonate and sodium bicarbonate, but there is usually also a quantity of sodium sulphate and sodium chloride (common salt). Indeed, some samples consist chiefly of sodium chloride, and, as laboratory experiments have shown that this could achieve mummification almost as effectively as natron, it is possible that it was used as an alternative by Egyptian embalmers. However, since several of the samples tested represent embalmers' refuse, it is possible that the chemical make-up of the salts had undergone alteration during the mummification process and do not represent their original composition.

26. Linen package containing the crystalline salts used to extract moisture from the corpse. Large numbers of these packages were stuffed inside the body cavity to absorb fluids from within, while the exterior of the corpse was covered with a heap of salts in dry, powder form. Probably Third Intermediate Period, about 1069–664 BC. From Deir el-Bahri, Thebes. 14.8×11.6 cm.

Although natron in solution has been found in some tombs, the bulk of archaeological evidence and the results of modern laboratory experiments indicate that the salts were usually employed in the form of a dry powder. Small linen packages of natron were stuffed inside the body cavity, perhaps together with temporary packing materials such as rags and wood shavings (see fig. 26). The body was then completely covered with natron, and was set aside for a prescribed period, during which its entire fluid content was absorbed by the natron, leaving the corpse thoroughly desiccated. Several texts indicate that this part of the process would have lasted about forty days, and modern experimental mummification carried out on the bodies of birds and small animals has confirmed that complete dehydration can be effectively achieved in this time; the seventy days mentioned by Herodotus actually refers to the duration of the entire mummification process, including the wrapping and the various ritual acts (see below). It is possible that, at its most sophisticated, the drying process involved more than one stuffing with natron in order to ensure thorough desiccation of the body.

Packing

Dehydration resulted in the disappearance of most of the muscle tissues and subcutaneous fat, leaving the body as little more than a skeleton covered with dark, rather wrinkled skin. Once the natron had been removed, the embalmers set about restoring some of the lost substance of the corpse to compensate for its shrunken appearance. The body cavities were rinsed and filled with packing materials to provide support and to lend a pleasant smell. These materials often included linen, sawdust and earth, as well as aromatic resins. In many mummies of the Late to Roman periods molten resin was poured into the interior. Occasionally dried lichen was used. In the 21st Dynasty, packing materials were also inserted beneath the skin in an attempt to render the corpse more lifelike (see below).

Anointing and cosmetic treatments

The exterior of the body was anointed with oils and perfumes, to provide a pleasant odour and to restore some degree of suppleness to the dried limbs. The *Ritual of Embalming* emphasises the religious significance of these operations. According to this text, the anointing sought to endow the body with the 'odour of a god'. The *Ritual* enumerates several applications of oils at this stage. These included an anointing of the body from the shoulders to the feet with oils identical to those used in the Opening of the Mouth (see Chapter 6). The substances most extensively used were coniferous resins, which were applied in large quantities, both in liquid form and as a viscous paste. In addition to their lubricating and aromatic qualities, the resins served to protect the body from the destructive effects of moisture, and for this reason they were applied generously to the exterior of the corpse before wrapping began. In many mummies liquefied resin was also poured into the body and the cranium after the extraction of the brain and viscera, probably both to arrest bacterial activity and to provide a filling for the cavities. Some mummies were filled with a mixture of solidified resin and resin-impregnated linen. Various coniferous resins, including cedar oil, were used in ancient Egypt. Modern analyses have also demonstrated that some of the resin was obtained from the *pistacia*, and that the incense used by the Egyptians in religious rituals came from the same source. Since incense (in Egyptian *senetjer*, 'that which makes divine') played a part in conferring divine status, a symbolic dimension may also have been present in its use in mummification – to assist in the transfiguration of the deceased.

Bitumen or asphalt, the source of the modern term 'mummy' (see above, p. 47) was sometimes used as well as or instead of resin. Bitumen has in fact been identified on some mummies, such as that of the priest Djedhor from Akhmim (*c.* 250 BC) (see fig. 51), though its use in earlier periods was rare.

Before beginning the wrapping of the body, the embalmers paid attention to its adornment. The hair was carefully arranged, and bald patches were concealed by the attachment of false plaits and other hair extensions. Artificial eyes were placed into the sockets. Features which had been lost in life or had disappeared in the embalming process, such as eyebrows, were sometimes added in paint. A

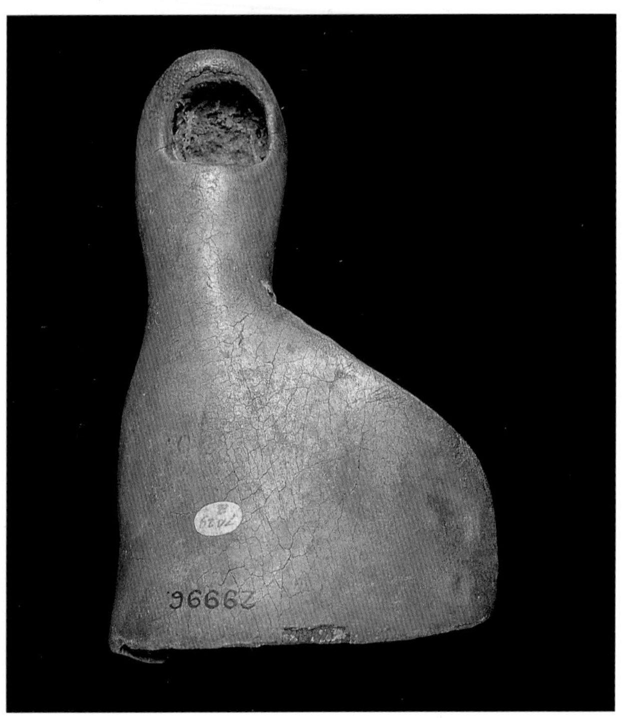

28. Finger of an unidentified mummy with gilded silver stall in place. Finger- and toe-stalls were fitted to mummies of persons of high rank. 26th to 30th Dynasties, about 664–323 BC. From Memphis. L. 7.2 cm.

27. Prosthetic toe made of cartonnage, originally fitted with a toe-nail made of a different material. This is one of the earliest known examples of an artificial limb. It is reported to have been found on a mummy, but signs of wear and refurbishment show that the prosthesis had probably been worn in life, and that it was adapted to be attached to the body after death. Probably 21st to early 26th Dynasties, about 1069–600 BC. From Thebes. L. 11.9 cm.

few cases are known in which missing limbs were replaced by artificial substitutes. These include crude imitations of arms and legs using sticks, and elaborate items such as the artificial toe found within the wrappings of a mummy of the Third Intermediate Period (see fig. 27). In the most elaborate treatments, gold or silver stalls were placed over the tips of the fingers and the toes (see fig. 28).

Wrappings

The standard material for mummy wrappings was linen; as the textile of everyday use for clothing and bed-covers it was produced in large quantities. Wrapping the corpse in strips and sheets of linen is attested as early as *c.* 3400 BC in graves at Hierakonpolis. It had apparently become an element of the formal treatment of the dead by the 1st Dynasty, even before the development of true mummification.

Wrapping the body, of course, helped to preserve its integrity, but texts indicate that in the pharaonic period the wrapping also possessed religious significance. Several texts explain that the wrappings were supposed to be provided by Tayet, the goddess of weaving, or by the weavers of the goddess Neith:

> One gives to you your bandages (*seshed*)
> and your mummy-wrappings (*wetyu*)
> Which the weavers of Neith have woven,
> You clothe yourself in a pure garment and lay aside the other.
> The arms of Tayet clothe you.

29. The cloth used to wrap mummies was almost invariably linen. Coloured threads woven into the fabric are often indicative of reuse, as on these pieces. The roll on the left formed part of the mummy of the lady Takush (25th Dynasty, about 680 BC, from Thebes); the other pieces are from unidentified mummies of uncertain date.

The reality was often rather different. Some royal mummies were indeed wrapped in the finest quality linen, but in many instances the cloth used was recycled, having previously seen service as clothing or bed-covers. Garments were found among the wrappings of the mummy of Sety II (*c.* 1200–1194 BC) (one bore the name of Sety's predecessor Merenptah, *c.* 1213–1203 BC, and hence must have been a piece from the royal household), and names and identification marks have been found on the linen used to wrap the bodies of private individuals. Perhaps families kept a store of discarded household cloth for this purpose. Whereas some garments were used in a virtually complete state, others were torn into strips; surviving portions of decorated borders (woven patterns and fringes) betray the original function of some of the cloths as parts of garments, and incidentally show that ancient Egyptian clothing was often more colourful than artistic depictions suggest (see fig. 29). The wrappings of a mummy in the museum at Lyons were found to incorporate substantial parts of the sail of a boat, prompting speculation that the dead man might have been a sailor.

In general, the head and the limbs were first wrapped individually, and the wrapping often proceeded with large sheets and narrow strips of cloth applied in alternating layers. Folded sheets and wads of linen were inserted from time to time to help to create the standard shape for the mummy. In many 21st Dynasty mummies a dense layer of resin was applied during the wrapping, to distinguish the outer and inner layers of cloth. The process was completed by the application of a large outer shroud covering the entire body from head to foot. In mummies of the New Kingdom and Third Intermediate Period, this shroud was often dyed a deep pink colour, using plant-dyes such as that of the saff flower (*Carthamus tinctorius L*). The use of a reddish pink – a solar colour – may have conveyed the notion of resurrection by the life-giving rays of the sun. In most cases this colour has faded owing to exposure to light, but depictions of mummies in contemporary paintings show the red shroud distinctly. Long strips of linen, arranged vertically, laterally and diagonally, held the outer shroud in place, and were dyed in colours to contrast with the shade of the shroud.

The wrapping was as much a ritual activity as the rest of the embalming, occupying a substantial part of the time devoted to the process. Incantations were uttered as each piece of linen was put in place; the words to be spoken are recorded in the *Ritual of Embalming*, which also describes the shape, colour and proper positioning of various cloths. Some of these had special names associating them with particular deities such as Ra-Horakhty, Hathor and Thoth. Both this text and the *Book of the Dead* include directions for the placing of amulets within the wrappings to protect the deceased and assist them towards rebirth. An enormous variety of funerary amulets was produced (see pp. 201–7), and pieces of jewellery were also placed on the body. In the case of a wealthy individual these might include collars, pectorals, earrings, bracelets and finger rings of gold, silver and precious stones.

The quantity of linen used to wrap a body varied, and was not necessarily related to the wealth or status of the deceased. An exceptional instance was the mummy of Wah, a minor Theban official of the 11th Dynasty, which was wrapped in approximately 375 square metres of linen.

30. The funerary mask represented the deceased in the transfigured state, with the shining golden skin appropriate to a divine being (the flesh of the gods was believed to be of gold). It also provided magical protection for the head of the deceased, and assured his transfiguration through an association between his bodily members and those of various gods. Gilded cartonnage mask, Late Ptolemaic to early Roman Period, first century BC to first century AD. Provenance unknown. H. 44 cm.

External trappings and masks

In the Old Kingdom, the body was prepared as a living image of the dead person, with facial features reproduced and clothing applied. From the First Intermediate Period, a different iconography was adopted, in which the body was enveloped and provided with important trappings which served to represent the deceased in the transfigured state – a visible sign that he had successfully reached the afterlife. The most important of these trappings was a mask which fitted over the head like a helmet (see fig. 30). By the principle of sympathetic magic the donning of a mask identified the wearer – whether living or dead – with the entity represented by the mask; so, for example, animal masks representing gods were worn by magicians and priests. The funerary masks placed over the heads of the dead performed an analogous function, representing them in the state aspired to after death, as transfigured beings, equipped with divine qualities.

The features were for the most part idealised depictions of a deceased person in the divine state, and should not be regarded as portraits; the only possible exceptions are the masks made for royal individuals (such as the gold mask of Tutankhamun, *c.* 1336–1327 BC), where facial features distinctive of the sculpture of a particular ruler might be reproduced (though to what extent this image was a likeness of the actual person is debatable). Placing magical power around the head reflects a particular concern in the minds of the Egyptians. The

29472

loss of the head, depriving the deceased of the ability to see, hear, eat, speak and breathe, was one of the most feared dangers of the netherworld. Spell 43 of the *Book of the Dead*, 'for preventing a man's decapitation in the realm of the dead', includes the words: 'The head of Osiris shall not be taken from him; my head shall not be taken from me.' The mask protected against the loss of the head – but also had a more specific function in ensuring continued existence after death. This is expressed in spell 531 of the *Coffin Texts* (revised and incorporated into the *Book of the Dead* as spell 151B), in which the individual parts of the mask are identified with the bodily members of particular deities or with the barques of the sun god: 'Your right eye is the Night-barque, your left eye is the Day-barque, your eyebrows are (those of) the Ennead, your forehead is (that of) Anubis, the nape of your neck is (that of) Horus . . .' The text also contains allusions to the deceased's association with Osiris and Ra, providing additional assurance of rebirth. The mask thus emphasised the deceased's elevation to a divine state, and this is reflected in certain common features of the iconography of mummy masks, notably the gold colouring of the skin and the blue wig, imitations of the attributes of gods.

While the funerary masks of kings were made of solid gold, those of persons of lower rank were usually constructed of cartonnage, an inexpensive yet durable material, composed of linen and plaster moulded into shape over a disposable core. Masks of this type enjoyed several phases of popularity until the Roman

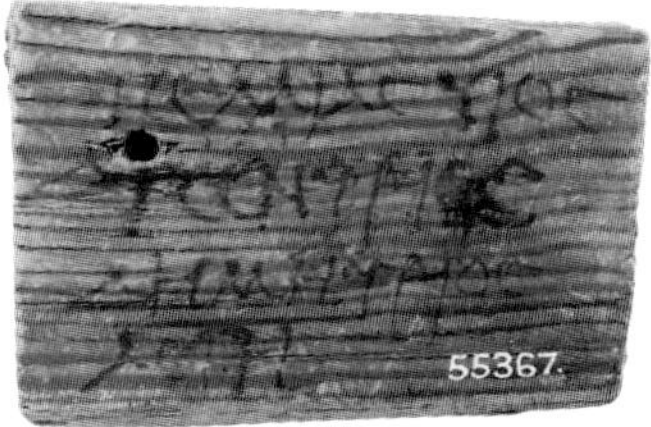

31. Mummies of the Ptolemaic and Roman Periods were frequently identified by wooden labels inscribed in ink with the name and parentage of the deceased, and often his or her place of abode. These tags were attached to the outer wrappings by cords, and served to ensure that the mummy was transported to the correct place of burial. Roman Period, after 30 BC. L. of largest label 16 cm.

Period. At that time, several alternative types of funerary image were in vogue, including plaster heads and panel-portraits, painted in encaustic (a technique in which hot wax is used as a medium) or tempera (see figs 52 and 180).

Other trappings were used at different periods. During the Third Intermediate Period a dyed red-leather *stola* was often placed around the mummy's neck, either within the wrappings or on their surface. This 'stole' was often represented in art as one of the trappings of deities, and perhaps conferred protection and divine status on the deceased. It also became part of the iconography of mummiform coffins (see Chapter 7). From the 25th Dynasty to the Ptolemaic Period a network of blue-green faience tubular beads, threaded in a lozenge pattern, was placed on the front of the body, over the outer wrappings (see Chapter 6). These nets appear to have carried celestial significance, the colour and patterning recalling the starry sky. Such patterning appears on dresses worn by the goddesses Isis and Nephthys in their role as protectors of Osiris, and a garment with this design is often depicted as worn by Osiris himself. The placing of the bead-nets over mummies therefore conferred the protection of the goddesses as well as identifying the deceased as Osiris. During the Roman Period the outer linen shroud of the mummy was frequently painted with a full-length image of the deceased, usually in Hellenistic dress, accompanied by Egyptian deities.

Disposal of waste

Excavations in the Theban necropolis have brought to light numerous caches of embalming materials which represent the leftovers from mummification. These usually consist of pottery jars containing cloths and rags stained with body fluids and embalming oils, natron salts and packing materials. Most of these were evidently used in eviscerating, drying and cleansing the body. The correct disposal of this material was a matter of some importance. The cloths and salts had been in contact with the body and had probably absorbed some of its fluids, in addition to being contaminated with small fragments of skin, hair or fingernails. Perhaps because such material was considered unclean from the ritual viewpoint, it was buried near but not actually in the tomb. Moreover, as it contained part of the corpse it required proper disposal to ensure the integrity of the deceased's body, and to prevent any portions of it falling into the hands of persons ill-disposed to the deceased who might use them to work magical spells which would threaten the wellbeing of the spirit. This formal disposal of the residue of mummification may underlie an enigmatic element of the funerary rituals depicted in New Kingdom tombs. This focuses on an object called the *tekenu*, which is drawn on a sledge with the coffin and canopic containers to the place of burial. The *tekenu* is depicted as an amorphous bundle with a human head, resembling the form of a contracted human body, and it is conjectured that it represents the portions of the corpse which were not included in the mummy or the canopic containers (see below, pp. 64–76). In the 25th and 26th Dynasties, these leftovers were sometimes wrapped in a large shroud imitating the appearance of an authentic mummified body, and buried close to the tomb in a coffin inscribed with the name of the deceased, further emphasising the personification of the remains.

Preservation of the Viscera

The manner of treatment accorded to the different internal organs of the body varied according to the ancient Egyptians' perceptions of their significance. As noted above, the brain was discarded, apparently because its function was not understood, whereas the heart – regarded as the physical 'centre' of the individual and the location of the intelligence – was deliberately left in place within the chest cavity. Of the organs which were extracted during mummification, four were singled out for separate preservation. These were the liver, the lungs, the stomach and the intestines. The kidneys were sometimes preserved as well, but have been less frequently identified in mummies than the four just mentioned. The reason for the selection of these particular organs is not fully understood, but in view of the importance attached to nourishing the dead it is probably no coincidence that the organs connected with digestion were among those most consistently preserved. Each of the organs was also regarded as an independent embodiment of the deceased himself, and this is reflected in the manner of their treatment. The visceral packages were treated as miniature mummies, separately preserved and encased in containers which have affinities with full-sized coffins. Occasionally they were even wrapped in the shape of a mummy and provided with small cartonnage masks in precise imitation of the type placed over the head of the corpse.

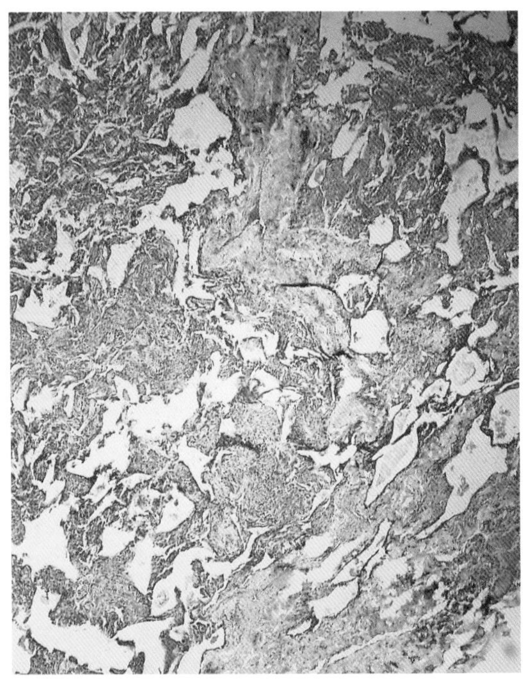

32. The organs which were extracted from the body during mummification were preserved and placed in special containers in the tomb. Examination of these remains using scientific techniques has yielded important evidence for patterns of health and disease in ancient Egypt. This histological section of lung tissue, from a canopic container of the Ramesside period (about 1295–1069 BC), shows evidence that the deceased suffered from pulmonary fibrosis.

According to Diodorus, the internal organs extracted by the embalmers were rinsed with palm wine and treated with spices. This statement may be correct, but has not been confirmed by archaeology. Examination of the viscera of mummies indicates that in many cases they were preserved in a similar manner to the body itself, first being dried with natron and coated with resin, before being wrapped in linen. The degree of success achieved in the preservation of these fragile organs varied. A number of specimens from the New Kingdom and Third Intermediate Period are sufficiently well-preserved to have yielded data about various diseases from which the deceased had suffered. These include lung complaints such as anthracosis and pulmonary oedema, and parasitic worm infections like schistosomiasis (see fig. 32). However, some visceral packages have turned out to contain mainly resin and other preservatives, with little trace of the actual organs, suggesting that the embalmers were sometimes unsuccessful in preserving the soft tissues themselves. They may in fact have been unable to distinguish one organ from another in their desiccated state, a possibility supported by burials in which parts of the same organs are found to have been included in more than one of the packages, as observed in mummies in the Munich museum. The fact that the formalities of creating and burying such packages were still observed under these circumstances is a strong indication of the predominantly ritualistic importance of the act.

Canopic jars and their protective deities

The embalmed organs were placed in the burial chamber of the tomb, close to the coffin containing the corpse. Special receptacles were designed to house them. The earliest of these, dating to the Old Kingdom, took the form of a cubic chest of stone or wood, divided internally into four compartments. Later chests imitated the shape of a *naos* or shrine. The evolving form of these chests conforms closely to the development of outer coffins and sarcophagi, emphasising their conceptual role as 'coffins' for the viscera. At first, the organ packages were placed directly into the chest without additional protection, but beginning in the late 4th Dynasty the practice arose of providing a set of four jars of stone, pottery or wood, each to contain one of the major organs preserved. These jars were either placed inside the chest, or deposited on the floor of the burial chamber or in a special niche.

The ancient Egyptians do not seem to have had a specific term for these containers. They are referred to in inscriptions simply as *qebu en wet*, 'jars of embalming'. They have become known in Egyptological parlance, however, as canopic jars. The term derives from the town of Canopus in the Delta, where, according to Rufinus (fourth century AD), a vase-shaped object was worshipped which probably represented a local form of Osiris. Classical writers linked the city and the vase-fetish with Canopus, the pilot of Menelaus, who was supposed to have drowned in a storm and been buried near the city to which his name was given. Though this image had no direct connection with the jars made to hold embalmed viscera, the term 'canopic' has since become firmly attached to them.

It was important that the organs be protected in order to ensure their continued usefulness to the deceased. Their safety was entrusted to four divinities: Imsety, Hapy, Qebehsenuef and Duamutef, collectively known as the Sons of Horus. These were very ancient deities, who are mentioned in the *Pyramid Texts* as performing a wide range of actions on behalf of the deceased king; they supported him, joined his limbs together, washed his face, opened his mouth, and also warded off hunger and thirst from his body, the latter role associating them closely with the digestive organs. In these early sources, at least two of the 'sons' were pairs of gods, male and female counterparts, an original status reflected in the survival of the grammatical dual-endings -ty/-wy in the name of Imsety, and probably also that of Hapy (which seems originally to have been Hepwy). By the Middle Kingdom, both their function and their individual characters had evolved, and the canonical tradition of four singular gods had been established. By this date their principal role was that of protecting the internal organs contained in the canopic jars. They were regularly invoked in inscriptions on the jars and chests, and from the New Kingdom onwards, each god had his distinctive iconography. In the most common tradition Imsety was depicted with a human head, Hapy with that of a baboon, and Qebehsenuef and Duamutef with the heads of a falcon and a jackal respectively. The jackal and falcon heads were probably adopted from the iconography of the 'Souls' (*bau*) of Buto and Hierakonpolis (representing the primeval kings of Egypt), with whom the Sons of Horus had associations. Variations on this iconographic pattern occurred from time to time, particularly in the Third Intermediate Period, when Qebehsenuef was frequently depicted as jackal-headed and Duamutef as falcon-headed.

The Sons of Horus were themselves guarded by four goddesses. Two of these, Isis and Nephthys, were prominent as protectors of the dead, having – according to the myth – played an important part in the resurrection of the murdered Osiris. They protected Imsety and Hapy, while Duamutef and Qebehsenuef were guarded, respectively, by Neith and Selkis. These four goddesses are often invoked in inscriptions on the sides of coffins and canopic chests, though at Deir el-Bersha, a necropolis of the city of Ashmunein, the association of the Sons of Horus with goddesses followed an independent local tradition, with Sendjet and Renenutet replacing Isis and Nephthys.

No inscription states which organs were supposed to be protected by which deity. The only evidence for this comes from examinations of the contents of undisturbed canopic jars and (for mummies of the 21st to 22nd Dynasties) identification of organs found inside the body accompanied by wax or resin figures of the Sons of Horus. Generally speaking, this evidence indicates that Imsety protected the liver, Hapy the lungs, Duamutef the stomach, and Qebehsenuef the intestines. However, only a minority of burials have yielded evidence on this, and there are a number of exceptions to the above pattern, suggesting that variant traditions may have been operating at different periods or in different parts of Egypt.

The evolution of canopic containers

Because it was important that canopic jars should function properly to magically protect the body organs, a canonical form for them was established at an early date, undergoing only relatively minor variations over a period of 2500 years. In the same way, other vessels with strong ritual associations – such as the *hes*-vase used for making libations – retained their characteristic shape for long periods. This ritual import probably explains why in a large number of instances the jars were placed in the tomb empty, as is the case in the Old and Middle Kingdoms, when evisceration of the corpse was not always carried out, and again in the Third Intermediate Period when the organs were replaced in the body but jars were still provided.

Apart from possible emplacements for canopic chests in some 2nd–3rd

Dynasty tombs at Saqqara and elsewhere, the tombs of high officials of the early 4th Dynasty at Meidum are the earliest to include a special place specifically for the viscera. These are niches cut into the south wall of the burial chamber. Wall-niches or pits occur in the same location in tombs of the reigns of Khufu (*c.* 2589–2566 BC) and Khafra (*c.* 2558–2532 BC) at Giza. Most were found empty but in the tomb of Ranefer at Meidum remains of viscera, wrapped in linen, were still in place.

33. Calcite canopic jar with painted wooden stopper in the form of a human head. The squat form of the jar, with widely flaring shoulder, is typical of the Middle Kingdom. At this period, all four lids of a set of jars usually represented human faces, which were probably those of the Sons of Horus. 12th Dynasty, about 1900 BC. From Deir el-Bersha. H. 29.5 cm.

The canopic niche or pit was usually no longer provided in the tomb after the 4th Dynasty. The viscera were placed instead in separate receptacles. The earliest is the calcite (Egyptian alabaster) chest made for the burial of Queen Hetepheres I, mother of Khufu. It was found in her tomb at Giza, placed in a niche cut in the southern end of the burial chamber's west wall. The chest was divided internally into four compartments into which the viscera were placed directly. When the tomb was found in 1925, the chest still contained the remains of the linen-wrapped packages, which lay in a dilute solution of natron in water.

The earliest datable canopic jars are the limestone set made for Queen Meresankh III (*c.* 2500 BC), found in her tomb at Giza. The canopic jars of the Old Kingdom were simple in design. They were usually made from limestone or calcite, and are distinguished by their shallow, convex disc-shaped lids. The jars were usually undecorated and uninscribed – though the vizier Kagemni, who was buried in a tomb at Saqqara in the 6th Dynasty, was provided with a fine set of calcite canopic jars incised with his name and titles.

By the Middle Kingdom, sets of four jars had become usual in élite burials. The jars were made of pottery, wood, limestone or calcite – the latter notable for their high exterior polish. They usually have a pronounced shoulder and a tapering profile. Jars with disc-shaped lids in the Old Kingdom tradition continued to be made in this period, but now the lids more usually took the form of human heads (see fig. 33). An early example of one of these human-headed lids, dating from the late 11th Dynasty, was found at the temple-tomb of King Mentuhotep II (*c.* 2055–2004 BC) at Deir el-Bahri. The appearance of the complete jars with their lids in place clearly reflects that of the canonical mummy image introduced in the First Intermediate Period (see p. 81), underlining the conception of the viscera as embodiments of the deceased. This idea was expressed explicitly in a set of canopic jars made of cartonnage for Djehutynakht of Bersha, which represented the human body with arms and feet individually depicted. In the majority of cases, however, the jars have a smooth surface, and the lids in all probability represent not the deceased but the Sons of Horus. Early depictions of these gods vary; on the interiors of canopic chests from Deir el-Bersha they are all represented with the head of a falcon (appropriate to the offspring of Horus), but on coffins of the 12th Dynasty from Asyut all four consistently have human heads, and this became their standard iconography in the Middle Kingdom. In several sets of canopic jars, three of the lids have bearded heads, while one is beardless and has a lighter skin-colouring than the others, an indication of female sex. Such jars are sometimes specifically identified as Imsety, whose originally feminine character is indicated by the grammatical form of the name. The role of the Sons as guardians was further emphasised in this period by the addition of inscriptions on the jars invoking their protection. This concept was sometimes graphically illustrated by the depiction of human arms on the sides of the jar, as though embracing the contents. A redware jar of this type in the British Museum, bearing a formula naming Duamutef, has the god's arms modelled in high relief, the hands grasping the *ankh* and *was* sceptre (see fig. 34).

34. Redware canopic jar made for the official Wahka. The inscription invokes the aid of the god Duamutef, whose protective embrace is graphically represented by the human arms carved on the sides of the jar; the god's hands grasp the *ankh* (sign of life) and the *was* sceptre, symbolising his authority. Probably from the tomb of Wahka II at Qaw el-Kebir. 12th Dynasty, reign of Amenemhat III, about 1800 BC. H. 28.6 cm.

The outer chests for canopic jars continued to imitate contemporary coffins in form, decoration and inscriptions. During the Middle Kingdom the chests, like the coffins, developed from a flat-lidded type to one with a vaulted top. The canopic chests from the necropolis of Bersha are particularly interesting in this respect; several of them are decorated internally with passages from the *Coffin Texts*, among which are the earliest instances of the *shabti* spell (see Chapter 4), and there are also figures of the Sons of Horus and tutelary goddesses.

The evolution of the canopic chest continued during the Second Intermediate Period. Several burials found at Thebes included wooden canopic chests of distinctive type, having vaulted lids with end-boards, and images of the Anubis-jackal painted on the sides. The chest made for King Sebekemsaf (*c.* 1600 BC), now in Leiden, had an internal lid on which the four canopic jars were painted in profile. Curiously, actual jars from this period are rather rare, and it may be that in many cases the linen-wrapped viscera were placed directly into the wooden chest.

In the 18th Dynasty the provision of canopic jars underwent a revival. They were often made of clay, fashioned on a potter's wheel, and sometimes of stone or wood. The body of the jar was usually squat, with a prominent shoulder, and the lids followed the tradition of the Middle Kingdom in representing all four Sons of Horus with human heads (see fig. 35). The lids of a few 18th Dynasty jars, however, represented the distinctive animal-heads of the Sons, and this became standard practice in the reign of Ramesses II (*c.* 1279–1213 BC) in the 19th Dynasty. The form and material of the jars also changed in the Ramesside Period, with limestone and calcite the favoured materials rather than pottery or

35. Canopic jars made for the Child of the Royal Nursery, Ahmose (left), an unidentified owner (centre) and Renseneb (right). 18th Dynasty canopic jars were frequently made of painted pottery, as these examples illustrate. Early to mid-18th Dynasty, about 1550–1450 BC. Provenance unknown. H. (left to right) 33 cm, 32 cm, 31 cm.

36. Calcite canopic jar from a set inscribed for Queen Mutnedjmet, the wife of the pharaoh Horemheb. The shape is typical of jars dating to the 19th and 20th Dynasties. The hieroglyphic text is the speech of the goddess Isis, and refers to her protection of Imsety, one of the Sons of Horus who in turn guarded the internal organs. Early 19th Dynasty, about 1290 BC. Probably from Saqqara. H. 41 cm.

wood, while blue-glazed faience was occasionally used. The distinctive 'Ramesside shape' is tall and slender, and without the pronounced shoulder of 18th Dynasty jars (see fig. 36). A standardised inscriptional formula also emerged, painted or incised on the jar in three or four vertical columns, in which the organ within the jar was identified both with the deceased and with its protective genius, around which protection is extended by the four goddesses.

The protection of the Sons of Horus by the four goddesses was also reflected in the depiction of the goddesses on the sides of canopic chests in the New Kingdom. The chests themselves regularly imitated the shape of a shrine with a cavetto cornice and sloping roof. They were usually mounted on runners to

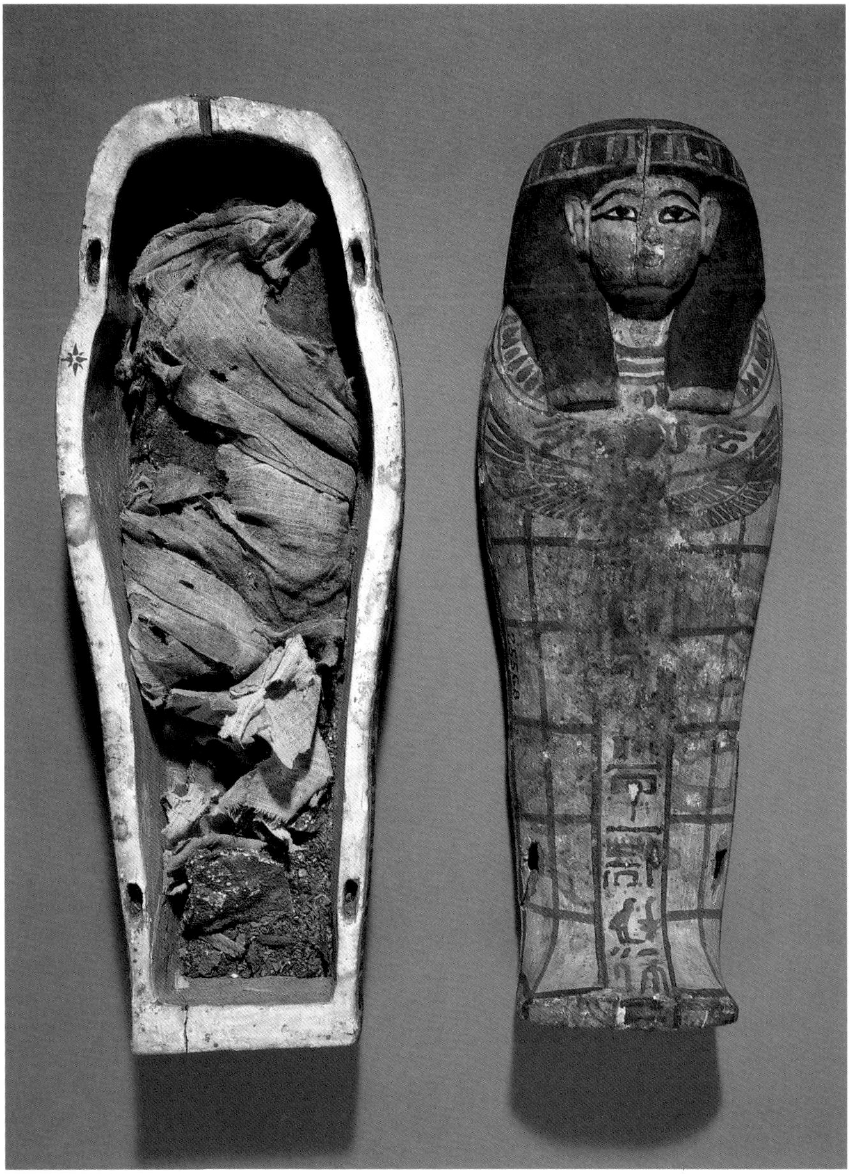

37. Painted wooden canopic chest containing four jars of Neby. The shape of the box resembles that of a shrine, with a cornice and a sloping roof. It is mounted on sledge-runners, on which it could be drawn to the tomb during the funeral procession. On the sides are protective figures of the Sons of Horus and the goddesses Isis, Nephthys, Neith and Selkis. The four jars, also of wood, have stoppers in the form of human heads. 18th Dynasty, about 1380 BC. From Thebes. H. 63.5 cm.

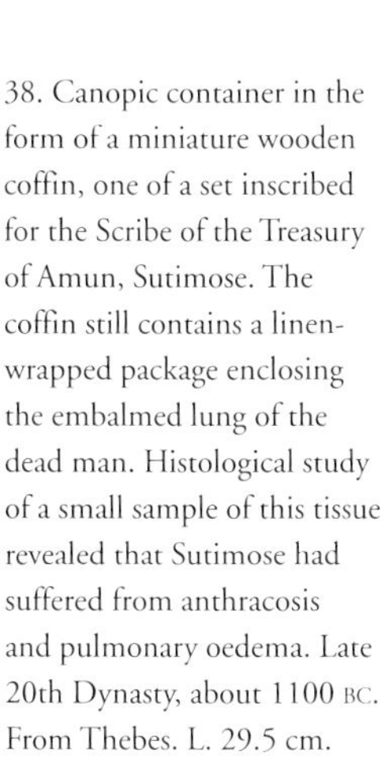

38. Canopic container in the form of a miniature wooden coffin, one of a set inscribed for the Scribe of the Treasury of Amun, Sutimose. The coffin still contains a linen-wrapped package enclosing the embalmed lung of the dead man. Histological study of a small sample of this tissue revealed that Sutimose had suffered from anthracosis and pulmonary oedema. Late 20th Dynasty, about 1100 BC. From Thebes. L. 29.5 cm.

enable them to be drawn along the ground, and indeed are depicted being pulled in this way (often surmounted by an image of Anubis) in representations of the funeral procession (see fig. 37). The chests made for private individuals were usually of painted wood; those for kings were of calcite. Examples found in the Valley of the Kings contain four cylindrical cavities, each covered by a human-headed stopper. In the calcite canopic chest found in the tomb of Tutankhamun (*c.* 1336–1327 BC), each cavity contained a miniature gold anthropoid coffin with glass and semiprecious inlays, inside which was a visceral package. After the 19th Dynasty, kings seem to have returned to using individual jars, but canopic coffinettes were used sporadically for non-royal burials. The treasury

39. Mummy of a priest of Amun. The chest cavity has been exposed to reveal the linen-wrapped packages containing the internal organs, which were regularly replaced inside the body by the embalmers in the 21st Dynasty. From the tomb of the priests of Amun (Bab el-Gasus) at Thebes. 21st Dynasty, about 1069–945 BC.

scribe Sutimose (20th Dynasty) possessed a set of such miniature coffins, all of which were human-headed (see fig. 38); another set in the Turin Museum bears the heads of the Sons of Horus.

At the end of the New Kingdom the manner of preparing the mummified viscera changed. Each of the preserved organs was wrapped in a separate package accompanied by a small figurine of one of the Sons of Horus, and placed inside the body cavity before the mummy was wrapped. The replacing of viscera within the body is first attested in the mummy of Ramesses V (mid-20th Dynasty, *c.* 1147–1143 BC), and became the standard method in the Third Intermediate Period, when the organs were contained in four (or occasionally seven) packages (see fig. 39). The reason for the change is unknown, but a desire to restore the physical integrity of the corpse may have been an influential factor. The figurines of the Sons of Horus which accompanied the packages were commonly made of beeswax; other examples were made from resin or from wax over a core of clay or resin (see fig. 40). The majority of the images represent the deities in mummy-shape and adorned with *stolae* crossing on the front and back of the body; other examples, however, depict them as living beings, wearing divine costume. The colour of these figures was deliberately altered using pigments or bleaching; hence some are yellow (imitating gold and suggesting divine – perhaps specifically solar – associations); some are red (perhaps again denoting solar associations, or protection); some black (the colour most frequently associated with death and rebirth), and others white (indicative of ritual purity, the colour of the garments worn by the blessed dead). Good examples of these figures have been found in the Royal Cache and the Bab el Gasus cache-tomb at Deir el-Bahri (21st Dynasty), and they remained in use until the end of the Third Intermediate Period. One of the latest known sets of wax figures comes from the mummy of the woman Irtyru from Thebes (25th Dynasty); in this case, the figures were not placed inside the body but within the wrappings, a variant practice also known from the 21st Dynasty.

As a consequence of the change in the method of depositing the viscera, canopic jars became superfluous. However, they continued to be provided in well-appointed

40. Wax figurines representing the Sons of Horus, the deities who guarded the internal organs of the dead. During the Third Intermediate Period, when the viscera of mummies were replaced in the body cavity in linen bundles (see fig. 39), each package was provided with a figure of this type to confer magical protection. 21st to 25th Dynasties, about 1069–664 BC. H. of largest 13.3 cm.

burials of the Third Intermediate Period. The kings buried at Tanis and the members of the family of the Theban rulers of the 21st Dynasty were provided with sets of jars. These jars were fully functional but were of course empty (see fig. 41); in many other cases, however, dummy jars of stone or painted wood were provided. Some of these were carved in one piece with integral heads; others have detachable lids but contain only a shallow cavity, too small to accommodate organ-packages. It appears that the jars were retained on account of their ritual significance and out of respect for the longstanding tradition that a set of jars was a necessary component of a proper burial outfit. The association of the names of the genii with the heads on the jars exhibits a number of variations on the traditional pattern during this period, particularly with respect to Duamutef and Qebehsenuef, who frequently appear with the heads of a falcon and jackal respectively (see fig. 42). The widespread occurrence of this change on canopic jars and also in coffin decoration suggests the existence of alternative traditions, rather than error on the part of ancient scribes.

59197
59198
59199
59200

41. Calcite canopic jars with painted wooden lids representing the heads of the four Sons of Horus: Imsety (man), Hapy (baboon), Duamutef (jackal) and Qebehsenuef (falcon). This set was made for the lady Neskhons, wife of the high priest of Amun Pinedjem II. 21st Dynasty, about 1000 BC. From the 'Royal Cache' at Deir el-Bahri, Thebes. H. 36.5–40 cm.

The practice of placing visceral packages in canopic jars was revived in the late 25th Dynasty; the jars of the Kushite rulers buried at el-Kurru and Nuri show that this development occurred (at least for kings' burials) in the reign of Taharqo (690–664 BC). The reintroduction of functional jars, perhaps reflecting the archaising trends which were manifested in art and material culture at the period, was quickly adopted throughout Egypt, 26th Dynasty examples being attested at Thebes, Abydos and Saqqara. 26th Dynasty canopic jars were frequently made of calcite. They are often of large size and are barrel-shaped, being widest a little above the middle (see fig. 43). The lids usually represent the zoomorphic heads of the Sons of Horus (now identified once more according to the traditions of the New Kingdom), but are occasionally uniformly human. A more elaborate formulaic text was devised for the inscriptions. This is first

42. Set of dummy canopic jars of painted wood. During the Third Intermediate Period, when the internal organs were replaced inside the body, canopic jars continued to be placed in the tomb, though many were solid imitations. These specimens also illustrate the breakdown of the traditional pattern of iconography for the Sons of Horus at this time; here the falcon head is associated with Duamutef, and that of the jackal with Qebehsenuef. 25th Dynasty, about 700 BC. Provenance unknown. H. 28–35.5 cm.

43. Calcite canopic jars of the army commander Neferibre-emakhet. The owner was the son of another general named Psamtek-sa-Neit. The inscriptions promise the protection of the goddesses Isis, Nephthys, Neith and Selkis, and that of the four Sons of Horus. Late 26th Dynasty, about 570–525 BC. From Saqqara. H. 33–5 cm.

encountered with the royal jars of the 25th Dynasty and continues to the Ptolemaic Period. However, the return of functional jars did not completely supersede the replacing of the viscera within the body or in the mummy wrappings. In some cases, the viscera were placed on the thighs; in other cases returned to the body cavity, as in the mummy of Hornedjitef in the British Museum (see front cover), dating to the late third century BC. In the latter case, a wooden shrine-shaped canopic chest was also included in the tomb, but its four compartments contained only potsherds wrapped in linen, as 'dummy' viscera.

THE EMBALMERS AT WORK

The embalmers were organised in a hierarchy, like the priests of a temple, and those who carried out the more important tasks held sacerdotal titles. The operations were supervised by the *hery seshta*, or 'Master of Secrets', the 'secrets' being the specialised treatments performed on the corpse to preserve it. The *hery seshta* was closely linked with the god Anubis, who had mummified Osiris, according to mythology. In the ritualised process of mummification the deceased was identified with Osiris and, accordingly, the *hery seshta* played the part of Anubis; it is possible that he wore a jackal-headed mask during the proceedings to emphasise this association. However, the depictions of a jackal-headed man in scenes such as figs 20 and 133 more probably represent a hypothetical ideal in which Anubis himself performed the mummification and its rituals. References to embalming several times mention the deceased being 'in (or under) the hands of Anubis'.

Other participants included the *khetemu netjer*, or 'seal-bearer of the god' and the *khery-hebet* ('keeper of the sacred book', or lector-priest), who read out the appropriate words at different stages of the ritual. The practical aspects of the work were carried out by embalmers called *wetyu*, of whom there were doubtless many. Their tasks would have included the preparation of water, oils, resin, natron and cloth. Greek texts identify two specialist types of embalmer – the *paraschistes* ('incision maker' or 'ripper-up') and the *taricheutes* ('pickler'), though these are not distinguished in Egyptian sources.

As embalming became widespread, the personnel involved gradually increased in numbers; according to Diodorus, the office was hereditary. In the Old and Middle Kingdoms, when mummification was usually reserved chiefly for the royal family and persons of high rank, it is likely that only privileged individuals were permitted to carry out the necessary operations. At this period, mummification could be awarded by the king as a favour in recognition of good service or an exemplary act of piety by a subordinate. The biography in the tomb of Sabni at Aswan (6th Dynasty) records the sending from the Residence of officials to carry out the mummification of Sabni's father Mekhu (see Chapter 1). These comprised two embalmers, a chief lector-priest, besides other officials, mourners, various oils and utensils, and the ritual knowledge (literally the 'secrets') of the two embalming workshops or *wabety* (at this period there was a Northern and a Southern *wabet*). With the passage of time, the techniques and the special knowledge required probably became established in provincial centres, leading to local traditions of embalming.

After ritual purification in the *ibu* (see p. 52), the body was transferred to the place of embalming. This is often termed the *wabet*, literally the 'pure place' or 'place of purification'. Another term frequently used is *per-nefer*, often translated 'Good/Beautiful House', but perhaps best rendered as 'House of rejuvenation'. In the Old Kingdom, part or all of the embalming of the dead king took place in the valley temple of the royal pyramid. The embalming of other individuals was carried out in a temporary structure erected close to the tomb. The work performed in these places occupied a specified period of time, which is often mentioned in texts: from the 18th Dynasty onwards, the figure of seventy days is mentioned several times as the length of time between death and burial:

> A good burial comes in peace, your seventy days having been completed in your place of embalming (*wabet*).

44. Document written in demotic on papyrus, containing the statement of Phagonis, probably a lector-priest, who acknowledges receipt of quantities of natron and linen for the mummification of a corpse, with a promise to hand over the body to the *choachytes* (the officials responsible for burials and the service of the dead) on the 72nd day after death. Year 16 of the reign of Ptolemy II, December 270 to January 269 BC. From Thebes. H. 20 cm.

There are several texts, ranging in date from the 5th Dynasty to the Ptolemaic Period, which show that the duration of the mummification process was variable. The seventy-day period is perhaps to be understood as the length of time during which mourning for the deceased took place, within which period the body was embalmed. Only for an elaborate mummification would seventy days be required. This would have comprised about thirty-five to forty days for the evisceration and drying of the body and a further thirty to thirty-five days for anointing and wrapping. The length of time occupied by the latter operations would have depended more on ritual requirements than practical necessity. Sometimes considerably longer treatments are documented. The body of the father of the vizier Senedjemib, whose tomb was at Giza, was in the *wabet* for one year and two-thirds (see Chapter 5). Inscriptions in the tomb chapel of Queen Meresankh III in the Eastern Cemetery at Giza (late 4th Dynasty) mention the dates of death and burial: 'Year 1, first month of *shemu* [harvest-season], day 21. The resting of her *ka* and her proceeding to the house of purification' and 'Year after 1 [i.e. Year 2], second month of *peret* [season of sowing], day 18. Her proceeding to her beautiful tomb'. The interval between these two dates amounts to 273 or 274 days. If this time was spent entirely in the place of embalming an exceptionally long mummification would be indicated. The skeleton of the queen, however, showed no evidence of special treatment.

Mummification was not always carried out by professionals. Within a close-knit community such as the workmen's village of Deir el-Medina it could be done by a relative or work colleague. Much more information about the organisation of embalmers is available for the Ptolemaic and Roman periods, from which survive contracts made between embalmers and relatives of the deceased. Some of these documents on papyrus include receipts for materials used and a promise to deliver the completed mummy to the family on a specified day (see fig. 44).

Despite the ritual framework in which mummification was supposed to take place, the realities of the embalmers' workshop must have been hideous, particularly when large numbers of corpses were being processed simultaneously for it would have been impossible to maintain a sterile environment within the tent-like working-areas. Insects certainly had access to the workshops, and were able to lay their eggs on the bodies, as is clear from the many beetles and larval skins which have been discovered when mummies have been unwrapped (see fig. 45). Even the bodies of small rodents have been found between layers of wrappings, where they had presumably crept while the partly-wrapped body was unattended, only to become trapped.

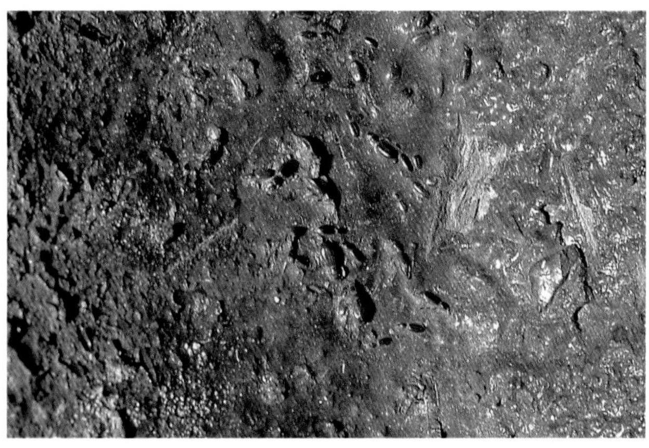

45. Beetles adhering to the resinous coating on the interior of the wooden coffin of King Nubkheperra Intef. The substance apparently remained glutinous for some time after the body was placed in the coffin, and entrapped a number of carrion beetles (*dermestes*), which had perhaps escaped through the wrappings of the corpse. 17th Dynasty, about 1600 BC. From Dra Abu el-Naga, Thebes. H. of coffin 170 cm.

Instances of carelessness and dishonest practice on the part of the embalmers are also numerous. Radiography has revealed that many mummies of the Roman Period, though elaborately wrapped and adorned, are very poorly preserved and were probably in an advanced state of decomposition before the embalmers began their work. The bones are frequently in disarray and some body parts are found to be missing altogether. Some Theban mummies of the 21st Dynasty, though found undisturbed by archaeologists, had been plundered of their jewellery and amulets while still in the embalming workshop, only the impressions being left in the bandages, which had been unwound and then replaced.

The reputation of the embalmers seems to have varied. According to Diodorus, they were 'considered worthy of every honour and consideration, associating with the priests and even coming and going in the temples without hindrance, as being undefiled'. Herodotus, however, perceived them as artisans, neither deserving of respect nor altogether trustworthy. The most explicit statement of the irregular behaviour of embalmers comes from Herodotus, who recorded a scurrilous story that necrophilia was practised by some among them:

> Now the wives of important men, when they die, are not handed over to be embalmed at once, nor women who are especially beautiful or famous. Not until the third or fourth day has elapsed are they given to the embalmers. They do this to prevent the embalmers violating the corpse. For they say that one of them was caught who had actually abused a newly-dead woman; a workmate denounced him.

The evolution of mummification

The procedures used in mummification changed over time. It is generally supposed that technical innovations were introduced by those who embalmed the bodies of the king and his relatives, and were subsequently extended to non-royal persons. At some periods, different techniques were practised simultaneously, as noted by Herodotus, but a chronological development is apparent.

Pre-Old Kingdom

The Egyptians of the Predynastic period buried their dead in simple shallow pits, oval or circular in shape, scooped out of the desert sand. The corpse was laid on its side with the arms and legs tightly flexed and the hands placed in front of the face – an apparently embryonic posture, which may point to the early development of a concept of rebirth. The body was sometimes wrapped in matting or hides, but was otherwise in direct contact with the sand. The body fluids were rapidly absorbed by the sand, leaving skin, bones, hair, nails and internal organs all well preserved.

During the second half of the fourth millennium BC, burials began to be more elaborately prepared, and greater efforts were made to protect the body. Besides wrapping it in hides or matting, basket trays and simple wooden box-coffins were introduced, and the grave-pit itself was more carefully made, with vertical sides and a wooden roof. These well-intentioned arrangements unfortunately proved detrimental to the body's survival, since they insulated it from the sand filling of the grave – the main agent of natural preservation. Most corpses buried in this manner decomposed together with their wrappings, leaving only the bones.

Provision of a coffin and a roofed grave with internal facings became marks of status, and were particularly significant in the formative stages of the pharaonic state, around 3000 BC, when the hierarchy of Egyptian society was becoming progressively emphasised. Once these improvements had been introduced, it was no longer acceptable to the élite members of society to be buried in a simpler style. No less important was the transformation of the corpse into an idealised body which would serve the deceased in the new life. Hence more and more attention began to be focused on preserving the body by artificial methods. Experimentation along these lines had already begun in the late Predynastic period; burials dating to about 3500 BC discovered at Hierakonpolis in 1997 already showed the use of linen, both in strips to wrap the corpse and in the form of bundles acting as padding, perhaps to help retain the shape of the body. Moreover, traces of resin on the skin of these corpses hint at efforts to achieve more elaborate preservation. The few surviving remains from high-status graves of the 1st and 2nd Dynasties show that wrapping the body in linen was a well-developed practice. Linen bandages were found on a disembodied arm from the tomb of King Djer (*c.* 3000 BC) at Abydos, and early dynastic burials from Saqqara had all the limbs wrapped separately in linen bandages; in one case eight layers were counted on the limbs and up to fourteen over the chest. In these cases the soft tissues usually did not survive, with only the bones being preserved inside the wrappings. Some burials of this period reflect the alternative tradition (see p. 48) of dismembering the corpse and wrapping the dry bones.

Old Kingdom

In the Old Kingdom, important advances were made in the procedure of mummification, though at this period the most elaborate treatments were probably available only to members of the royal family and to officials of very high status. For this reason, and on account of the robbery of most Old Kingdom tombs, very few mummies from this period have survived. Those that have illustrate a well-defined methodology. Although the brain was left undisturbed, the viscera were extracted from the body cavity and preserved separately. This practice had been introduced at least by the beginning of the 4th Dynasty (*c.* 2600 BC), since a calcite chest for the viscera was found in the tomb of Queen Hetepheres I, mother of King Khufu (*c.* 2589–2566 BC) (see above, p. 67). Some method of drying the corpse must have been employed during this period, probably involving the use of natron, but precise details are lacking. It became customary for the corpse to be laid out with the limbs fully extended, a practice which coincides roughly with the adoption of the evisceration of the deceased. This 'extended' posture had already been introduced during the 3rd Dynasty, at which date the first full-length coffins are attested (see p. 218). The soft tissues were not well-preserved, and the embalmers seem to have devoted most of their efforts towards the external appearance of the wrapped mummy, which was fashioned into a lifelike but idealised image of the deceased, rather like a statue. Linen padding was inserted under and over the skin, to fill out the shape of the body, particularly the facial features, which were carefully modelled in layers of linen impregnated with resin. Arms, legs, ears, fingers and toes were individually modelled, and hair was rendered in a naturalistic manner. The fragmentary human remains discovered in the pyramids of Djoser, Sneferu, Raneferef, Djedkara-Isesi and Unis, at Saqqara, Abusir and Dahshur, indicate that the bodies of Old Kingdom rulers were prepared in this manner. A similar treatment is attested in the case of non-royal individuals. The mummy of Ranefer from Meidum was padded with linen and coated with resin, the individual limbs and the head moulded, and the eyes and eyebrows painted on the outer wrappings.

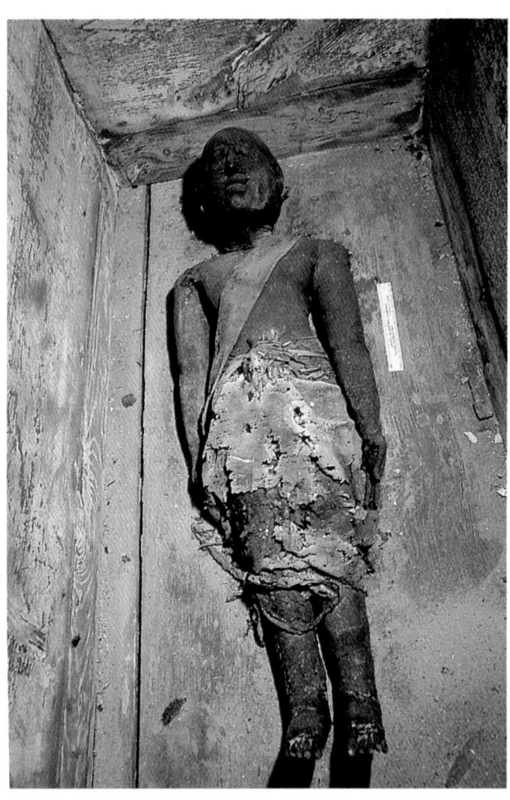

46. Mummy of a man found in a shaft-tomb near the causeway of the pyramid of Unis at Saqqara. Using linen soaked in resin, the body has been fashioned into an idealised image of the deceased as a living being, with arms and legs separately prepared. Facial features have been added in paint, and the body has been dressed in a linen kilt and priest's shoulder-strap. This method of mummification was characteristic of the Old Kingdom. 5th Dynasty, about 2494–2345 BC.

In an alternative treatment, applied to mummies found in tombs of the 5th and 6th Dynasties at Giza, a coating of fine plaster was added to the outer wrappings. This coating, sometimes painted, was often confined to the head, but occasionally extended over the entire body, which was represented naturalistically, with the limbs delineated.

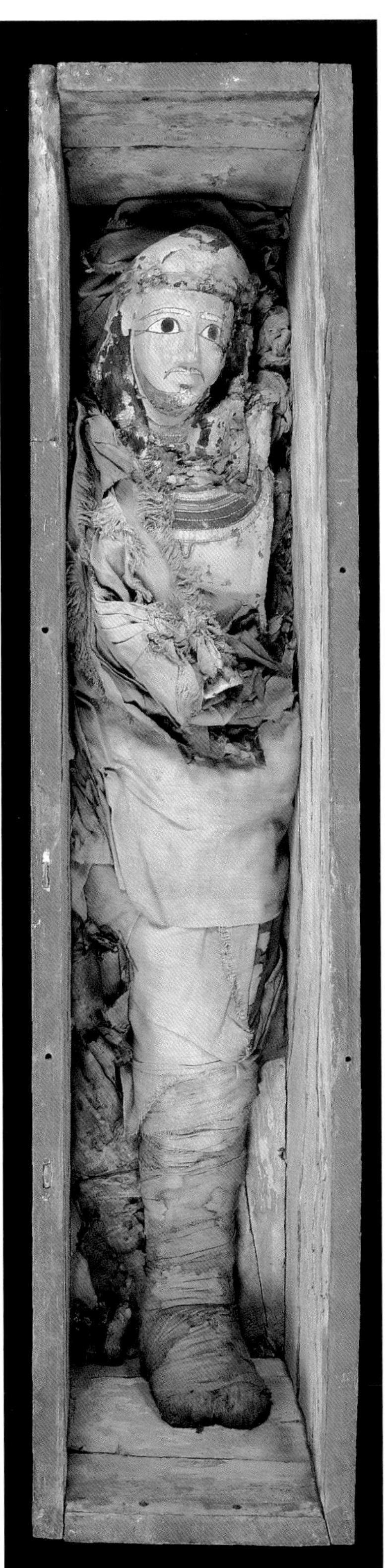

The lifelike appearance of Old Kingdom mummies was enhanced in some cases by the addition of clothing and other trappings. The body of an unidentified woman found in a 5th Dynasty tomb at Giza wore a sheath-dress and had realistic breasts elaborately fashioned from layers of linen. Another female from a Giza tomb wore an inlaid gold fillet, gold and bronze necklaces and bracelets, and a faience bead-net dress. In this case, the fingers were individually modelled in clay. A male mummy found at Saqqara (see fig. 46) was dressed in the linen kilt and priestly shoulder-strap familiar from artistic representations of the period, and traces of a kilt on one of the plaster coverings from Giza show that some mummies prepared by this method were also represented clothed. The bodies of the kings were apparently treated in the same manner. In the pyramid of Pepy I (*c.* 2321–2287 BC) at Saqqara were found part of a pleated kilt and a gilded wooden sandal, on the sole of which were carved the 'Nine Bows' representing the traditional enemies which the Egyptian king symbolically trod underfoot. These finds suggest that the mummy of this king, at least, was prepared in a lifelike form, equipped with royal trappings.

First Intermediate Period

An important innovation of this period was the creation of a new iconography for the mummified body. While evisceration and drying continued to be practised according to the principles established in the Old Kingdom, the external appearance of the body was changed. Instead of a lifelike image of the deceased, with limbs, fingers and toes and naturalistic facial features, the embalmers enveloped the entire body in a cocoon of linen, concealing the individual members, and completed it with a mask of painted cartonnage placed over the head (see fig. 47). This is the form which was known by the name *sah* (see Chapter 1). The earliest examples of bodies prepared in this way are known from provincial cemeteries such as Sheikh Farag and Hagarsa, but the style rapidly spread throughout Egypt.

47. Mummy of a man named Ankhef. The mask of painted cartonnage depicts an idealised image of the deceased wearing a wig and collar and with a beard and moustache. It extends beneath the outer wrappings to cover the upper body. In the time at which Ankhef lived, the mummy was usually placed on its left side, the face aligned with the eyes painted on the exterior of the coffin (see fig. 104). Early 12th Dynasty, about 1950 BC. From Asyut. L. 170 cm.

Middle Kingdom

The number of well-preserved mummies from this period is relatively small, but those found provide indications that several different techniques were in use at this period. The mummies of some of the wives and courtiers of Mentuhotep II (*c.* 2055–2004 BC), found in tombs at Deir el-Bahri, had been prepared in a simple manner. They showed no abdominal incisions to extract the viscera, which in most cases were found still within the body cavities. There were some signs that oil or resin might have been injected via the anus, but the evidence was inconclusive and it may be that the bodies had simply been wrapped, without any attempt at evisceration. The preservation of the soft tissues and hair of these mummies was consistent with a process of drying by means of an external application of natron and oil or resin. Fingernails, epidermis and – in some cases – hair had been lost, but the bodies had evidently been wrapped while the soft tissues were still flexible; jewellery placed on the body of the woman Ashait had left its imprint in the flesh. Another mummy from Deir el-Bahri, dating from the late 11th or early 12th Dynasty, is that of the official Wah. In this case, the organs of the abdominal cavity had been extracted via an incision in the flank, and the soft tissues were well preserved. As with the other mummies discussed here, however, more attention had been devoted to the wrappings and external adornments. Wah's mummy was provided with a gilded mask and enveloped in a huge amount of linen (see p. 60). At several points during the wrapping, the textile had been coated with resin, as though to provide a sealant, and jewellery and amulets were placed between some of the many layers of linen.

Middle Kingdom mummies from other sites exhibit signs of different methods of treatment. Evisceration was frequently performed, as indicated by the provision of canopic containers in many tombs of the 11th and 12th Dynasties. The modelling of the facial features over the skull by means of layers of linen, as in the Old Kingdom, continued, as exemplified by the head of the provincial governor Djehutynakht, found in his tomb at Deir el-Bersha. In this case, details such as the eyebrows were added in black paint on an outer layer of linen. The mummies from this tomb, however, were also provided with masks, so that the facial modelling on the bodies may ultimately have been concealed. In general, the mummification process in the Middle Kingdom did not result in consistent survival of the soft tissues, and the majority of bodies from this period were reduced to skeletons.

The embalmers may have attempted to remove the brain as early as the Old Kingdom, but it was not until the Middle Kingdom that this practice became more widespread, although the procedure was still at an experimental stage. CT-scanning of the skull of Djehutynakht, mentioned above, showed that the brain had been extracted not via the nostrils as in later periods, but through holes made in the maxillary sinuses. This technique resulted in damage to the eye-sockets of the skull, and was not continued after the Middle Kingdom.

A striking indication of the range of mummification techniques in use at this period is provided by the bodies of about sixty soldiers, who had been killed in battle and were brought back to Thebes for burial in a collective tomb at Deir el-Bahri (see p. 41). Several exhibit fatal wounds, including arrows *in situ*; other mutilations were probably caused by birds of prey before the bodies were removed from the battlefield. The preservation of these corpses had been carried out in a simple but effective manner, by burying them temporarily in sand (traces of which still adhered to the skin) and wrapping them in linen. They are thus counterparts to the naturally-preserved bodies of the Predynastic period, which they resemble in terms of the state of their preservation.

Second Intermediate Period

The embalming techniques of the 12th Dynasty seem to have continued in use in the 13th, although evidence is scanty. The mummies of King Hor (*c.* 1750 BC) and the king's daughter Nubheteptikhered, who were buried at Dahshur, had evidently been eviscerated, since canopic containers were provided. The bodies themselves, however, consisted of little more than the bones when found.

The Hyksos chieftains who ruled northern Egypt during the later Second Intermediate Period (*c.* 1650–1550 BC) appear to have followed the burial customs of their Palestinian homeland, to judge from the tombs excavated at Tell el-Daba in the north-east Delta. Mummification has not been identified at that site, although it continued to be practised at Thebes, the power-base of the indigenous 17th Dynasty rulers. The few specimens which survive from this period, however, are not well preserved. The mummy of King Seqenenra Taa (*c.* 1560 BC), dating to the end of this period, consists essentially of skin and a disarticulated skeleton. In this case, the poor preservation perhaps resulted in part from the exceptional circumstances of the king's death. A series of severe wounds in the skull show that he had been the victim of a violent attack, probably on the battlefield. The mummy of his successor Kamose (*c.* 1555–1550 BC) was apparently also inefficiently embalmed, since it is reported to have fallen to pieces when discovered at Thebes in 1857. Another burial of this period, found at Qurna, was enclosed in a richly gilded anthropoid coffin but, in spite of elaborate wrappings, only the bones survived.

New Kingdom

Important advances in embalming were achieved in the New Kingdom, doubtless facilitated by the long-term stability and prosperity which Egypt enjoyed during this 500-year period, and the availability of a wider range of materials from abroad (particularly oils and resins) through improved commercial contacts. The developments are traceable via the mummies of the kings and queens of the period, many of whom were buried at Thebes. It is a reasonable assumption that these bodies represent the best methods available at the time of their preparation, and they illustrate the fact that the most skilled embalmers were now able consistently to preserve the soft tissues of the body as well as the bones (see fig. 48).

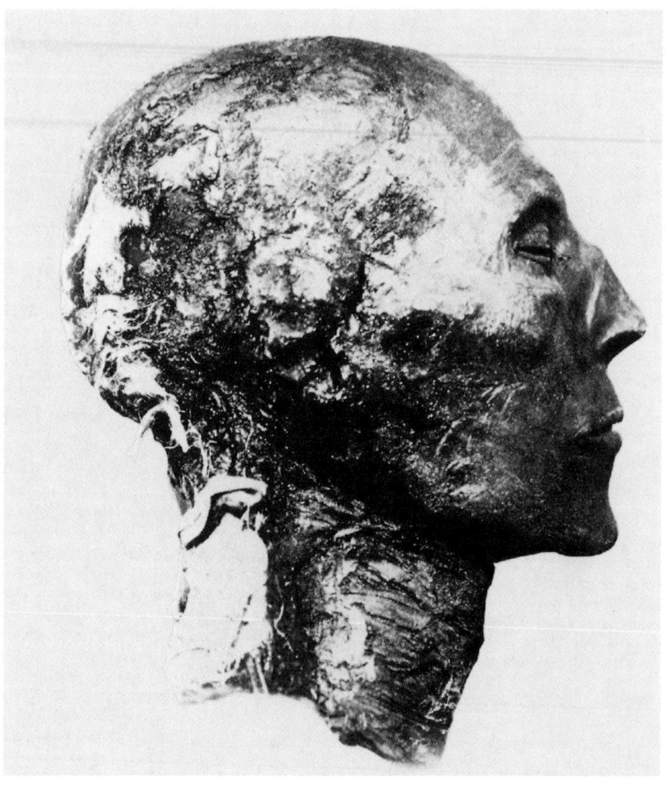

48. Head of the mummy of King Sety I. This specimen is the most perfectly preserved of the royal mummies of the New Kingdom, discovered in the cache at Deir el-Bahri on the Theban West Bank in 1881. Early 19th Dynasty, about 1279 BC.

The extraction of the brain became a regular feature of sophisticated embalming at this period. The embalmers who carried out the mummification of King Ahmose I (*c.* 1550–1525 BC) at the beginning of the 18th Dynasty removed the atlas vertebra from the neck, and extracted the brain through the *foramen magnum* at the base of the skull. This difficult technique was not repeated and subsequently the standard method of removing the brain was that described by Herodotus – by piercing the ethmoid bone and inserting a metal hook into the cranial cavity, after which the brain tissue was drawn down through the nose.

Evisceration continued to be a standard practice and was usually performed via the abdominal incision. The position of the incision changed through time. After the removal of the organs the body cavity was stuffed with packing material. The incision was often left open, though a leaf-shaped plaque of gold foil might be placed over it.

Large quantities of resin were applied over the body, and in many cases, skin, hair and nails were well preserved. However, the loss of the subcutaneous fat and the muscle tissue during the dehydration process often caused severe creasing and wrinkling of the skin. In some cases the epidermis was lost during the drying process, and fingernails became loosened. A number of mummies exhibit threads around the finger-ends, apparently tied on to prevent the loss of the nails during embalming.

The position of the arms of kings' mummies changed during the 18th Dynasty. Ahmose I and Amenhotep I (*c.* 1525–1504 BC) appear to have been prepared with their arms at their sides. From the reign of Tuthmosis II (*c.* 1492–1479 BC), however, the arms were crossed on the breast. Royal sceptres were placed in the hands of Tutankhamun (*c.* 1336–1327 BC), and were probably provided for other kings besides. The crossed-arms position seems to have been reserved for kings at this period; in the mummies of non-royal individuals the arms are usually placed by the sides, with the hands covering the genital area.

The body cavities of the royal mummies were filled with a variety of materials – usually resin-soaked linen but in a few cases of the 19th and 20th Dynasties with lichen, sawdust or a fatty substance apparently mixed with natron. Resin was extensively applied to the surfaces to exclude moisture and help to prevent bacterial activity. The fact that in some cases the resin has penetrated into the

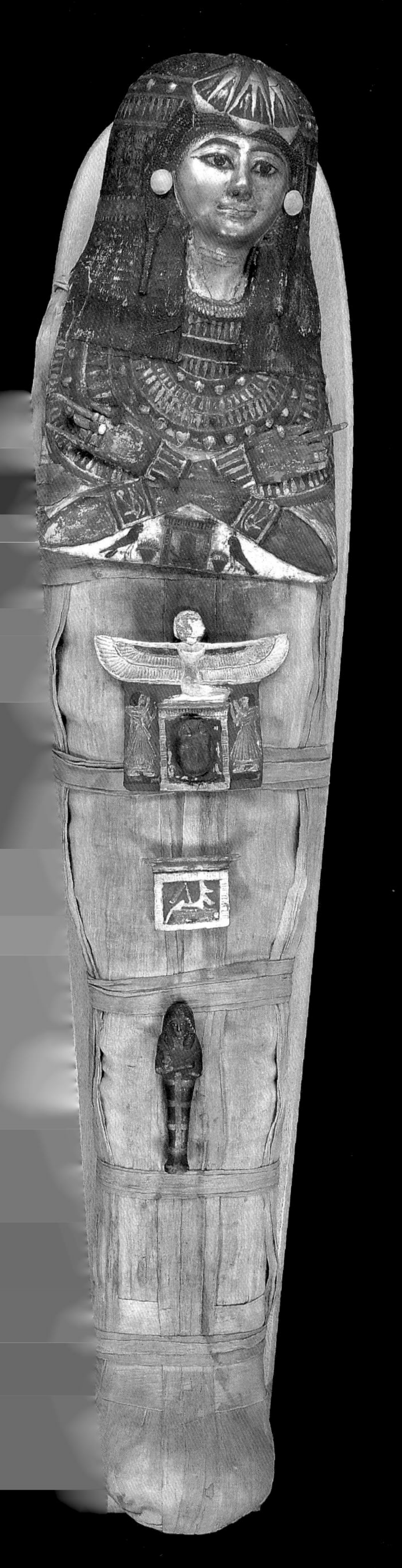

interior of the bones indicates that it was applied in a heated state. In the case of the mummy believed to be that of Amenhotep III (*c.* 1390–1352 BC), who had been obese at death, resin was inserted beneath the skin to restore substance to the features. Other cosmetic treatments are attested in this period. Several elderly queens were suffering from thinning hair at the time of their deaths, and artificial extensions were added. Hair and fingernails were stained with henna, and artificial eyes were provided. These were sometimes fashioned from linen, but in some instances small onions were used as substitutes for the eyes themselves, which usually shrank to the back of the orbits during the drying process.

These elaborate techniques were evidently available to the highest ranking members of the court, but the majority of mummies of non-royal individuals of the New Kingdom present a different picture. Although the external trappings may appear impressive, the actual techniques of mummification employed were rudimentary; often the corpse was simply dried and wrapped, without any attempt to extract the brain or viscera. This method was observed in the mummies of the parents and other members of the family of Senenmut, one of the most influential officials in the reign of Hatshepsut. An example in the British Museum is the mummy of Katebet, an elderly woman who probably died around the end of the 18th Dynasty (see fig. 49). Considerable expense seems to have been lavished on her beautiful gilded mask and other adornments, but radiography has demonstrated that the brain was not removed, that little soft tissue survived and that large quantities of mud had been

49. Mummy of an elderly woman named Katebet. The head is covered by a mask of gilded cartonnage, and pectoral ornaments and a *shabti* figure lie over the torso. CT-scanning has revealed that mummification was rudimentary; the brain was not extracted, and large amounts of dense packing material, probably mud, were applied to the exterior of the corpse before wrapping, perhaps to prevent it from falling to pieces. Late 18th or early 19th Dynasty, about 1300–1280 BC. Found in an unidentified tomb at Thebes. L. 165 cm.

used to prevent the body falling apart – suggesting that embalming had been rudimentary at best. Written references show that mummification was not always done by professional embalmers, but could be carried out by relatives or colleagues. The bodies of the family of the necropolis workman Sennedjem from Deir el-Medina had been prepared very simply; a contemporary reference from the same community mentions that the workman Neferabet 'wrapped up' his deceased brother. Doubtless such unprofessional operations did not represent the highest standards of embalming.

Third Intermediate Period

The years following the end of the New Kingdom represented the technical peak of Egyptian mummification procedures. The processes of evisceration and drying used in the New Kingdom had been perfected and had become standard practice, and the embalmers of the 21st Dynasty turned their attention increasingly to recreating the natural appearance of the body. In an effort to restore fullness to the shrivelled features and limbs, the embalmers inserted packing under the skin. Mud, linen, sand, sawdust, and occasionally other materials were used for this purpose. The neck, chest, back and legs were stuffed via the flank incision made to remove the viscera. Additional incisions were sometimes made to facilitate the stuffing of the back and legs: the shoulders and arms were stuffed via incisions in the shoulders, and the cheeks packed via the mouth (see fig. 50). Overstuffing sometimes caused skin to burst, as occurred in the case of Henuttawy, the wife of Pinedjem I (*c.* 1050 BC).

The treatment of the viscera changed at the end of the New Kingdom. Instead of being placed in canopic jars, the preserved liver, lungs, stomach and intestines were replaced in the body cavity. Each organ was wrapped in a separate linen package and accompanied by a wax figure of one of the Sons of Horus to confer

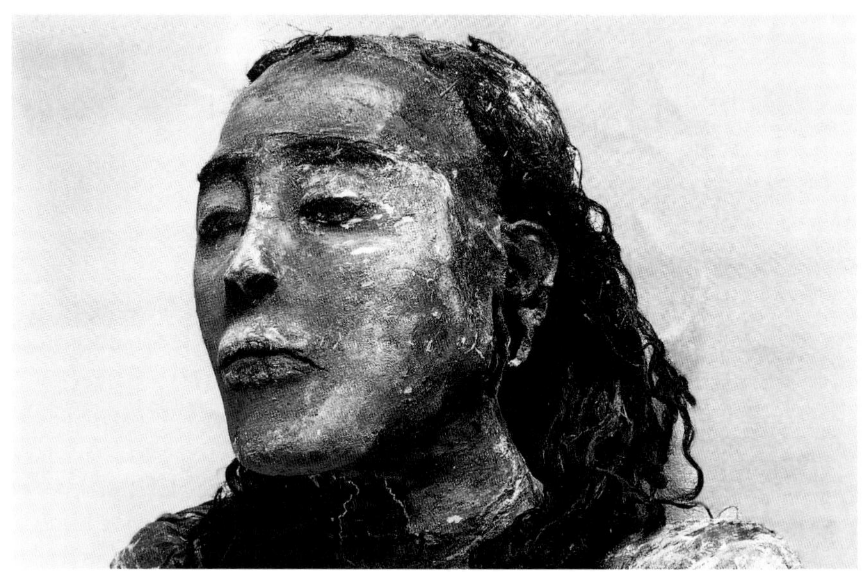

50. Head of the mummy of the lady Nany, a member of the ruling family of the high priests of Amun at Thebes in the early 21st Dynasty, about 1050 BC. The body exemplifies the sophisticated embalming techniques of the period, including subcutaneous packing to restore substance to the shrunken features, and careful arrangement of the hair. From an intrusive burial in the 18th Dynasty tomb of Queen Merytamun at Deir el-Bahri, Thebes.

magical protection. Although the canonical number of packages was four, this custom was not always observed, several mummies of the 21st Dynasty containing seven packages.

Elaborate cosmetic treatments were carried out. The skin of male mummies was painted red, that of female bodies yellow (in conformity with the artistic convention for distinguishing male from female). Thinning hair was eked out by extensions, and artificial eyes of glass or stone were inserted into the eye-sockets. Repairs were even made to the skin, where damage had occurred. Defects in the skin of an elderly woman, probably caused by bedsores, were repaired by sewing on leather patches. Injuries in life which had resulted in the loss of bodily members were sometimes made good by the use of prosthetics. A finely made artificial toe, discovered in the wrappings of a mummy, may have been worn in life to conceal a disfigured foot before being incorporated into the mummy.

After the 21st Dynasty, a decline in the standards of mummification began. Although subcutaneous packing and the replacing of viscera inside the body continued into the 22nd Dynasty, the range of other treatments employed seems to have narrowed with the passage of time.

Late Period

Mummies of the 26th Dynasty and later exhibit signs of deteriorating standards of preservation. Subcutaneous packing was less frequently employed, and there was an increasing tendency to rely on the use of large quantities of molten resin to preserve the body. The distinction of methods according to cost mentioned by Herodotus is exemplified by several bodies which seem to have been prepared according to his 'cheaper' method. An example is the mummy of the woman Irtyersenu (late 26th Dynasty) which was dissected and examined in 1821 by Augustus Granville. This mummy had no flank incision and contained a substantial portion of the viscera, which had perhaps been preserved by means of an anal injection. Canopic jars were reintroduced during this period, but did not attain universal use; in many mummies the viscera were placed on or between the thighs and held in position by the outer wrappings. The positioning of the arms began to change at this period, the arms more frequently being crossed on the breast, instead of the fully extended position which had been usual in earlier centuries.

Ptolemaic Period

The often inferior standards of embalming continued into the Ptolemaic Period, when many bodies were crudely preserved by being coated in a thick layer of resin, although for persons of wealth and high status elaborate treatments were still available (see fig. 51). The mummy of the priest Hornedjitef from Thebes (late third century BC) appears to have been carefully preserved. Radiography showed that the brain had been extracted and the skull cavity partly filled with molten resin. The viscera had been wrapped separately and replaced in the body cavity as in the Third Intermediate Period.

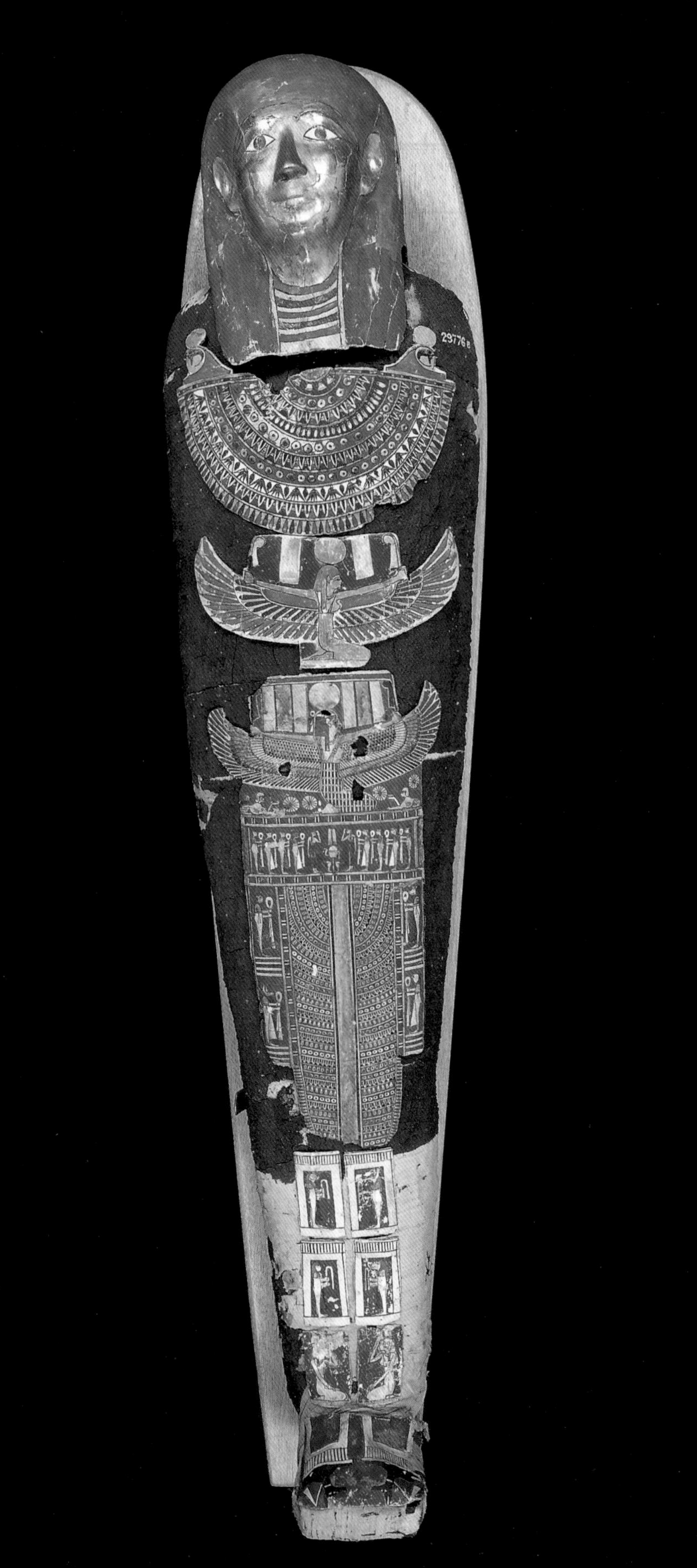

51. Mummy of a man named Djedhor. The outer wrappings have been carefully coated with a black substance, which has been identified chemically as bitumen from the Dead Sea. Over this black coating have been placed a gilded mask and a group of painted cartonnage plaques, representing the goddess Nut with outspread wings, the Sons of Horus, Isis and Nephthys and other deities. Ptolemaic Period, about 250 BC. From Akhmim. L. 156 cm.

52. Mummy of a young man named Artemidorus in a painted and gilded stucco case. The portrait-panel shows the deceased dressed in a tunic and mantle of Roman style, and with his hair brushed forward in the manner of the Trajanic period (second century AD). Traditional Egyptian funerary scenes in gold leaf appear on the body, the case as a whole exemplifying the mixing of classical and Egyptian styles characteristic of the Graeco-Roman period. CT-scanning has revealed that the developmental state of Artemidorus' bones and teeth is consistent with an age at death of around the early twenties, as the portrait implies. AD 100–120. From Hawara. L. 167 cm.

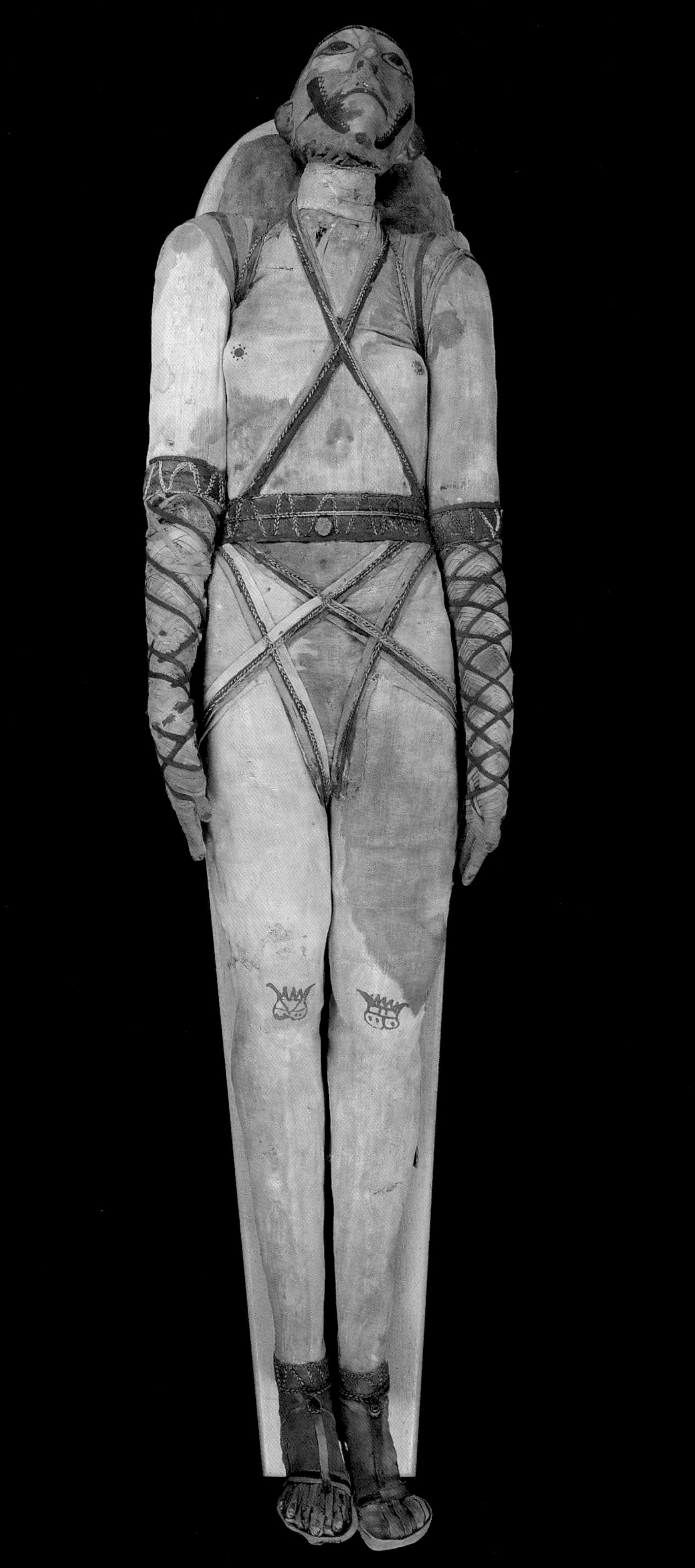

53. Mummy of a young adult man, found at Thebes. Radiography has shown that the brain has been extracted through the nose, and the viscera via an abdominal incision. The external preparation of the body recalls the methods used in the Old Kingdom. The facial features have been carefully modelled using resin-soaked linen, and the limbs filled out with a granular packing material. The arms, legs, fingers and toes have been individually wrapped, and the eyes, eyebrows and mouth painted on the wrappings. The natural hair of the deceased has been intentionally left exposed. Finely patterned wrapping has been applied to the forearms, and the body adorned with a belt, armlets and straps. Ptolemaic or Roman Period, after 305 BC. L. 162 cm.

Roman Period

A large number of mummies from the Roman Period have survived, and the rich decoration which many of them exhibit testifies to the importance attached to the external appearance of the wrapped body and its trappings. As in some earlier periods, such lavish adornment is often associated with crude and inferior preservation of the body itself (see fig. 52). Unwrapping and radiography of mummies of this period has revealed that the corpse is often poorly preserved. The bones are sometimes disarticulated and disordered; some parts of the body are missing altogether and sometimes a single 'mummy' contains parts of more than one body. This suggests that the embalmers often carried out their work in a rudimentary fashion and that many of the bodies were in an advanced state of decomposition before work on them began. Although 'restorations' of damaged or incomplete bodies were carried out, these were usually crude efforts using wooden splints, rolls of linen, mud and pottery – a far cry from the sophisticated cosmetic treatments used in the Third Intermediate Period.

More elaborate treatments were, however, available at this period, as one unidentified male mummy in the British Museum illustrates (see fig. 53). The brain was removed via the nose and the organs extracted from the body cavity. Before wrapping, the embalmer carefully modelled the facial features and the shape of the limbs to create a lifelike appearance, using resin-soaked linen for the face, and a granular packing material to emphasise the breasts. The facial features were painted on the wrappings, and the crown of the head was intentionally left uncovered so that the natural hair could remain visible. The limbs were wrapped separately and the fingers and toes individually bandaged, the feet being wrapped to imitate sandals. Finally, patterned wrapping was applied to the forearms, and the body was adorned with a belt, armlets and straps. Despite the prominent breasts, the body is that of an adult man, and the elaborate preparation, though exceptional for the period, is highly idiosyncratic, and recalls the style of mummification used in the Old Kingdom. Several other mummies prepared in the same style are known, and it is possible that all these individuals were mummified in the same embalming workshop.

The end of mummification

The latest well-dated mummies are attributable to the second and third centuries AD. After this date the traditions of pharaonic burial customs declined. Mummification was condemned as a pagan practice by the Coptic church, whose bishops preached against it, and much simpler styles of burial were increasingly adopted. However, in spite of official disapproval, crude mummification continued in the Christian era – the bodies of Coptic monks found at Thebes show signs of having been dried using salts (perhaps natron) and wrapped in bandages and shrouds, and the practice may have survived until the Islamic conquest in AD 641.

CHAPTER 3

Provisioning the Dead

The custom of providing the dead with material things for their comfort and wellbeing has been practically universal in all societies. Even today, the placing of gifts or treasured possessions in the coffin may help to assuage the sense of loss or ameliorate feelings of guilt on the part of those left behind. In ancient Egypt, providing for the dead was not merely a reaction to bereavement – it was essential to survival beyond the grave. Without proper provisioning there could be no afterlife.

Nourishing the dead

The most basic requirement for human survival, the need for food and drink, was a major consideration in funerary preparations at all periods. For the Egyptians, the simplest way to satisfy this need on behalf of the dead was to place supplies of foodstuffs in the grave or burial chamber. This practice is well attested during the late Predynastic and early Dynastic periods, when all but the poorest graves contained storage jars of stone or pottery filled with grain, water, beer or wine. Substantial quantities of such supplies have been found in some graves of the 1st and 2nd Dynasties. In some of these, the raw materials for food production, rather than the finished product, were provided, but there were exceptions. Loaves of bread, cakes, and cooked meats were sometimes placed in the grave, and occasionally the food was laid out on plates and in bowls as a meal, consisting of several courses. One such feast for the dead, found in a tomb of a woman of the 2nd Dynasty at Saqqara, included a porridge of ground barley, a quail, a pigeon stew, a cooked fish, ribs of beef, cooked kidneys, wheaten loaves and cakes, fruit and cheese.

Trussed birds, joints of meat (including ox and calf), bread and cakes were placed in tombs of the Old Kingdom, sometimes enclosed in limestone boxes carved to represent their contents. By this period, however, the nourishing of the dead was usually being taken care of by magic and ritual, and the custom of providing real comestibles appears to have waned until the New Kingdom, when there was a resurgence of the practice. Many loaves, cakes, fruits and other items have been found in tombs of the 18th to 20th Dynasties, particularly at Thebes, where local conditions are especially favourable to the survival of such impermanent items (see figs 54–5). The tombs of the kings and other individuals of high status also contained portions of meat which had been mummified and wrapped in linen, sometimes coated with resin or oil. These provisions were enclosed in wooden cases carved in the shape of the contents, which usually included geese, ducks, pigeons, joints of beef and portions of sheep or goat. A black-painted wooden box in the British Museum, perhaps from the burial of the high-ranking Theban woman Henutmehyt (*c.* 1250 BC) contains enough meat for a substantial meal, comprising a selection of linen-wrapped fowl and joints cut from a small quadruped, possibly a goat.

Clearly, limited food supplies of this kind were not meant to be replenished,

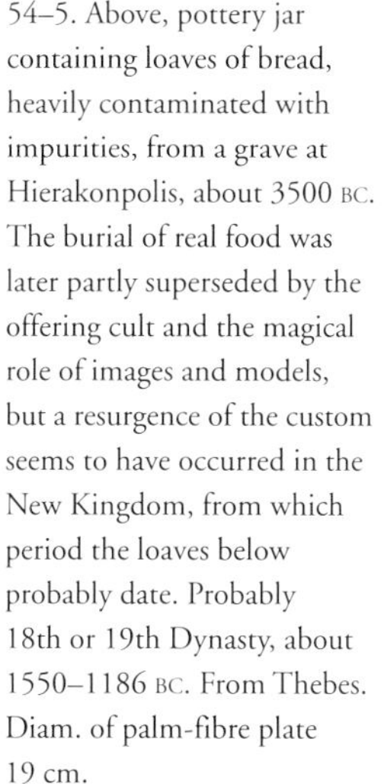

54–5. Above, pottery jar containing loaves of bread, heavily contaminated with impurities, from a grave at Hierakonpolis, about 3500 BC. The burial of real food was later partly superseded by the offering cult and the magical role of images and models, but a resurgence of the custom seems to have occurred in the New Kingdom, from which period the loaves below probably date. Probably 18th or 19th Dynasty, about 1550–1186 BC. From Thebes. Diam. of palm-fibre plate 19 cm.

and therefore could not be expected to nourish the deceased for eternity. Such food must in fact have fulfilled a symbolic rather than a functional role. This has been borne out by microscopic examinations of samples of the loaves and cakes recovered from tombs. These are frequently found to be composed of substandard ingredients, heavily contaminated with waste products which would have made them extremely unappetising. However, this would not pose a problem if the food-offerings were regarded simply as tokens, and there is evidence to suggest that this attitude was indeed held from the earliest times; loaves found in jars in the Predynastic cemetery at Hierakonpolis, dating to about 3500 BC, proved to be made predominantly of chaff, and hence would have been inedible (see fig. 54). Bread and cakes from New Kingdom tombs in the British Museum have also been discovered to contain a high proportion of chaff, in addition to other contaminants.

56. Painted limestone relief from the shrine or funerary chapel of Kemsit, one of the wives of King Mentuhotep II (about 2055–2004 BC). Kemsit is depicted savouring the scent of a jar of perfumed ointment and stretching out her hand to receive offerings. On the right, a servant, whose figure is lost, was shown pouring a drink into a cup and uttering the words inscribed in a vertical line: 'For your *ka*, gifts and offerings'. From Deir el-Bahri, Thebes. H. 37.5 cm.

Provisioning by magic

The offering cult

Throughout most of the pharaonic period the sustenance of the dead was taken care of by magical means. Funerary texts indicate that it was not the physical body but the *ka* which required feeding (see Chapter 1) (see fig. 56). The *ka* was dependent on the world of the living to make this possible. This need was met chiefly through the establishment of a mortuary cult, served by relatives of the deceased or by priests, whose duty it was to present offerings to the dead in the context of a formal ritual. This took place in the tomb chapel, to which the *ka* ascended from the burial chamber below (see Chapter 5), passing through the false-door and taking up temporary residence within the statue of the deceased in order to receive its sustenance. In terms of its procedures, the offering ritual was closely related to the magical purification and provisioning of the images of the gods which took place every day in the great cult temples. The *ka* of the deceased, like the divinity embodied within the cult-statue in the temple, consumed only the essence of the foodstuffs placed on the offering table. The offerings then 'reverted', or, in other words, were eaten by the priests or by those who had performed the ritual. The underlying notion that physical digestion did not take place removed the obligation to 'neutralise' (through offering them to the dead) much-needed provisions which might otherwise be consumed by the living.

Mortuary cults were established with great care to ensure that the funerary rituals would continue to be performed from one generation to the next (see Chapter 5). However, despite the most elaborate precautions, it was the fate of all such cults ultimately to fall into abeyance. Though the spirits of long-dead kings might continue to be maintained through temple cults, with the support or consent of the reigning pharaoh, for non-royal individuals cults of remote ancestors (even grandparents) were probably rarely maintained for more than a generation or two. The Egyptians were well aware of the futility of trusting to tomb and cult for eternal survival, as literary compositions often emphasise (see p. 45).

One text exhorts the reader to make himself remembered by his writings; only thus are the names of the wise men of the past recalled, for 'their portals and mansions have crumbled, their *ka*-servants are [gone]; their tombstones are covered with soil, their graves are forgotten'.

The written word: the offering formula

To circumvent this difficulty, recourse was had to the magical power of word and image. The most important part of the offering ritual was the invocation to the gods to provide supplies, which was expressed in a standard form of words. This 'offering formula' encapsulated the relationship between gods, men and king which was crucial to the survival of the dead. In its simplest form the wording runs:

> An offering which the king gives to Osiris so that he may give a voice-offering consisting of one thousand loaves of bread, one thousand jugs of beer, one thousand fowl, one thousand oxen, and every good and pure thing on which a god lives, for the *ka* of [the deceased].

The introductory phrase here alludes to the concept that, in theory at least, offerings to the dead came from the king or the gods. Under a reciprocal arrangement the king made offerings to the gods, who in turn provided for the dead (alternatively, it may have been supposed that the king and the god together presented the offering to the deceased). Of the many deities who are invoked in the formula on different monuments, Osiris and Anubis, on account of their special connections with the dead, are the most frequently encountered. The offering itself is termed a *peret-kheru*, i.e. 'going forth at the voice' (or 'voice-offering'), an expression which stresses the importance attached to the speaking of the words aloud in order to accomplish the purpose of the ritual. The offerings requested generally begin with bread, beer, oxen and fowl – regarded by the Egyptians as the staples of a good diet – and are often accompanied by 'alabaster [vessels], incense, and clothing'. Sometimes other commodities such as wine or milk are added to the list. The goods are usually enumerated in quantities of one thousand to symbolise the notion of abundance.

This text was inscribed on the stela in the tomb chapel, and often on the coffin, on statues and on other monuments besides. Every time the words were spoken the beneficiary received a renewed supply of the articles named. All those who entered the tomb chapel were expected to pronounce the formula, and on many stelae the owner of the tomb personally addresses future visitors with an appeal to recite the appropriate words for his benefit. The appeal on the stela of Minnefer (12th Dynasty) reads:

> O living ones upon the earth, the *hem*-priests and *hem*-priestesses, and the *wab*-priests of this temple, may you say: 'One thousand of bread and beer, oxen and fowl, for the revered one, the overseer of the chamber Minnefer, justified.'

The exhortation is often preceded by an account of the deceased's exemplary conduct on earth to assure the visitor that the desired offerings were indeed well-deserved. As an added incitement the visitor who speaks the formula is promised benefits to himself, as on the stela of Nebipusenusret (12th Dynasty).

> You shall be in the favour of your sovereign, you shall hand over your offices to your children . . . you shall not hunger, you shall not thirst . . . according as you shall say: 'An offering which the king gives . . .'

57. Part of a list of offerings from the limestone false door in the tomb of Rahotep at Meidum. The compartments contain the names of items of furniture and sacred unguents. This piece was originally situated to the left of the offering scene (see fig. 109). Early 4th Dynasty, about 2600 BC. H. 105 cm.

The mere presence of the text in the tomb was itself of value, for it was a fundamental tenet of Egyptian magical practice that the written word itself possessed the power to bring about desired results, and to bring what was written into substantial existence. So the offering formula was inscribed on a wide range of objects destined for the tomb, including items which were not intended to be seen by visitors, such as the coffins. The presence of the words in the deceased's funerary environment sufficed to activate the spell and to produce a limitless supply of food and other necessaries.

While the offering formula concentrated on the most essential commodities, a wider range of offerings was specified in other texts. The walls of many tomb chapels and coffins of the Old and Middle Kingdoms are inscribed with extensive lists of offerings which the deceased required for his survival and comfort in the next world. Among the items mentioned are various kinds of bread, meat, fruits and wines, together with the 'seven sacred oils' used in the ritual of the Opening of the Mouth (see Chapter 5). These are often arranged in tabular form, each compartment specifying a particular commodity needed for the afterlife or for the adequate performance of the offering ritual (see fig. 57).

Two and three-dimensional images

No less efficacious was the image, which – like the written word – was believed to embody the power to become reality. Depictions of food, drink and other items were therefore an important part of the environment of the tomb (see fig. 58). Among the earliest images to appear in this context was that of the deceased seated before a table of offerings, a scene which first occurs on the slab-shaped limestone funerary stelae of the 2nd to 4th Dynasties. It was subsequently incorporated into the decoration of the false door, the focal point of the offering chapel (see Chapter 5). The deceased stretches forth one hand towards the offering table, which may be temptingly heaped with a variety of foodstuffs, or may support a rather more austere row of stylised conical loaves of bread. The scene is usually accompanied by the offering formula and offering list.

58. Images of food offerings for the deceased, carved on the false door from the *mastaba* of Ptahshepses. 5th Dynasty, about 2400 BC. From Saqqara. H. of false door 366 cm.

By the early Old Kingdom, new scenes were added to the false door and to the walls of the tomb chapel. These showed rows of servants bringing supplies for the tomb owner. These figures are usually female, and personify the mortuary estates which (in the case of a person of wealth) provided the supplies for the offering cult and the stipends for its personnel. Other scenes show representative stages in the production of food and other essentials, a logical extension of the compartmentalised lists of provisions found in earlier tombs (see fig. 59). Chief among these are the standardised depictions of agricultural activities – servants harvesting crops, making bread and beer, and butchering cattle – but the weaving of cloth and the construction of household and funerary objects by craftsmen are also shown. By the principle of magical substitution it was believed that the things and the people depicted would come into existence in the tomb and serve the owner eternally, providing him with a staff of attendants who would go about the tasks which they were depicted performing for as long as he required them. The introduction of these representations in about the Third Dynasty coincides with the disappearance of the custom of filling tomb-magazines with large quantities of foodstuffs and furniture.

The inscriptions which accompany the activities sometimes include the statement that it is for the *ka* of the owner that the actions are carried out. Occasionally there is even a hint as to the Egyptians' attitude towards these representations. In the *mastaba* tomb of Nefermaat at Meidum (4th Dynasty), one of the earliest tombs to possess a chapel with full wall-decoration, the enduring quality of the images (which are referred to as 'gods') is expressed in a eulogy of the tomb owner: 'It is he who made his gods as representation that cannot be obliterated.' A later Old Kingdom tomb inscription from Saqqara identifies the carved figure of a funerary priest as the medium (literally 'door') by which the priest is to 'go forth' to serve the master. These statements emphasise that for the Egyptians the images carved and painted in tombs and on coffins were primarily functional. This does not of course mean that they did not take pleasure in fine draughtsman-

59. Limestone relief showing two servants leading an ox which is to provide sustenance for the *ka* of the owner of the tomb. The figures are carved in the style of provincial workshops of the First Intermediate Period, about 2181–2025 BC. From the tomb of Mereriqer at Dendera. H. 34.3 cm.

ship and skilful sculpting – some scenes even contain humorous details probably placed there for the amusement of future visitors.

Model figures for the tomb

The notion that images of servants could act as substitutes for real ones marks an important step forward in cultural development. During the 1st Dynasty the king had been accompanied in death by attendants whose graves were located around that of their master. They were in all probability put to death at the time of the royal burial so that the ruler would not be deprived of their service in the afterlife. This practice had been abandoned in Egypt by the beginning of the Old Kingdom (although it occurred in Nubia during the Classic Kerma phase *c.* 1750–1600 BC) and the prevalence of images in the tombs of the élite during the following centuries indicates that magical substitution had become the norm. In the 4th to 6th Dynasties, further developments took place. The two-dimensional figures of servants on the walls of the tomb chapel began to be augmented by statuettes which represented a comparable range of activities. The earliest of these are limestone figures of the 4th to 6th Dynasties, examples of which have been

60. Limestone statuette of a servant grinding corn on a quern. Individual servant statuettes of this type stand at the beginning of the tradition of providing substitute servants in the tomb to supply the needs of the deceased in the afterlife. 6th Dynasty, about 2345–2181 BC. Provenance unknown. H. 22 cm.

found chiefly in tombs at Giza and Saqqara. Each represents an individual male or female servant; several are kneeling in the act of grinding grain on a quern (see fig. 60); others are represented straining mash through a sieve into a vat to make beer. Less common types depict other activities including baking, butchery and the manufacture of stone and pottery vessels.

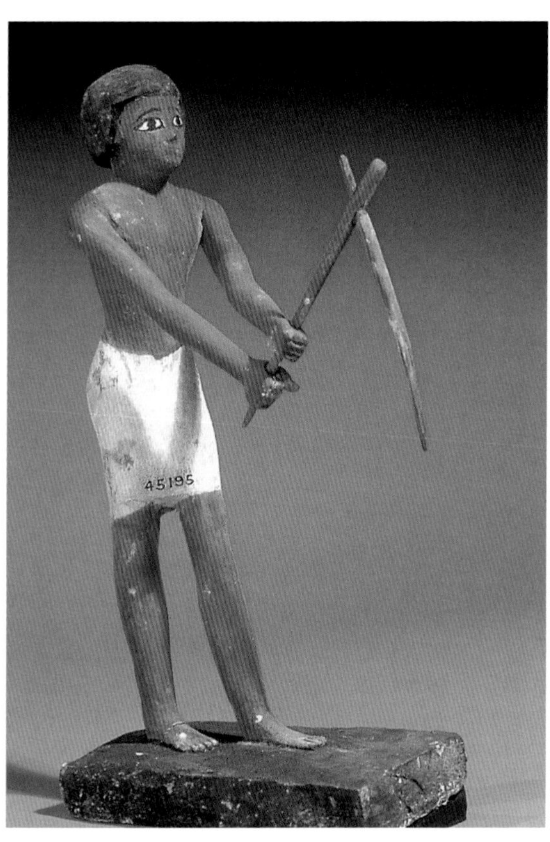

61. Painted wooden model of a peasant wielding a hoe with which to break up the ground for the planting of crops. Limestone figures were superseded by wooden models from the late Old Kingdom. 6th Dynasty, about 2345–2181 BC. From Asyut, tomb 45B. H. 33 cm.

After the Old Kingdom, the limestone figures were replaced by statuettes of painted wood, which had first begun to appear during the 6th Dynasty. These statuettes represented servants both singly and in groups, engaged on various tasks. Examples have been found at sites throughout Egypt, and date chiefly to the First Intermediate Period and the early Middle Kingdom. In undisturbed tombs, the models have been found placed on top of the coffin or at its side. A single tomb might contain many models; the tomb of the provincial governor Djehutynakht at Bersha was stocked with forty-five models of scenes and servants and fifty-five model boats. The most imposing group are the twenty-four models found in the tomb of the official Meketra at Thebes, dating to the late 11th Dynasty. These encompass a wide range of activities, and the models are exceptional for their detail and fine workmanship.

An astonishing range of activities is represented in tomb-models. The quality of craftsmanship varies enormously, from crude stick-like figures with angular faces and hastily-daubed painted features, to exquisitely modelled sculptures finished in painstaking detail. Even the crudest groups present a vivid picture of the everyday lives and activities of the ancient Egyptians, and the models are of inestimable value for understanding how basic activities were carried out.

The production of foodstuffs is depicted in great episodic detail, with models of various stages in the agricultural process. The preparation of the ground for sowing is represented by a single figure from a tomb at Asyut. He wields a hoe, the standard agricultural tool of the Egyptian peasant (see fig. 61). Several group-models represent ploughing with a pair of horned oxen yoked to a simple wooden plough; one man is shown guiding the plough as it cuts the furrow, while a second urges the draught beasts onward with a goad. The rest of the cultivation process is not usually depicted in models, though ploughing scenes sometimes include a figure scattering seed. Other models represent animal husbandry, chiefly the management and slaughtering of cattle. The most elaborate model of this type is a large group from the tomb of Meketra, showing the tomb

62. By the First Intermediate Period, servant models had evolved; they were now usually made of painted wood and very often represented groups of servants engaged in a variety of activities. This group from the tomb of Sebekhetepi at Beni Hasan shows male and female servants grinding corn and baking bread, brewing beer in vats and slaughtering an ox. Another man carried two jars slung over his shoulders on a yoke. Probably late 11th Dynasty, about 2000 BC. 49.6×24.3 cm.

owner and attendant scribes inspecting a herd of nineteen cows – a substantial number which reflects the high status of their owner. This model, however, is unique; most models of cattle show the process of butchering, the animal lying on the ground, its legs bound together and its throat cut (or about to be). In the most detailed models of butchery, such as that of Meketra, cuts of meat are seen hanging up to dry on strings on the upper level of the abattoir.

The preparation of bread and beer are among the most commonly depicted tasks, and after the Old Kingdom both processes were usually represented in a single group (see fig. 62). Several models depict bakers modelling loaves and cakes and tending an oven or a stack of filled breadmoulds heated over a fire. The making of beer is usually represented by one or more standing figures straining mash through a sieve or cloth into a large vat.

A highly important category of model is the granary – a miniature storehouse filled with samples of grains used to make bread and beer. These models are among the most informative of all for they often represent the complete building with walls and working door, ramps, ladders and grain silos with movable hatches. A granary from the tomb of Sebekhetepi at Beni Hasan is occupied by figures of men carrying the grain while a scribe records the quantities on a writing board (see fig. 63). An example from Thebes has a courtyard in which a

63. This granary, which comes from the same tomb as the group in fig. 62, depicts men depositing or removing sacks, while a scribe holds a writing board, on which he is keeping a record of the quantities of grain. The storage bins are filled with actual grains and with juniper berries. Probably late 11th Dynasty. From Beni Hasan, tomb 723. H. 21 cm.

64. Model of a female servant grinding corn on a quern supported on a table. The figure comes from a model of a granary found in a tomb at Thebes. 12th Dynasty, about 1850 BC. H. 13 cm.

65. Model of a female servant bringing offerings for the owner of the tomb. On her head she carries a basket of bread and cakes and the head and foreleg of an ox. The right hand probably held a bird (now lost). The figure is made from an indigenous timber, probably tamarisk. Said to come from the tomb of the physician Gua at Deir el-Bersha. 12th Dynasty, about 1850 BC. H. 39 cm.

woman stands grinding corn on a quern set on a legged stand (see fig. 64); the master, seated under a canopy on an upper level, keeps a careful watch over the activities below. In some granary models the silos are labelled with ink inscriptions identifying different varieties of corn. Less common, but nonetheless instructive, are scenes of weaving, carpentry and brick-making.

Particularly striking are the carriers of offerings, usually female, pairs of which were supplied in many tombs (see fig. 65). The commonest type is depicted walking, supporting with her left hand a provision-basket on her head and holding a bird in her right hand. They are frequently larger than the other models and are often of superior craftsmanship to that of others from the same tomb. The reason for their special significance is debatable. It may reflect their role as personifications of mortuary estates, the fundamental basis of provisioning for the dead. There is no doubt that the iconography of the figures closely resembles that of the personified estates depicted on the walls of Old Kingdom tomb chapels (see p. 98).

These models were produced in large numbers during the First Intermediate Period and the Middle Kingdom, but seem to have fallen out of fashion after the 12th Dynasty, their role being partly taken over by *shabti*s (see Chapter 4).

Model boats

The boat was of great importance in ancient Egypt, not only as the principal means of transport, but also for fishing and fowling. Boats also played a major role in religion, being conceived as the main means by which the gods travelled across the sky and through the netherworld. It is hardly surprising, then, that miniature boats form the largest single category of models found in the tombs of the Old to Middle Kingdoms. Three broad categories can be distinguished. The first comprised vessels designed for everyday transport (see fig. 66). Most of these models represent boats built of wooden planks, and the hulls are often carefully painted with details of the deck planking and structural beams emphasised in red. These boats are directed by one or two steering oars mounted at the stern. Besides the helmsman, crew members are represented rowing or setting the sail; there is usually a lookout-man at the prow, holding a lead-line or a pole to test the depth of the water. Some of the transport

66. Painted wooden model of a sailing boat. Under a canopy sits the owner with two boxes or storage-chests. At the stern sits the helmsman and in the bows stands the pilot, who tests the depth of water with a lead-line. Three of the crew are hauling on the rigging, while two others are depicted using poles (now lost), as if levering the boat off a sandbank – a regular obstacle to navigation on the Nile. Late 11th Dynasty, about 2000 BC. From the tomb of Sebekhetepi at Beni Hasan (no. 723). L. 69.8 cm.

boats incorporate a cabin or canopy, beneath which sits a figure of the owner, often squatting in an enveloping cloak in the manner of later block-statues. He is sometimes attended by servants or soldiers. A smaller number of boat models represent craft used for fishing and fowling. Among the models of Meketra are two papyrus skiffs, from which fishermen are shown casting nets. Most tombs were supplied with two boat models, one with its sail set and the other propelled simply by oars. The different modes of propulsion were those appropriate to travelling north and south, respectively, and this idea is sometimes emphasised by the positioning of the two vessels within the tomb, one with its prow facing north and the other in the opposite direction.

A second class of model consisted of the type of boats used at funerals or for making pilgrimages to holy sites such as Abydos. The appearance of these craft indicates that they were ideally supposed to be made of papyrus, although in reality the full-size boats would probably have been made of wood (see fig. 67). Hence the prow and stern are raised up out of the water, and the hull is usually painted green to suggest the colour of the bundles of papyrus reeds of which it

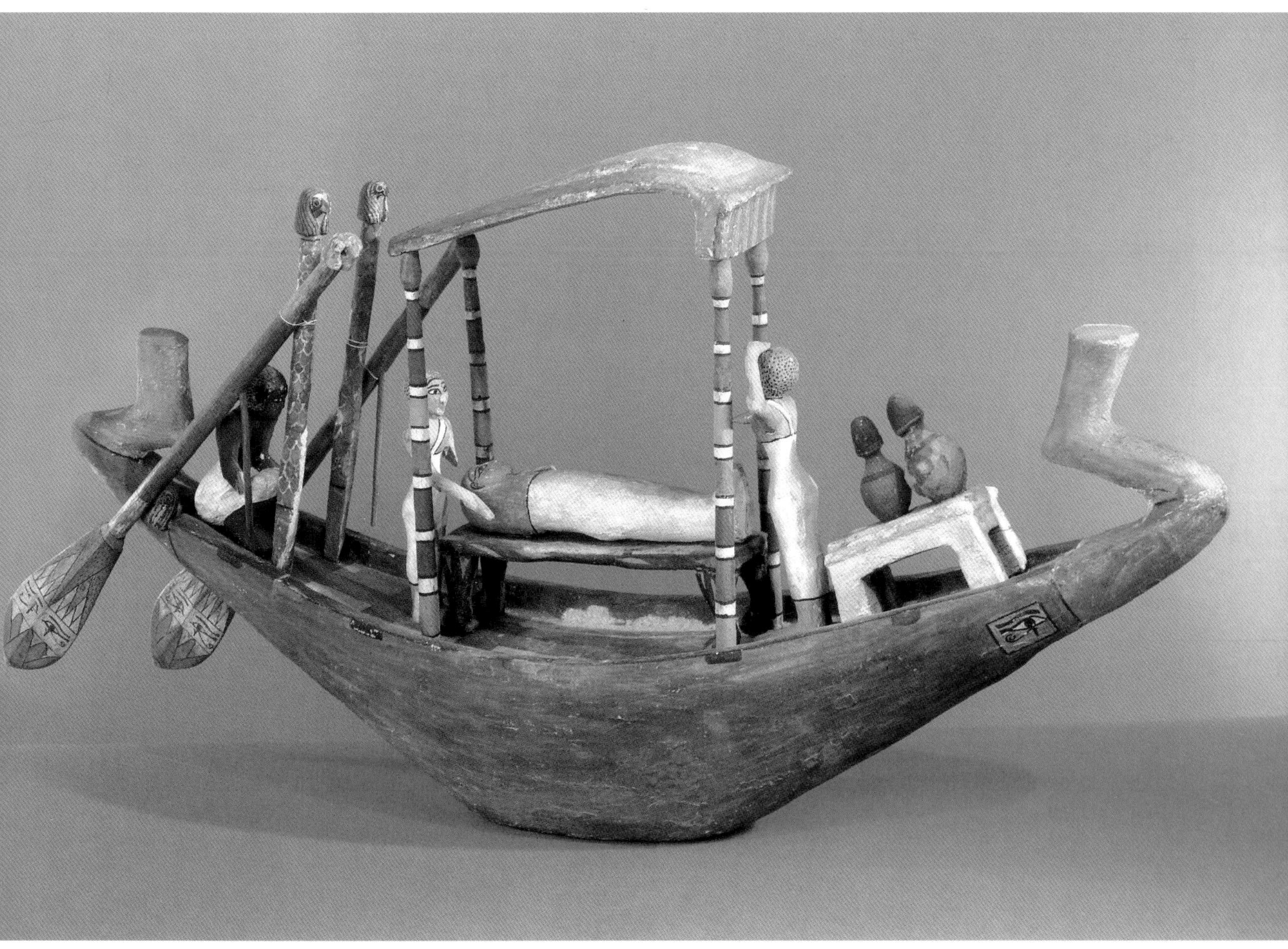

67. Painted wooden model of a funerary boat. The hull is painted green to suggest the papyrus reeds of which such craft were traditionally made. On the deck is a canopy, beneath which lies the mummy on a bier, attended by female mourners who represent Isis and Nephthys lamenting the death of Osiris. 12th Dynasty, about 1850 BC. From Thebes. L. 66.7 cm.

was made. These boats usually have a canopy amidships under which lies a mummy on a bier. Female mourners personifying the sister goddesses Isis and Nephthys stand at the foot and head of the bier, sometimes in traditional attitudes of lamentation. It is difficult to determine whether such models represent an episode in the funeral, during which the corpse was ferried across the Nile from its habitation on the east bank to the tomb in the west, or are meant to symbolise the journey to Abydos, the holy city of Osiris.

The third category of boat model comprised representations of the solar barque in which the sun god was believed to travel. The importance of this concept was dramatically revealed in 1954 by the discovery of the full-size ship buried in a pit alongside the pyramid of Khufu (*c.* 2589–2566 BC) at Giza. This vessel was intended to enable the dead king to traverse the heavens with the sun god; finds from other royal burials from as early as the 1st Dynasty indicate that one or more boats were often provided for the dead king's use. Small scale models of solar barques were also included among the tomb equipment of some private individuals in the Middle Kingdom.

68–9. The graves of poorer individuals of the Middle Kingdom were often simple shafts, without any mortuary-chapel or offering table to act as a focus for the ritual provisioning of the dead. To supply this need cheaply, a pottery offering-platter or model house was often deposited at the mouth of the shaft. The main feature of these was a representation of a courtyard containing a water basin and a range of food offerings – usually an ox and a variety of loaves, cakes, fruit and vegetables. More elaborate examples, termed 'soul houses' by Egyptologists, incorporated a representation of a house. Offering platter, Middle Kingdom, about 2050–1650 BC. Provenance unknown. L. 30.5 cm. 'Soul house', 12th Dynasty, about 1985–1795 BC. Provenance unknown. 25 × 23.5 cm.

Offering platters and 'soul houses'

For those who could not afford a cult place and the range of images described above, access to offerings could be obtained through the medium of a pottery model which combined the functions of the tomb chapel and the offering table. These date principally to the Middle Kingdom and examples have been found at many sites throughout Egypt, notably at Deir Rifa, where Flinders Petrie was able to establish through excavation that they had been placed at surface level above the burial shaft, and hence acted as the focus for offerings in the absence of a tomb chapel.

These models varied in the amount of detail they contained. The simpler type is a round or oval pottery plate with raised edges and a simple T-shaped runnel impressed into the clay, terminating in a small spout (see fig. 68); this served to carry away the water-offerings which were to be poured on to the plate. The rest of the space was occupied by clay models of food offerings, usually including a trussed ox, a loaf of bread or cake and a bunch of vegetables. Other models are more elaborate and usually incorporate a representation of a house, and a courtyard containing a wide range of offerings. Earlier Egyptologists supposed that the miniature structures were intended as homes for the spirit, giving rise to the modern term 'soul houses' (see fig. 69). Although this was probably not their true purpose, the models are highly informative for the study of ancient Egyptian domestic architecture, ranging as they do from simple domed huts to elaborate houses with columned porticos and stairways leading to a roof terrace. The courtyards contain large quantities of offerings and usually a libation basin or pool. Some examples have holes in the base of the courtyard or along the top of the enclosure wall, suggesting that model trees may have been inserted to add to the realistic effect. Comparable Middle Kingdom houses with walled gardens and pools have been excavated near Lahun, and funerary texts repeatedly allude to the desirability of having water and shady trees for the comfort of the deceased.

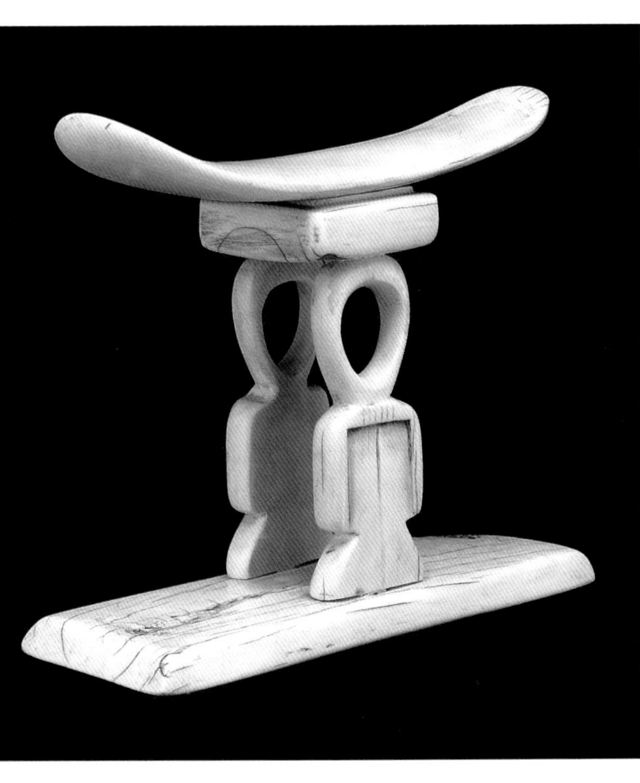

70. An ivory headrest. The two sides of the central support are carved in the shape of the *Tit*, or 'girdle of Isis', which symbolises the protection of the goddess. Said to be from the tomb of the physician Gua at Deir el-Bersha. 12th Dynasty, about 1850 BC. H. 16 cm.

Other provisions for the tomb

Since the existence beyond the grave paralleled that on earth in many ways, other necessaries were provided for the dead. These often included objects of everyday use, provided so that the lifestyle to which the owner had been accustomed on earth could be continued after death. Furniture was placed in the grave as early as the 1st Dynasty. Fragments of decorated beds, chairs and stools have been found in the royal tombs of the early dynasties at Abydos, and in other tombs of later periods. The tomb of Tutankhamun contained a range of chairs, stools and beds – even a folding camp-bed – and private tombs of the New Kingdom have yielded a large number of comparable items made for officials and humbler folk. Among the commoner items were beds and headrests (see fig. 70). Here again symbolic significance was doubtless important, since in texts death was often likened to a sleep. In some cultures – notably in Nubia – the dead were actually laid on beds in the tomb, as though to awaken to a new life. Although this custom was not generally observed in Egypt, during the Old and Middle Kingdoms mummies were regularly placed in coffins on their left sides, with a headrest supporting the head (see p. 219). This position may have been intended to reflect the conception of death as a sleep. The headrest also possessed amuletic significance. In the New Kingdom, spell 166 of the *Book of the Dead*, often written on an amulet representing the headrest in miniature, assures the deceased peaceful sleep and that his head will not be taken away in the netherworld.

71. Pair of wooden sandals with leather thongs. The delicate construction indicates that these sandals were not worn in life, but were probably made specifically for the tomb. They would assist the deceased magically in walking in the afterlife, and symbolically enable him to tread down hostile entities. This pair was found placed on the lid of the inner coffin in the undisturbed tomb of Sebekhetepi at Beni Hasan (see fig. 73). Late 11th Dynasty, about 2000 BC. L. (left) 25.3, (right) 25 cm.

Clothing was also provided. Some tombs have yielded enormous quantities of garments, mostly of linen. The tomb of Kha at Deir el-Medina, dating to the reign of Amenhotep III (*c.* 1390–1352 BC), included over 100 items. Sandals were regarded as particularly important items. As pointed out in Chapter 2, these were sometimes worn by the mummy in the Old Kingdom, and in later periods pairs of sandals were regularly placed in the coffin (see fig. 71). The provision of sandals magically gave the deceased the ability to leave the tomb at will; their importance is further emphasised by the fact that they were regularly painted on the interior of coffins. They also magically enabled the deceased to tread his enemies underfoot, as the example from the burial of Pepy I (*c.* 2321–2287 BC) illustrates (see p. 81). In the context of a non-royal burial, this defeat of foes was a symbolic act which reaffirmed the triumph of order over chaos, and hence perpetuated *maat*. The predominantly symbolic significance of funerary sandals becomes even clearer when it is realised that many of those found in tombs are 'dummies', equal in size to functional examples but made from inflexible or fragile materials which would have made them impractical to wear. The theme of the victory of order over chaos was taken up again in the Ptolemaic and Roman periods, when many mummies were provided with sandal soles or footcases of cartonnage, the under-surfaces of which carry painted images of bound prisoners, representing the traditional enemies of Egypt.

Most tombs, even those of the very poor, contained some personal jewellery and cosmetic implements. Cosmetics were used in life to adorn, beautify and protect the body against the effects of the extreme climate of Egypt, and cosmetic materials and applicators were among the earliest everyday items to be

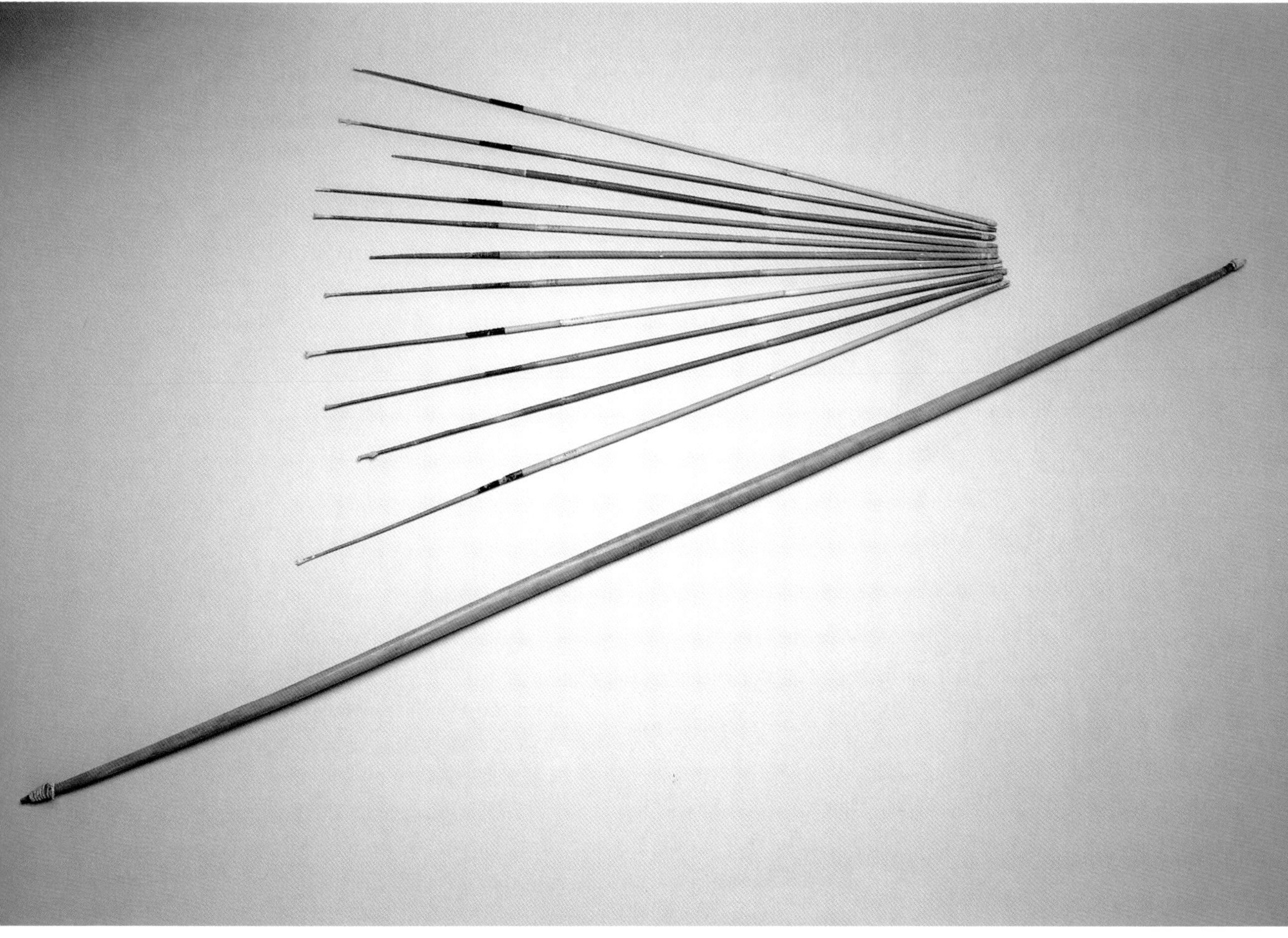

72. Acacia-wood bow and flint-tipped arrows, found on the top of the coffin of Ankhef (see figs 104, 160). Weapons were commonly placed in tombs from the Predynastic period onwards. Some items, such as axes and daggers, may have served principally as status symbols, but the provision of archery equipment was essentially practical in intent, to enable the dead to enjoy the pleasures of hunting in the afterlife. Early 12th Dynasty, about 1950 BC. From Asyut. L. of bow 160 cm.

placed in graves. Predynastic burials contain slate palettes, often in the shape of a fish, bird or other creature, for grinding the pigments used as cosmetics, and in many graves powdered malachite has been found in a separate container, or may even be still visible on the palette. Combs, hairpins, copper or bronze mirrors, stone and pottery vessels containing oils and perfumes, and other containers made of more expensive materials such as glass, are also regular finds in tombs. However, some of these items – perhaps too valuable to consign to the tomb – were at times replaced by dummies. In some tombs of the 18th and 19th Dynasties, wooden, pottery and limestone dummy vessels were included, imitating the forms and distinctive colouring of containers made of more costly materials. Many of these jars were completely solid, their surfaces intricately painted to represent the veined appearance of calcite, the mottled surface of breccia or granite, or the brightly-coloured festoon-patterns of glass.

Tombs have also yielded items of professional equipment, such as scribe's palettes, cubit rods, writing boards, tools, weapons and hunting equipment (see fig. 72). The pharaohs of the New Kingdom were even provided with chariots, and a room in the tomb was designated as the 'chariot hall'. Six dismantled chariots were found in Tutankhamun's tomb, and fragments from other tombs show that this was not an isolated instance. Chariots have also been found in a few non-royal tombs, though this is rare. The tomb of Yuya and Tjuyu, the parents-in-law of Amenhotep III (*c.* 1390–1352 BC), contained a small chariot, apparently made specifically for the tomb.

To complete the atmosphere of comfort and luxury in which the deceased hoped to find themselves, musical instruments and games were also supplied. Board games were placed in tombs as early as the 1st Dynasty, and many playing pieces and boards from different games have been found. The board-game *senet* ('passing') was one of the most popular leisure-time activities of the ancient Egyptians, and gaming-boards and sets of playing pieces for them have been discovered in many tombs. The object of the game appears to have been to follow a pathway of thirty squares or 'houses', eventually bearing one's playing-pieces off the board in a manner reminiscent of the game of backgammon. Naturally, the placement of *senet* sets in the grave reflected a desire to continue this enjoyable pastime in the next life, but from the New Kingdom the game acquired a religious significance as well. The journey around the board came to be equated with the passage to the afterlife; after successfully reaching the goal, the player is rewarded by the gods with food and water. According to spell 17 of the *Book of the Dead* winning a game of *senet* was synonymous with successful attainment of the afterlife in the form of 'a living *ba*'.

Some of these 'everyday' objects had clearly been used in life. Headrests show signs of wear, other objects had been broken and repaired. They were not necessarily the best or newest the deceased had owned; many goods would descend to the heirs and continue in use, perhaps only being consigned to the tomb several generations after their manufacture, when they had outlived their usefulness or were considered old-fashioned.

73. Reconstruction of the contents of the burial chamber of Sebekhetepi (tomb 723 at Beni Hasan) as found. The tomb possessed no offering chapel, and the coffin was placed in a small rock-cut chamber, reached by a shaft. Inside the coffins were Sebekhetepi's sandals (see fig. 71), a set of model tools and a funerary statuette. On the lid of the outer coffin had been placed a range of models including the servant-group, granary and sailing boat illustrated in figs 62–3 and 66. Late 11th Dynasty, about 2000 BC.

CHAPTER 4

Funerary Figurines: Servants for the Afterlife

The concept and function of *shabtis*

74. Painted limestone *shabti* figure of Pamerihu, a scribe. 18th Dynasty, about 1370 BC. From Saqqara. H. 30.5 cm.

The use of magic to meet the needs of the dead and to improve the quality of their existence in the afterlife led to the creation of a wide range of images for inclusion among the furnishings of the tomb. Chief among these was the statue, in which the deceased's *ka* resided to receive offerings (see Chapters 1 and 5), while the servant statuettes of the Old and Middle Kingdoms (see Chapter 3) provided a magically-operated workforce for their master in the hereafter. In the course of the Middle Kingdom, these servant figures were superseded by a new type of human image, which was to become one of the most important categories of the tomb's furnishings. These were the funerary figurines which were known by the three alternative names *shabti*, *shawabti* and *ushebti*. These statuettes, usually mummiform in shape, were first introduced around 2100 BC, and had become a standard element of burials by the first millennium BC, at which time they were being mass-produced in their thousands.

The figures range in size from tiny specimens a few centimetres in length to large and finely crafted sculptures over 50 cm tall. They were made from a variety of materials: wood, stone, wax, metal, glass, faience, pottery, and even ivory. The importance attached to these images is clear from their survival as part of the burial assemblage for almost two thousand years, and by the fact that at the height of their popularity, kings as well as their subjects required *shabti*s for their tombs.

The significance of the figurines was complex, and changed with the passage of time. Since they took over the function of the earlier tomb models, the *shabti*s possessed the character of servants of the deceased. But whereas the models were at all times regarded as separate entities, distinct from their owner, the *shabti* was more than this, acting also as a personal substitute for its master. Placed in the tomb (or, occasionally deposited at a cult place of special sanctity; see p. 133–5), the figurine provided an additional home for the *ka*, a reserve body in which its owner could exist and receive nourishment in the afterlife. Hence the *shabti*'s role was in some ways analogous to that of the mummy itself, the *ka*-statue or the

anthropoid coffin (see Chapters 5 and 7) (see fig. 75). This role dictated the main iconographical features of the figures, which represent not a living individual, but the deceased in the transfigured state, shrouded like a mummy and equipped with divine attributes. In keeping with this notion, the *shabti*s of the Middle and New Kingdoms were placed in the tomb either inside a miniature coffin, just like a mummy, or inside a shrine-shaped box, a type of container appropriate to a

75. Mummiform images of deceased individuals carved in high relief on a portion of a limestone stela or funerary monument. This idealised image of the dead was adopted for *shabti* figures in the Middle Kingdom. 12th Dynasty, about 1985–1795 BC. Provenance unknown. H. 12.8 cm.

divine image. As with other images of the deceased, the *shabti* was an idealised representation and cannot be regarded as a likeness of the owner.

However, the notion which ultimately came to dominate was that of the *shabti* taking the owner's place in carrying out manual labour in the afterlife. Ancient Egyptian civilisation was based essentially on agriculture, and this in turn depended on irrigation to water and fertilise the fields along the banks of the Nile. In order that this system might function smoothly, all Egyptians were subject to statutory labour by the authority of the king, and were required to spend a certain period each year maintaining dykes, channels and irrigation basins. Since the afterlife was thought to replicate many of the features of the earthly environment and its social hierarchy, it was expected that a similar obligation to carry out agrarian labour might be imposed by the gods on the transfigured dead. Naturally, the deceased hoped to avoid this unpleasant contingency, and it became the *shabti*'s role to relieve the owner of this duty. During the New Kingdom and later, *shabtis* were equipped for their work with hoes, grain baskets and sometimes a yoke and water pots; these tools were sometimes provided as models of the real thing, or, more often, carved or painted on the figures. Beginning in the New Kingdom, *shabti*s came to be regarded principally as slaves of their owner. This is reflected in texts such as the bill of sale (see p. 116), where they are described as 'male and female slaves', and in the adoption of the term *ushebti* – derived from the verb 'to answer', and recalling the figure's response to the summons to work.

The functioning of *shabti*s was dependent on a magical incantation (the so-called '*shabti* spell'), first attested in the 12th Dynasty (*c.* 1900 BC), when it appears as spell 472 in the great collection of funerary literature known as the *Coffin Texts*. The earliest copies of the spell so far known are found on two coffins from Deir el-Bersha, one of Gua (in the British Museum) and one of Sepi (in the Louvre). The text underwent development during the succeeding centuries, and was later incorporated into the *Book of the Dead* as spell 6. It ensured that the *shabti*s performed their duties. There are many variations in wording. One of the commonest versions of the spell reads:

> O *shabti*, allotted to me, if I be summoned or if I be detailed to do any work which has to be done in the realm of the dead; if indeed obstacles are implanted for you therewith as a man at his duties, you shall detail yourself for me on every occasion of making arable the fields, of flooding the banks or of conveying sand from east to west; 'Here I am,' you shall say.

The *shabti*'s task was thus particularly to carry out the more onerous and unpleasant tasks involved in the production of food: breaking up the ground, watering it and transporting sand. The significance of this 'sand' is uncertain. It is possibly to be equated with the *sebakh* used by modern Egyptian farmers as fertiliser; or it may have been used to make irrigation-dykes and field boundaries. These were the parts of the cultivation process which the deceased most wished to escape, and it is probably significant that scenes in tombs and on papyri showing the agricultural labours of the deceased in the Field of Reeds (see Chapter 1) usually omit these aspects of the work, concentrating on the less burdensome ploughing, sowing and reaping.

Many smaller *shabti*s bear only the name and title of the owner, often preceded by the introductory formula *sehedj Wsir* 'glorifying (or 'illuminating') the Osiris', or 'the illuminated one, the Osiris . . .'. This seems to be a reference to the transfiguration of the deceased by means of the sun's rays. Other texts sometimes occurring on *shabti*s allude to the owner's desire to see the life-giving sun, or commemorate the presentation of the figure to the owner by favour of the king.

The three terms for the figurines, *shabti*, *shawabti* and *ushebti*, are distinct and were not used interchangeably. *Shabti* occurs in the late Middle Kingdom and New Kingdom. *Shawabti* appears in the 17th Dynasty, but it was never as widely used as the other words and is chiefly found on figurines made in the 19th Dynasty at Deir el-Medina on the Theban West Bank. *Ushebti* is used from the 21st Dynasty to the Ptolemaic Period. The exact interpretation of the terms *shabti* and *shawabti* remains debatable. Two quite different etymologies for *shabti* are possible, one deriving from a word for 'stick' (perhaps alluding to wood as the prescribed material for the figures), the other from the word *shabt*, 'food', perhaps designating the statuettes as procurers of sustenance for the deceased.

Shawabti may also derive from 'stick'; a connection with *shawab*, 'persea tree' has also been suggested, though there is no firm evidence that the figures were actually made from this wood. *Ushebti* first occurred in the 21st Dynasty and remains the standard term until the figurines ceased to be made. It has been plausibly connected with the verb *wesheb*, 'to answer' – particularly appropriate in view of the figures' duty to respond to the call to work.

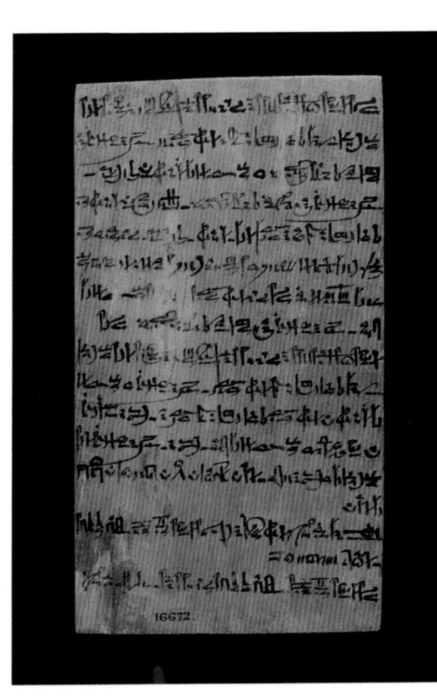

76. Wooden tablet inscribed with a hieratic text recording an oracular decree issued by the god Amun on behalf of Neskhons, wife of the high priest of Amun Pinedjem II (21st Dynasty, about 990–969 BC). The text states that the *shabti* figures have been paid for, and confirms that they shall perform their allotted tasks only for Neskhons. It is one of two copies of the decree, originally from the 'Royal Cache' at Deir el-Bahri, Thebes, in which Neskhons was buried. H. 28.9 cm.

The *shabti*, then, like the tomb and the coffin (see Chapters 5 and 7), was effective on several different levels. It was an image of the deceased and, as such, could serve as a vehicle for his *ka*, through which to receive offerings. It was also a servant, deputed to carry out tasks which provided sustenance for the deceased and which he himself wished to escape. The progressive depersonalisation of the *shabti*s which took place during the New Kingdom led to the predominance of the latter role, in which the *shabti*s were viewed merely as slaves of the owner, whose services were bought and sold. This notion is clearly revealed in documents relating to the purchase of *shabti*s.

*Shabti*s were made by craftsmen operating in workshops attached to the temples. A small hieratic papyrus in the British Museum, dating to the 22nd Dynasty, records that the priest Nesperennub had purchased a set of *shabti*s for his deceased father Ihafy. They had been supplied by the 'chief modeller of amulets of the temple of Amun', Padikhons, who (as his title implies) probably also made the faience amulets worn for protection by the living and included in the wrappings of mummies (see Chapter 6). In this document, Padikhons declares:

> I have received from you the silver [i.e. the payment] of these 365 *shabti*s and their 36 overseers, 401 in all, to my satisfaction. Male and female slaves are they, and I have received from you their [value in] refined silver, [the price] of the 401 *shabti*s. [O *shabti*s] go quickly to work on behalf of Osiris, for the beloved of the god, the *wab*-priest Ihafy. Say, 'we are ready' whenever he will summon you for service of the day.

The payment which the relatives made for the set of *shabti*s was both the vendor's remuneration and the 'wages' of the figures.

Further light on the acquisition and function of *shabti*s comes from a decree, recording a judgement given by an oracle of Amun at the temple of Karnak, concerning the *shabti* figures prepared for Neskhons, wife of the high priest of Amun Pinedjem II (*c.* 990–969 BC) in the late 21st Dynasty. The text survives in two copies written on wooden boards, which were probably deposited with Neskhons' *shabti*s in the 'Royal Cache' at Deir el-Bahri (see fig. 76). It states that the *shabti*s have been paid for and confirms that they shall perform their appointed duties on behalf of Neskhons alone. The document thus lends divine

77. Wax figurine in miniature wooden coffin. Figures such as this, representing the human body naked and unmummified, were the precursors of the first *shabti* figures. This specimen was made for the king's wife Kawit, who was buried early in the reign of Mentuhotep II (about 2020 BC) in a tomb incorporated into the king's funerary monument at Deir el-Bahri, Thebes. L. of figurine 6.4 cm.

sanction to an agreement essentially similar to that described in the hieratic papyrus, and confirms the right of Neskhons to command the *shabtis*.

THE EVOLUTION OF *SHABTIS*

Shabti*s in the Middle Kingdom*

The precursors of the *shabtis* date to the phase of political decentralisation called the First Intermediate Period and the early part of the 11th Dynasty before the reunification of Egypt under King Mentuhotep II. They were small, crudely modelled figurines made of wax or mud, which represent the naked body of the deceased, with the arms stretched at the sides and the feet together (see fig. 77). They were sometimes wrapped in scraps of linen in imitation of mummy wrappings, and were placed in small wooden boxes reproducing the shape and decoration of the coffins of the period, with standard funerary inscriptions and a pair of eyes painted on the eastern side (see Chapter 7). The use of this type of container, and the resemblance of the figurines to a mummy, emphasised the original concept of the images as substitutes for the physical body of the deceased. Examples of this type of figure have been found both in the Memphite region, at Saqqara, and in Upper Egypt at Deir el-Bahri. The figures are uninscribed, but their magical function is clear from the use of wax, a substance which played a prominent role in magical practices of the ancient Egyptians; it was supposed to have divine associations and was regularly employed to make figurines used in magic, both for positive and negative purposes (see Chapter 2).

The first figurines in mummiform shape occurred in burials of the 12th and 13th Dynasties. Their iconography represents the deceased as *sah*, a being who had entered the transfigured state through the process of mummification, and was thereby endowed with the attributes of divinity (see Chapter 1). It is not surprising then that these Middle Kingdom *shabtis* are often barely distinguishable in appearance from other mummiform images of the deceased, which served as substitutes for the owner's body – tomb statues, mummiform coffins, and mummy figures from model boats. Possession of *shabtis* was evidently a mark of high status at this period, and only one or two *shabtis* were provided for each burial. All of them were individually sculpted, and the majority are fine works of art (see fig. 78). They were generally made of hard stone, although a few examples made of wood or faience are known. On some, only the head, wearing a wig, protrudes from the mummy-wrappings; on others, the arms are folded across the breast and the hands grasp vases (the hieroglyphic sign

78. The *shabtis* of the Middle Kingdom were made in a range of materials, including stone and wood, and were varied in their iconography and inscriptional content. Left to right: Renseneb, painted limestone, with mutilated hieroglyphs (see p. 200), from Abydos, about 1750 BC, H. 23 cm; User, serpentine, provenance unknown, 12th Dynasty, about 1985–1795 BC; Senbi, painted wood, from Meir, 12th Dynasty, about 1985–1795 BC; Iwy, priest of Amun, gilded steatite, provenance unknown, 13th Dynasty, about 1795–1650 BC; name omitted, stone, 12th Dynasty, about 1985–1795 BC.

for the word *hes*, signifying 'favour'), *ankh* signs, a sceptre or a piece of folded cloth. Some of these figures are uninscribed; others simply carry the owner's name preceded by the offering formula. The *shabti* spell is encountered on only a few examples at this date, and it is a simple version of the text. One of the earliest *shabtis* to be inscribed with the spell is that of Renseneb, dating to the 13th Dynasty (see fig. 78).

In keeping with the role of the figures as images of the deceased, each was provided with its own miniature coffin, closely imitating the full-size coffins in which mummies were placed.

Late Second Intermediate Period

The production of fine *shabtis* seems to have declined after the 13th Dynasty, and there may even have been a hiatus in the tradition. However, *shabti* production revived at Thebes towards the end of the 17th Dynasty. Some of the figurines produced at this period were inferior imitations of *shabtis* of the Middle Kingdom, but the most characteristic specimens were figures of sycomore wood (or tamarisk), the majority of which were of extremely crude workmanship. Many of the figures were mere sticks or offcuts roughly shaped with an adze into a rudimentary likeness of the mummy. The face was suggested simply by a crude wedge-shaped projection, and the body was rapidly inscribed in black ink with the owner's name or the *shabti* spell. The surprising crudeness of these 'peg' *shabti*s does not disguise the fact that a clear pattern was being followed in their production, in which prescribed shape (however simplified), material, and words of power took precedence over fine craftsmanship in making the figures effective. Like the earlier *shabti*s, these examples were generally enclosed in a miniature coffin, either of wood or mud. These containers were usually rectangular but sometimes roughly imitated the anthropoid *rishi* style in vogue at the time (see Chapter 7) (see fig. 79). Relatively few examples of this type have been found in context and it is apparent that not all were placed in the burial chamber. At the tomb of Tetiky at Thebes (early 18th Dynasty), *shabti*s were discovered buried in the courtyard of the tomb. Their inscriptions contained the names of relatives who had evidently dedicated the figures to the deceased.

79. Crudely shaped wooden *shabti* with miniature rectangular coffin. These rough figurines were placed in tombs in the 17th and early 18th Dynasties. They were frequently inscribed in ink with the *shabti* spell. Late 17th to early 18th Dynasty, about 1600–1500 BC. Provenance unknown. L. 17.5 cm.

New Kingdom

In the 18th Dynasty, the production of fine *shabti*s was resumed, and the figurines were provided for a wider range of individuals (see fig. 74). One of the most significant innovations of the period was that *shabti*s began to be provided for kings. The earliest is a large limestone figurine inscribed for King Ahmose I (*c.* 1550–1525 BC), founder of the 18th Dynasty and inscribed with the *shabti* spell (see fig. 80). From the reign of Amenhotep II (*c.* 1427–1400 BC) the number of *shabti*s placed in the king's tomb began to increase steadily.

*Shabti*s of the early 18th Dynasty resembled those of the Middle Kingdom, but there was much greater variety in material and form (see fig. 81). The majority were made in stone and painted wood, but faience and pottery grew in popularity. The period is particularly notable for the significant developments which occurred in iconography. After the middle of the 18th Dynasty the crossed hands – previously an optional feature – were regularly depicted. The most important innovation was the representation of the agricultural tools which were required for the *shabti* to perform its tasks. These were hoes, and baskets or bags for grain suspended from a yoke. At first individual models of these tools were made from bronze or faience, and placed in the tomb for the figures to take up when required. Within a short time, however, these items began to be carved or painted on the *shabti* itself, which was generally represented holding two hoes in its hands

80. Limestone *shabti* figure of King Ahmose I. The piece is in the austere style of the early New Kingdom, and the inscription consists of the *shabti* spell. This is the earliest known *shabti* figure to have been made for a king. 18th Dynasty, about 1550–1525 BC. H. 30 cm.

81. Limestone *shabti* of the priest Nefer, with the *shabti* spell inscribed on the body. This example is typical of the finer figurines of the 18th Dynasty. About 1500–1400 BC. H. 24.5 cm.

and grasping cords from which one or two grain baskets hung. This development seems to have begun about the reign of Tuthmosis IV (*c.* 1400–1390 BC), whose *shabtis* are the first datable ones to have the tools. The baskets were at first shown at the front, but by the reign of Tutankhamun (*c.* 1336–1327 BC) they had been transferred to the back, hanging over the shoulder.

The figures were often inscribed with the text of the *shabti* spell in horizontal lines around the body and legs. During the 18th Dynasty the version of the text codified as spell 6 of the *Book of the Dead* became the standard text for *shabtis*. This emphasised the role of the *shabti* as a servant, just as did the inclusion of tools, but the older notion of it as a substitute for its owner still remained strong. One manifestation of this is the continuing close parallelism between the iconography of *shabtis* and that of anthropoid coffins which also acted as eternal images of their owners. Many *shabtis* of the early 18th Dynasty bore painted images and texts in blue, yellow and red on a white background, closely resembling the coffins of the same period; on some *shabtis* the similarity was enhanced by the depiction of transverse 'mummy-bands' and a vulture on the breast, again features of contemporary coffins. Later specimens had details in gold leaf or yellow paint on a black background in clear imitation of the coffins of the later

82. Miniature double *shabti* coffin of Montu. In keeping with their role as substitutes for the deceased, the figurines were often enclosed in miniature coffins, modelled on those used for human bodies. In this case the fine gilded steatite *shabti* of Montu was placed in a small anthropoid coffin, which in turn lay inside a rectangular coffin carved with figures of protective deities. Mid to late 18th Dynasty, about 1450–1380 BC. From a tomb shaft at Sheikh Abd-el-Qurna, Thebes. L. of outer coffin 11.4 cm.

18th to early 19th Dynasties (see Chapter 7). On others the natural colour of the stone or wood was left exposed. The containers for *shabtis* also continued to imitate coffins, both anthropoid and rectangular types. A few *shabtis* for persons of high status were even enclosed in nests of miniature coffins comprising a rectangular outer case and an inner one of anthropoid shape (see fig. 82).

Although under Akhenaten (*c.* 1352–1336 BC), traditional conceptions of the

83. Four wooden *shabtis* of Khons, captain of the barque of Amun, with their original boxes. The tall, shrine-shaped box was introduced as a container for *shabtis* in about the reign of Amenhotep III, and gradually superseded the use of miniature coffins. Late 18th Dynasty, about 1400–1300 BC. From Thebes. H. of boxes 30.5, 35.5 cm.

afterlife based on Osiris were repudiated, *shabtis* continued to be made, both for the king and his subjects. The *shabtis* of Akhenaten himself usually bear only the king's names and titles and avoid standard features of *shabti* iconography, but those of non-royal persons were more conventional, retaining their agricultural tools. Some are inscribed with the *shabti* spell, although others have a special formula in which the Aten (the divine solar disc) is invoked to provide funerary offerings, and the deceased is promised the benefits of the 'gentle breeze of the north wind' (see fig. 84). According to Akhenaten's doctrine, resurrection was to be obtained not through Osiris but through the daily rising (i.e. rebirth) of the Aten, although the precise role of the *shabti* in this system of belief remains unclear.

A legacy of the Amarna period was the appearance of more richly detailed *shabtis*, often with large elaborate wigs of the kind worn on festal occasions. At the height of the New Kingdom some unusual forms were created, including the double *shabti* (see fig. 85), often comprising figures of a husband and wife side by side as though together on a bed, and the *shabti* kneeling and grinding corn. At the same period, several fine *shabtis* included a representation of the *ba* bird spreading its wings over the body (as in the vignette from the *Book of the Dead* showing the *ba* rejoining the mummy: fig. 10). This image reinforced the notion

84. Painted ebony wood *shabti* of Hatsherit, Chantress of the Aten. The owner's title suggests that the figurine was made during the reign of Akhenaten (about 1352–1336 BC). A number of examples from this period were inscribed with a modified version of the *shabti* spell, created in order to reflect the unorthodox concept of the afterlife which was promoted by the king. This specimen, however, retains the traditional form of words and even describes Hatsherit as 'revered with Osiris', indicating that proscription of orthodox funerary beliefs was not total in the Amarna period. H. 23 cm.

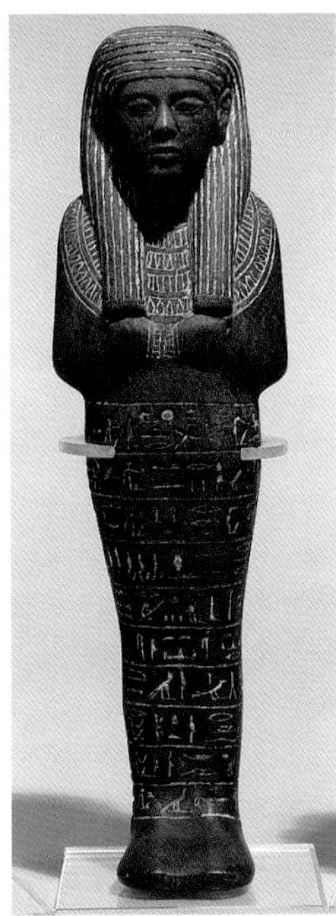

86. Steatite *shabti* of the Master of the Horse, Sunur. In the 19th Dynasty, a number of *shabtis* abandoned the mummiform appearance and represented the owner as a living individual – a phenomenon also encountered in the development of coffins at that period. This example shows Sunur dressed in the wig, pleated robe and sandals of a man of high rank. His crossed arms embrace his *ba*. 19th Dynasty, about 1275 BC. Provenance unknown. H. 21.4 cm.

85. Another innovation of the New Kingdom was the double *shabti* figure representing a male and a female – probably husband and wife – side by side. Such groups, as this example shows, usually rest on a flat support. This double *shabti* of painted limestone is uninscribed. 19th to 20th Dynasty, about 1295–1070 BC. From Thebes. H. 14 cm.

of the *shabti* as the substitute of its owner; a further variation on this theme was the *shabti* lying on a lion-bier, again accompanied by the *ba*. A fine specimen of this type was found in the tomb of Tutankhamun (*c.* 1336–1327 BC).

Fine, individually crafted *shabti*s of stone and painted wood continued to be made in the 19th Dynasty. Among the finest were those produced for the members of the royal tomb-builders community at Deir el-Medina. These often had polychrome decoration on a white or yellow background. Many *shabti*s continued the iconography of the 18th Dynasty, with crossed arms, hoes, baskets and the *shabti* spell. A new type was also introduced at the beginning of the 19th Dynasty, representing the owner as a living person in the elaborate pleated robes and full wig, collar and bracelets of festal occasions (see fig. 86). This development again reflects a comparable trend in coffins and sarcophagi, which seems to focus particularly in the reigns of Ramesses I, Sety I and Ramesses II (*c.* 1295–1213 BC) (see Chapter 7). Sometimes the iconography of the standard *shabti* was completely transcended by depicting the hands laid flat on the thighs, but in most instances the hands were still crossed on the breast. Some hold hoes, while others grasp amulets or embrace the *ba*-bird which is carved in high relief on the breast.

During this period there was a marked increase in the number of *shabti*s provided for each burial. This coincided with a reduction in the size of figures and a simplification of the manufacturing techniques. Many *shabti*s were now crudely modelled, and were often of painted pottery or faience (see fig. 87). Among the largest known teams from the 19th Dynasty is the set made for Henutmehyt, comprising forty wooden and pottery *shabti*s in four boxes (see fig. 88). Here already, quantity takes precedence over quality, for in workmanship Henutmehyt's figures are inferior to those of the Deir el-Medina craftsmen. The painted wooden type

87. Blue-glazed faience *shabti* of King Sety I. The number of *shabti*s provided for kings steadily increased during the New Kingdom. Sety I possessed several hundred specimens in wood and faience. This, one of the finest examples, represents the mummiform ruler wearing the royal *nemes* headdress and grasping agricultural implements. Early 19th Dynasty, about 1279 BC. From the tomb of Sety I in the Valley of the Kings, Thebes. H. 14.5 cm.

88. Painted wooden *shabti* box of Henutmehyt, a high-ranking woman, with the figurines which it contained. The box is made in the shape of two conjoined shrines (the *per-nu* shrine of Lower Egypt), and is decorated with scenes showing Henutmehyt receiving food and drink from the goddess Nut, and adoring the Sons of Horus. The polychrome painted *shabti*s are typical of the later years of the New Kingdom. 19th Dynasty, about 1250 BC. From Thebes. H. 34.3 cm.

89. *Shabtis* for (left to right) Heqasekheperi, Sety I, Pypyu, Bakwerner and Ramesses VI. A substantial number of *shabtis* produced during the 19th and 20th Dynasties were made of faience, glazed in a variety of colours including light and dark blue, white and red, as the four specimens from the left illustrate. At the same period, very roughly modelled *shabtis* were made in calcite, and crudely inscribed in paint or with a wax-based green pigment (far right). H. 13.3, 14, 14.2, 13.4, 11.4 cm.

was particularly characteristic of the 19th Dynasty, and was largely superseded in the 20th Dynasty by faience and pottery figurines. The faience *shabti*s of the 19th to 20th Dynasties were of various colours (see fig. 89). The ground colour was often white with details in red, purple or black; others were bright blue with details in black, and some were red. The inscriptions were often restricted to the simple *sehedj*-formula followed by the owner's name. Crude pottery *shabti*s were often painted in rough imitation of the finer stone and wooden examples. Strangest of all was a series of amorphous calcite *shabti*s made in the 20th Dynasty for kings and officials. These make only the most rudimentary pretence towards form, and are very crudely decorated and inscribed, usually with a bright green pigment probably made by heating wax in a copper vessel.

Until the Amarna period it was still customary to provide only one or two *shabti*s for persons of non-royal status. The custom of placing them in miniature coffins also continued, and these followed the pattern of full size coffins, reflecting the same evolutionary changes. However, beginning around the reign of Amenhotep III (*c.* 1390–1352 BC), special boxes for the storage of *shabti*s began to be used. These were tall wooden chests with vaulted lids, imitating the appearance of a shrine. Such boxes appear in Theban tomb paintings showing the bringing of funerary goods to the tomb, and actual examples of boxes of this type were provided in the tomb of Yuya and Tjuyu, the parents of Queen Tiy, each box containing one or two *shabtis*. The British Museum possesses a good early example of a set housed in this manner, comprising four wooden *shabtis* made for Khons, captain of the barque of Amun (see fig. 83). These were finely carved, and each pair was stored in the tomb in a tall unpainted wooden box. Oddly, the boxes are not a matching pair, being of unequal height. Some of the earlier shrine-shaped boxes have panelled 'palace façade' decoration or a single line of inscription, while others carry depictions of mummiform figures. The shrine-shaped box remained the standard *shabti* container during the 19th and 20th Dynasties, and to accommodate the increasing number of *shabtis* in these periods it took the form of two or three (occasionally even four) such shrines joined side by side. The boxes were mounted on flat or sledge-shaped bases, and decorated with figured scenes in polychrome or yellow on a black background. The subjects most commonly represented include the deceased seated with his wife, offering to deities, or receiving food and drink from a goddess in a sycomore-tree. In place of wooden boxes, pottery jars were sometimes used as containers for *shabtis* in burials of the 19th to 20th Dynasties, notably at Abydos, el-Amra, Gurob and Sedment. These '*shabti* jars' resemble canopic jars, with lids in the form of the heads of the Sons of Horus (here perhaps acting as representatives of the cardinal points of the heavens, rather than as protectors of the viscera), and contained from six to twelve crude pottery *shabtis* (see fig. 90).

90. Painted pottery '*shabti* jar' with lid representing the head of a jackal. Although similar in appearance to canopic containers, these jars were used to hold crude *shabti* figures in some burials of the later New Kingdom, particularly at the cemeteries of Abydos. 19th to 20th Dynasty, about 1295–1070 BC. From Abydos. H. 25 cm.

Third Intermediate Period

As the New Kingdom proceeded, the concept of the *shabti* changed. They became ever more 'depersonalised', being regarded less as substitutes for the owner, and more as slaves to do his bidding.The increase in the number of *shabtis* per person reached its culmination in the Third Intermediate Period with the establishment of a canonical organisation. According to this pattern, a full complement of figurines comprised 365 workers, one for each day of the year, which were organised in thirty-six gangs of ten, each supervised by an overseer. The two types were clearly distinguished by their iconography – 'worker' *shabtis* followed the traditional form of the mummified body holding agricultural tools, while 'overseer' *shabtis* were depicted as alive, wearing daily dress, with a kilt with projecting apron; one arm was held at the side, the other flexed across the chest, the hand holding a whip to impose authority on the workers. This division and the resultant total of 401 is mentioned in the bill of sale referred to on p. 116, which also makes clear the perceived status of the figurines as 'male and female slaves'. At the same time, the standard word for the figurines becomes *ushebti* – 'answerer' – a term clearly related to the figures' response to the call to work.

Not surprisingly, in view of the vastly increased numbers of *ushebtis* now required, the methods of manufacturing them were standardised and the

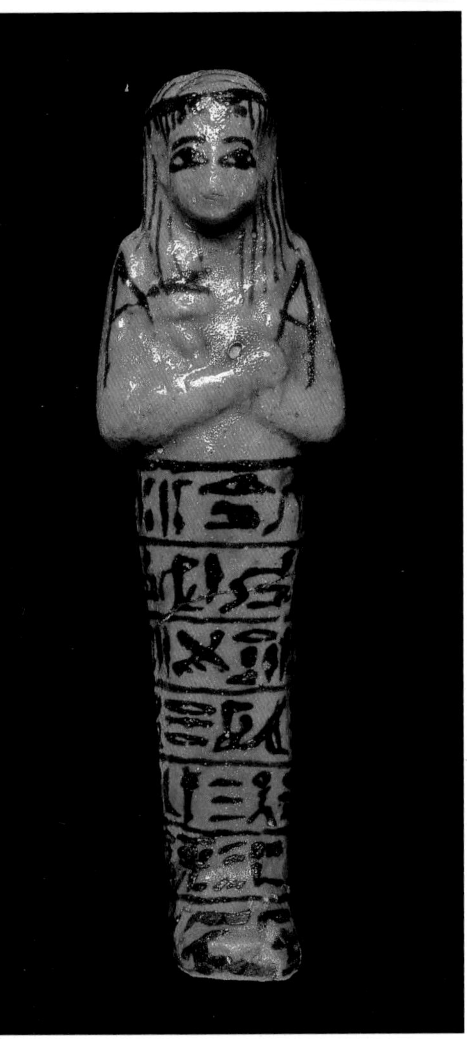

91. Blue-glazed faience 'worker' *ushebti* of the high priest of Amun Pinedjem II. After the New Kingdom, the concept of *ushebtis* as slaves of their owner, rather than personal substitutes, predominated. Late 21st Dynasty, about 990–969 BC. From the 'Royal Cache' at Deir el-Bahri, Thebes. H. 16.8 cm.

individual figures were usually small in size and crudely made (see fig. 91). The majority of examples were made of faience, and both workers and overseers were mass-produced in moulds. Their proportions were often poor, with large heads and feet and flat backs; the details of face, wig and tools were crudely painted. They wear a tripartite wig, and from the middle of the 21st Dynasty this is bound by a fillet tied at the back of the head; otherwise only the hoes and basket were represented. Although the *shabti* spell continued to be included, the text was often garbled or incomplete, and on many examples it was replaced by the short *sehedj*-formula, simply followed by the title and name of the deceased.

Most *shabtis* of this period were covered with a blue or green glaze. Figurines of the 21st Dynasty were usually blue, and among them may be distinguished those made for the ruling high priests of Amun and their relatives, most of whom were ultimately buried in the 'Royal Cache' at Deir el-Bahri. The glaze of these *ushebtis* is of an intense blue ('Deir el-Bahri blue'). Comparable *ushebtis* of paler colour were provided for the kings of the 21st Dynasty buried at Tanis, and the royal tombs there also yielded a number of very small *ushebtis* of bronze. This type, however, seems to have been short-lived, and in the 22nd Dynasty faience *shabtis*, often with a predominantly green glaze, remained the norm. The finest specimens of this period have the text of the *shabti* spell written in horizontal lines on the body and legs but many bear only the owner's name and titles in a vertical column on the front.

With the growing number of figurines, their containers increased in size commensurately. The double or triple shrine-shaped boxes continued into the 21st Dynasty, although the decoration was often austere, with a single panel of inscription in black on a white background. The multiple shrine form was often illusory, and frequently the boxes contained no internal division, the *shabtis* being unceremoniously heaped inside. During the 21st and 22nd Dynasties the shape of the boxes was further simplified. New types had flat lids and shallow rounded end-boards, the exterior painted white or black, with a simple panel of inscription containing the deceased's name and titles.

Ushebtis *in the Late Period*

By the end of the Third Intermediate Period, the faience and pottery *ushebtis* had declined in size and craftsmanship to an unprecedented degree. The typical figurines of the 25th Dynasty were small and very crudely shaped, often without glaze, and uninscribed. They were usually stored in pairs of wooden boxes with a flat lid, on which one or two boats were painted. The sides of the box usually carried an inscription in vertical or horizontal lines, sometimes accompanied by a figured scene. An alternative type of *ushebti* box imitated the shape of the rec-

92. Hardstone *ushebtis* made for the Theban governor Montuemhat and the chief lector priest Pedeamenemope. The production of large, finely-sculpted funerary figurines with extensive inscriptions was a phenomenon of the early seventh century BC, and was evidently influenced by archaising trends in art and funerary practices at that period. Early 26th Dynasty, about 650 BC. From Thebes. H. (left to right) 13 cm, 17 cm.

tangular outer coffins of the 25th to 26th Dynasties, with vaulted lid and posts at the corners (see Chapter 7).

The Kushite rulers who dominated Egypt throughout the 25th Dynasty fostered a revival of earlier traditions in art, architecture and literature. This 'archaising' tendency was already present in the eighth century BC but was accelerated in the Kushite period and extended to embrace a wide range of manifestations of material culture. One consequence of this trend was a major change in the iconography of *ushebtis*. The *ushebtis* made for the earlier Kushite kings Piy, Shabaqo and Shabitqo (*c.* 747–690 BC), discovered in their pyramid tombs at el-Kurru in Nubia, show the evolution of a new form. The mummiform 'worker' *ushebtis* are very simplified in shape, having no arms, hands or tools, although overseer figures were still represented as living individuals. Shabaqo's workers especially show the emergence of a new mummiform image soon to be more widely used. It is characterised by a large, broad face with a heavy beard, and a

93. Two faience *ushebti*s of the 26th Dynasty, illustrating the characteristic iconography of the period: long striped wig, plaited beard, smiling face, back pillar, and pedestal supporting the feet. Each grasps a hoe in the right hand and a mattock in the left, while a grain-basket is suspended over the left shoulder on a cord. The standard *ushebti* spell is inscribed on the body. The *ushebti* on the left is inscribed for a high official named Neferibre-sa-neith. That on the right belonged to Psamtek, son of Sebarekhyt. Late 26th Dynasty, about 550 BC. From Saqqara. H. (left) 9.2 cm, (right) 8.4 cm.

flat-topped tripartite wig. The proportions and features of these 25th Dynasty royal *ushebti*s clearly drew inspiration from sculptures of the Middle Kingdom, and this became even more apparent in the reign of Taharqo (*c.* 690–664 BC), whose pyramid at Nuri yielded a remarkable series of stone *ushebti*s in granite, calcite and serpentine. These were of large size, with a bold iconography and they were inscribed with a clearly 'archaising' version of the *shabti* spell, which revived the full phraseology of earlier periods. Comparable figures were made for the highest ranking officials at Thebes, including the God's Wives of Amun, and the officials Montuemhat, Pedeamenemope and Harwa (see fig. 92).

The production of stone *ushebti*s did not continue for long after the 25th Dynasty, but the innovations of that period brought about the establishment of a new standardised type, which was extensively produced in faience and which remained in use from the reign of Psamtek I (664–610 BC) until the Ptolemaic

Period. These figures, usually of green (less often blue) faience, are distinguished by the tall, slender body, long plaited beard, long tripartite wig without fillet, a pronounced smile and by the inclusion of elements derived from stone sculpture – a pedestal beneath the feet and a rectangular pillar supporting the back (see fig. 93). The toolkit of most early examples is restricted to two hoes and a basket suspended over the left shoulder on a cord, but after the reign of Psamtek II many figures hold a hoe in the right hand and a pointed pick in the left. The inscription is often the *shabti* spell incised in horizontal lines around the body, or a shorter vertical text on the front, giving the name and parentage of the deceased. Both types occur within a single burial outfit.

94. Faience *ushebti* figures as found in the undisturbed tomb of the Kanefer family at Saqqara. The increase in number of figures per burial after the New Kingdom led to the production of large wooden boxes, in which *ushebti*s were stored in the tomb. In some cases, as here, the figures were arranged standing in rows around the walls of the burial chamber, as though awaiting the summons to work for their master. Late Period, about 664–305 BC.

These figures, like their precursors, were produced in moulds, and the quality of the workmanship varies. Full sets of 401 have been found in several tombs of the 26th to 27th Dynasties at Saqqara and Abusir, notably those of Hekaemsaf, Tjanehebu, Psamtek-meryptah and Iufaa. The iconographic distinction between workers and overseers soon disappeared – the latest examples of overseers occur among the *ushebti*s made for Divine Adoratresses of Amun of the 26th Dynasty, buried at Medinet Habu – but the concept may have persisted. Possibly the variations in inscription (or its absence in a proportion of examples) might reflect the difference. The figures were stored in wooden boxes, sometimes placed in special niches in the walls of the tomb, or arrayed standing in ranks around the tomb chamber (see fig. 94).

The majority of these late *ushebti*s have been found at sites in the north of Egypt. There are relatively few from Thebes, and those are of inferior type, such as the *ushebtis* of Ankh-hor the Chief Steward of the Divine Adoratress, who was buried about 586 BC. This reflects the steady decline in the importance of Thebes which followed the reunification of Egypt by Psamtek I (664–610 BC). Most of the *ushebtis* of this period were made for men, in striking contrast to the situation in the New Kingdom and Third Intermediate Period, when a high proportion of *ushebtis* were provided for women. Kings continued to be provided with *ushebtis* at least until the 29th Dynasty; examples have the royal *nemes* headdress but otherwise are not distinguished from non-royal specimens.

Stylistic evolution of *ushebtis* during the Late Period was limited, and was confined mainly to variations in the disposition of the text. A T-shaped arrangement, with one horizontal line above one vertical line on the front, appears to be characteristic of the Persian period, having been introduced during the mid-5th century BC.

The last ushebtis

The final innovations in *ushebti*-design occurred during the early years of the Ptolemaic Period, with the introduction of a two-tone pattern of colouring. *Ushebtis* with this feature are distinguished by the dark blue colouring of the wig and inscription on a pale blue or green background. This pattern was not, however, adopted universally, and otherwise the styles of the preceding period were copied with increasing carelessness and lack of comprehension. Fine detail is usually wanting, and the inscriptions are often full of mistakes. The Ptolemaic Period witnessed a change in attitude to the dead and to their experience of the afterlife. In this changed environment, the relevance of *ushebtis* was diminished and the custom of including them in tombs steadily declined. Perhaps one of the last *ushebtis* is that made for the sailor Soter, a grotesque and unconventional figurine in which only the basic mummy form betrays any link with its precursors.

ANIMAL-HEADED *SHABTIS*

One of the most remarkable variations on the basic form of these figurines is that of the animal-headed *shabti*. Some of these owed their existence to the practice of burying sacred animals in a fashion modelled on the ritual burial of humans, a custom which was carried out with increasing elaboration from the New Kingdom to the Roman Period, as described in Chapter 8. The most elaborate of these animal burials was that of the Apis bull, which was mummified and interred in a sarcophagus, accompanied by many of the trappings of a human burial, including canopic jars, amulets and jewellery. Some Apis bull burials at Saqqara included *shabtis* with a mummiform human body and the head of the bull. The provision of these figurines probably reflects the intention to assimilate the burial of the bull to that of a human corpse.

A few other animal-headed *shabtis* are known, but a different explanation for these is required, since they were inscribed with the names and titles of officials of the New Kingdom. The Overseer of Cattle of Amun Thutmose (19th

Dynasty), whose tomb was at Tuna el-Gebel, had *shabti* figures with baboon and jackal heads, which were probably part of a set representing the Sons of Horus. Although the principal role of these deities was to protect the internal organs (see Chapter 2), they, like the *shabti*, also ensured that the deceased was provided with nourishment, and the figurines of Thutmose may have been a concrete representation of this notion. Another canine-headed *shabti* was found at Asyut, the cult-centre of the jackal-god Wepwawet. This example was perhaps dedicated by its owner, the scribe Nahuher, as a votive offering to the local deity.

Non-sepulchral *shabtis*

Despite the increasing emphasis, from the New Kingdom onwards, on the *shabti* as a servant or slave for the deceased in the afterlife, the concept of the figurines as substitutes or representatives of their owners persisted throughout this period. The strong belief in this function led to the depositing of *shabti*s in places of special sanctity other than in the tomb, in order to enable the owner to participate in the rituals and benefit from the offerings made at the holy place of a god such as Osiris. In consequence, deposits of *shabti*s have been found buried at sites such as Abydos and the Memphite necropolis. This practice had already begun in the Middle Kingdom. The owners of the figurines were mainly kings or officials of high rank, and the *shabti*s could be deposited in a container, such as a jar or miniature coffin, in holes in the ground or close to a monument such as a tomb or stela.

Large numbers of *shabti*s were found in the Serapeum at Saqqara, the burial place of the Apis bulls. In an intact sepulchre containing the mummy of a bull which died in year thirty of the reign of Ramesses II (*c.* 1279–1213 BC), *shabti*s inscribed with the names and titles of many high officials of the realm were discovered. Some of these were in the burial chamber and others actually inside the sarcophagus of the bull. Many bore the name of Prince Khaemwaset, who displayed special interest in the burial place of the bulls, while others commemorated high ranking Memphite officials and their wives. The *shabti*s seem to have been placed there to give their owners a physical presence at this holy place.

Caches of *shabti*s have also been found elsewhere in the Memphite necropolis, at Giza and Saqqara. The placing of *shabti*s there brought the owner close to 'the great tribunal of Rosetjau'. The term Rosetjau ('The Entrance of subterraean passages') denoted any hole or shaft in the ground (principally tomb shafts but also natural features) which was believed to be an entrance to the netherworld. The Memphite necropolis was 'the domain of the god Sokar who was called "Lord of Rosetjau"', and it is likely that the depositing of *shabti*s close to the entrances to the subterranean realm was done in order to bring the deceased into direct proximity to the god as he entered the netherworld.

Another site where many non-sepulchral *shabti*s have been discovered is Abydos. This was important as the traditional burial place of the god Osiris. As early as the Middle Kingdom, the tomb of King Djer (*c.* 3000 BC) in the royal cemetery of the Early Dynastic Period at Umm el-Qa'ab was re-identified as the sepulchre of Osiris, and Abydos became a place of pilgrimage. Many stelae and chapels were set up on the terrace of the temple of Osiris during this period (see Chapter 5). Some of these incorporated statuettes in high relief representing the dedicator and relatives as living persons or as mummies, and these were probably the forerunners of the use of *shabti*s in this context. Individual statuettes inscribed with the *shabti* spell were being buried in holes in the area of the Umm el-Qa'ab in the late 12th and early 13th Dynasties, and this tradition continued in the New Kingdom. Small hills near the tomb of Djer have yielded many *shabti*s of officials of the 18th and 19th Dynasties, some of them placed in jars. The archaeologist Flinders Petrie found many very fine *shabti*s with bronze hoes, baskets and yokes in a mound near the Old Kingdom *mastaba* tomb of Emdjadja. He named it Heqreshu Hill after the owner of some of the finest *shabti*s and tools (see fig. 95). A number of *shabti*s from Abydos are inscribed with a special text, in which the gods who are with Osiris (perhaps meaning the dead kings of the Early Dynastic Period buried at Umm el-Qa'ab) are petitioned to intercede on the deceased's behalf so that he should obtain a share of the food offerings made to Osiris at the *wag*-festival (an annual festival of Osiris which took place at Peqer, the god's traditional burial place at Umm el-Qa'ab). The text also emphasises that it is the deceased's *shabti*s who shall labour in his place when the summons to work comes. This text is known as the Amenhotep III formula, since it is chiefly on *shabti*s of that king that it occurs, but variants of it are occasionally found on *shabti*s of private individuals.

The multi-titled official Qenamun, who served Amenhotep II (*c.* 1427–1400 BC), possessed a large number of exceptionally fine *shabti*s. Besides those from his tomb at Thebes, he also had groups of *shabti*s in model coffins buried close to the royal tombs at Umm el-Qa'ab. Another large group of about sixty *shabti*s or *shabti*-like figures with his name and titles were found at Zawiyet Abu Mesallam, between Giza and Abu Gurob. Many of these figures are inscribed with a text-formula stating that they were a donation to Qenamun from the king, and hence they must have been made in the royal workshops (see fig. 96).

Another series of extra-sepulchral *shabti*s comes from the Theban necropolis. Several of these limestone and wooden figures

95. Copper *shabti* of Iuny. The eyes were inlaid with glass and the stripes of the wig originally contained a blue pigment. Apart from a few examples made for kings, bronze *shabti*s are rare, and this example was dedicated at the holy city of Abydos as a means of enabling its owner to share in the offerings made to Osiris there. 18th to 19th Dynasty, about 1300–1200 BC. H. 17.7 cm.

96. Two votive mummiform figures of Qenamun. This high official possessed a large number of fine wooden *shabtis* which were buried in ritual deposits at Abydos and in the vicinity of Giza. The formulaic inscriptions record that the figures were donated to Qenamun by the king as a mark of honour. The absence of agricultural tools, and the projecting tangs which indicate that the figures stood on separate plinths, distinguish them from the conventional *shabtis* of the period. 18th Dynasty, reign of Amenhotep II, about 1427–1400 BC. H. 37 cm.

are inscribed with the names of kings including Ramesses II (*c.* 1279–1213 BC), Merenptah (*c.* 1213–1203 BC) and Ramesses IX (*c.* 1126–1108 BC). Figures of this type are associated with deposits in the Wadi Qubbanet el-Qirud, south of Deir el-Bahri, a spot later used as a burial place for corn-mummies and hence perhaps related to the Osirian Khoiak mysteries (see Chapters 1 and 6). This interpretation is supported by the inscriptions, which mention the god Sokar, who was prominent in the mysteries, and most of the statuettes have the white crown, the headgear prescribed in texts relating to the ritual. Since none of these statuettes actually carry the *shabti* spell, their identification as *shabtis* might even be questioned, although, as the preceding survey has shown, those figurines could fulfil a wide range of magical functions on behalf of the individual represented.

CHAPTER 5

The Threshold of Eternity: Tombs, Cemeteries and Mortuary Cults

The function of the tomb

The tomb was the physical setting for the eternal afterlife of the deceased. It fulfilled the two most essential requirements, those of providing a permanent resting-place in which the body lay protected from thieves and scavengers, and a setting for the cult, where the ritual acts which were intended to ensure eternal life could be performed (see fig. 97). The importance of constructing and equipping a tomb is emphasised repeatedly in ancient Egyptian writings. The 'instructions' attributed to Prince Hardjedef (probably 5th Dynasty, *c.* 2300 BC) state: 'Make good your dwelling in the graveyard, make worthy your station in the West . . . the house of death is for life'. Since this new life was to be unending, the tomb ideally should last for ever, and this was reflected in the ancient terminology, which described it as the 'House of Eternity' (see Chapter 1).

The dual function of the Egyptian tomb is clearly reflected in its architecture, in spite of the many changes in form and construction which occurred over a period of approximately 3000 years. In all but the poorest graves, two components can be recognised. The first is the burial chamber, sealed after the funeral, which contained the body, the coffin and the most essential funerary equipment; this was usually located below ground level (although in a few kings' pyramids of the 4th Dynasty the burial chamber was in the mass of the superstructure). The second was a cult place – usually a chapel located within the superstructure of the tomb – which remained accessible to relatives, priests and casual visitors. For kings, a temple, built adjacent to or close by the tomb, replaced the chapel. The focus of the cult place was the false door or stela, the point of transition between this world and the next. Here, at the performance of the offering ritual, food, drink and other essentials were placed on the offering table, accompanied by appropriate words and actions, and the *ka* of the deceased was believed to pass in disembodied state from the burial chamber to the offering-place. There it could inhabit a statue (either in the chapel itself or in an adjacent chamber, the *serdab*), in order to partake of the provisions. This ritual was supposed to be performed

97. Rituals performed on the day of burial. At the right is the entrance to the tomb, with a schematised depiction of a frieze of funerary cones over the door. In front of this, priests support the mummies of the two tomb-owners in their black-varnished anthropoid coffins. Libations of purifying water are poured, and at the foot of each coffin crouches the lamenting widow. The woman on the left has exposed her breast and is casting dust on her head as a sign of mourning. Copy of a scene in the tomb chapel of Nebamun and Ipuky at Thebes, late 18th Dynasty, about 1380 BC.

regularly, but even if it were neglected the architecture, decoration and equipment of the tomb encompassed alternative methods of ensuring that the service of the dead continued.

The arrangement of the different components of the tomb changed through time, and differed according to the status and personal wealth of the owner. The earliest burials, both of kings and their subjects, comprised a pit dug in the level ground of the desert fringe, covered by a superstructure of earth, mud-brick or stone. The most developed form of this type, the *mastaba* tomb, remained in use for non-royal persons as late as the Middle Kingdom, but tombs with free-standing superstructures continued until the end of the pharaonic period. The most elaborate examples reproduced many of the architectural features of a cult temple.

From the Old Kingdom to the beginning of the New Kingdom, kings were buried in pyramid tombs, comprising a massive superstructure of stone or mud-brick with adjacent mortuary temple or chapel. In the New Kingdom, the pyramid ceased to be a royal prerogative, and small brick pyramids were incorporated into private tombs.

A third major type of sepulchre was the rock-cut tomb. These were hewn into the cliffs and wadis bordering the Nile. Originally made for non-royal persons only, the type was adapted in the New Kingdom for the burials of kings.

Cosmogonic symbolism of Egyptian tombs

The tomb – as the architectural setting for important cult practices – had affinities with the temples of the gods, the mortuary temples of the kings, and chapels for the maintenance of the royal *ka*. The ritual acts performed in these structures centred on a statue which served as the physical embodiment of a deity or a king, and the maintenance of these cults was directly linked with the survival of the universe, and the perpetuation of *maat* (see Chapter 1). Because of this role, temples and chapels, in one way or another, were conceived as cosmograms, i. e. miniaturised representations of the Egyptian cosmos. This was a means of relating the cult acts performed within the temple or chapel to the universe as a whole, and of ensuring thereby the effectiveness of those rites. This underlying significance accounts for much of the architectural form, layout and wall-decoration of the cult temples of the gods.

In a differing degree the same principles underlay the design and decoration of tomb chapels of the élite at several periods of Egyptian history. The tomb, like the temple, was a place in which cult practices were performed, here before a statue of the deceased. The ritual not only guaranteed the rebirth and nourishment of the dead in the afterlife but placed this rebirth in the broader context of the perpetuation of the cosmos, a feature highly characteristic of Egyptian notions of human existence (see Chapter 1).

Because of this cosmogonic significance, the location, architecture, 'decoration' and fittings of the tomb had to conform to prescribed patterns. The most fundamental condition to be fulfilled was the orientation of the burial place, and attention to this aspect is apparent from prehistoric times. Predynastic graves, as well as *mastaba* tombs of the pharaonic period, were deliberately orientated north-south. The positioning of the body was the factor which determined the orientation of the grave-mound or tomb superstructure. In the Predynastic period, the body might be placed with the head to the south or to the north, and with the face turned either to the west or to the east, but the importance of the north-south alignment remained consistent. In the dynastic period, it became standard to position the body with the head to the north and the face towards the east, a consequence of the growing importance of solar aspects of the afterlife. The deceased was thus positioned looking from the west, the realm of the setting sun and the dead, towards the rising sun (symbol of rebirth) and the world of the living, from which direction his offerings were brought. The importance attached to this east-west orientation led to the painting of a pair of eyes on the eastern side of the coffin in the late Old Kingdom and Middle Kingdom, and the placing of the mummy itself on its left side in order to align the face with the eyes on the coffin (see Chapter 7). Moreover, although the superstructure of tombs might continue to be orientated north-south, like the corpse, the principal internal features of the tomb came to be arranged on an east-west axis, so that visitors and officiating priests entered the chapel from the east and proceeded towards the stela, which was both the focal point of the cult and the interface between the worlds of the living and the dead.

The local orientation of the Nile was often used as a guide to the establishment of the cardinal points, just as is done today in Egyptian villages. Deviations from a north-south flow coincide with variations in the positioning of tombs;

this is clear at sites such as Abydos and Naga ed-Deir, where Early Dynastic tombs are aligned north-west: south-east, precisely reflecting the orientation of the river in this area. For major monuments such as the pyramids of kings, however, it is clear that orientation was not dependent solely on the position of the Nile, but on astronomical observations.

The architecture and iconography of the tomb also conveyed the notion of its cosmic significance. At various periods tombs resembled temples in architecture, design and iconography. Already in the 12th Dynasty, the tombs of provincial governors at Qaw display architectural features characteristic of temples, and more developed versions are represented by élite tombs of the New Kingdom and Late Period. Not only the architecture, but also the wall-decoration of the tomb played a major part in realising its cosmogonic significance. The 12th Dynasty tomb chapel of the official Khnumhotep II at Beni Hasan illustrates this. Scenes of hunting, fowling and agriculture in river, floodplain, marsh and desert reproduce the local environment in which Khnumhotep lived (his 'personal cosmos'). In some scenes he carries out roles appropriate to the king – the 'royal cosmos'. The wall scenes representing the earthly environment also served as the basis for a projection of the cosmos as a whole, supplemented by more indirect allusions to the celestial regions in which the sun god travels, and the subterranean *Duat* or underworld. Hence a tomb chapel can be interpreted as a projection of several cosmoi simultaneously – scenes such as the deceased fishing and fowling in the marshes can be read both as 'good wishes' for the future state and also as symbols of the establishing of order over chaos, in which the dead man fulfills the role of the king and the gods, subduing and controlling the 'disorder' of the natural world. Many of these scenes, of course, also functioned as magical substitutes for the objects depicted so as to provide for the needs of the deceased in the afterlife (as explained in Chapter 3), but this in no way conflicts with the interpretation of the tomb chapel as cosmogram, since a recurrent characteristic of Egyptian representations is that they convey meaning on more than one symbolic level simultaneously. With the continued development of tombs in the New Kingdom and Late Period, the cosmogonic symbolism was increasingly reflective of the parallelism and interaction between the realms of Ra and Osiris, through whom rebirth was expected to be achieved (see below).

Location of tombs and spatial layout of cemeteries

Most people were buried near to the community in which they had spent their lives. Generally, only the bodies of kings and persons of exalted rank were taken after death to be buried at places of special sanctity, such as Abydos or the Valley of the Kings. Tombs were rarely isolated, but instead were grouped in cemeteries, usually located along the desert fringe bordering the floodplain, but not on the cultivated land, which was too valuable and limited in extent to be used for burials. The proximity of cemeteries to settlements facilitated contact between the living and the dead members of a community. These contacts were maintained particularly on the occasion of the numerous religious festivals which were held throughout the year. The regions in which the dead were buried were regarded as enjoying the special protection of the gods, a notion which is reflected in the standard term for 'cemetery', *kheret-netjer* (literally, 'that which is under the god' or 'that which the god possesses'). Most cemeteries lay on the west bank of the Nile, the region of the setting sun, regarded symbolically as the realm of the dead. A few cemeteries, however, were located on the east bank. The situation of some of these may have been influenced by the availability of cliffs and wadis there suitable for the cutting of rock-tombs, as at Beni Hasan and Deir el-Bersha. In special cases, such as the tombs at el-Amarna, unusual religious concepts dictated the choice of site.

Since the tomb was to reflect the owner's position in the cosmos, it had to manifest his place within the structure of Egyptian society. The persistence of social hierarchies beyond death is manifested in the positioning of tombs, both at national and local levels. Persons of very high status, who formed the royal entourage, were buried close to the king at several periods, notably in the Early Dynastic Period, at the height of the Old Kingdom and during the 12th Dynasty. Other people were buried in the place where they had lived or held office. Within a particular cemetery, graves of important people generally occupied the more prominent locations, which acted as focal points around which the graves of persons of lower rank were grouped. In the First Intermediate Period, when the influence of the kings was reduced and that of local governors relatively high, provincial cemeteries show a progressive trend towards a spatial distribution based on links to persons of high status. This is even more clearly seen in the Middle Kingdom. At sites such as Deir el-Bersha, the tombs of the governors were architecturally the most elaborate and occupied the most imposing sites; in the forecourts of some of these tombs or on the slopes of the hillside below them were the burials of the attendants who constituted the governor's 'court'. One such official, interred below the tomb of the governor Ahanakht specifically records that he built his tomb 'at the feet of my lord'. The grouping of officials' tombs occurs also in the Theban necropolis in the New Kingdom. Some of these tombs were positioned in a relationship to major royal monuments, such as the mortuary temples of the deceased rulers on the west bank.

The degree to which cemeteries were artificially 'planned' varied. Different areas of a cemetery might be allotted to persons of different social groups, but such patterns sometimes changed over time, as the use of the site progressed. In many cases, the individual graves were probably dug only when required, and not prepared in advance. The excavation or building of a series of graves simultaneously with a view to future use was a relatively rare phenomenon. The most notable instances of this date to the early Old Kingdom, when the tombs of courtiers were sited close to the pyramids of their masters at Meidum, Dahshur and Giza, those at the latter site being constructed as part of a pre-planned installation, centred on the Great Pyramid and its temples. Here, *mastaba* tombs were laid out on a grid-plan of 'streets' and subsequently allotted to their eventual occupants. Although cemetery planning at this level was exceptional, simple shaft- and chamber-tombs of minor local officials of the Middle Kingdom do appear to have been constructed in series at sites such as Beni Hasan, perhaps to be allotted as a favour at the discretion of the governor.

The tombs of the kings

The death of the king

The death and burial of the Egyptian king was an event of cosmic significance. His death meant the temporary victory of chaos over order (*maat*), a situation which, potentially, might threaten the very foundations of the universe. A successor was appointed without delay, and if possible was proclaimed king at sunrise the day after the death of the previous ruler. On a pragmatic level, this helped to avoid the destabilising effects of disputes between rival claimants, and in ideological terms demonstrated the restoration of *maat*, with a new incarnation of Horus occupying the throne of his father Osiris.

Because of its religious significance, the death of the king was described in metaphorical terms which emphasised his divine nature, and provided reassurance that all would be well for Egypt. The *Pyramid Texts* contain various descriptions of the king's death: he flies to heaven as a bird; he climbs a ladder; he journeys by boat. Non-funerary texts take up the same themes. In the story of Sinuhe, King Amenemhat I 'flew to heaven and united with the sun-disc, the divine body merging with its maker.'

The cosmos was not set in order until the dead king had been buried with proper rites, and had successfully embarked on eternal life among the gods. His special nature was reflected in the structure and decoration of his burial place which, at most periods, differed from those of his subjects.

The evolution of the tombs of kings

Kings' graves of the late Predynastic period and the 1st and 2nd Dynasties were located close to the cliffs at the important cult centre of Abydos, in an area now called Umm el-Qa'ab. They comprised a subterranean burial chamber surrounded by storage rooms for offerings, and sometimes subsidiary graves containing the bodies of the king's servants. Over the grave were erected two brick mounds, one below ground and the other at surface level. This structure symbolised the primeval mound from which the creator-god emerged and via which the dead king would be reborn. The entire edifice was surrounded by an enclosure wall, and identified by pairs of stone stelae inscribed with the king's name. Separate brick enclosures, situated closer to the Nile, were associated with the graves, and probably served as eternal dwellings for the dead rulers and as the place where the mortuary rituals were carried out. By the late 2nd Dynasty, these enclosures included a rectangular feature, which may have been a stepped mound.

The reign of Djoser (Netjerikhet) (*c.* 2667–2648 BC), first king of the 3rd Dynasty, marked a major change in the royal burial. For the first time, the entire

98. The Step Pyramid of king Djoser at Saqqara. This monument, designed, according to later tradition, by the official Imhotep, united for the first time a number of elements of the royal burial which had previously been distinct: the stepped mound, the subterranean burial apartments, and the palace-like enclosure. Throughout the entire complex, constructional techniques which had originally been developed using wood, reed and brick were translated into stone with remarkable success. 3rd Dynasty, about 2670 BC.

complex was built of hewn stone, and the king's tomb was situated on the desert edge overlooking the city of Memphis, the principal royal residence and the centre of government. The enclosure replicated the features of the earlier brick funerary 'palaces' in stone. The rectangular mound of the 2nd Dynasty mortuary enclosures was developed by creating a series of superimposed '*mastabas*' to produce the Step Pyramid, a symbolic 'stairway to heaven' for the king's spirit (see fig. 98). The body was buried beneath the pyramid and the huge surrounding enclosure was the setting for the mortuary cult and for the *Sed* festival, a ritual in which the king's powers were eternally renewed.

Further development under later rulers produced the 'true' pyramid with smooth, angled sides, constructed of massive limestone blocks. It was set within a funerary complex consisting of a mortuary temple on the east side of the pyramid, to serve the cult of the dead ruler, and a 'valley temple' close to the Nile, in which among other activities the mummification of the king took place. The two cult units were linked by a covered causeway. The burial apartments were usually within the mass of the pyramid, or, in some cases, beneath it. The development of this type of tomb in the reign of Sneferu (*c.* 2613–2589 BC) culminated in the three pyramids of Khufu, Khafra and Menkaura (*c.* 2589–2503 BC), at Giza. The construction of these massive monuments took decades to complete and involved both professional builders and peasant conscripts. Contrary to

99. The pyramid of Khafra at Giza. During the reign of Sneferu, first king of the 4th Dynasty, the royal pyramid underwent trasnformation from a stepped structure to a true pyramid with smooth sides. This became the model for all subsequent kings' pyramids. 4th Dynasty, about 2558–2532 BC.

traditions recorded by classical authors, there is no evidence that the workmen were coerced. Modern calculation suggest that crews of 2000 men could have accomplished the quarrying, haulage and stone-setting required to complete even the largest pyramids at Giza (see fig. 99). Because of the traditional belief that the dead king would ascend to the circumpolar stars of the northern sky the entrance was usually still situated in the north face, but the east-west alignment of the cult structures emphasised that solar symbolism had also become important. This was further reflected in the shape of the true pyramid. Although it still reflected the notion of the primeval mound, the true pyramid was also a stylised replica of the *benben*, the conical sacred stone kept in the temple of Ra at Heliopolis. The dead king could ascend to the sky up its smooth faces, as up a ramp, and for his additional help sacred boats were buried in pits alongside the pyramid, to convey him to the sky each dawn so that he might travel with the sun god.

The pyramid form, with its associated temples, was retained for most kings' burials throughout the 4th, 5th and 6th Dynasties, although the size and constructional standard of the monuments declined after the reign of Menkaura (*c.* 2532–2503 BC). A major innovation, however, was the inclusion of hieroglyphic inscriptions on the chamber-walls of the pyramids of the late 5th and 6th Dynasties. The obscure kings of the First Intermediate Period appear also to have had

100. Funerary complex of King Mentuhotep II at Deir el-Bahri, Thebes. In place of the rock-cut tombs of his predecessors, Mentuhotep constructed a large free-standing funerary monument which combined the functions of tomb, mortuary chapel and cult temple. The rectangular terrace originally supported a superstructure, now destroyed, which may have been a pyramid or a flat-topped building. 11th Dynasty, about 2055–2004 BC.

pyramid-tombs, but to judge from the scanty traces which survive these were very small and of inferior construction.

King Mentuhotep II (*c.* 2055–2004 BC) of the 11th Dynasty reunited Egypt and constructed at Thebes a highly individual sepulchre of ambitious design. This was located in the great natural amphitheatre of Deir el-Bahri, and was fronted by a large cult monument dedicated not only to the king but to the deities Amun-Re and Montu-Re (see fig. 100). A stone platform supported a stylised divine booth surrounding a now-lost edifice which may have been a rectangular structure symbolising the primeval mound or, less plausibly, a pyramid. A descending passage led from the rear of the monument to the vaulted burial chamber, under the cliffs. His two successors, Mentuhotep III and IV (*c.* 2004–1985 BC), may have followed the same tradition, but their tombs have not been definitely identified.

Amenemhat I (*c.* 1985–1955 BC), founder of the 12th Dynasty, probably

101. The mortuary cults of the New Kingdom rulers were maintained in large temples which were physically separated from the tombs in the Valley of the Kings. These temples stretched in a line along the base of the cliffs on the Theban West Bank, facing across the Nile towards the temple of Karnak. Among the most elaborate was the Ramesseum, the mortuary temple of Ramesses II (about 1279–1213 BC).

began a funerary monument at Thebes, in the style of that of Mentuhotep II, but on transferring the court to Itj-tawy, in northern Upper Egypt, he abandoned his Theban tomb and constructed instead a pyramid complex at Lisht in the style of the late Old Kingdom monuments. His successors of the 12th and 13th Dynasties were also buried in pyramids, situated at various sites around and north of the Faiyum region: Dahshur, Lisht, Saqqara, Lahun and Hawara. These pyramids were relatively small in size, of inferior construction, and contained no inscriptions, but several of them possessed complex internal arrangements of passages and chambers intended to foil the attempts of robbers to plunder the burials (see below).

The tombs of the Asiatic Hyksos rulers (15th Dynasty), who controlled the Delta and northern Upper Egypt during the Second Intermediate Period, have not yet been found. They were perhaps buried in tombs of Canaanite type, non-royal examples of which have been found at their principal centre Tell el-Daba

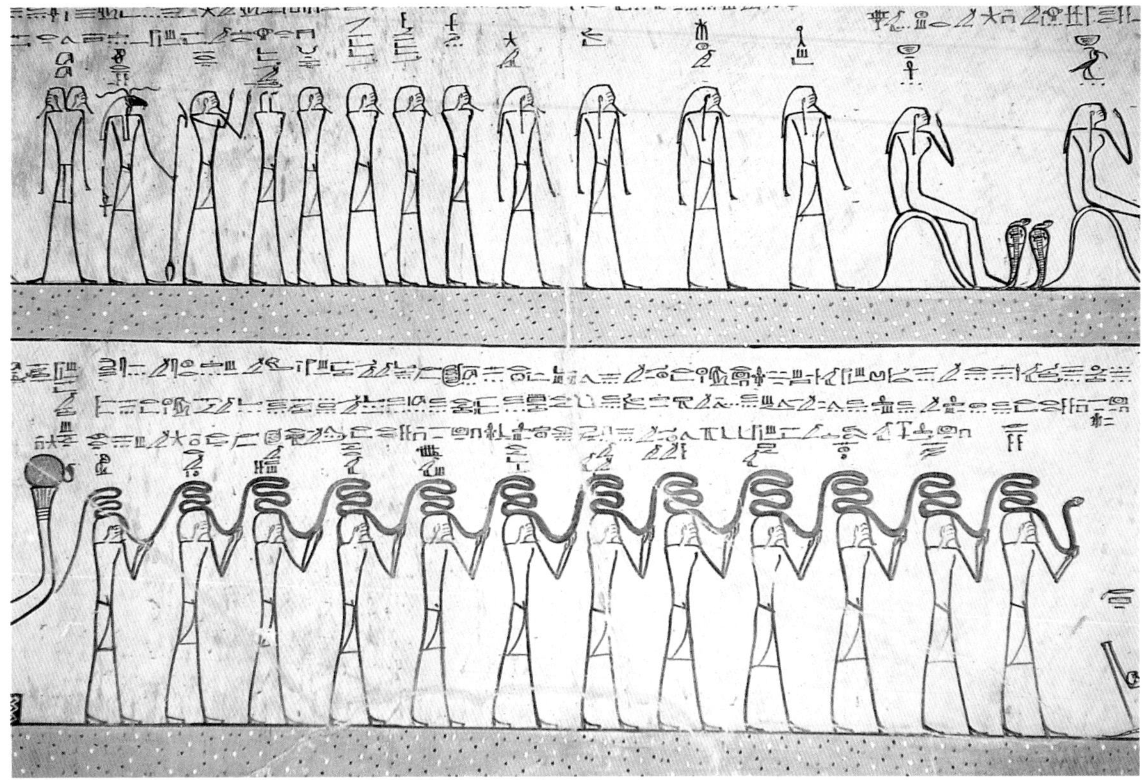

102. The pharaohs of the New Kingdom broke with the tradition of burial in pyramids. Their tombs, in the Valley of the Kings at Thebes, were extensive rock-cut sepulchres, decorated with texts and inscriptions describing the nocturnal journey and rejuvenation of the sun god, with whom the dead king was closely identified. This scene, painted on the wall of the burial chamber of Tuthmosis III (about 1479–1425 BC) shows gods towing the barque of the sun god in the underworld (*Book of Amduat*, eleventh hour).

(Avaris). The rise to power of the Hyksos compelled the native Egyptian rulers of the contemporaneous 13th Dynasty to abandon the capital of Itj-tawy and to take up residence at Thebes (from which point in time they are termed the 17th Dynasty). The last few of these kings were buried in tombs with small brick pyramid-superstructures, in the Dra Abu el-Naga area of the Theban necropolis. What appear to be the substructures of some of these tombs, comprising burial chamber, pillared hall and court, have been identified recently.

The New Kingdom rulers were buried in tombs of a new type, cut in the Valley of the Kings on the Theban West Bank. The tombs consisted of a series of rock-cut passages and chambers, without a superstructure; possibly the prominent local peak of El-Qurn, which dominates the Valley and resembles a natural pyramid, was regarded as a collective 'superstructure' for all the tombs there. The mortuary temples, to serve the cult of the dead kings, were physically separate from the tombs and were located in the plain on the other side of the cliffs (see fig. 101). The internal arrangements of the tombs provide one of the clearest examples of the tomb as cosmogram. They replicated the environment of the underworld through which the sun god journeyed by night (see fig. 102). The decoration of the walls illustrated and described the episodes of that journey, in the course of which the sun god (and hence the dead king also by assimilation) was rejuvenated. The sole exception to this pattern was the tomb of Akhenaten (*c.* 1352–1336 BC), who promoted a religious 'revolution' in which the solar disc was elevated to the status of sole god. Not only did Akhenaten's creed deny the existence of multiple deities, it negated traditional views of the afterlife based on the mythological cycles of Ra and Osiris. Hence the king's tomb was situated in the cliffs east of his new city of Akhetaten (el-Amarna), well away from those of his orthodox predecessors, and its decoration eschewed all the elements of traditional iconography. Under Tutankhamun (*c.* 1336–1327 BC), the orthodox religion was restored and the practice of burying the dead ruler in the Valley of the Kings was resumed.

The Valley of the Kings was abandoned at the end of the 20th Dynasty. The Delta became the political focus of the kings of the 21st and 22nd Dynasties, and they chose to be buried at Tanis, the main cult centre of the god Amun in the north. The tombs comprised stone-built subterranean burial chambers, probably with cult chapels (now destroyed) above, situated within the enclosure wall of the temple of Amun. The siting of tombs within temple enclosures also extended to the burials of royal relatives and high-ranking officials at this period. The custom was interrupted during the 25th Dynasty (consisting of rulers of Nubian extraction). Although resident in Egypt and adopting the trappings of pharaonic rule, they made their tombs in their Nubian homeland at el-Kurru and Nuri. The tombs themselves revived Egyptian traditions of the distant past, having small pyramid superstructures and adjacent mortuary temples. The 25th Dynasty sepulchres are the latest identifiable tombs of Egyptian kings. Textual evidence indicates that the rulers of the succeeding 26th Dynasty returned to the practice of constructing their tombs within the enclosure of a cult temple (in this case, that of the goddess Neith at Sais), but no archaeological remains of them have been found. It may be that this tradition was continued by later rulers, but of this there is no proof.

THE EVOLUTION OF NON-ROYAL TOMBS

Predynastic and Early Dynastic periods

The earliest non-royal graves were simple pits dug into the desert sand. Cemeteries of such graves first appeared around the end of the Palaeolithic Period (*c.* 12000–10000 BC). The bodies were placed in the grave in a contracted position, without funerary gifts. In the Neolithic period, graves continued to be circular or oval pits, apparently without superstructures. The corpse was sometimes wrapped in matting or animal skins; simple jewellery of shell, bone or stone was often provided and pottery vessels, probably to hold offerings, began to appear in graves. In the Badarian period (*c.* 4800–4200 BC), the custom of placing artifacts with the dead became fully established, with pottery and implements as regular features. In the succeeding Naqada I (or Amratian) period, graves increased in size and were oval in shape, while the goods supplied were more numerous and varied, including pottery and stone vessels, jewellery and figurines. In the Naqada II and Naqada III phases, oval grave pits were superseded by larger rectangular graves. Internal arrangements for the dead were improved, and some graves were lined with wood or brick. At this period the walls of an élite tomb at Hierakonpolis, perhaps that of an early ruler, were decorated with painted scenes of ships, animals and human figures, the earliest dated instance of wall-decoration in an Egyptian tomb.

The unification of Egypt under a single ruler in about 3100 BC, brought centralised government and rapid acceleration in the evolution of social organisation, writing, and religious practices. This is reflected in the development of tomb-types at this period, which show greatly increased variation according to the rank of the owner. The tombs of kings, queens and high officials of the first two dynasties were much larger than earlier versions, having enormous mud-brick superstructures containing storage magazines for the vastly increased quantity of funerary equipment now thought necessary. The external faces of these structures were decorated with palace façade panelling, imitating the recessed decoration of contemporary élite dwellings. The body was placed in a subterranean burial chamber excavated in the rock and reached by a descending stairway. Some tombs at this period incorporated hewn stone, the earliest attested use of stonework in Egypt. Some of the tombs of the kings were surrounded by the graves of servants, who were apparently buried at the time of the king's interment, suggesting that they may have been put to death in order to accompany their master into the afterlife. This practice steadily declined and was abandoned at the end of the 1st Dynasty.

The notion that the deceased dwelt in the grave in physical form – implicit in the Predynastic custom of placing food, clothing, tools and weapons in the grave – survived into the Early Dynastic Period, and is manifested in the architecture of large tombs. The 'palace façade' design of early tombs probably reflects this concept, and the idea was carried further in some large *mastaba* tombs of the 2nd and 3rd Dynasties at Saqqara, Giza and Helwan. The substructures of these comprise a complex of chambers strongly reminiscent of the plans of the houses of the living, as exemplified by surviving structures of New Kingdom date at el-Amarna. In the tombs, the burial chamber is equated with the main bedroom (suggesting an early conceptual association between death and sleep), while other chambers represent storerooms, servants' quarters and even bathrooms and lavatories.

Old Kingdom

From the 3rd Dynasty, tombs with stone- or brick-built superstructures were the norm for non-royal individuals of high rank. Like the earlier brick graves, these tombs had rectangular superstructures, but with the sides inclined at a slight angle and usually without panelled decoration. This type of tomb was dubbed a *mastaba* (Arabic for 'bench') by Egyptian workers of the 19th century, after a perceived resemblance to a type of bench found in front of Egyptian peasant houses. The substructure of these tombs dispensed with the notion of replicating living quarters for the dead, and comprised a single large burial chamber reached by a vertical shaft (see fig. 103). Instead of the continuous panelled decoration of the earlier superstructures, the early Old Kingdom *mastabas* had two niches, one at the northern end, one at the southern end; these served as suitable places for

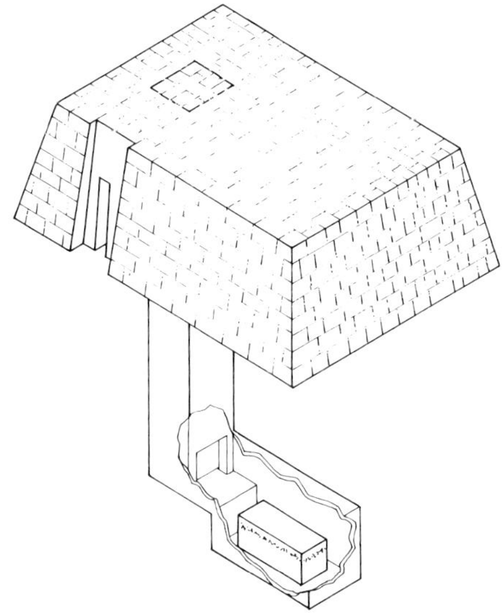

offerings to be made. With the passage of time, this section of the tomb developed to become the chapel for the cult of the dead.

In the 4th Dynasty, stone began to be regularly used in the construction of élite tombs. The courtiers of Khufu (*c.* 2589–2566 BC) were buried in limestone *mastaba*s laid out on a grid-plan close to the king's pyramid at Giza. The burial chamber was reached via a vertical shaft which opened in the roof of the *mastaba*, passing through the superstructure into the rock beneath. After the burial, the burial chamber was sealed with a wall of brick or stone, or sometimes a slab of stone lowered like a portcullis in slots. The shaft was filled with stone blocks or masons' debris. An alternative style of substructure, exemplified at Meidum, was characterised by a passage and burial chamber built of stone within a trench specially excavated in the rock; emplacements for a sarcophagus and canopic chest were cut into the walls or floor.

103. A typical *mastaba* tomb for an official of the Old Kingdom, about 2650 BC. The stone-built superstructure contained the offering chapel where the mortuary rituals for the deceased were carried out. The subterranean burial chamber was reached via a vertical shaft, blocked after the funeral, which passed through the mass of the superstructure.

In earlier tombs, the offering cult was centred in a niche in the eastern external façade of the *mastaba*. The special sanctity of this spot led to the enclosing of the space, creating the prototype of the cult chapel. On some examples, a structure of brick walls abutted against the external face of the superstructure; on others, a long corridor was created against the external wall, providing access to the offering niches. A more significant development was the situation of the offering niche within the solid mass of the superstructure, thus creating the mortuary chapel as a separate chamber. The false door was the focal point of the chapel, but the plan of the chapels varied; some were cruciform, others rectangular or L-shaped. Once the trend had been established, the number of chambers within the *mastaba* multiplied, the cult place becoming only the most important of a series of chambers. By the late 5th/early 6th Dynasty, some chapels had complex arrangements of halls, storerooms and *serdab*s (statue chambers) occupying the whole of the superstructure. The tombs of Ptahhotep, Mereruka and Khentika at Saqqara exemplify this type, and that of Mereruka comprised thirty-two chambers. The storerooms in these *mastaba*s contained food and ritual equipment for use by priests in the offering cult, rather than supplies for the deceased's own use, as in tomb-magazines of earlier periods.

The introduction of internal chambers and the progressive expansion of the rooms created wall-surfaces which could be decorated. Isolated instances of wall-painting in tombs had occurred as early as the middle Naqada II period (such as the 'painted tomb' at Hierakonpolis, mentioned above) but the tradition only became firmly established in private tombs in the 3rd Dynasty. The earliest wall-decoration consisted of images of the tomb-owner before offerings, and paintings of furniture, tools and other goods required for the afterlife; but by the early years of the 4th Dynasty, agricultural scenes, hunting scenes and personified estates were being added to the repertoire. This trend was interrupted during the reigns of Khufu and Khafra (*c.* 2589–2566 and *c.* 2558–2532 BC), when the tombs of the king's courtiers at Giza were characterised by a simple, austere monumentality (echoing that of the ruler's pyramid), without internal chapels and pictorial wall-decoration, and having only a slab-stela with an offering-scene (see below). This simplification of the tombs of the officials is probably partly due to the fact that they were built as a pre-planned cemetery, and only subsequently assigned to particular occupants – and it has been suggested that this was related to a move to emphasise the unique quality of the monarchy by restricting the grandeur of officials' tombs. In the late 4th Dynasty the pictorial treatment of the internal walls was resumed, with the development of scenes representing various activities: servants (personified estates) bringing goods, butchery, agriculture, fishing and fowling. All these activities were shown taking place in sight of the deceased, whose figure dominates the scene. The repertoire of scenes increased during the Old Kingdom, as did the narrative character of the representations, but – with the exception of scenes representing the funeral rituals – all the wall-decoration of Old Kingdom tombs reflects the earthly life of the deceased and shows nothing of the existence in the afterlife. The scenes acted both as a magical means of sustaining and provisioning the deceased and also served to perpetuate magically the world in which he had lived, and to confirm his status within it.

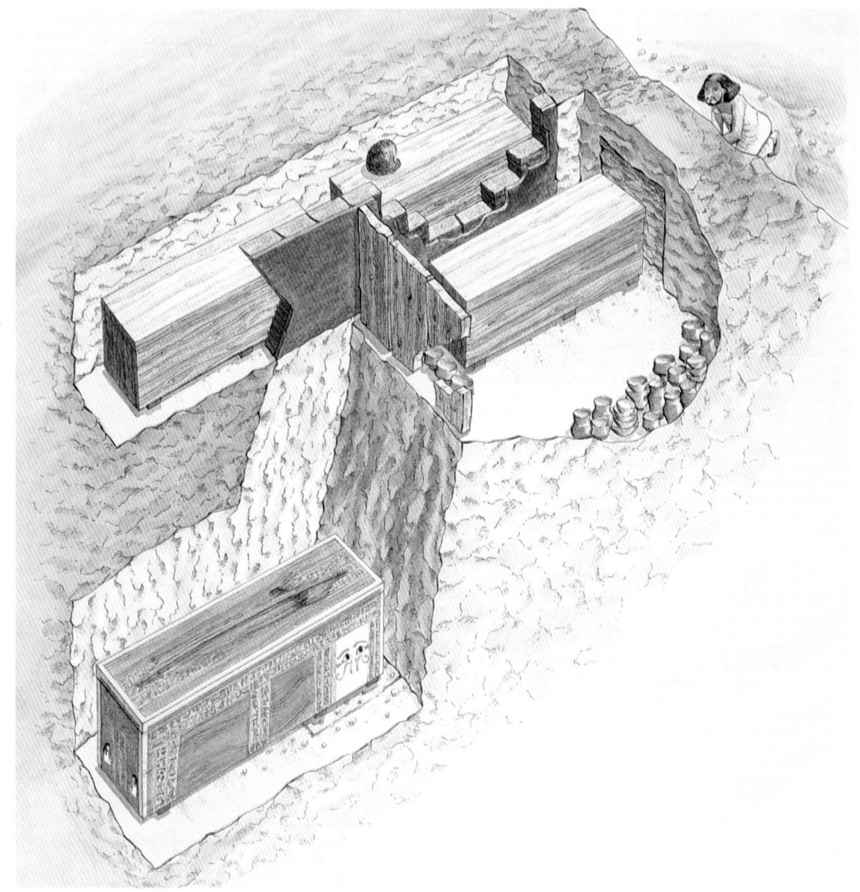

104. Interior of tomb 9 at Asyut, excavated by David Hogarth in 1906–7. This reconstruction of the tomb as found, based on the excavator's plan and field notes, shows burials on two levels (an additional burial at a third, lower level, is not shown). It is a typical rock-cut chamber tomb, without a superstructure, divided internally with a brick wall and a wooden partition. The outer chamber contained three uninscribed wooden coffins and a group of pottery offering-vessels. The richest burial, that of a man named Ankhef, lay in a separate chamber reached via a steeply inclined ramp. The coffin was painted and inscribed, and a bow and arrows had been placed on the lid. The mummy inside was provided with a cartonnage mask and a headrest (see figs 47, 72 and 160). Early 12th Dynasty, about 1950 BC.

The alternative to a *mastaba* was a rock-cut tomb. These became popular in the late Old Kingdom, and are mainly found at provincial cemeteries in Upper Egypt, where the steep cliffs along the Nile valley were often close to the Nile, allowing limited space for the construction of *mastaba*s. Tombs were thus cut into the cliffs facing the river, or in wadis. Some rock-cut tombs were made as early as the 4th Dynasty, but became common only in the late 5th Dynasty. The rock-cut tomb, though physically different from the *mastaba*, fulfilled the same functions. It comprised an offering chapel, where the funerary cult was maintained, and shafts leading to burial chambers (see fig. 104). The chapels of rock-cut tombs were usually large and adapted architectural features from *mastaba*s, such as architraves supported on pillars, but they comprised fewer chambers than those in *mastaba*s. They were equipped with a false door and *serdab* for statues; sometimes, instead of occupying a separate room, statues were carved out of the wall of the chapel.

First Intermediate Period and Middle Kingdom

The breakdown of central authority in the First Intermediate Period had repercussions on tomb design. Large elaborate superstructures and extensive rock-cut chapels ceased to be made, and even the tombs of élite individuals were inferior in quality to those of the Old Kingdom. Rock-cut tombs predominated, and there was usually no decoration except a small stela located at the mouth of the shaft or passage. Even the largest rock-cut tomb of the period, that of Ankhtifi at Moalla, was of crude construction, with an irregularly-shaped cult-chamber, supported by uneven pillars. The wall-paintings were executed in a provincial style, with figures floating free of register lines. At other sites, such as Naga el-Deir, simple brick superstructures were erected, with small chapels containing stelae. Wooden models largely replaced relief scenes on chapel walls (see Chapter 3).

The re-establishment of central authority in the early Middle Kingdom brought more settled conditions and the opportunity for local officials to exploit resources and craftsmen's skills to create more imposing tombs. The great rock-cut tombs of the 12th Dynasty had a courtyard and chapel, often with a pillared portico, a shrine or niche and passages leading to burial chambers, as exemplified at Beni Hasan, Deir el-Bersha, Asyut, Meir and Aswan. At Thebes there was a local development now known as a *saff* tomb, comprising a very large court with pillared or plain façades, with a corridor leading to a small shrine or chapel, and a passage to the burial chamber. Although rock-cut tombs now predominated, *mastaba*s continued to be built for very high-ranking officials, such as those buried in the vicinity of the royal pyramids at Lisht.

New Kingdom

Rock-cut tombs (often with little decoration) remained the norm during the Second Intermediate Period, but important innovations occurred in the New Kingdom. The early 18th Dynasty tombs in the Theban necropolis developed from the *saff* tombs constructed there in the Middle Kingdom; some early New

Kingdom tombs were unfinished *saff* tombs of earlier date, adapted and modified, such as those of the officials Ineni and Hapuseneb. The *saff* type was subsequently developed by transforming the long narrow space behind the façade into a self-contained transverse hall – this, together with an axial passage beyond, constituted the basic type of Theban tomb of the 18th Dynasty, the plan of which suggested an inverted 'T'-shape. The walls of the chambers were painted and sometimes carved in relief. The transverse entrance hall mainly had scenes reflecting the environment in which the deceased had lived; these included agricultual scenes, the deceased hunting and fowling, enjoying a banquet, and carrying out his official duties (such as inspecting the products of craftsmen in their workshops). It is these 'daily life' scenes which provide us with much of our detailed knowledge of ancient Egyptian dress, industries and manners and customs. The scenes however were not merely commemorative of a life on earth well-spent. As usual, they conveyed meaning on different levels. They emphasised the status of the deceased, reflecting his position in society, and symbolised aspects of the future existence he hoped for. Fowling in the marshes, for example, signified the subjection of chaotic forces by order, in which the deceased fulfills the crucial role of the king in maintaining the cosmos. On the walls of the axial passage the images were usually concerned with funerary themes, mainly the burial rites and cult of the deceased. This section terminated in a false door or statue niche, where the rituals were performed. The burial chamber was subterranean, reached via a shaft or passage, and was usually undecorated, though funerary texts and scenes were occasionally placed there.

During the short-lived religious 'revolution' instigated by the pharaoh Akhenaten many of the king's principal courtiers had rock-cut tombs made for themselves in the cliffs surrounding the new royal residence city of Akhetaten. Architecturally these tombs continued the tradition established in the early 18th Dynasty, but the decoration of the chapels concentrates on the adoration of the royal family by their subjects, and events in the lives of the tomb-owner. Akhenaten's religion offered mortals only the hope of continuing to exist on earth under the rays of the sun. Images and texts relating to traditional concepts of the afterlife were avoided.

After the 18th Dynasty the concept of the tomb changed. There was a shift away from the earlier 'commemorative' function, by which the decoration sought to confirm the deceased's setting in the hierarchy of earthly society, and a corresponding emphasis on the tomb's religious role, setting the deceased in the divine environment in which he was to exist after death. The equation of tomb with temple, a holy place where the deceased adored the gods, already foreshadowed in the Middle Kingdom, became more pronounced. This development was manifested by innovations both in the wall-decoration of the chapel and in the architecture of the tombs. The chapels of 18th Dynasty tombs were characterised by the concentration of a single subject or scene on one wall (as demarcated by the corners of the chamber, doorways and other architectural features); internal organisation of components within scenes was done by the use of regis-

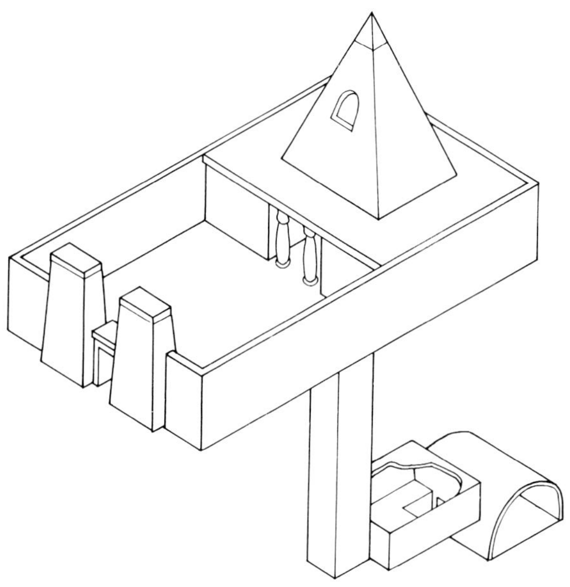

105. A private tomb of the Ramesside period (about 1295–1069 BC). A wall with a small pylon-gateway encloses a courtyard, at the rear of which is the cult chapel, surmounted by a small brick pyramid (by this date no longer the prerogative of royalty). A shaft leads to the subterranean burial apartments.

ter lines. This was supplanted by the 'Bildstreifenstils', in which the subject matter was arranged sequentially in a horizontal pictorial strip (which on occasion extended around a corner on to an adjacent wall). The arrangement of two of these strips on a given wall offered the painter the opportunity to realise a conceptual parallelism. Scenes of the funerary cult usually occupied the lower strip, and those relating to the afterlife and the world of the gods the upper one. This upper-lower parallelism clearly derived from the decorative layout of funerary stelae; already in the 18th Dynasty stelae show the adoration of the gods above, and the funerary cult below (see figs 115 and 116). The architectural form of the tomb also changed in response to this functional shift. Pre-Ramesside tombs consisted only of two main parts, however elaborate these might be: the (always accesible) cult place for the performance of the mortuary ritual, and the burial place (inaccessible after the funeral). Ramesside tombs, by contrast, have been shown to comprise five distinct sections: the outer parts (pyramid and court), and the inner parts (cult place, sloping passage and burial place) (see fig. 105).

The architecture of the court and chapel of the tombs, with its close links with temple architecture, emphasised the parallelism between the cult of the gods and that of the dead. This became much more marked in the post-Amarna phase, both at the Theban and Memphite necropoleis. Tombs such as that of the general (later king) Horemheb (*c.* 1323–1295 BC) at Saqqara are characterised by a pylon entrance, colonnaded court, chapel, and more elaborate subterranean parts, and this style also became established at Thebes, where the funerary temple of Amenhotep, son of Hapu (*c.* 1370 BC), probably acted as an important influence on this development. At the same period, the pyramid form, having now been abandoned as a royal prerogative, was taken over by non-royal persons in their tombs, on a much smaller scale, and is regularly manifested as part of the superstructure of private tombs both at Memphis and Thebes.

In addition to the five-part architectural composition of the Ramesside tombs, mentioned above, the conceptual aspect of them can be interpreted as manifested in three 'levels', an upper, middle and lower section which symbolically reflect the religious background. The subterranean part consisting of a sloping passage leading to a series of rooms including the burial chamber, was a realisation of the realm of Osiris (i.e. the topography of the underworld and the burial place of the god). These rooms were blocked by walls of brick or rubble. The superstructure of the tomb had solar associations, manifested through the pyramid and the placing in a niche of a statue of the deceased, supporting a stela inscribed with a hymn to the sun god. This part of the tomb was usually built of mud brick, and relatively few survive in good condition, but fragments and representations of tombs in paintings help to clarify the picture. The middle part (court, transverse and axial halls and chapel) was that chiefly inspired by temple architecture. This was the cult place, the site for the adoration of the gods, and here the funerary rites were performed.

This scheme represents a further development of the conceptual function of the tomb, of which that of Khnumhotep at Beni Hasan (see above) is an early example. It is a monumental reflection of the role of the deceased, placing him as a participant in the sun god's journey, and identifying him with both Ra and Osiris. The Ra/Osiris connection is manifested in many ways in the whole tomb layout. The pyramidion (capstone of the pyramid) usually shows the adoration of the sun god. On the stelae, the left (i.e. eastern) side has depictions of Ra-Horakhty with associated texts; the right (western) side has depictions and text relating to Osiris (or sometimes vice versa). Among other Osirian features of the New Kingdom tomb was a garden with trees. These would provide shelter and nourishment for the deceased's *ba*, as described on a New Kingdom tomb stela: 'May my *ba* alight upon the branches of the trees which I have planted, may I refresh myself under my sycomore trees and eat the fruit which they give.'

Post New Kingdom

The construction of new tombs waned towards the end of the New Kingdom, and in the succeeding Third Intermediate Period relatively few were built. Instead, older tombs were reused, often without any alteration of the wall-decoration, and there was an increased tendency to group burials together. Nonetheless, some original funerary structures were built, but most of these were rather modest brick chapels, with shafts leading to small undecorated burial chambers. There are numerous examples at Thebes, particularly in the enclosure of the Ramesseum, and indeed the siting of tombs within the compounds of cult temples was a characteristic feature of the period. Although some of the chapels were adorned with painted and carved relief-blocks, coffins and papyri became the main vehicles for the continuing tradition of funerary texts and images, the coffin in particular acting as a miniature tomb (see Chapter 7).

The 25th and 26th Dynasties witnessed a revival of earlier traditions in art, architecture and religious practices, and this trend is also apparent in tomb design. Benefitting from the resurgence in architectural construction which the re-establishment of centralised government brought, high officials at Thebes and Memphis had large and elaborate tombs constructed. At Thebes the great tombs of Montuemhat and the officials of the Divine Adoratress of Amun were built along the processional route to the temple of Hatshepsut (*c.* 1473–1458 BC), which had probably acquired renewed importance as the focus of the revived Festival of the Valley. These enormous 'palace tombs' belonged functionally to the same tradition as the Ramesside tombs. At Saqqara and Giza, high-ranking officials were buried in great shaft tombs, their bodies protected by enormous stone sarcophagi (see fig. 106). Persons of lower status continued to reuse older tombs, and to be buried in large groups.

The tendency of the tomb-chapel to imitate a cult temple culminated in the fourth to third centuries BC, with the creation of tombs such as that of Petosiris at Tuna el-Gebel. Elsewhere the arrangements for the disposal of the dead varied. Burial catacombs were in use at Alexandria (Kom el Shugafa), adorned with painted and relief decoration, in which Egyptian imagery was intermingled with Graeco-Roman elements. In the Faiyum, mummies were interred in large pits, perhaps following temporary storage in some type of mortuary structure. At Kom Abu Billo there were brick tombs with vaulted roofs, and a niche at the eastern end containing a limestone stela. With the advent of Christianity burials were increasingly simplified, often comprising no more than a pit grave.

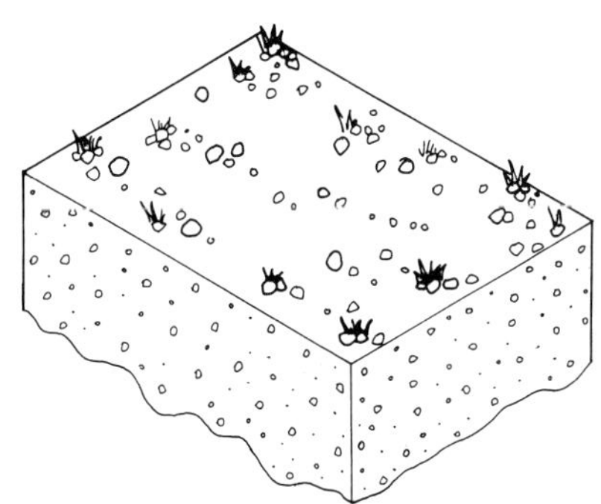

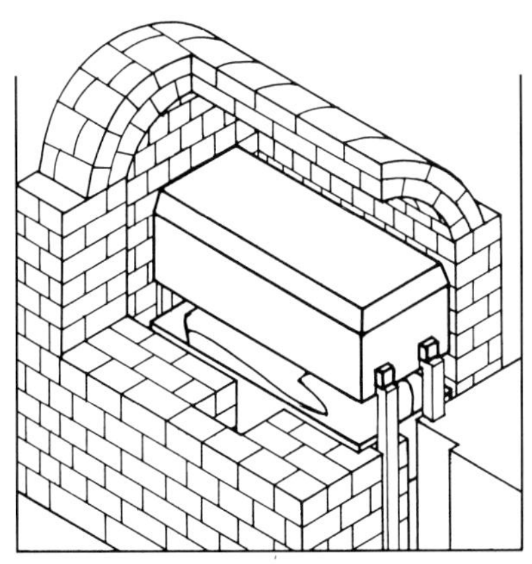

106. During the Late Period (664–305 BC), rock-cut sepulchres and tombs with large, free-standing superstructures continued to be built. Another type of burial place, of which examples were constructed in the Memphite necropolis, was the shaft tomb. The burial was located inside a massive sarcophagus beneath a vaulted structure of stone, built at the bottom of a deep excavation in the rock. After the funeral, the shaft was filled to ground-level with sand and rubble. This technique successfully defeated attempts at robbery.

The fittings of the tomb

The objects which accompanied the dead in their graves changed over time. Variations occurred for economic reasons (the status and/or wealth of the deceased and his relatives) and according to changing ideas of what was considered necessary for the welfare of the deceased. The most consistently important fittings were those which acted as the focus for the funerary cult: the stela and the offering table, together with one or more statues of the deceased – receptacles in which the *ka* could reside to receive offerings.

Tomb stelae and offering tables

Stelae were essentially commemorative tablets, which were usually made of stone, and sometimes of wood or other materials. They were used in various contexts. Some were set up in temples to record the acts of kings in fulfillment of their role as champions of *maat*; others were carved on the rocks to mark the limits of royal power or to record expeditions to extract raw materials. The largest category is that of funerary stelae, which were set up in tombs or mortuary temples. The stela, together with the offering table, were essential pieces of cult furniture. The food offerings and libations which would ensure the survival of the *ka* were placed on the offering table, which was located in front of the stela.

The earliest stelae known were small limestone tablets which have been found at 1st Dynasty graves at Abydos. They perhaps served to mark the place of the funerary cult, though it is uncertain whether they were free-standing or set into the superstructure. Both rectangular and round-topped varieties occur. The majority simply bear the owner's name in hieroglyphs, sometimes with a figure of the deceased serving as a determinative to the writing of the name (see fig. 107). These were succeeded by rectangular slab-stelae with a figure of the deceased seated before a table of offerings – the first examples of which are from tombs of the 2nd Dynasty at Saqqara, where they appear to have been set into the southernmost of the two niches in the eastern façade of the superstructure.

107. Limestone stela from the burial of a dwarf named Nefer, whose distinctive bodily proportions are illustrated in the hieroglyphic determinative accompanying the name. The stela, together with another almost identical in design, comes from the subsidiary chambers of the tomb of King Semerkhet at Abydos. These chambers contained the bones of two achondroplastic dwarfs, who were probably members of the king's entourage. The simple design of the piece is typical of the earliest funerary stelae from Egypt. Late 1st Dynasty, about 2900 BC. H. 45 cm.

The principal type of funerary stela from the Old Kingdom was the 'false door' – a sculptural representation of a panelled doorway, complete with central opening and lintel. A development from the slab-stelae of the 2nd Dynasty, the false door was at first located on the exterior of the *mastaba* superstructure, marking the cult place. In later tombs it was incorporated into a niche, and ultimately became the focal feature of the chapel, set into the west wall. The false door stela was called the *r-per* (literally 'mouth of the house', i.e. tomb) and, as the name suggests it allowed the deceased to enter the chapel to receive offerings and to return again to the burial chamber. The early false door stelae also maintained a tradition of representing the standing figure of the deceased, exemplified in niches in some 3rd Dynasty tombs, particularly that of Hesy-Re at Saqqara, where the figures were carved on wooden panels. The majority of false doors come from Giza and Saqqara. They vary in size and degree of elaboration, but certain standard features recur. At the top was a lintel, below which came a rectangular tablet with a scene of the deceased seated before offerings (see fig. 109). Below this again was the niched doorway; the central opening was usually plain, whereas in reality it would have been covered with a hanging mat, and on some false doors this was represented rolled up above the aperture (see figs 108 and

108. Painted limestone false door from the tomb of Bateti. The lintel and side panels are unfinished, but the central aperture includes a depiction of the rolled mat which would have 'closed' the door and – unusually – a figure of the deceased represented as though emerging from the burial chamber into the tomb-chapel to receive his offerings. 4th or 5th Dynasty, about 2613–2345 BC. Possibly from Saqqara. H. 131 cm.

109. Panel from the limestone false door of the king's son and high priest of Ra at Heliopolis Rahotep. The central scene shows the dead man seated on a bull-legged chair, extending his right hand towards a table on which are stylised conical loaves of bread. The names of other offerings (including incense, eye paint, wine and figs) are inscribed above and below the table, and at the right, in tabular form, is a list of different kinds of linen cloth. The large hieroglyphic texts framing the scene give the name and titles of the deceased. Early 4th Dynasty, about 2600 BC. From the tomb chapel of Rahotep at Meidum. H. 79 cm.

110. Limestone false door from the tomb of Kaihap. At the top is an inscription in which offerings are requested for the deceased at various festivals in the religious calendar. Below this in the centre is a tablet showing Kaihap and his wife seated before an offering table. The central aperture of the door is again occupied by figures of Kaihap and his wife, while on the panels at each side relatives and mortuary priests burn incense and present offerings. 5th Dynasty, about 2494–2345 BC. From Saqqara. H. 209 cm.

110). The recessed sides of the niche carried representations of the deceased, relatives, offering bearers or offerings. At Giza in the reigns of Khufu and Khafra (*c.* 2589–2566 and *c.* 2558–2532 BC) false doors were usually omitted from tombs, and instead a slab bearing the offering-table scene alone was set into the eastern side of the *mastaba*.

The development of stelae was accompanied by an evolution in the offering table. In graves of the first two dynasties a circular table on a central support, usually of calcite, was placed within the burial chamber, close to the corpse. This served to support the food offerings and is exactly the type of table which appeared in the offering scene on stelae. As the provision of food supplies within the grave was gradually superseded by a formal offering cult situated in the tomb superstructure, offering tables began to be placed in front of the false door or stela. In the 3rd to 4th Dynasties the circular type continued in use and a stone trough for offerings of water, wine or beer was added (though these could also act symbolically as pools for the deceased to sail on in the next life) (see fig. 111). At this period, a rectangular type of offering-slab also appeared, combining the libation-trough with a representation of the circular table carved in relief. From the 5th Dynasty onward the standard type was the offering table in the shape of the hieroglyphic sign *hetep* ('offering'), which in origin represented a loaf of bread standing on a reed mat.

111. Limestone offering table of rectangular shape incorporating the hieroglyphic sign *hetep* ('offering'), two circular depressions probably representing individual offering tables and two miniature libation-troughs. The basic function of the troughs was to receive drink-offerings of water, beer or wine, but they also played a symbolic role as miniature pools on which the deceased might travel by boat in the afterlife. In the centre of the upper portion is a carved figure of the deceased, identified in the text as the Overseer of the Storehouse Seneb. Possibly from Saqqara, 6th Dynasty. 39×37 cm.

In the years immediately following the Old Kingdom, the design of stelae became simpler as Egypt became politically decentralised and provincial traditions of craftsmanship rose to prominence. A common type of the First Intermediate Period was the 'slab stela', a rectangular tablet with a representation of the deceased before an offering table as the principal feature (see fig. 113), with the frequent addition of figures of relatives and servants bringing offerings. The rigid graphic framework of earlier stelae gave way to a more haphazard arrangement with figures and offerings 'floating' in the field (see fig. 112).

Following the reunification of Egypt under Mentuhotep II (*c.* 2055–2004 BC), greater uniformity in the design of funerary stelae returned. Examples from the 11th and 12th Dynasties were rectangular in basic shape, and included both the false door type and a type with a rounded top. This marked a significant development away from the false door (symbolising the threshold of the netherworld) to a type of stela which represnted the cosmos. The curved upper portion suggested the vault of heaven, and was frequently occupied by celestial symbols, such as the winged solar disc or *wedjat* eyes. The main scene again showed the deceased before the offering table, often accompanied by relatives and servants presenting offerings. The text, often inscribed above the

113. Stela of the granary official Sarenenutet, showing the deceased seated before an offering table. The tall bread-loaves of earlier offering scenes (see fig. 109) have been transformed into reed-leaves, a change which occurs on such scenes in the 5th to 6th Dynasties. This was probably a conscious development on the part of the sculptor, to link the basic image of sustenance with an allusion to the Field of Reeds, a region of the hereafter in which the deceased obtained food (see Chapter 1). Early 12th Dynasty, about 1970 BC. H. 52 cm.

112. Stela of the lector priest Inhur-nakht, who is shown standing with his wife Hu to receive offerings from a son and servants. The inscription requests offerings and contains formulaic phrases descriptive of Inhur-nakht's virtues while alive. The absence of register-lines in the scene, and the informal placing of the small figures of servants and groups of offerings are characteristic features of funerary stelae dating to the First Intermediate Period. Probably from Naga ed-Deir. H. 77 cm.

scene, usually comprised the offering formula, but some examples include autobiographical passages and an appeal to the living (see Chapter 3). Offering tables generally continued to take the form of the hieroglyphic sign *hetep* and bore carved images of foodstuffs and libation vessels – images which, like those on the chapel walls, were to satisfy the deceased's needs should the real offerings cease to be provided (see fig. 114). Some examples also incorporated miniature libation troughs.

In the later Middle Kingdom, stelae were characterised by the subdivision of the surface into small rectangular compartments, each occupied by a figure of an individual related to the deceased (children, brothers, sisters, etc.). This type continued into the Second Intermediate Period. A number of crudely painted rectangular wooden stelae were also included in burials in this period.

In private tombs of the New Kingdom stelae were usually tall and round-

114. Limestone offering table. The upper surface incorporates images of food offerings and depictions of libation vessels, from which liquid is shown pouring through one of three miniature troughs and out via a large spout. An offering formula is inscribed around the edge, and the inscription names three beneficiaries: two men named Wepwawethetepi and Djefaihapi, and a woman named In. From Asyut, tomb 13A. Probably 12th Dynasty. L. 24 cm.

115. Limestone stela of Bakkay. The rounded top symbolises the vault of heaven. The surface is divided in a manner characteristic of funerary stelae of the New Kingdom. Above, Bakkay and his wife offer flowers and a libation to the god Osiris; below, offerings are made to a couple named Huy and Henutnofret by four members of their family. At the bottom is an inscription containing an offering formula. 18th Dynasty, reign of Amenhotep III, about 1390–1352 BC. Provenance unknown. H. 54 cm.

topped, and were frequently large. They were often made of limestone and were brightly painted. While free-standing stelae were common, many were also hewn from the rock. The stelae stood in pairs in the courtyard of the tomb, and also at one or both ends of the transverse hall. Many of them continued to show the deceased and his wife receiving offerings, but this scene was now usually at the top. A major innovation of the period was the regular depiction of deities (who appeared only occasionally in the Middle Kingdom) (see fig. 115). Osiris and Anubis often appeared, sometimes accompanied by Isis, Nephthys or Horus, receiving offerings or incense from the deceased. The scene of the deceased receiving gifts often itself appeared in a lower register. Stelae from the later New Kingdom sometimes incorporated a pyramid-shaped top, emphasising the solar aspects which at this period rose to greater prominence in the tomb (see fig. 116).

The general reduction in the scale and complexity of tomb superstructures during the Third Intermediate Period was accompanied by a simplification of the stela. Most burials were provided with a small round-topped stela of painted wood, usually showing a scene of the deceased adoring Osiris or Ra-Horakhty. A few of these are known from the 21st Dynasty, but the vast majority date to the 22nd Dynasty. The concept of the stela as a miniature cosmos was still prominent in these examples: the curved upper surface was often decorated with the hieroglyphic sign for 'sky' and the field below was framed by the signs for 'east' and 'west', with the baseline representing the earth (see fig. 117). On some examples of the 25th Dynasty the entire frame was formed of the arched body of the goddess Nut. This type continued in use under the 25th to 26th

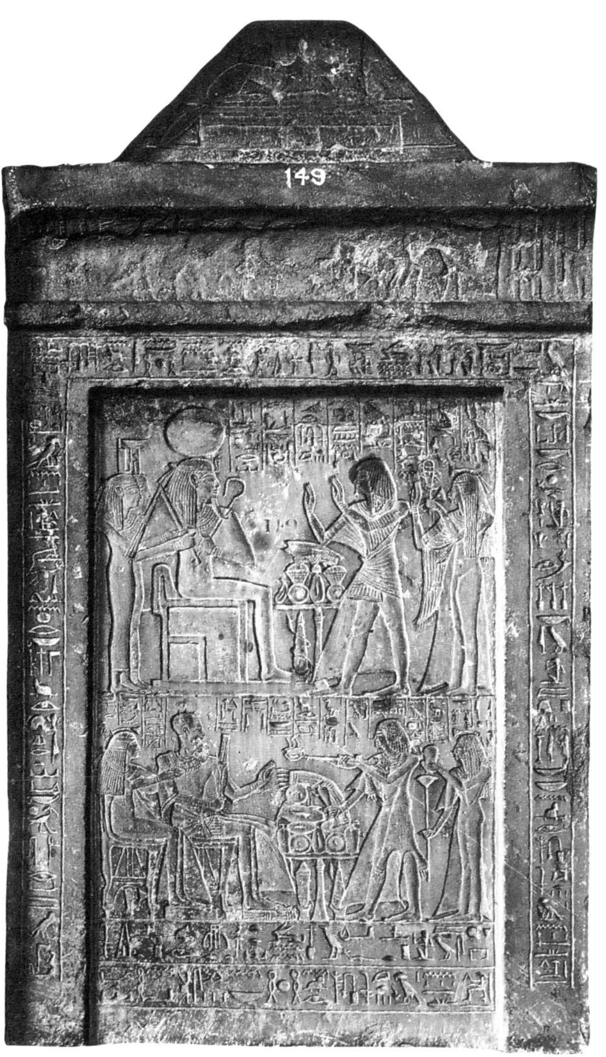

116. Limestone stela of Benaa. This example, dating to the early part of the reign of Ramesses II, illustrates the uniting of solar and Osirian concepts in the context of the tomb in this period. Solar associations are manifest in the pyramidion which tops the stela, and in the sun disc worn as a headdress by Osiris in the upper scene. As in the stela of Bakkay (see fig. 115), the adoration of the gods occupies the upper register, and the funerary cult the lower. H. 121 cm.

117. Painted wooden funerary stelae. Left: the priest of Amun Nakhtefmut and his daughter Tashepenese adore Ra-Horakhty. 22nd Dynasty, about 850 BC. H. 27.5 cm. Right: the woman Tjentdiashakhet seated before an offering table. The 'sky' hieroglyph above and the signs for 'west' and 'east' which form the frame of the scene define the stela as a miniature version of the cosmos. The iconography of the scene and the arrangement and wording of the inscription deliberately imitate models from the Old Kingdom. From Qurna, 25th Dynasty, about 680 BC. H. 21 cm.

Dynasties, when substantial texts reappeared below the scene, which often included a solar barque. Some of these were installed in chapels, but others were probably located inside the burial chamber.

Private funerary stelae made of stone were rare after the New Kingdom, when wooden tablets were the norm, but examples of stone began to reappear in the Late Period. Both stone and wooden stelae were used in the Ptolemaic Period (see fig. 118). Some of these were inscribed with a Greek text, and there was a tendency towards the inclusion of more Hellenistic features noticeable particularly in the dress and pose of the deceased. Some examples represent architectural doorways, such as those from Kom Abu Billo (Terenuthis). They were ultimately succeeded by Coptic Christian gravestones.

Statues of the deceased

The statue was regarded as a physical embodiment of the individual, a base which the *ka* could occupy in order to receive offerings. A common word for statue, *shesep*, probably means literally 'receiver', and when used in the phrase *shesep r ankh* ('receiver in order to live') it denotes the capacity of the image to serve as a receptacle for the vital essence of the deceased. Another function

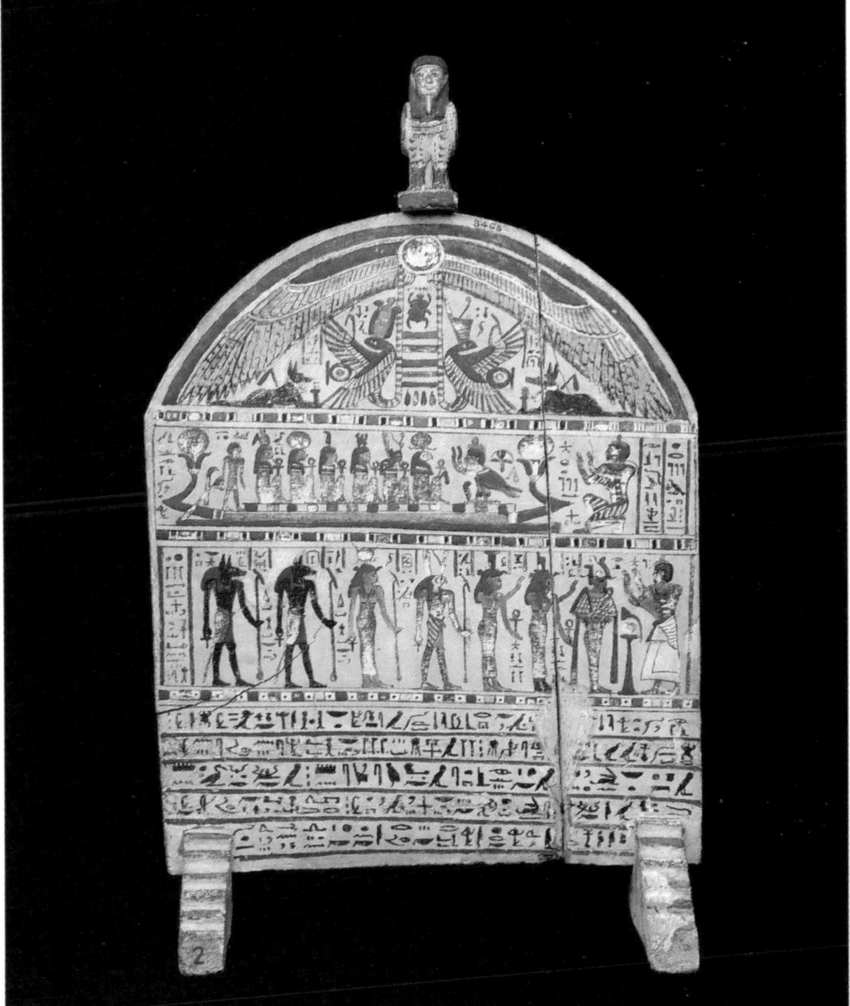

118. Painted sycomore fig funerary stela of Neswy (see also fig. 156). The *ba* of the deceased is perched on the top of the vault, stressing the role of the stela as a miniature representation of the tomb. Beneath the schematic vault of heaven, adorned with a winged sun disc and two jackals representing Anubis, are scenes of the deceased adoring the sun god and other deities in the solar barque, and a row of gods. Early Ptolemaic Period, about third century BC. From Thebes. H. 53.5 cm.

of the statue was as a reserve body to act as a base for the *ba*, since this aspect of the individual could not exist independently without a physical form (see Chapter 1).

All human images produced by Egyptian artists were created according to a canon of proportions. The figure was laid out on a grid, and standing figures were divided from hairline to foot into (for most of the pharaonic period) eighteen squares. This allowed consistency in reproducing the human image, which was heavily idealised. Figures were usually depicted in a formal pose, in which symmetry was important (though not invariable). Most figures were positioned squarely on the base, looking forward. Stone statues were usually provided with a back pillar and carried an inscription on the base, pillar or seat. Certain poses were applicable to the different sexes. Standing figures of men usually show the left leg advanced, those of women represent the feet together.

The principal materials used to make statues for the tomb were stone and wood. A range of stones was obtained from quarries in Egypt – limestone, granite, quartzite, serpentine – while the woods used included both native and imported varieties (sycomore fig, acacia, tamarisk, ebony and cedar). The particular qualities of the different materials encouraged different treatments by the craftsmen; hence stone statues often represent the subject seated, whereas wooden ones are more frequently standing. The size of the figure varied, from a few centimetres in height to over lifesize.

Ancient Egyptian sculptures were not portraits, but rather idealised images. This is demonstrated by the strong standardisation apparent in statues produced in the same period, and by the fact that where numerous statues represent the same owner there are usually no similarities which can be attributed to a likeness to the subject. The majority of statues were probably carved without reference to the actual appearance of the person depicted. Resemblance between statues probably reflects the prevalent sculptural style of the period and/or local craft tradition.

119. Scenes from the rock-tomb of Pepiankh at Meir, showing the production of statues of the tomb owner. On the left, the lector-priest and scribe Pepi-ihyemsa paints a standing statue. On the right, the 'overseer of sculptors' Itjau and the sculptor Sebekemhat use chisels to carve the finer details of a seated statue. 6th Dynasty, about 2200 BC.

Since a statue could enable the owner to be physically present in some location outside his body, there was in theory no limit to the number of images by which an individual might be represented, although most people probably had only one. A statue set up in a temple put the owner in the vicinity of the god of that place; in the same way as in the tomb, the person depicted could receive some of the offerings presented in the temple ritual. It is somewhat less easy to explain the presence of numerous statues in the tomb, a phenomenon particularly associated with the Old Kingdom. Possibly some of these figures acted as reserves in case of damage. Other possibilities are that they depicted the owner at different ages, or as the holder of different offices.

Since the statue was made of inert materials, it had to be transformed into an object which had the properties of a living being. The eyes must be given the capacity to see, the mouth to speak and to eat and drink. This animation of the statue could be done only by the performance of the ritual known as the 'Opening of the Mouth', or sometimes more fully the 'Opening of the Mouth and Eyes'. This ritual was performed at the completion of the statues, while in the workshop. Its main features were the touching of the eyes and mouth with a range of instruments: three types of adze, an instrument called the *weret-hekau* (also imitating an adze), a chisel and a finger-shaped instrument. Each episode in the ritual was accompanied by appropriate incantations. It is no accident that most of the instruments involved are sculptors' tools. The rite therefore incorporates the animation of the image within the process of creating it, as in fact an indispensable conclusion to the creative process. Once the ritual had been performed, the statue became linked to the *ka* of the person represented. In the same way the 'Opening of the Mouth' was performed on other types of image which served to support the *ka* of the owner, such as anthropoid coffins (see Chapter 7), and even on two-dimensional images carved in relief. Most importantly it was carried out on the mummified body itself at the completion of the embalming, in order to revivify it (see Chapter 6).

The evolution of tomb statuary

Although fragmentary remains point to the existence of funerary statues as early as the 1st Dynasty, the earliest well-preserved tomb figures date to the 3rd Dynasty. The mortuary temples of the Old Kingdom rulers, built adjacent to their pyramids, have preserved some of the finest early examples of funerary statues. The earliest is the seated limestone statue of King Netjerikhet Djoser (*c.* 2667–2648 BC), founder of the 3rd Dynasty, which was discovered still walled up in its *serdab*, or statue chamber, against the north side of the Step Pyramid at Saqqara. Two holes cut into the north wall of the *serdab* enabled the royal *ka*, via the medium of the statue, to look out to the place where the rituals were performed for his benefit. Royal mortuary temples of the Old Kingdom contained many statues of the king, varying in size, material and attitude; all, however, fulfilled the same function, as receptacles for the *ka*.

It was also in the 3rd Dynasty that private tombs began to contain one or more statues of their occupants. They could range from life-size examples of supreme workmanship, such as the seated figures of Rahotep and his wife Nofret, from Meidum, to smaller pieces of humbler quality. Examples from the 3rd Dynasty represent men and women, seated and standing, but always individually (see fig. 120). During the 4th to 6th Dynasties, the number and range of the statues increased. In the chapels of rock-cut tombs statues were carved out of the living rock; in *mastaba* tombs they were usually concealed in the *serdab*, a special

120. Painted limestone statue of Nofretmin. In some tombs, pair-statues represented a married couple seated or standing together. In others, individual statues of the owner of the tomb and his wife were positioned side by side. This statue perhaps comes from the otherwise unknown tomb of Nofretmin's husband. The straight hairstyle and simple, unpleated dress are typical of the period. Although the statue is made from limestone, the high-backed seat has been painted in imitation of a harder and more costly stone, perhaps granite. From Meidum or Dahshur. 6th Dynasty, about 2300 BC. H. 46 cm.

121. Wooden statue of Tjeti, a provincial official of high status. The figure is finely carved from a dark wood, originally painted, and attached to a base of a different wood, on which is carved an inscription giving the name and titles of Tjeti. The bodily form has been carved with exceptional skill, and the muscular structure beneath the skin has been faithfully rendered. The inlaid eyes are made from limestone and obsidian set in copper surrounds. Such wooden figures were frequently provided as tomb statues for persons of rank in the Old Kingdom. Probably from Akhmim. 6th Dynasty, about 2345–2181 BC. H. 75.5 cm (modern staff).

122. Cedarwood statuette, said to be from the shaft tomb of Gua, physician to the provincial governor Djehutyhotep. Although uninscribed, the pose and costume of the figure, together with the use of an expensive imported timber, suggest that it represents the owner of the tomb. Small-scale wooden figurines, placed in or near the coffin, sometimes served as a repository for the *ka* in burials which did not possess an offering chapel. 12th Dynasty, about 1850 BC. From Deir el-Bersha. H. 35 cm.

chamber in the superstructure in which the statue was placed. It was usually concealed from the view of visitors to the chapel; a small slit in the wall, level with the eyes of the statue, permitted communication with the offering chapel. The *serdab* was sometimes located directly behind the false door, before which the offering ritual was performed, so that the deceased's *ka*, within the statue, faced the participants. In some tombs the participation of the deceased in the ritual was emphasised by having the statue carved within the central aperture of the false door itself, either standing (see fig. 108) or advancing as though entering the chapel to partake of his offerings. Most freestanding statues represented the deceased or his wife standing or seated. Some were life-size, but the majority were smaller. Some images of men were in the pose of a scribe, emphasising literacy; this was an important prerequisite for an official to hold high office, and the scribal statue would help to ensure that this privileged position would be perpetuated in the afterlife. Pair statues show husband and wife seated or standing, some with children on a smaller scale. There were also many statues of wood, mostly on a small scale (see figs 121 and 122).

A well-publicised but enigmatic group of early tomb sculptures are the so-called 'reserve heads', the majority of which have been found in early 4th Dynasty *mastaba* tombs of persons of high status in the west cemetery at Giza, adjacent to the pyramid of Khufu (*c.* 2589–2566 BC). These are limestone representations of the head and neck, without details of hair or wig, and with only a simple carved line marking its outline. The eyes are sometimes turned upwards.

The significance of these sculptures is uncertain. They may have been intended as substitutes for the head in case of its loss (by analogy with later mummy-masks), or as a receptacle for the *ka* to receive offerings, but it is unusual for Egyptian representations of the deceased to omit the body. It is notable that they occur mainly in the tombs of Khufu's courtiers, which are otherwise distinguished by the austerity of their decoration (for example, there are no wall-images and false doors are usually omitted; see above, p. 150). Since these tombs usually contained no *ka* statue, the reserve head may have been a substitute for the statue and two-dimensional wall-images of the deceased, representing only the most important part of the body. The puzzle of the heads' significance is complicated by the distinctive mutilations found on many of them – the ears are always damaged or entirely destroyed, and on many there is a vertical incision down the back of the head. This has suggested to some scholars that they were sculptor's models from which plaster casts were taken, and that the mutilations occurred during the removal of the casts. However, it is at least as likely that they were related to the plaster head-coverings of the mummy (see Chapter 2) or were intended to function in funerary rituals.

During the First Intermediate Period, funerary statues from provincial centres such as Asyut were mainly made of wood. There is no evidence for royal funerary sculpture between the 6th Dynasty and the late 11th Dynasty, when a series of painted sandstone statues were carved for installation at the temple-tomb of Mentuhotep II (*c.* 2055–2004 BC) at Deir el-Bahri. These figures, both standing and seated, are the earliest to represent the dead king in the so-called 'Osirian' pose, with feet together and arms crossed on the breast. His garment, however, is not the enveloping shroud of later statues, but the short knee-length robe worn at the *sed* festival, emphasising the notion of renewed life and powers inherent in these images. Non-royal burials of this period were sometimes provided with small limestone figures.

At the height of the Middle Kingdom, royal mortuary temples continued to contain statues of the king as a living individual, but alongside these, true mummiform figures were also installed. Both types were found at the pyramid complex of Senusret I (*c.* 1965–1920 BC) at Lisht, and the mummiform statue was also installed in cult temple contexts at Karnak at this period. The more imposing private tomb chapels of this period contained a seated statue of the owner set in a niche at the end, while others contained mummiform figures lining the walls of the passage, as in the tomb of Sarenput at Aswan. In smaller tombs, where the surfaces of the coffin replicated the chapel wall-decoration of richer burials, a small wooden statuette of the deceased was placed in the coffin or burial chamber.

In private tombs of the 18th Dynasty it became more usual for the statue to be positioned in the chapel, where it was fully visible to the visitor. The figures were often lifesize, usually representing the owner and his wife, sometimes with his mother or a group of relatives. These statues were often cut from the living rock, but there were also freestanding statues (usually smaller than lifesize) which were placed in a niche in the chapel (see fig. 123). Many figures were of painted limestone, although other stones were used. Besides the familiar seated type, the range of sculptural forms used in tombs was expanded. Block statues and stelophorous figures became more common. Whereas the dress of earlier statues was generally traditional, tomb sculptures now began to reflect changing fashions of dress. This is exemplified well in the post-Amarna period by such pieces as the large limestone statues from Saqqara (see fig. 124). In the later New Kingdom, stelophorous statues were often placed in the tomb superstructure.

After the New Kingdom, many burials were grouped in family vaults or in earlier rock-cut tombs, often without an adjacent mortuary chapel. The entire burial outfit was simplified, and among the items which disappeared from the fittings of the tomb was the statue of the owner. At the same period, there was an increase in the number of statues of non-royal individuals which were set up in the precincts of cult-temples, a phenomenon particularly well-documented at Thebes. The poses and attributes of these sculptures followed traditional models (mainly seated or block statues). Their inscriptions request offerings and often proclaim the devotion of sons in setting up the statues to preserve the memory of fathers, very much in the manner of tomb-statues of earlier periods. It may be

123. Painted sandstone pair-statue of Itu, a priest of Amun and his wife Henutweret. The couple are represented sitting on a plain seat, clasping each other by the shoulders. A small figure between the man and wife represents their son Neferhebef. Groups such as this were set up in the offering chapels of tombs to provide a physical form for the *ka* of the dead person to receive sustenance. The hairstyles and the simple costumes of these figures are characteristic of the middle years of the 18th Dynasty, about 1400 BC. From Thebes. H. 74 cm.

124. Limestone pair-statue of an unnamed man and wife. The function and design of this piece are essentially the same as that illustrated in fig. 123, but this example illustrates the artistic legacies of the Amarna period (mid-fourteenth century BC). The poses of the couple are more relaxed, their mutual affection is more naturalistically suggested by the clasping of their hands and the sculptor has represented luxuriant curled wigs and elaborately pleated gowns. They are seated on a wooden chair with leonine legs. Late 18th Dynasty, about 1300 BC. Probably from the Memphite necropolis. H. 132 cm.

is possible that some of the many other New Kingdom tombs there may have been built by craftsmen from Deir el-Medina, but evidence is almost totally lacking, and there is a strong possibility that other groups of workers were responsible for many of the sepulchres. It has been estimated that outside Deir el-Medina at this period perhaps two to four tombs would be under construction at Thebes at a given time, with possibly four or five craftsmen at work on each. The wall-decoration of the tomb of Amenemhat includes a rare acknowledgement of the craftsmen who built his tomb. Amenemhat is shown making offerings to them, and although most of the names and figures are destroyed they included a son 'who directed the work upon this tomb', an 'outline-draughtsman' and 'the sculptor who made the statues'.

It can be safely assumed that the prospective occupant would regularly inspect the work on his tomb, for a fine funerary chapel confirmed the status of the owner in the eyes of posterity. As the 'appeal to the living' implies (see Chapter 3), it was expected that the chapel would be visited by future generations, who might then recite the offering formula for the benefit of the deceased. A finely-decorated chapel with wall-scenes would attract admirers, and many tomb scenes include amusing details which might appeal to a casual visitor. Thus, in a market scene in the tomb of Tepemankh at Saqqara (5th Dynasty) a baboon seizes a thief by the leg; in the 18th Dynasty tomb of Menna two young girls fight, tearing at each other's hair; in the tomb of Iduit (6th Dynasty) a predatory crocodile watches hungrily as a hippopotamus gives birth. In scenes of peasants and craftsmen dialogue is often included, freezing for ever the banter and jocular insults of daily life. Visitors' graffiti in Old Kingdom pyramid temples show they were visited as tourist attractions as early as the New Kingdom.

The ownership of a tomb was often indicated by inscriptions on the door-jambs or lintel. Another medium by which the owner was identified was baked clay cones, the bases of which were stamped with hieroglyphic texts giving the names and titles of the deceased. These objects were arranged in friezes above the entrance to the tomb with their inscribed surfaces visible.

Great care was devoted to the equipping of the tomb. Some of the various objects placed in the tomb had been used in life (clothing, containers, tools, weapons, jewellery, games and musical instruments), but the majority of items were made specifically for the grave. Apart from those items made as a special concession in the royal workshops, coffins, canopic containers, *shabti*s and other items were made by local craftsmen. Most of these were attached to temples. Those items which carried detailed religious iconography and texts – particularly coffins and papyri – were probably produced in workshops attached to the 'House of Life', i.e. the temple library. Sculptors, joiners, painters and scribes worked in teams to produce objects (see fig. 126). Such teamwork is depicted in a famous scene from the tomb of Ipuy at Thebes, in which craftsmen are shown making a shrine. Scenes such as this are rare, but scrutiny of finished works reveals (in spite of a basic uniformity of style) the mark of different hands, besides errors and corrections. The limestone architrave of Akhethotep in the University

126. Craftsmen in the workshop of the temple of Amun. Among the objects being made are some which were probably intended for the tomb. Part of a scene in the tomb chapel of Nebamun and Ipuky at Thebes, in which one of the owners inspects the work under his authority. 18th Dynasty, about 1380 BC.

Museum, Liverpool (6th Dynasty) exhibits technical variations between figures and hieroglyphs suggesting the hands of both master(s) and apprentices.

Informal notes on hieratic ostraca from Deir el-Medina show that skilled craftsmen could make funerary items for neighbours and colleagues as private commissions. One such transaction is recorded as follows:

> 'What the draughtsman Neferhotep gave to Horemwia (namely):
> one painted stela of (Nofretari), May she live! (And) he gave me
> a wooden coffer in exchange for it. In addition, (I) decorated two
> coffins for the Riverbank (*meryt*) for him, and he made a bed for me . . .'

The mortuary cult

As explained in Chapters 1 and 3, the continued survival of the dead depended largely on the maintainance of a mortuary cult. This would ensure that the deceased was nourished by a supply of offerings in perpetuity, presented in the prescribed context of the funerary ritual, and involving the pronouncement of the name of the dead. This cult might be performed by the relatives of the deceased or by priests, but it required some means of long-term support. This often took the form of an endowment, usually a plot of cultivable land which was dedicated by the deceased as his mortuary estate. The profits of the land yielded the offerings of food, drink, incense and other items to be presented to the deceased, and also provided payment for the officials of the cult. The importance of making these preparations is expressed in the instruction of Prince Hardjedef, who urges his son: 'Choose for him [i.e. the mortuary priest who will serve his cult after death] a plot among your fields, well-watered every year. He profits you more than your own son; prefer him even to your [heir].' The mortuary estates are depicted in tomb chapels of the Old Kingdom, personified as female servants carrying goods to the tomb. In some tombs endowment documents are carved on the walls, recording the duties of the personnel, the content of the endowment, and sometimes ways of protecting the interests of the cult personnel to prevent interference or attempts to divert the funds elsewhere.

Ideally the main cult officiant was the son of the owner. Ideologically, this reflected the myth of Osiris, in which Horus performed the funerary offices for his dead father. It played an important role in the royal succession, since carrying out the funerary rites for a dead king legitimised the officiant as his successor, irrespective of his relationship to the deceased. In the wall-paintings in the burial chamber of Tutankhamun (who died without a male heir) the funerary rituals for the dead pharaoh are performed by the official Ay, who is accordingly represented as the new king. In the private sphere there was a link between the mortuary cult and the inheritance of property. Inheritance was conditional upon the son's fulfillment of duties towards the father's cult (see p. 171), and as the mortuary cult was intended to last in perpetuity it might have been hoped that the land set aside for the endowment would remain in the family from generation to generation.

127. *Ka* priests (*hemu-ka*) bringing 'choice cuts' of meat, birds and other foodstuffs to sustain the owner of the tomb. Scene carved on the jamb of a false door from the *mastaba* of Werirenptah, priest in the sun temple of King Neferirkara. 5th Dynasty, about 2400 BC. From Saqqara.

Besides the eldest son the main personnel of the mortuary cult were priests called *hemu-ka* (literally servants of the *ka*) (see fig. 127). Their task was to keep the *ka* of the deceased supplied, and in return for fulfilling this duty they received the largest share of the endowment. They served in rotation. Besides these priests a lector priest was necessary to direct the cult proceedings. His title – *khery-hebet* – means literally 'the keeper of the sacred book' and he read the words of the ritual from a papyrus scroll.

Information on the organisation of mortuary cults varies in degree from period to period. We are comparatively well informed about the administration of certain royal mortuary establishments of the Old Kingdom because archives on papyrus have been found at Abu Sir in the funerary temples of kings Neferirkara (*c.* 2475–2455 BC) and Raneferef (*c.* 2448–2445 BC). These sources show that each cult was run by priests divided into five rotating shifts, or *phyles* – each *phyle* having its own storeroom within the temple. Each *phyle* was divided into two sub-groups, which served for a month. Hence a ten-month cycle of rotation operated. The duties of the priests, as recorded in the papyri, included making two daily processions around the pyramid, looking after the cult statues, maintaining goods belonging to the cult, and guarding the temple. To ensure the long-term continuation of the king's cult, settlements were founded near to the royal tomb. These 'pyramid towns' housed the priests, administrators and labourers who served the cult.

In the later Old Kingdom (5th to 6th Dynasties), tomb chapels of some non-royal persons in the Memphite necropolis were served by priests organised in *phyles*, on a basis comparable to that operating in the royal mortuary cults. This was evidently a special privilege. Most of the persons who enjoyed this system were very high-ranking officials (such as viziers) or were closely linked to the royal family in some way. The *phyle* system was not used in private cults after the 6th Dynasty.

Generally, the operation of non-royal mortuary cults seems to have been organised on simpler lines, involving fewer personnel. Information about the functioning of these is uneven, but for the Middle Kingdom we have several groups of documents which throw light on the arrangements. Hekanakht, author of a famous series of letters, was a *hem-ka* priest of the mortuary cult of the vizier Ipy, who was buried at Thebes in the 11th Dynasty. Hekanakht's family occupied a farm which was probably the mortuary estate that provided the profits for the running of the cult. Hekanakht was frequently away from Thebes, and his son seems to have carried out the duties of mortuary priest in his absence. The letters were found close to the tomb chapel of Ipy, where they had perhaps been stored or abandoned (one of them was unopened) by Hekanakht's son.

Another means of ensuring the continuation of a private mortuary cult was to arrange to have it perfomed by the priests of the local temple. Since, it was hoped, the cult of the local god would survive indefinitely (whereas that of a deceased official might not) such an arrangement improved the chance of one's cult being maintained over many generations. A well-documented instance comes from the tomb of Djefahapy, provincial governor and high priest of the god Wepwawet at Asyut. The inscriptions in his tomb record the contracts he made with the priests of Wepwawet. Djefahapy's own endowments would provide funds to the cult of the god, in return for which the god's priests would also take on the maintainance of the dead man's mortuary cult. The duty of priest and the endowment which maintained it were to be passed from generation to generation to ensure perpetual service of the dead.

Another example of a contract recorded on stone is the limestone stela of

Intef, son of Myt, dating to the late 11th Dynasty, from Thebes, in the British Museum. The relevant passage reads:

> I have made a contract with the *hem-ka* priest Nekhtiu, son of Irmeh . . . son of Nekhtu, for the pouring of water and the pouring out of libations, while the *mhwnw*-attendant holds out his arms to him, and the *khent-wer* [officiant] holds the offering-cakes and the jar in which they go forth, and make offering therewith to my statue in the course of every day. Moreover, I have made a contract with the lector priest Intef, son of Mentunesu, son of Intef, son of Tjetu in order that service may be performed in the tomb and that the liturgy may be read by the *hem-*[*ka*] at every monthly festival and at every half-monthly festival, in order that my name may be beautiful and that my memory may exist up to this day, and in order that the chapel of this excellent *sah* may be established. Moreover I have given twenty garments to this mortuary priest and I have given ten garments to this lector priest, and a man-servant and a maid-servant to each . . .

Evidence from later periods is less informative. Judicial papyri of the Late Period/Ptolemaic period mention mortuary priests called *wah mu*, 'water pourers', who are more generally termed *choachytes* (the Greek version of *wah mu*). They maintained the cult of the dead, fulfilling the traditional role of the eldest son, and they seem to have been the successors of the *hemu-ka* of earlier periods. Though not explicit in the records, it is likely that their responsibilities extended beyond a basic water-pouring ritual, and that they were in fact professional mortuary priests, paid by the family of the deceased, perhaps with the profits of a land endowment, as in earlier periods.

Ritual purity had to be observed when performing the cult of the dead. The necropolis, like the temple precinct of a god was a sacred area, not to be entered in a state of impurity. Inscriptions in some tombs of the Old Kingdom warn against this. In the tomb of Harkhuf (6th Dynasty) we read:

> As for any man who enters this tomb unclean,
> I shall seize him by the neck like a bird,
> He will be judged for it by the great god!

The mortuary priests underwent purification at the *ibu* or *seh netjer*, the place where the body of the deceased was purified before being embalmed. In the tomb of Rekhmira at Thebes there is a depiction of the lector priest and other mortuary personnel undergoing this ablution before entering the necropolis. Even the funerary equipment and offerings had to be purified in order to prevent any unwelcome influences entering the realm of the dead.

The mortuary cult was inaugurated on the day of burial, when the first offerings to the dead were made, and the ritual was repeated at the numerous religious festivals in the calendar. On these occasions offerings were made to gods in their cult temples and, by the process of 'reversion', these offerings could then be presented to the dead so that they might receive a share of the nourishment which they provided. For this reason, inscriptions on false doors and tomb stelae often request offerings at specified festivals – the feasts of particular gods, and secular ones such as the new year festival, and the monthly and half-monthly festivals. In the tomb of Princess Ni-sedjer-kai at Giza the text runs: 'May offerings be given her on the New Year's festival, the Thoth festival, the First-of-the-Year feast, the *wag*-festival [a celebration of the vindication of Osiris], the Sokar festival, the Great Flame festival, the Brazier festival, the Procession-of-Min festival, the monthly *sadj*-festival, the Beginning-of-the-Month festival, the Beginning of the Half-Month festival, every festival, every day . . .'. On each of these occasions the offering ritual would be performed at the tomb. The most important of all these events during the New Kingdom was the annual Festival of the Valley, which took place at Thebes. On this occasion, the cult image of the god Amun was taken from his shrine in the temple of Karnak and ferried by barge across the Nile to the west bank to visit the mortuary temples of the deceased rulers (see Chapter 1). The people of Thebes followed the image of the god in his procession, and visited the tombs of their dead relatives in the necropolis. Here they would hold a feast at which the dead were honoured guests. Besides ensuring that the dead were nourished, this event was crucial to maintaining the links between the living and the dead members of the community. The importance of the Valley Festival for the dead is amply illustrated by texts such as the following, inscribed in the now-lost 18th Dynasty tomb of a man named Amenhotep:

> May you see the lord of the gods Amun on his beautiful Festival of the Valley, may you follow him in the sanctuaries of the temples. And when your name is invoked at the offering table every time the rite is performed, may your *ba* cry aloud so that it may be heard. It shall not be kept back from the great place, and you will partake of the offerings brought forward and drink water at the edge of the pool.

Robbery

The intention to provide the dead with commodities and objects of value brought with it the threat of tomb robbery. The tombs of the élite were most at risk, since they contained a higher proportion of valuable objects, but even poor graves were robbed for the sake of the meagre offerings and adornments placed with the dead. Grave robbery was present from the very earliest times, and, as the equipping of the dead grew progressively more elaborate, so the threat of tomb robbery increased. Some aspects of the evolution of tomb architecture can be viewed as attempts to defeat robbers; for example, the storing of goods in the superstructure in early tombs was abandoned in favour of placing them in subterranean magazines. The entrance stairway leading to the burial chamber in Early Dynastic and Old Kingdom *mastaba* tombs was blocked by one or more stone slabs, which slid into place in vertical slots like a portcullis. The entrance passage (or shaft, in later tombs) was also blocked with rubble. The entrance passage in Old Kingdom pyramids had always been a security risk because religious reasons dictated that it should be located consistently in the north face (see above). 12th Dynasty rulers broke with this tradition and varied the position of the entrance to their pyramids, but this failed to protect their mummies; robbers tunnelled into the masonry of the pyramids at random, until they broke into one of the internal passages, which led them to the burial chamber. Towards the end of the 12th Dynasty, the architects, as though engaged in a battle of wits with the robbers, changed the internal arrangements of the king's pyramid with each successive reign. The most ingenious and complex of all these structures was the pyramid of Amenemhat III (*c.* 1855–1808 BC) at Hawara, in which a series of blind passages and concealed trapdoors was cunningly deployed to outwit and frustrate the robbers. Modern archaeologists found that they had, however, successfully negotiated these puzzles to reach the burial chamber. This room had been carved out of a single enormous quartzite block, set into place during the construction of the pyramid and covered by three huge slabs of quartzite. The robbers, no doubt after immense efforts in conditions of great discomfort, had succeeded in mining their way through one of the roof-blocks to gain access to the king's sarcophagus. When the chamber was first entered in modern times (by a boy employed by Flinders Petrie in 1888–9) only minute traces of the original burial equipment were recovered.

In addition to architectural devices to foil robbers, the Egyptians made use of several ingenious locking-systems to secure doorways and coffin-lids. The burial chamber in the tomb of Senusret-ankh at Lisht (12th Dynasty) was protected by a series of stone 'portcullis' slabs, the first of which, once lowered into place, could not be forced upwards again on account of the metal or wooden 'bolts' which were released from holes in the lateral grooves as the slab was lowered, effectively 'locking' it. Locking mechanisms were also incorporated into kings' sarcophagi in the Old Kingdom and on the wooden coffins of high-ranking persons in the Middle Kingdom. These latter, of course, would not deter most robbers, but would perhaps have prevented pilfering by officials responsible for the burial.

The ingenuity of the precautions taken to protect the body was sometimes self-defeating. In several of the kings' pyramids of the 12th and 13th Dynasties, the huge stone trapdoors were left open by the masons after the burial, perhaps having found that the effort required to move them was too great. In some tombs, robbery was committed at the time of burial, probably by the undertakers or cemetery guardians. A number of intact burials have been found in tombs where the entrance blockings were intact, yet the bodies had clearly been searched and valuables removed before the coffin lids had been replaced. Elsewhere, bodies had clearly been thrown out of their coffins while still articulated, indicating that the disturbance had occurred soon after the burial. In cemeteries where many tombs were cut into the rock, it was relatively easy for robbers to tunnel from tomb to tomb. In the small, closed communities of ancient Egypt the position and internal arrangements of a wealthy burial could not easily be kept secret, and those with specialist knowledge – notably the masons who cut the tombs and the undertakers who supervised the burials – were advantageously placed to carry out robberies. There were also opportunities for pilfering during the embalming process and when the mummy was placed in the tomb, at which periods the deceased's relatives probably had little chance of detecting dishonest practice. A group of mummies of high-ranking women of the 21st Dynasty, discovered in a tomb at Thebes, was apparently undisturbed, yet examination revealed that the gilded faces had been removed from the coffins, and items of jewellery taken from the mummies before the wrapping was completed, thefts which could only have been perpetrated by those responsible for the burials and the embalming.

An additional means of protecting the mummy was by placing it in a stone sarcophagus. These were sometimes enormously thick and those provided for the élite were made of hard stones such as granite, quartzite or basalt, but in few cases did these defeat the robbers, who levered the lids off, or even tunnelled through the sides or floors of the sarcophagi to reach the contents.

Tomb robbery was reviled because it harmed the deceased's chances of reaching the afterlife. Inscriptions in some Old Kingdom tombs included warnings that robbers would be judged by the gods in the hereafter. Fear of divine retribution, however, clearly did not outweigh temptation, as the extent of plundering makes clear. For those who were caught, severe punishments could be applied. One of the most famous collections of legal documents to survive from ancient Egypt concerns the trials of men accused of robbing both royal and private tombs in the Theban necropolis. The texts, dating to the reigns of Ramesses IX–XI (*c.* 1126–1069 BC), purport to give verbatim accounts of the confessions of the defendants and the statements of witnesses, from which it appears that private tombs were regularly robbed, although most of the royal tombs had not been disturbed. The severe punishments meted out to those found guilty served as a deterrent. Referring back to the trials under Ramesses IX, a later witness recalled: 'I saw the punishment of the thieves in the time of the vizier Khaemwaset. Is it then likely that I should seek such a death?' It is interesting that there is no indication of fear of retribution from the dead or the gods. This is clear enough from the disrespectful way in which corpses were stripped and hacked to pieces or burned to facilitate the extraction of valuable jewellery or amulets.

Reuse and recycling

Reuse and recycling are attested at all periods. When a tomb-owner's descendants died, the tomb and its chapel were often neglected, falling into disrepair. Some such old tombs were appropriated for new owners and reoccupied; others were simply exploited as convenient sources of building materials for new monuments, since to do this was more economical than quarrying new stone. Texts, however, warned against this practice. The *Instruction for Merykare*, a Middle

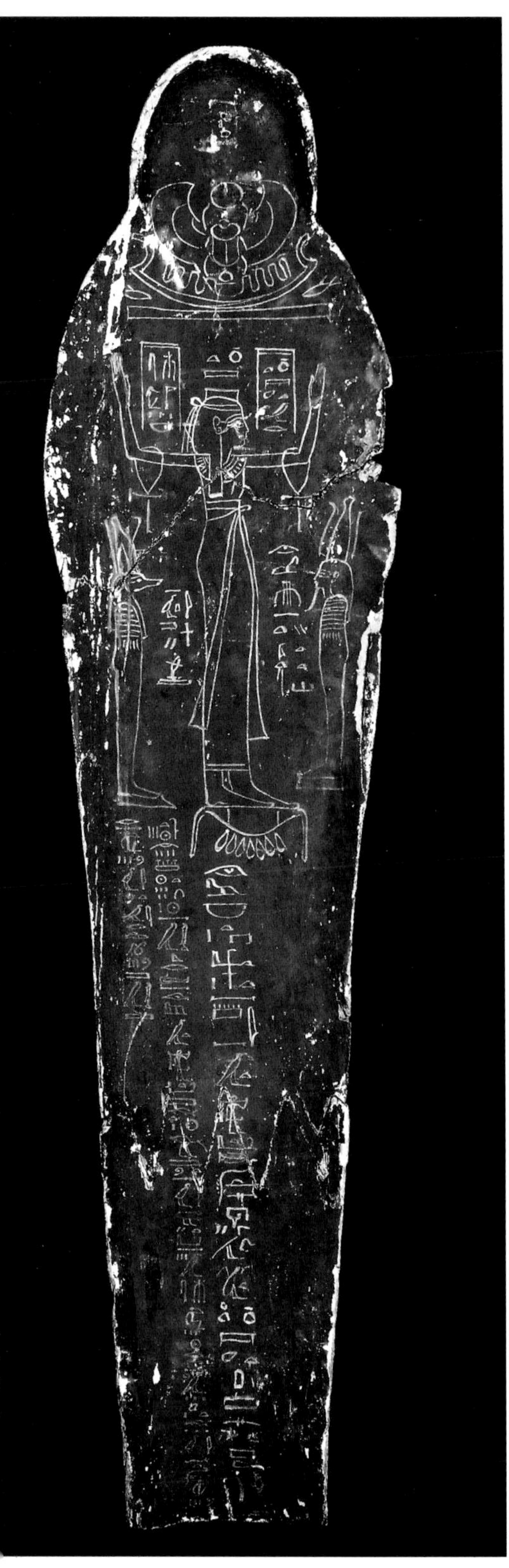

Kingdom wisdom text, advises: 'Do not despoil the monument of another, but quarry stone in Tura. Do not build your tomb out of ruins, (using) what had been made for what is to be made'. Yet the practice was widespread, and there was even an attempt to justify it, on the grounds that the original owner of the tomb reused in this way would himself benefit.

While reoccupation of an ancient or plundered tomb might be justified, the reuse of coffins was a common practice which was less easy to defend. Occasionally a coffin prepared for its owner in advance might be adapted for a close relative who had died prematurely, while the original had a new coffin made (see above, p. 171). Often, however, coffins were simply purloined from earlier burials and reinscribed. There are numerous examples from the Middle Kingdom, and the practice became especially common at Thebes in the 21st Dynasty. Many coffins of this period show alteration of the name of the occupant and changes to the main sex-indicators (hands, face, wig) in order to adapt the object for a new owner. This prevalence of coffin usurpation coincides with the widespread emptying of tombs and moving of burials which occurred in the 21st Dynasty, and was probably unsanctioned. A mummy-board in the British Museum testifies to the illicit nature of the procedure. The names on the front were altered and subsequently restored, and an inscription added on the back shows that the necropolis workers were responsible (see fig. 128).

There are also examples of the restoration of earlier burials for less selfish motives. During the middle of the first millennium BC attempts were evidently made to restore some of the royal burials of the Old Kingdom in their pyramids at Giza and Saqqara. Inside the pyramid of Menkaura (*c.* 2532–2503 BC) at Giza was found a damaged wooden coffin, whose anthropoid shape, together with the wording of its inscription indicate that it had been made in the late Third Intermediate Period or 26th Dynasty to rehouse the plundered remains of the king .

In spite of the prevalence of tomb robbery – particularly, it would appear at times of economic stress when food and other

128. Rear of the mummy-board of a woman named Tameniut. In addition to images of deities and a text invoking the protection of Nut, a secondary inscription (lower left) records the restoration of the lid to its rightful owner after necropolis officials had removed it from the tomb and re-inscribed it for another individual. Early 21st Dynasty, about 1050 BC. From Thebes. H. 165 cm.

basic necessities were in short supply – most of the royal burials of the New Kingdom seem to have survived with little serious disturbance until the end of the New Kingdom. Around the end of the 20th Dynasty, however, economic weakness forced the authorities to begin a process of official dismantling of the royal burials in the Valley of the Kings. The mummies and coffins of the dead kings were stripped of items of intrinsic value, which were then recycled to support the ailing economy. The bodies themselves were secreted in caches in various parts of the Theban necropolis. The early stages in this process are documented in letters sent by the army commander Piankh (virtual ruler of Upper Egypt at this time) to the scribe of the Theban necropolis Butehamun, instructing him to open a tomb, and by numerous graffiti written on the rocks by Butehamun and his colleagues – records of the process of searching for and identifying older tombs. A part of the funds recovered in this way may have been used to finance military operations against Nubia. Some items were perhaps retained for inclusion in the burials of the 21st Dynasty kings at Tanis, while others were recycled for use by individuals buried at Thebes. Pinedjem I (*c.* 1054–1032 BC) was buried in a coffin which had originally contained the mummy of Tuthmosis I (*c.* 1504–1492 BC), while a *shabti* of Ramesses II (*c.* 1279–1213 BC) was converted into an Osirian statuette for a private burial .

The opening of tombs and the reorganisation of burials at Thebes during the 21st and early 22nd Dynasties led to the creation of collective burials in earlier tombs. Royal mummies were moved several times, from one tomb to another in the Valley of the Kings, a large group finally coming to rest in the tomb of Amenhotep II (*c.* 1427–1400 BC). Others were grouped in tombs at Deir el-Bahri, which had become an especially sacred spot in the 21st Dynasty, highly favoured for burials – perhaps on account of its association with the cult of Hathor. The most famous of these was the so-called 'Royal Cache', the largest single group of royal mummies of the New Kingdom which survived undetected until 1871.

Secondary memorials to the dead

The cult of the dead was also maintained at locations outside the tomb. By setting up an ex-voto statue or a stela of the deceased at a cult temple or a place of pilgrimage it was believed that the deceased would be able to benefit from the offerings made at these places. They would receive a share of the daily offerings made to the local deity, and at festivals such memorials would be seen by large numbers of people who might then pronounce the owner's name or recite the offering formula, ensuring benefits for them.

The placing of a statue in a temple or the deposition of *shabti*s at a sacred spot could serve to represent the owner for this purpose. In some cases, however, the secondary memorial to the dead took the form of a complete tomb, comprising cult place, burial chamber and a sarcophagus, which of course was empty. These secondary tombs, or 'cenotaphs', were erected on behalf of several kings and private persons at important cult centres. King Senusret III (*c.* 1874–1855 BC) and King Ahmose I (*c.* 1550–1525 BC) erected 'cenotaphs' of this kind at Abydos. Like a real burial place, these dummy-tombs had a mortuary temple with an associated town to accommodate the officials who served the cult. A more common type of monument was a chapel without a dummy burial, in which a statue served as the focus for devotion.

During the Middle Kingdom a large number of memorial chapels were set up at Abydos. The importance of this site was not due to any economic significance. It was the burial place of the kings of the 1st Dynasty and of two of those of the 2nd Dynasty, and later became the centre of the cult of Osiris. Although the original god of Abydos was Khentimentiu, it became the chief cult centre of Osiris in the late Old Kingdom. The most important event at Abydos was the annual festival of Osiris. This celebrated the resurrection of Osiris and the overthrow of his enemies, and records of the festival state that the image of Osiris was brought out of his temple in a sacred barge borne by priests and carried in procession. At a place on the desert fringe called Peqer a dramatic performance took place in which the main elements of the myth of Osiris were re-enacted. One of the tombs of the 1st Dynasty kings (that of King Djer, *c.* 3000 BC) came to be identified as the tomb of Osiris. The spot attracted thousands of pilgrims who made offerings in pottery vessels. The remains of these still cover the area and are responsible for the modern Arabic name Umm el-Qa'ab, 'Mother of Pots'. After the 'burial' of Osiris, the defeat of Seth was enacted and the procession returned triumphantly to the temple. Every Egyptian made – or desired to make – a pilgrimage to be present at this festival. It is depicted in some tombs of the Middle and New Kingdoms. Some even aspired to be buried at Abydos itself, but this was possible only for the privileged few.

In order to participate vicariously in the rituals and to receive a share of the offerings made to Osiris, commemorative monuments were set up in the locality known as the Terrace of the Great God (see fig. 129). This was a raised area close to the western entrance to the cult temple of Osiris. The location was doubtless chosen because it was on the processional route along which the cult image of Osiris (preceded by that of the jackal-god Wepwawet) was carried at the annual festival. The spirits of the individuals whose chapels stood on the Terrace could thus participate in this all-important ritual – seeing the images of the gods pass on the outward and return journeys, and themselves sharing in the rejuvenation experienced by Osiris. The stelae generally have an image of the deceased receiving offerings. The *hetep di nesu* formula is included, often with an appeal to the living to recite the words for the deceased's benefit. Autobiographical passages recount the owner's virtues and achievements. Several stelae might be set up at different times by the same individual or by members of the same family, and occasionally work colleagues might also be commemorated as a personal favour. Some of the monuments commemorated an actual visit to Abydos, but the mere presence of a monument recording one's name was sufficient to enable one to participate in the rituals. Hence the stela of Nebipusenusret in the British

Museum was not set up by the man in person, but was taken to Abydos by another official. Another stela was deposited at Abydos on the way home from an official visit to Upper Egypt.

Only scanty details of the appearance of the memorial chapels at Abydos are available. The area in which most of them stood was intensively mined for antiquities by the collectors of the 1820s and 1830s. Records of the context of the finds are meagre and little now remains on the ground; fortunately a few chapels were partially preserved by later structures built over them, and these were excavated by the Pennsylvania-Yale Expedition in the 1960s. The chapels were closely packed together. They were of brick, with stelae set in niches in the structure, and some had courtyards in the manner of a tomb-chapel.

From the New Kingdom to the Late Period, memorials more often took the form of ex-voto statues set up in temples. Many of these were naophorous or statue-bearing images, i.e. showing the owner holding a shrine or an image of the god of the temple where they were placed. In the Late Period these statues were extensively inscribed with autobiographical texts, stressing the achievements and piety of the owner. An alternative to the statues, in the Late Period, was to set up stelae at cult centres, especially at the burial places of sacred animals, such as the Serapeum at Saqqara. Hundreds of stelae were installed there by pilgrims, recording their adoration of the Apis bull, and requesting the god's protection or assistance (see Chapter 8).

The dead themselves were sometimes the focus of cult activity. The 'ancestor busts' have been

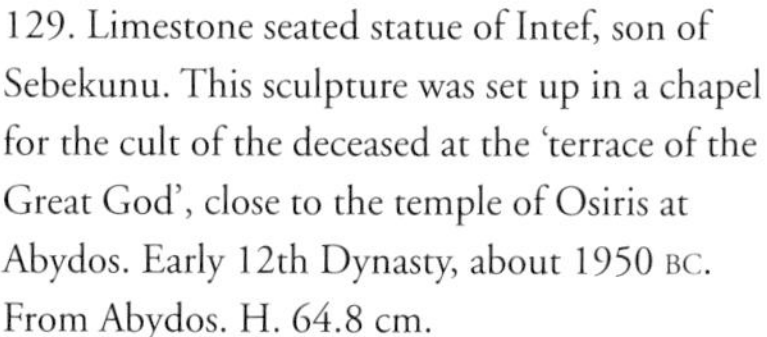

129. Limestone seated statue of Intef, son of Sebekunu. This sculpture was set up in a chapel for the cult of the deceased at the 'terrace of the Great God', close to the temple of Osiris at Abydos. Early 12th Dynasty, about 1950 BC. From Abydos. H. 64.8 cm.

132. Group of female mourners, detail of the scene illustrated in fig. 131. Their exposed breasts and vigorous gestures are conventional expressions of grief. Early 22nd Dynasty, about 945–900 BC. From Thebes. H. of coffin 210 cm.

men generally adopted a less dramatic pose, squatting on the ground with their faces downcast, a gesture described in the story of Sinuhe, where the courtiers who lament the death of the king sit 'head-on-knee'. In addition to these groups, there were sometimes two women who personified Isis and Nephthys, the mourners for Osiris.

The procession also included the embalmer and various priests, headed by the lector priest carrying a scroll, from which the appropriate incantations were read out. Servants brought the burial goods, particular attention being given to the canopic container, which was dragged on a sledge. Since most tombs were on the west bank, it was usually necessary to cross the Nile. At the river the coffin was placed on a boat, towed by rowing boats. The coffin was laid beneath a canopy in the middle, with the two principal lamenting women at the prow and stern. The boat crossed the river and arrived at the west bank, where it was received into the *wabet*. This structure (perhaps the same in which the embalming had been carried out) was the place in which the mummy was subjected to purifying rituals, before resuming the journey to the tomb.

At the tomb a further series of rituals took place. Here the *muu* dancers performed a ritual dance wearing tall headdresses made of vegetal material. Brief processions were made representing journeys to different cult centres in Egypt, which were represented by chapels. These included a visit to Sais, with rituals believed to derive from the ceremonies enacted at the burials of the Predynastic rulers of Buto in Lower Egypt. Finally, both the *tekenu* (see Chapter 2) and the canopic container were brought to the tomb entrance.

The Opening of the Mouth

Once the deceased had arrived at his tomb, the threshold of the next world, the *sakhu* rituals were performed, to bring about his transfiguration. This was the moment for the most important of the funerary rites, the Opening of the Mouth, the basic purpose of which was to re-animate the mummy. As described in Chapter 5, this originated as a ritual to endow statues with the capacity to support the living *ka*, and so to receive offerings. By the Old Kingdom it had been adapted from a statue-rite to one performed on the mummy, its purpose being to restore to the dead person the use of his mouth, eyes, ears and nose, enabling him to see, hear, breathe, and receive nourishment to sustain the *ka*. Texts offer no clear indications as to what became of the *ka*, *ba* and other non-physical aspects of a person during the seventy-day interval between death and

133. The ritual of the Opening of the Mouth. The mummy is supported by Anubis in front of a schematised depiction of the tomb, with inscribed stela and pyramid superstructure. Female relatives lament the death of Hunefer and priests burn incense and perform the prescribed ritual acts using the appropriate instruments. Vignette from the papyrus of Hunefer. Early 19th Dynasty, about 1280 BC. From Thebes. H. 31.9 cm.

burial; possibly their activity was imagined to be suspended until the mummification process was complete. The Opening of the Mouth, however, renewed the relationship of these aspects with the corpse.

134. Sets of model ceremonial implements (left and above right) for use in the Opening of the Mouth. The objects include the *pesesh-kef*, a bifurcate instrument possibly used to support the lower jaw of the corpse, miniature tools and libation vessels. At lower right is a calcite tablet with wells for the seven sacred oils prescribed for use in the ritual. Larger Opening of the Mouth set and oil-tablet, from the tomb of the lector priest Idy at Abydos, 6th Dynasty, about 2300 BC. L. (left) 17 cm, (right) 13 cm. Smaller Opening of the Mouth set, 5th to 6th Dynasty, about 2494–2181 BC. 11×9 cm.

Depictions of the ritual from the New Kingdom show the mummy placed upright on a patch of clean sand at the entrance to the tomb (see fig. 133). The liturgy was recited while the appropriate acts were carried out; in its fullest form, the ritual incorporated elements from a number of different sources. Purifications and offerings similar to those performed in temple rites were enacted. The most important episodes were those adapted from the original statue-ritual, involving the priest touching the mouth of the mummy-mask with a chisel, an adze and other implements, including a bifurcate object called the *pesesh-kef*, by which the faculties were symbolically renewed. The ritual was directed by an official called the *sem*-priest. This individual, originally the eldest son of the king, acted as the intermediary between the deceased and the netherworld; through his filial relationship to the deceased, like that of Horus to Osiris, the identification of the dead man with the resurrected god was strengthened. From the New Kingdom onwards this role was often conceived as being carried out by Anubis; at least, he is often depicted taking part, either holding the mummy upright while the ritual is performed (see fig. 133) or bending over the mummy on its bier, holding the adze and actually carrying out the ritual himself.

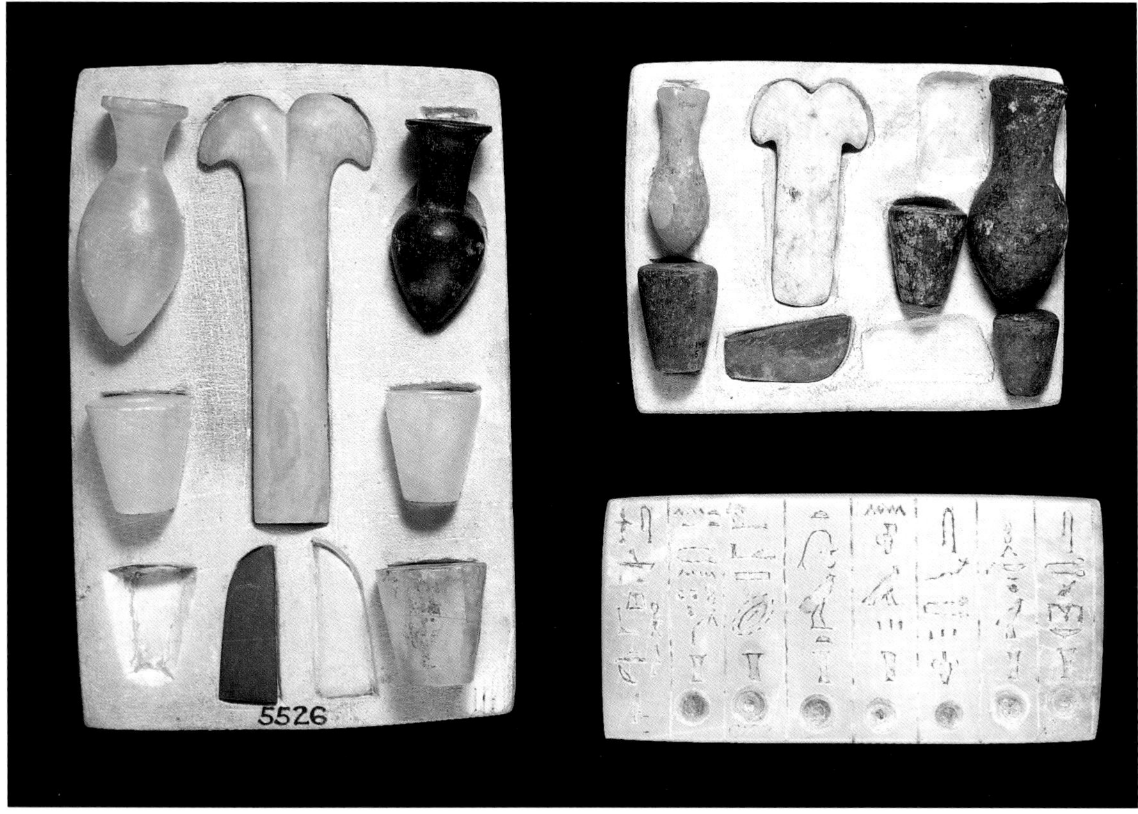

135. Gessoed and gilded dummy vessels of carved wood, bearing the cartouches of Ramesses II, possibly from a royal burial. One represents a globular jar, and the others are in the shape of bags tied at the neck. Each is inscribed with the name of one of the substances used in the ritual of the Opening of the Mouth. 19th Dynasty, reign of Ramesses II, about 1279–1213 BC. Provenance unknown. H. (left to right) 11.5 cm, 7.2 cm, 12.2 cm.

The words of the Opening of the Mouth ritual occur in the *Pyramid Texts*. In the New Kingdom, a revised version of the ritual was produced, illustrated with seventy-five individual scenes, copies of which are found in several tombs, notably that of Sety I (*c.* 1294–1279 BC) in the Valley of the Kings. The main elements of this revised version were purification, the sacrifice of a bull, the mouth-opening itself, and the presentation of offerings. The ritual ended with an invocation to the gods at the placing of the mummy or statue in the tomb.

Because of the importance of the Opening of the Mouth, tombs were sometimes supplied with sets of implements which enabled the deceased to perform the ritual for himself if the need should arise. In the Old Kingdom, these implements are usually models, set into stone slabs with receptacles specially cut to receive them (see fig. 134). More elaborate models of some of the implements and vessels are known from the New Kingdom (see fig. 135), and some tombs of the Late Period have also been found to contain groups of objects relating to the ritual. The tomb of Tjanehebu at Saqqara (26th Dynasty) contained a group of these, including a *sekhem* sceptre, the ram-headed serpent rods called *wer-hekau* instruments, and models of vessels in faience, calcite and wood.

The Offering Ritual

As noted in Chapter 3, the Offering Ritual supplied the deceased with nourishment for eternity. It was performed for the first time immediately after the Opening of the Mouth, and, like the latter, was composed of several individual rituals: purifications, libations, the burning of incense, and the presentation of food and drink. Actual food and drink were placed on the offering table of the chapel, and the *hetep di nesu* formula (see p. 00) was pronounced. This was the most important ritual in the long term, since it was the one which would ensure the continued survival of the deceased. It was accordingly repeated at intervals after the burial.

The last element in the 'funeral' was the actual burial. The body and its funerary goods were placed in the tomb and the entrance to the burial chamber was sealed. Cattle were slaughtered, and the choicest parts of the animal were offered to the dead. The remainder was consumed by the relatives and mourners at a feast. The remnants of this banquet were sometimes ritually buried, and from such a deposit found in the Valley of the Kings we know that the guests at Tutankhamun's funeral feast consumed beef, sheep or goat, duck and goose. The participants then withdrew, returning to their homes, while final rituals to protect the tomb were performed.

Funerary texts

The collective term for all ancient Egyptian funerary texts was *sakhu* (literally, 'that which makes *akh*'). This emphasises the principal purpose of all the texts, which was to enable the deceased to make the successful transition to the transfigured state, *akh*. The placing of funerary texts in the tomb – on the walls of the chapel, on papyri, on coffins, stelae and amulets, or on the mummy wrappings – sought to make possible the replication by magic of the ritual acts which the texts described. The deceased was thereby equipped with the special knowledge needed to attain the afterlife.

Funerary texts in ancient Egypt had a long history, stretching from the late third millennium BC to the early centuries AD. Originally reserved for the sole use of the dead king, they ultimately became available to a broader range of the population.

The Pyramid Texts

The earliest collection is the texts inscribed on the internal walls of pyramids of kings and queens buried in the Memphite necropolis, from Unis, last ruler of the 5th Dynasty, to Ibi, an obscure king of the 8th Dynasty (early First Intermediate Period), i.e. *c.* 2350–2150 BC. They are carved in vertical columns on the walls chiefly of the burial chamber and antechamber. The hieroglyphic signs were filled with green pigment, symbolising regeneration, but there were no images. Although principally for royal use, some sections of the *Pyramid Texts* were used in non-royal burials even before the end of the Old Kingdom, and sporadically at later periods. It is possible that the entire corpus derived from a 'master' source in which the main protagonist was not consistently the king.

These texts are in fact a compilation of earlier sources, and represent various traditions which apparently arose at different times, though they probably do not (as was once believed) go back to the Predynastic period. Some allude to the dead king's ascent to the stars, others to his association with Osiris, while others place emphasis on his connections with the sun god. Hence already at this formative stage in the tradition of Egyptian funerary literature we observe the 'multiplicity of approaches' which characterises so much of Egyptian religious belief and practice. Apparently contradictory doctrines are accommodated simultaneously. Far from being a random compilation of old spells, the *Pyramid Texts* are structured, and organised into three different categories. Their function is expressed not only through the wording of the spells but also through their positioning on the walls of the pyramid's internal chambers.

One category consists of 'incantations' of a protective nature, designed to ward off the attacks of dangerous creatures such as snakes, or other hostile entities. A second category comprises the words to be spoken at the enactment of important funerary rituals carried out for the benefit of the dead. In these texts the deceased is equated with Osiris, the ruler of the Underworld, and the words are put into the mouth of the king's son, who takes the role of Horus. Within this group of texts – which are inscribed in the burial chamber – are 'offering' rituals and 'resurrection' rituals. The former, written on the north wall, gives the words to accompany the Opening of the Mouth to revitalise the deceased, and the offering of food and drink to sustain the spirit. The 'resurrection' ritual, inscribed on the facing wall, consists of spells relating to the dead king's passage from earth to the afterlife.

The third category comprises the 'personal' spells designed for the deceased's own use. They cover a variety of themes, particularly the transition to the next world expressed in metaphorical terms (such as crossing water, or ascending a ladder to the sky). These are inscribed on the walls of the antechamber and the passage leading to the exterior of the pyramid; it is important to recognise that the spatial arrangement of the texts is for the convenience of the dead king in leaving his sarcophagus and making his way *out* of the pyramid to the next world. Spells from the *Pyramid Texts* were also inscribed in the tombs and on the sarcophagi of some officials in the Middle Kingdom and the New Kingdom, and more extensively in the Late Period.

The Coffin Texts

After the end of the Old Kingdom, the corpus of Egyptian funerary literature underwent further development. This period saw the emergence of another compilation of funerary texts, known to modern scholars as the *Coffin Texts*. The name derives from the circumstance that the majority of examples are found inscribed in cursive hieroglyphic script on the surfaces of wooden coffins (see fig. 136), but they also occur on tomb walls, on mummy masks and occasionally on papyri. Many of these texts were identical to, or adapted versions of spells from the *Pyramid Texts* corpus, with additions from other sources. During the First Intermediate Period and Middle Kingdom, these texts were not restricted to royalty and occurred in the burials of officials and their families in various parts of Egypt. These texts articulate, for the first time, the possibility that all Egyptians, and not the king alone, could attain divine status in the afterlife.

This adoption by private individuals of funerary texts previously reserved for royalty is commonly termed 'democratisation of the afterlife'. It is a somewhat

136. The *Coffin Texts* were so-called because they were most frequently inscribed on the internal surfaces of rectangular wooden coffins. Unlike the *Pyramid Texts*, the use of these spells was not restricted to the king. They provided the ordinary person with the knowledge required to reach the afterlife in safety. False door, offerings and *Coffin Text* spells on the interior of the inner coffin of Gua From Deir el-Bersha. 12th Dynasty, about 1850 BC. L. 225 cm.

misleading term, as it implies a removal of the distinction between king and subject which the evidence does not warrant. The king continued to be distinguished from his subjects both in life and in the provision made for him after death, as exemplified by the restriction of the pyramid-tomb for the use of royalty alone. What funerary texts were used for Middle Kingdom rulers is not known, but they were not necessarily the same as those provided for non-royal persons. It is noteworthy that several centuries later, in the New Kingdom, new royal funerary texts were created, but that these were, as a rule, distinct from those of private individuals.

The organisation of the *Coffin Texts* is related to that of the *Pyramid Texts*, the internal surfaces of the wooden coffin equating to the stone interior walls of the king's pyramid. The 'resurrection' ritual continues to be used, while in place of the 'offering' ritual an offering-list is often included; the offerings are further illustrated in the 'frieze of objects', a narrow band of pictures of various commodities which is one of the most characteristic features of coffin decoration in the Middle Kingdom (see Chapter 7).

The *Coffin Texts* develop the notion of the two main contrasting concepts of the afterlife: the heavenly travels of the *ba*, and existence in the earthly netherworld, through the preservation of the corpse and the nourishing of the *ka*. The content of the *Coffin Texts* is heavily indebted to that of the *Pyramid Texts*, and includes many of the 'personal' spells. There were, however, innovations, the most important of which was a new genre of spells, collectively termed 'guides to the hereafter'. These texts were usually accompanied by a map showing the topography of the netherworld, and the means of access to it. The texts provided information and special knowledge to assist the deceased in making a safe journey into the next life. The most important of these guides was the *Book of Two Ways*. This composition was probably formulated at the

Residence and first employed in the cemeteries of Dahshur and Lisht. From here it seems to have spread to other regions, most notably to the province of Hermopolis. The rectangular wooden coffins of governors and officials from Deir el-Bersha, the necropolis of that city, are the major source for the *Book of Two Ways*. On the coffins, the floor is usually occupied by the map, generally presenting two paths consisting of earth and water. The coffins of the physician Gua in the British Museum are among the finest examples (see fig. 15). Different versions of the book were in use simultaneously. In the version painted on the outer and inner coffins of Gua, the main goal of the deceased is to join the sun god Ra.

137. Painted and inscribed linen shroud made for the mummy of a woman named Resti. The *Coffin Texts* were superseded in the 17th to 18th Dynasties by a new collection of funerary spells, now known as the *Book of the Dead*. These texts, accompanied by vignettes, were at first written on mummy-shrouds. 18th Dynasty, about 1500 BC. Provenance unknown.

The Book of the Dead

The Second Intermediate Period brought an interruption in the funerary text tradition, but by the beginning of the New Kingdom, a series of new corpora of texts had been assembled. The main composition developed at this time was the collection of texts called the *Spells for Going Forth by Day*, better known by the modern term, the *Book of the Dead*. This comprised approximately 200 spells, the bulk of which can be traced back in earlier guises to the *Pyramid Texts* and *Coffin Texts*, although new spells were also added. The *Book of the Dead* was probably created at Thebes in the 17th Dynasty. It perhaps owed its existence to the need for a new compilation of funerary texts when the transfer of the court from Itj-tawy to Thebes severed direct contact with the sources of older text-traditions based at Memphis and Heliopolis. Early examples of *Book of the Dead* texts were written on coffins and on linen mummy-shrouds (see fig. 137). These texts on shrouds were succeeded in the middle years of the 18th Dynasty by the *Book of the Dead* written in ink on a roll of papyrus (see fig. 138). The spells were also inscribed on tomb walls, coffins and mummy-bandages .

The *Book of the Dead* provided instructions and access to magical power to assist the deceased in his passage to the afterlife and in his existence there. Most of the texts are 'personal' spells. Unlike its precursors, the *Book of the Dead* was extensively illustrated with vignettes. The most important addition to the text corpus was spell 125, relating to the judgement of the deceased to determine his worthiness to receive new life (see Chapter 1). Many of the spells begin with rubrics giving instructions for their proper use. Certain spells were inscribed separately on objects, such as chapter 6 on *shabti*s, and chapters 30 or 30B, 26, 27 and 29B on heart scarabs.

138. From the reigns of Tuthmosis III and Amenhotep II (about 1479–1400 BC) the usual medium for the *Book of the Dead* was a roll of papyrus, on which a selection of spells was written in a cursive form of the hieroglyphic script. This section shows the vignette of spell 151B, a schematic representation of the burial chamber, in which the mummy of the deceased, equated with that of Osiris, lies on a lion-shaped bier. Stationed around him as protectors are the goddesses Isis and Nephthys, the god Anubis and the Sons of Horus. Papyrus of Nakht, late 18th Dynasty, about 1300 BC. H. 35.5 cm.

139. Sheet of fine-quality papyrus inscribed with a funerary text for the lady Henutmehyt, 19th Dynasty, about 1250 BC (see figs 88, 149 and 167). The text is spell 100 of the *Book of the Dead*. The rubric of the chapter directs that it should be written on a clean sheet of papyrus and placed on the front of the mummy, not in direct contact with the body. The papyrus was indeed found placed over the outer wrappings of the mummy. This is an exceptionally early instance of the preparation of such texts as charms for the dead, which are otherwise mainly attested after the New Kingdom. H. 41cm.

Although the whole corpus of *Book of the Dead* spells comprised about 200 separate texts, it was usual for only a selection of these to be made and inscribed on a roll of papyrus. Certain spells were meant to function as charms to protect or assist the deceased, and according to the rubrics, were to be written out on a separate sheet. The rubric to spell 100 states that the words were to be pronounced over the appropriate design which was to be drawn on a clean, unused sheet of papyrus with powder of green glaze mixed with myrrh-water, the sheet to be placed on the breast of the deceased without coming into direct contact with the body. If this is done, the text states, the deceased will be able to enter the barque of Ra. A rare example of the carrying out of these instructions in a New Kingdom burial is the papyrus from the mummy of Henutmehyt, which bears the text and vignette of spell 100 written unusually in red and white inks (see fig. 139).

The *Book of the Dead* remained the most important collection of funerary texts until the Ptolemaic Period. In the version used in the New Kingdom (the 'Theban recension') the spells do not occur in a standard sequence. A major revision of the corpus in the 25th to 26th Dynasties (the 'Saite recension') resulted in a fixed sequence of chapters dealing in turn with the burial of the dead, their equipping with divine power and knowledge, their judgement and, finally, transfiguration. It is this later version that is the basis of the numbering sequence used today.

Books of the Underworld

Whereas the *Pyramid Texts*, *Coffin Texts* and *Book of the Dead* were concerned primarily with the destiny of the deceased in the afterlife, the other major set of compositions of the New Kingdom deal chiefly with the sun god's nightly journey and rejuvenation. These are the *Books of the Underworld*, the most important texts used in kings' tombs of the New Kingdom. They were descended from the 'guides to the hereafter' of the Middle Kingdom. The major ones, in chronological order of their appearance, are: the *Amduat*, the *Book of Gates* and the *Book of Caverns*. All these 'books' are concerned with the journey of the sun through the subterranean underworld during the twelve hours of the night. The god is envisaged as travelling from the western to the eastern horizon by barque along an underworld river (the counterpart of the Nile) (see fig. 140). In the course of this journey the god is united with Osiris (the two of them regarded as halves of a single divine being) and there takes place the all-important rejuvenation of the sun god, which makes possible the new day. The god's progress is opposed by the forces of chaos, chief among whom is the serpent Apep who has to be defeated and restrained. The books also provide details of the experience of the dead; the righteous are rewarded with new life, while the unrighteous are punished. As in earlier periods, there is a distinction between the texts supplied for the king's use and those available to his subjects. The *Books of the Underworld* were primarily a royal prerogative throughout the New Kingdom (although in rare cases they were used by private individuals). The king's rebirth is assured through his close identi-

140. Scene from the *Book of Gates*, showing the sun god's journey through the subterranean chambers of the underworld. In this composition, first introduced in royal tombs at the end of the 18th Dynasty (about 1300 BC), each hour of the god's nightly passage beneath the earth is spent in a different chamber, access to which is gained through enormous gates guarded by dangerous serpents. Copy by Henry Salt (1780–1827) of a scene in the tomb of Sety I (about 1294–1279 BC) in the Valley of the Kings, Thebes.

fication with the sun god throughout his journey. These compositions are primarily pictorial guides with commentaries. The *Amduat* and *Book of Gates* are distinguished by their layout in three registers, the central one representing the sun god's path. Each has twelve divisions corresponding to the hours of the night; this aspect is emphasised in the *Book of Gates* by the depiction of large fortified doorways guarded by serpents, at the entrance to each division – from which the composition takes its modern name.

Mortuary Liturgies

The three great corpora of funerary writings, the *Pyramid Texts*, the *Coffin Texts* and the *Book of the Dead*, represent the most conspicuous stages in the development of the textual tradition. Another important category of funerary texts, however, is that of the 'mortuary liturgies', the words of the rituals carried out at the time of burial. Although designed for the welfare of the dead, they were not primarily meant to be read by them for their own benefit, but were intended for use by the mortuary priests who carried out the rites. Although, as noted above, a substantial number of them are found incorporated within the *Pyramid Texts* and *Coffin Texts*, they are far more widely distributed in time, from the Old Kingdom to the Roman Period. They also occur in various contexts, being inscribed in tombs, on coffins, on stelae, on papyri and on statues. With the passage of time, the main funerary text corpora and the mortuary liturgies followed independent courses of development, and the two became more clearly differentiated.

Late funerary texts

Funerary texts of earlier periods were revived in the Late Period, including the *Pyramid Texts* and *Books of the Netherworld*, inscribed in sarcophagi and on tomb walls. The production of long *Book of the Dead* papyri declined in the late Ptolemaic Period, though short selections continued to be used until the Roman era. From the 4th century BC, the *Book of the Dead* was increasingly replaced by other texts. These included liturgies used in temple rituals, which were usually written on papyri. Some of these texts were originally mortuary liturgies. There were also new compositions such as the two *Books of Breathing* and the *Book of Traversing Eternity*. The opening phrases of the *Books of Breathing* demonstrate that the texts have the character of divine decrees to grant new life to the deceased, notably giving him the ability to breathe. They also acted as letters of

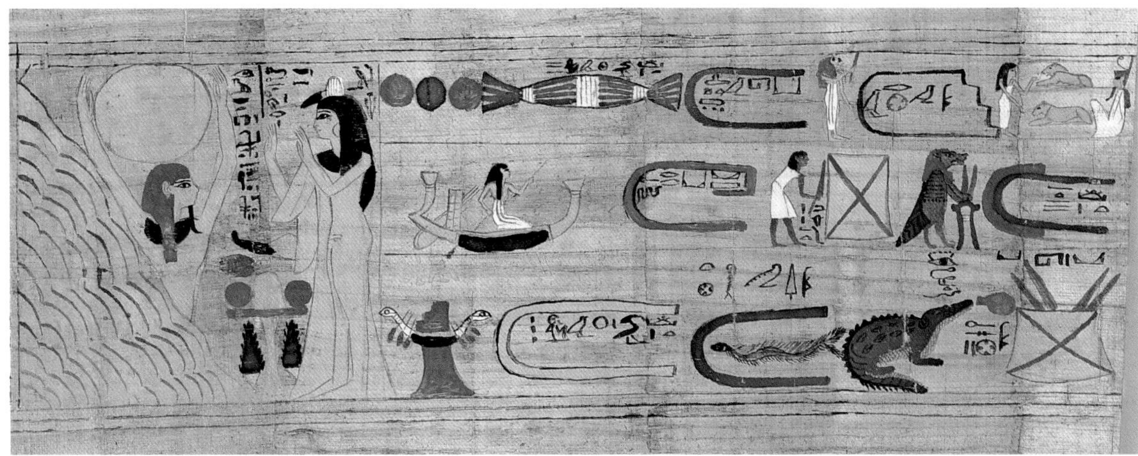

141. During the 21st and early 22nd Dynasty, burials of persons of high status were generally provided with two funerary papyri. One of these contained texts from the *Book of the Dead*, while the other often had only vignettes. This papyrus of the chantress of Amun-Ra, Tentosorkon, contains spells 125–130 of the *Book of the Dead*. Early 22nd Dynasty, about 945–900 BC. Probably from Thebes. H. 24.5 cm.

recommendation to the inhabitants of the hereafter. These 'passports' to the afterlife were sometimes folded up like letters and placed at the head and legs of the mummy, so that the deceased might present them to the gods on reaching the next world. Such late texts were also sometimes inscribed on wooden boards placed under the mummy.

The provision of funerary texts had been abandoned by the 4th century AD, together with most of the other features of traditional pharaonic burial practices.

Magical objects for the deceased

Objects were believed to convey magical power no less efficiently than texts. Magical objects and images placed in the tomb could function independently through the associations of their form, colour or material, as well as in conjunction with texts which would activate them. The strong belief in the power of the image is strikingly emphasised in some funerary inscriptions of the Middle Kingdom and Second Intermediate Period. In these texts, hieroglyphic signs representing potentially harmful creatures were deliberately 'mutilated' – snakes were drawn without tails or with the head severed from the body, birds appear without legs – as a precaution lest the images should inadvertently be activated within the tomb and cause harm to the deceased.

Funerary jewellery

Egyptian burials have yielded an enormous quantity of jewellery, and this was one of the main temptations to ancient tomb-robbers. From the point of view of the deceased, however, its importance was manifold. Jewellery not only beautified the body and marked the social status of the wearer for eternity; much of it also conveyed magical power and protection, through its form, its iconography, and the materials of which it was made. Some people were buried with treasured jewellery which they had worn when alive, but there was also jewellery made specifically for the tomb. This superficially resembled real jewellery but was

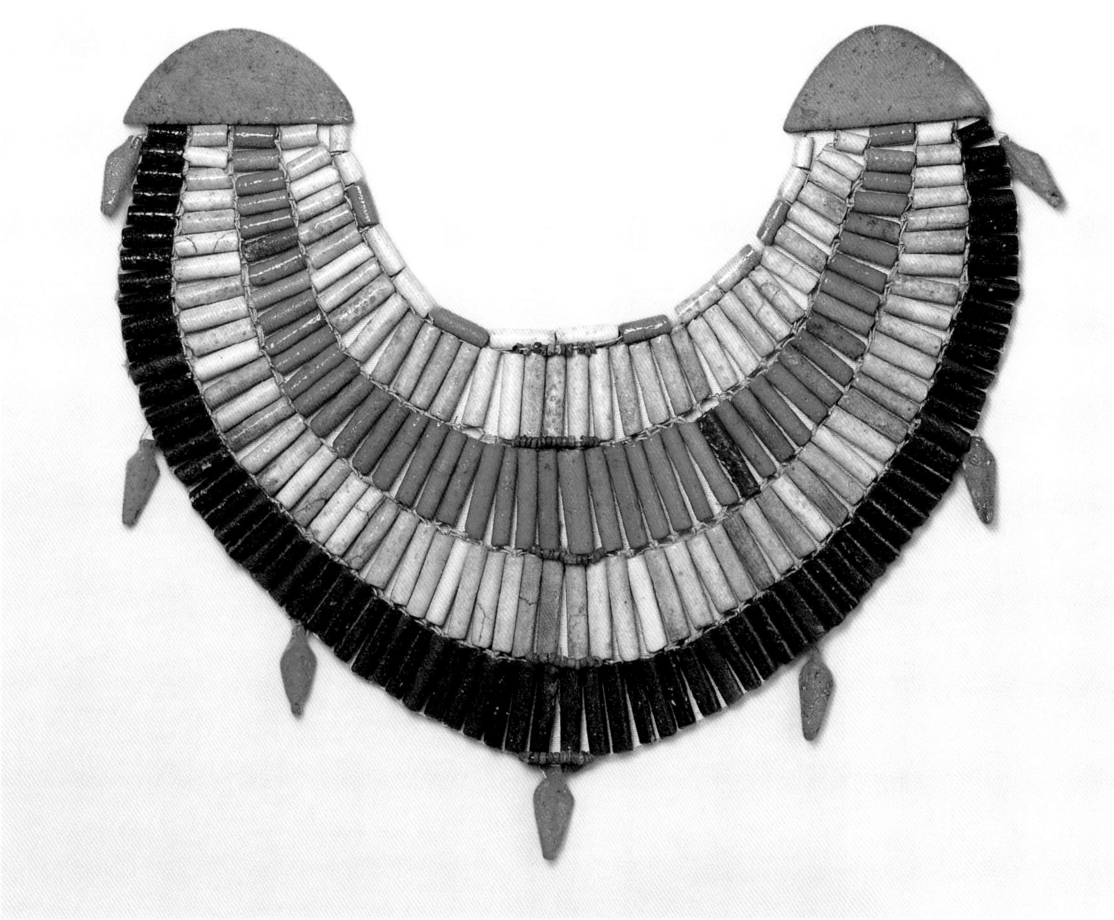

142. *Wesekh* or 'broad' collar made of faience beads. The pendants forming the outermost row are perhaps intended to represent leaves. From Deir el-Bahri, Thebes. 11th Dynasty, about 2020 BC. Max w. 25.5 cm.

flimsy in construction. Like the tomb models and model vessels, they were substitutes which would function as well as the real thing by magic.

The most important items of funerary jewellery were collars. The *wesekh*, or 'broad', collar (see fig. 142) usually had terminals in the shape of falcon heads. This collar conveyed magical protection over the deceased, as did the vulture collar. The magical functions of these collars, and the manner prescribed for their placing on the body are described in spells in the *Book of the Dead*.

Funerary amulets

Another important means of protecting and empowering the deceased was through amulets. In ancient Egypt, amulets were widely used by the living as well as by the dead. Their purpose was to give the wearer supernatural power or protection. They depended for their potency on their shape and colour, the material from which they were made, and the particular ritual acts and incantations associated with them which rendered them effective. Certain spells in the *Book of the Dead* prescribe the correct materials, form and colour of important

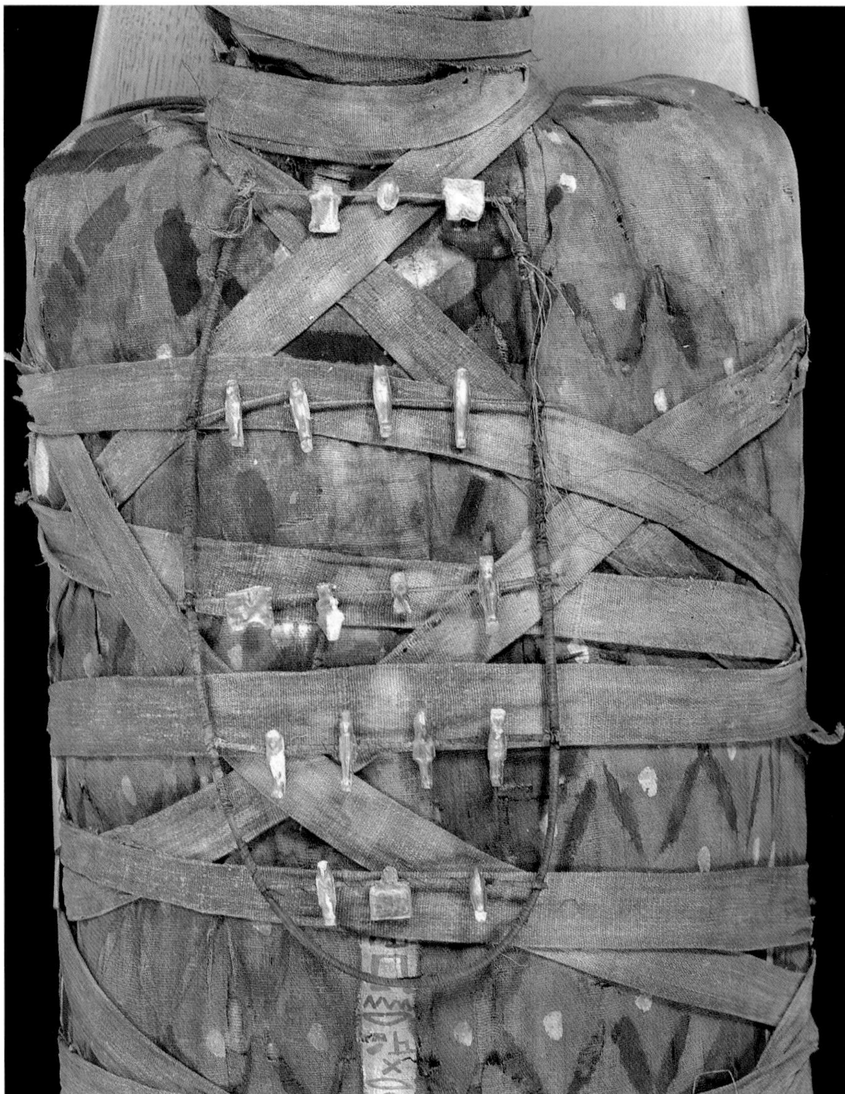

143. Small amulets of gilded wood, arranged on a frame placed on the breast of a mummy. The body is that of a man, and the outer shroud is painted in imitation of the bead-net garment worn by Osiris. Roman Period, after 30 BC. Provenance unknown. L. of mummy 164 cm.

amulets and how they were to be positioned on the body. Similar details are also included in the *Ritual of Embalming*.

Some amulets were placed within the wrappings during the mummification process, while others were laid on the outer surface (see fig. 143). Small numbers of simple amulets were being included with the dead even in the Predynastic period. They began to increase in number from the First Intermediate Period onwards. The growth in popularity of amulets in the Middle Kingdom was perhaps as a substitute for funerary literature, which was absent in many burials. By the New Kingdom, the wrappings of royal mummies were filled with a wide range of amulets, as the body of Tutankhamun (*c.* 1336–1327 BC) testifies (see fig. 144); in the burials of private individuals, however, amulets were generally few in number and restricted to a few types, such as the *tit*, the

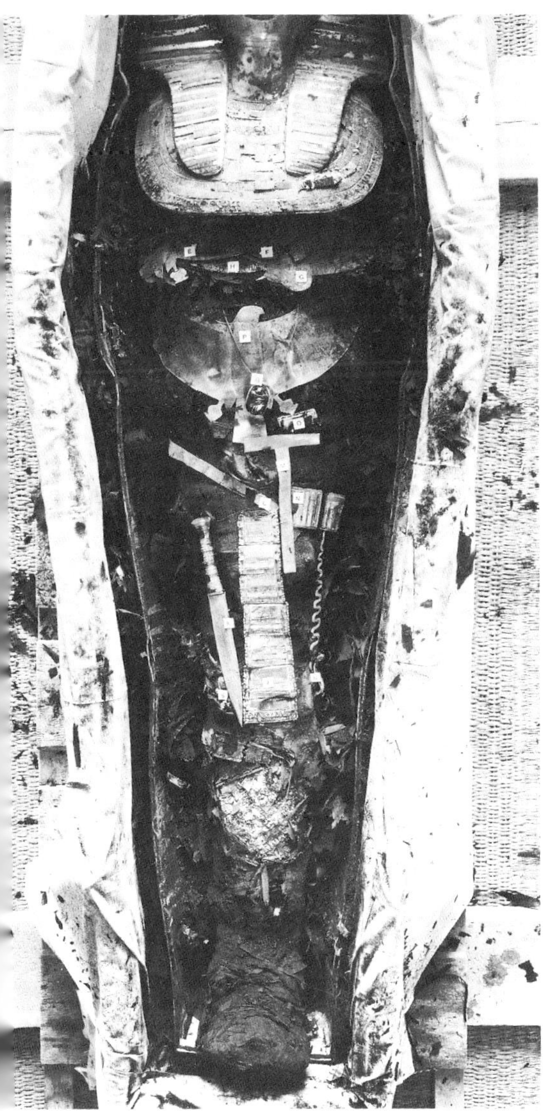

144. The mummy of Tutankhamun during the process of unwrapping in 1925. On the front of the body, below the gold mask, is a group of amulets including a sheet-gold falcon-collar and a resin heart scarab on a gold wire loop. Among the objects placed over the pelvic area and thighs are a decorative apron, a dagger with an iron blade and a gold *uraeus* serpent.

djed pillar, papyrus column and heart amulet (see below). After the New Kingdom there was a substantial increase in the range and quantity of amulets provided for the dead (see fig. 145); many mummies of the Late Period possessed a profusion of amulets, and a single body might even contain several groups positioned between different layers of the wrappings.

One of the commonest amulets, closely associated with Osiris, was the *djed*, a pillar or column, which perhaps originally represented a tree with lopped branches. Originally associated with Sokar and Ptah, it featured in an ancient ritual called the 'Raising of the *Djed*', in which the pillar was hauled into an upright position using ropes. Later it became a

145. Common types of funerary amulets, placed within the wrappings of mummies to protect and empower the deceased. Top row, left to right: faience hand (L. 3.1 cm), haematite headrest, faience papyrus column. Middle row, left to right: carnelian snake's head, haematite plummet and carpenter's square, faience staircase, carnelian leg. Bottom row, left to right: red glass heart, obsidian two fingers, red jasper *tit*. Old Kingdom to 26th Dynasty, about 2300–525 BC.

146. Large pectoral ornaments made of faience, metal or stone were a common attribute of mummies during the New Kingdom. The decoration of these often featured the scarab beetle or heart amulet, or showed the deceased adoring Osiris or Anubis. This group of pectorals dates to the 19th to 20th Dynasties, about 1295–1069 BC. Provenance unknown. L. of largest pectoral 12 cm.

symbol of Osiris and was reinterpreted as a representation of his backbone. As an amulet, it conferred stability on the deceased, and the ability to stand upright. The *djed* was often paralleled by the *tit*, a depiction of a girdle-tie, which was associated with Isis. Spell 156 of the *Book of the Dead* directed that it be made of red jasper, and explained that if placed on the mummy's throat it would convey the power of Isis to protect the body.

In the myths about Horus, originally a god of the skies, his eyes were equated with the sun and moon. Seth stole the eye of the moon, and the two gods came into conflict. Seth disposed of the eye, which was later found in pieces by Thoth and restored. This story perhaps enshrines the explanation of the name *wedjat*, 'that which is whole', which was assigned to the eye of Horus; eye amulets in the form of the *wedjat* became very common as protective devices, guaranteeing that the wearer, like the healed eye of the god, was whole and sound.

Symbols such as the *wadj*, or papyrus column, were usually made of green stone or blue-green faience. This amulet connoted rebirth and resurrection, as manifested in the new growth of plants, of which the papyrus was a familiar example to the ancient Egyptians. The predominantly green colouring of this amulet played a significant part in establishing its effectiveness.

A large number of amulets are miniature representations of a particular god or goddess. When used in funerary contexts these placed the wearer under the protection of that god, or identified him with the deity, so as to endow him with the god's powers or attributes. The most common deities represented in this form are those associated with the myth of Osiris: figures of Isis and Nephthys are common, either individually or as members of a miniature triad incorporating Horus. Amulets representing Osiris himself are rare, probably because the deceased was himself identified with Osiris in the context of the tomb.

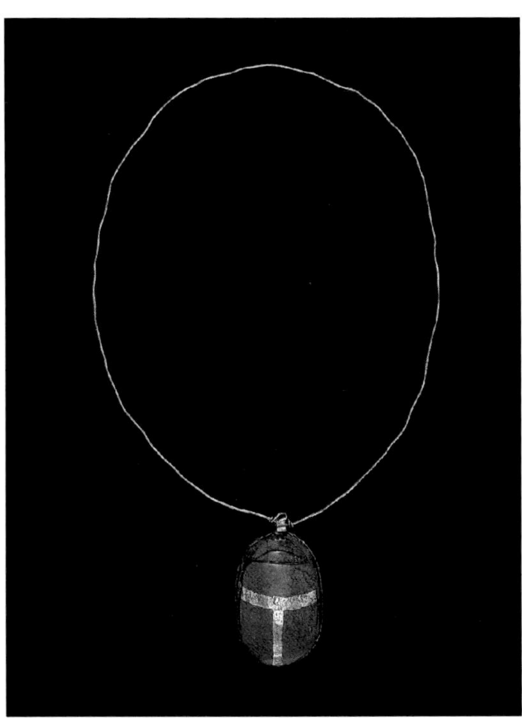

147. Green basalt heart scarab of Renseneb, suspended on a necklace of gold wire. This type of funerary amulet protected the deceased's heart, the centre of his physical and mental existence, and prevented it from revealing incriminating details of its owner's behaviour in life to the gods of the judgement hall. A magical spell to ensure this was inscribed on the base of the amulet. 18th Dynasty, about 1450 BC. L. 5.5 cm.

The scarab (a representation of the beetle *scarabeus sacer*) was another of the most popular amulets. Small representations of scarabs were commonly used by the living as seals, but they also served as funerary amulets to be placed on mummies. The scarab was associated both with the sun god and with the notion of rebirth. The adult beetle was observed to propel before it a ball of dung in which its eggs were embedded. The sight of the ball from which newly hatched beetles emerged apparently prompted in the minds of the Egyptians a comparison with the sun-disc at dawn as the source of renewed life. Hence the scarab was regarded as the form adopted by the sun god in the morning, and is depicted propelling the solar disc across the sky. This powerful image of rebirth occurred repeatedly on coffins, mummy-trappings and pectorals, sometimes showing the beetle alone, but often with outspread falcon-wings (see fig. 146).

One of the most important of all funerary amulets was a special type of scarab which protected the heart of the deceased (see fig. 147). The heart was regarded as one of the modes of human existence, and was considered to be the location of the human intelligence. Moreover, it contained a record of its owner's deeds and behaviour in life, and it would be examined by the gods of the judgement hall to determine whether or not its owner merited eternal life (see Chapter 1). It was therefore important that the heart should be retained in the hereafter. It was deliberately left inside the mummified body by the embalmers, and spells in the *Book of the Dead* were designed to guard against its loss. Since it could reveal potentially damning information about the deceased, texts such as spell 30B of the *Book of the Dead* also prevented the heart from testifying against its owner in the presence of the gods (see Chapter 1). This text was often inscribed on the 'heart scarab'. The rubric of the spell prescribed that this amulet should be carved from green stone and mounted in gold. It was to be anointed and

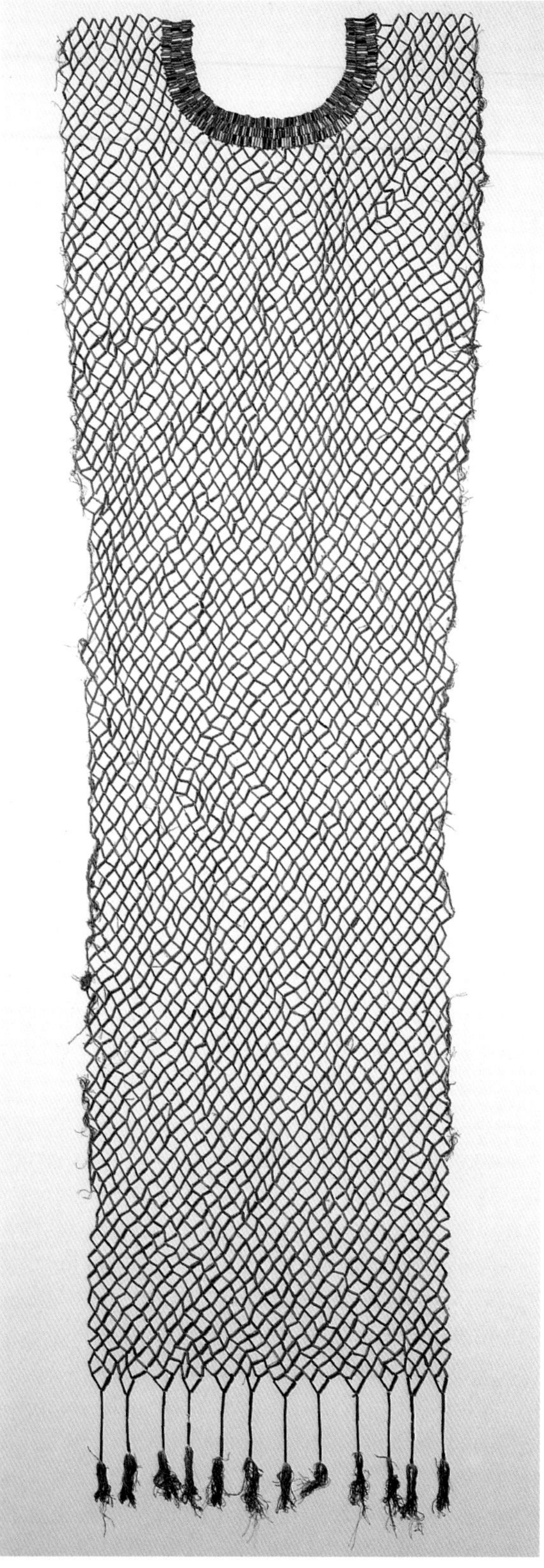

148. Network of blue faience tubular beads with collar of polychrome beads. Nets such as this were regularly placed over the outer wrappings of mummies from the 25th Dynasty to the Ptolemaic Period. The nets evidently conferred on the deceased the protection of the sky-goddess Nut, and their pattern imitates that of a bead garment often shown as worn by Osiris. Late Period, after 664 BC. Provenance unknown. H. 140 cm.

vitalised by the Opening of the Mouth, then placed on the breast of the mummy. Many heart scarabs are indeed of green stone (jasper seems to have been the preferred material), though others were of faience or Egyptian blue. One of the earliest known examples of a heart scarab is that inscribed for King Sebekemsaf of the 17th Dynasty (*c.* 1600 BC). It is mounted in gold, as prescribed in the spell-rubric, and bears a representation of a human face in place of the head of the beetle, emphasising that the heart encompasses the being of the deceased. A number of heart scarabs of the 18th Dynasty were also bound by gold bands, and were suspended on a gold wire or chain around the neck of the mummy.

While spell 30B is the most common, some heart scarabs carry other spells from the *Book of the Dead*, though the texts are always concerned with the heart. These include spell 26, to ensure that the deceased retains his heart in the netherworld; spell 27, to prevent the taking away of the deceased's heart in the netherworld; and spell 29B, relating to the *bennu*, or heron, which is identified as the *ba* of Ra. The *bennu* bird is frequently represented both on heart scarabs and on heart-shaped amulets. These latter also protected the heart. They were commonly placed inside the mummy wrappings, and the amulet was sometimes depicted being worn as a pendant by the deceased in scenes such as the weighing of the heart.

A characteristic feature of mummies of the middle and late 1st millennium BC was a large net of blue-green faience tubular beads, threaded in a lozenge pattern, with small spherical beads of different colours at the junctions and amuletic figures attached. These were placed on the front of the body, over the outer wrappings (see fig. 148). The bead-nets were evidently related to the bead-garment worn by Osiris, and hence the placing of such a net on the mummy probably enhanced the assimilation of the deceased with Osiris. The nets also carried celestial symbolism, illustrated in the blue colouring and the incorporation of the face of Nut into some examples. This also recalls the astral associations of Osiris; in at least one late depiction of Osiris wearing the net (in a tomb at Kom el-Shugafa) the lozenge spaces are occupied by moon, star and solar disc.

A few sporadic instances have been reported from the Third Intermediate Period, but it was only in the 25th Dynasty that the nets were introduced on a regular basis, continuing in use until the Ptolemaic Period. The earliest version of the net usually extended only from the shoulders to the ankles, and amuletic figures were limited to a faience winged scarab and the four Sons of Horus on the breast. Later examples (26th Dynasty and later) were more elaborate, covering the head as well as the body. The finest ones incorporate a face mask of gold (occasionally silver), often with a *wesekh* collar, and a wider range of amuletic figures. To the Sons of Horus were added a winged Nut, mourning Isis and Nephthys, and a band of inscription giving the name and titles of the deceased; these could be of gold leaf, gilded wood or cartonnage. Some Memphite examples incorporated a flat face of the goddess Nut, frontally depicted, recalling frontal images of the goddess on coffins. Particularly rich burials had more elaborate nets. That of the chief of royal ships Hekaemsaf, buried at Saqqara in the reign of Ahmose II (570–526 BC), consisted of beads of gold, lapis lazuli and amazonite, with an integral gold mask, bead-collar with gold falcon-head terminals, and figures of Nut and the Sons of Horus and an inscription all in gold. Another type of net incorporated a face of tiny coloured beads, directly over the face of the mummy. Some examples have a collar and divine figures in the same 'mosaic bead' technique threaded into the open lozenge-pattern net. These have been found at sites such as Saqqara, Abusir, Lahun and el-Hiba.

Magic bricks

Depictions of the mummy in the burial chamber occur in the *Book of the Dead*, and these illustrate the protection of the deceased by a range of deities and tutelary symbols. One important means of providing magical protection was the placing of four bricks of unbaked mud in niches in the burial chamber. These are attested for high status burials of the New Kingdom and 21st Dynasty, and were apparently reintroduced in the Late Period, the latest example dating to year 15 of Nectanebo I (*c.* 365 BC). They occur in both royal and private burials, so apparently no royal privilege was attached to them, though examples for kings usually have inscriptions in hieroglyphic, and those for non-royal persons in hieratic. The bricks have rarely survived in good condition, the best preserved set being those of Henutmehyt (reign of Ramesses II, *c.* 1279–1213 BC) (see fig. 149).

149. Set of magic bricks from the tomb of the chantress of Amun Henutmehyt, made of unbaked mud and each supporting an amuletic figure. The amulets represent a *djed* pillar of blue-glazed faience, a mud figure of the jackal-god Anubis, a wooden mummiform figure and a reed, intended to hold a wick. The inscriptions incised on the bricks contain the magical spells which describe their function, and indicate that each brick was to be placed facing one of the four cardinal points. 19th Dynasty, about 1250 BC. From Thebes. H. (left to right) 18, 9.5, 20.5, 9.5 cm.

Each brick supported an amulet – a *djed* pillar, jackal, torch, and mummiform figurine – and each had a text, which reveals that their purpose was to ward off hostile forces from the four cardinal points. This text, part of spell 151 of the *Book of the Dead*, contains specifications for the bricks and what the figures were to be made of. The *djed* brick was to be placed on the west, and the torch at the south – this was to be of reed, containing a wick. An Anubis of unbaked clay mixed with incense was to be placed on the brick for the east wall while the brick with the human figure guarded the north. The inscriptions and placing of the bricks seem to have confused the personnel who deposited them, for the texts often contain mistakes, and the positioning of the bricks in the tomb did not always follow the prescribed pattern. In some tombs the bricks were placed in two pairs of niches in opposite walls, and even in royal tombs, the pattern was not always followed, suggesting that the positioning may reflect notions of a localised geography within the burial chamber.

Other magical figures

At different periods, a range of other magical objects was placed in the tomb. Some of these, once introduced, became a fixed part of the standard burial outfit for centuries; others were in vogue only briefly. A complex methodology underlay the selection of objects; texts on coffin, mummy-shroud and papyrus were sometimes complementary, each component forming part of a ritual unit indispensable to the deceased's welfare. In the same way, at periods when funerary texts were rarely placed in the tomb, other types of object appeared, perhaps to compensate for the absence of the texts. Hence, from the middle of the 12th Dynasty

150. Ivory wand (apotropaion), used in the magical protection of the home, in particular the safeguarding of young children and mothers. The wands are carved with a series of protective deities and symbols, among whom can be recognised the hippopotamus-headed lion deity Ipi and the lion-headed Bes or Aha. 12th or 13th Dynasty, about 1985–1750 BC. Provenance unknown. L. 36.5 cm.

151. Limestone fertility figurine representing a woman, naked except for a full wig, lying on a bed with a male child at her side. 19th to 20th Dynasty, about 1295–1069 BC. Provenance unknown. L. 23.5 cm.

the custom of providing models of servants declined, while model food offerings were introduced and *shabtis* grew in importance. The same period witnessed a reduction in the use of *Coffin Texts*, corresponding with the addition to the burial outfit of a range of magical items.

Some of these were objects used in everyday life: serpent-shaped staffs, 'magical rods' bearing figures of turtles and other creatures, and curved ivory wands of apotropaic significance (see fig. 150). The latter carry carved figures of animal deities holding knives, with which they were to ward off harmful influences. Some examples are worn, or have been damaged and repaired in ancient times, so it is clear that they were used to protect the living – particularly mothers and young children. The placing of these wands in tombs in the Middle Kingdom and Second Intermediate Period indicates that they also protected the dead and promoted their rebirth. Some of these objects carried symbolic allusions to the victory of the sun god over his enemies. Because of this association they too might have functioned as replacements for the texts, now often absent from the tomb, which alluded to the same concepts.

It was also in the Middle Kingdom that fertility figurines began to be placed in tombs with frequency, a custom which continued into the New Kingdom (see fig. 151). These include figures representing naked females, often with the sexual organs emphasised, and others in the form of a woman lying on a bed, sometimes accompanied by a child. Such objects, which are also found in domestic contexts and at cult places, were probably intended to promote fecundity. Placed in tombs, they might have been intended to give the dead sexual powers as well – but more probably acted as symbols of rebirth and regeneration.

The kings' tombs of the New Kingdom contained a range of magical items and images all of which served to protect the dead king and assure his rebirth. Most of these objects are peculiar to royal burials. Notable among these are the pairs of lifesize or larger statues of the king (see fig. 152). The best preserved examples were found in the tomb of Tutankhamun (*c.* 1336–1327 BC). The statues were of wood, covered with black varnish and the headdresses, kilts and other trappings were originally gilded. In the tomb of Tutankhamun, the statues flanked the sealed doorway to the burial chamber. Similar statues, stripped of their gilding in antiquity, have been found in other tombs of the 18th to 20th Dynasties. The statues were differentiated by the types of royal headdress depicted: one wears the striped *nemes*, the other the bag-like *khat*. Those from Tutankhamun's tomb also bore different inscriptions. These indicate that the figures represented the two main aspects of the sun-god with whom the dead king was identified. The statue wearing the *nemes*, positioned on the eastern side, represented the king as the manifestation of Ra-Horakhty, the daytime form of the sun god, while that on the west (wearing the *khat*) was an image of the king as Osiris, equated with the nocturnal *ka* of the sun god.

Equally imposing are the couches in animal form. Three of these were found in Tutankhamun's tomb. Made of gilded wood, they have cow, lion and hippopotamus heads, and were intended to facilitate the king's passage to the afterlife. Heads from similar couches in black-varnished wood have been found in other tombs. Among the smaller figures were statuettes of the king as Horus, harpooning Seth, or riding on the back of a black panther, and standing and seated figures of deities. After the Amarna Period, the range of figures in the royal tomb was

152. Statue of king Ramesses I, one of a pair originally installed in his tomb. The statue is made from the wood of the sycomore fig and was coated with black resin. The king wears the bag-like *khat* headdress, and would originally have been depicted holding a staff and a mace. Headdress, collar, kilt and other details were originally gilded over a thin layer of gesso, and the eyes and eyebrows were inlaid. 19th Dynasty, about 1294 BC. From the tomb of Ramesses I in the Valley of the Kings, Thebes. H. 180 cm.

enlarged by the inclusion of a series of protective deities – often inaccurately termed 'demons of the underworld', but better described as apotropaic deities (see fig. 153). Most are in human form, but with a variety of heads, including those of a ram, gazelle or turtle. They grasp knives, snakes and lizards to symbolise their power over hostile forces. Some of these gods are deities well known from other contexts – such as the Sons of Horus, chiefly associated with the protection of the viscera – while others are cognate with deities listed in the *Book of the Dead*, who guarded the gateways that led to the netherworld, and turned back the unrighteous. Examples of this type were found in the tombs of Horemheb (*c.* 1323–1295 BC), Ramesses I (*c.* 1295–1294 BC) and other kings. Comparable figures were depicted on the walls of royal tombs of the 19th and 20th Dynasties, as well as on papyri, sarcophagi and coffins of the Third Intermediate Period. These sources throw light on the purpose of the images, which appear to have been arranged around the mummy as if forming a protective cordon. The later depictions show that access to this form of protection was no longer restricted to royalty after the New Kingdom, but sculptural representa-

153. Black-varnished wooden statuette representing an apotropaic deity. The seated ram-headed figure originally held either knives with which to ward off hostile entities, or snakes or lizards, symbolising his control of potentially dangerous forces which might harm the deceased. Groups of wooden figures of this type were a feature of royal burials of the New Kingdom. Probably from the tomb of King Horemheb in the Valley of the Kings, late 18th Dynasty, about 1295 BC. H. 51 cm.

tions occurred only once more; the Theban governor Montemhat (early 26th Dynasty, *c.* 650 BC) arranged for a set of statuettes of these guardians to be carved from stone and placed in his tomb in the Asasif.

Corn-mummies and Osirian statues

The god Osiris was closely associated with vegetation, and particularly with germinating grain. The emergence of young growth shoots from the fertile mud of Egypt was regarded as a powerful metaphor for human resurrection, and this notion was given physical form in Osirian images and figurines in which earth and corn were basic constituents. Some royal tombs of the New Kingdom contained an 'Osiris bed', a seed bed in a wooden frame or on a piece of textile, made in the shape of an image of Osiris. This bed was planted with barley, which germinated in the tomb, symbolising the renewal of life for the dead king via the agency of Osiris. A similar concept underlay the creation of 'corn mummies', figurines composed of earth or mud mixed with grains of barley and fashioned into a miniature mummiform image of Osiris. These figures were manufactured in an elaborate temple ritual during the month of Khoiak, and then buried in areas with sacred associations (see fig. 154). The majority of examples date to the Late and Ptolemaic periods, but comparable figures have occassionally been found in private tombs of earlier periods, and a few instances have been reported of small roughly shaped mummiform figurines found buried with mummies of the 22nd Dynasty.

154. A 'corn mummy' – an image of the god Osiris in the form of a miniature mummified body containing mud and grains of corn. The face is of green wax, and details of the eyes and beard have been added in gold leaf. These objects were made during the annual festival of Osiris in the month of Khoiak, and buried in specially designated sacred locations. Miniature ones were often placed in the hollow bases of Ptah-Sokar-Osiris statues (see figs 155–6). Late Period, 664 BC or later. H. 32 cm.

Towards the end of the Third Intermediate Period, a new type of funerary statuette was introduced. These mummiform figures of wood often had a cavity either within the figure or in the base to contain a rolled funerary papyrus. Their antecedents probably stretch back to the royal burials of the New Kingdom. As early as the reign of Amenhotep II (*c.* 1427–1400 BC), the king's burial included a mummiform statuette hollowed out to contain a papyrus. Similar figures, representing Osiris, were used in non-royal burials from the 19th Dynasty, but hollow figures fell out of use in the 22nd Dynasty, when the provision of funerary papyri temporarily ceased. The mummiform figures were re-introduced in the 25th Dynasty, now representing not Osiris alone but Ptah-Sokar-Osiris, a syncretistic deity who embodied the concept of resurrection (see fig. 155).

These statuettes possessed a standard range of attributes: a shrouded mummiform body, from which the hands occasionally protrude; a tripartite wig; a red, green or gilded face; and a headdress composed of twin plumes, ram's horns and a solar disc. The figure was supported on a long base (see fig. 156). Many of these images contain a cavity, either within the figure itself or in the plinth. Instead of a papyrus roll, they contained a small corn-mummy. This symbol of the deceased's resurrection, when placed in the base of the statue, was often covered by a miniature sarcophagus or an image of a mummified falcon. This last represented Sokar, the god who protected the necropolis. The tendency to merge Osiris and Sokar with Ptah had begun as early as the Middle Kingdom, but Osiris and Sokar predominated, Ptah always playing a minor role. The importance of this god as a symbol of resurrection is emphasised in the texts on the Late Period statuettes, according to which the deceased shared the renewal of life experienced by Osiris. In consequence, a Ptah-Sokar-Osiris statue became an indispensable feature of the standard burial assemblage in the Late-Ptolemaic periods.

155. Painted wooden statuettes of Ptah-Sokar-Osiris. That on the left was made for the burial of the vizier Pamiu (late eighth century BC), and represents an early form of this type of image, which remained popular until the late Ptolemaic Period. The statuette on the right is inscribed for a priest of Amun-Ra and scribe of the temple of Montu named Padimut, 25th Dynasty, about 700–670 BC. The texts on the front are a request to Osiris to provide funerary offerings, and speeches of the four Sons of Horus, whose figures appear at the sides. Both statuettes originally wore a feathered headdress or a crown. The cavity in the plinth of Padimut's figure probably contained a small corn-mummy. Both probably from Thebes. H. (left) 63.5 cm, (right) 64 cm.

156. Ptah-Sokar-Osiris figure from the burial of Neswy (see fig. 118). Early Ptolemaic Period, third century BC. From Thebes. H. 79.5 cm.

CHAPTER

The Chest of Life: Coffins and Sarcophagi

Evolving responses to the needs of the deceased led to many changes in the objects placed in the tomb for their well-being. Some categories of object remained in use for centuries, while others were quickly superseded. The coffin was, however, the single most important item of funerary equipment, and its provision was the most consistent feature of Egyptian burial practice throughout the pharaonic period. This is scarcely surprising when it is considered that the coffin fulfilled both practical and ritual roles, and frequently reproduced the functions of the tomb itself. Ancient names for the coffin included 'lord of life' and 'chest of life' – emphasising the importance of the object as a vehicle for resurrection.

Symbolism of the coffin

At its simplest, a coffin protected the buried corpse from the depredations of scavenging animals and tomb robbers, thereby helping to retain the integrity of the body. The earliest Egyptian coffins were simple boxes of reeds, clay or wood. Had physical protection been their only function, all later coffins might have been as plain and unadorned as were these primitive examples. But in fact Egyptian coffins were subject to an astonishingly rich variety of form, pictorial imagery and text. Through its shape and its surface imagery, texts and colouring, the Egyptian coffin was heavily endowed with symbolic meaning. Like the tombs discussed in Chapter 5, coffins created special environments or cosmoi in which the transfiguration of the dead was promoted: the extended cosmos (incorporating sky, earth and underworld) and the more restricted cosmos of the deceased's immediate surroundings represented by the burial place and cult-chapel. The coffins' evolution reflected changing attitudes to the afterlife, taking up, preserving and developing different notions, expressions of which came to be ultimately embedded within the complex iconography and texts of their surfaces.

The earliest attested symbolic role of the coffin was as a 'house' or eternal dwelling for the deceased. This is apparent in both the shape and decoration of the coffins of the Early Dynastic Period and Old Kingdom, which, like tomb superstructures, replicated the architectural features of early palace buildings (see fig. 158).

Development was relatively rapid. By the end of the Old Kingdom, the coffin had already begun to reproduce the immediate funerary environment of the deceased. The orientation of the coffin and its decoration were crucial to the fulfillment of this goal, the long front and back sides being aligned east and west respectively like the corresponding walls of the burial chamber, while the mummy within faced east, towards the rising sun. The tomb, of course, also took care of the sustenance and provisioning of the deceased, through the agency of the offering chapel with the false door stela as its focal point, and by means of images and lists of offerings on the walls. These magical 'tools' accordingly began to be depicted on the internal surfaces of the coffin, so that the space confined by its sides and lid was treated as a miniaturised reproduction of the tomb. The application of the bulk of the pictorial and textual material to the inside of the coffin, from the late Old Kingdom to the Middle Kingdom, emphasised the notion that it was arranged for the convenience of the dead person within. For the same reason, images and spells were positioned close to the part of the body to which they directly referred.

A more sophisticated role for the coffin or sarcophagus was already developing during the Old Kingdom, to set the deceased within a larger environment than that of the tomb alone – that of the universe itself. The lid of the coffin was symbolically associated with the sky; on examples from the Middle Kingdom, star-clocks and constellations are depicted on the under surface, and at later periods coffin lids, both rectangular and anthropoid, were identified with the sky-goddess Nut. Texts on the lid refer to the goddess stretching herself protectively above the deceased and placing him 'among the imperishable stars' – these of course were the circumpolar stars which were regarded as the destination of the dead king, in early concepts of the afterlife (see p. 25). The case of the coffin was associated with the earth. Thus the coffin recreated the universe around the deceased.

The dead man, inside the coffin, was identified with Osiris or Ra, each of whom were reborn within the cosmos, or with Shu, god of the atmosphere, whose place was between earth and sky. A significant element in this role was the occasional identification of the entire coffin, not just the lid, with the sky-goddess Nut. The sky-goddess was regarded as the mother of all the dead. As she was also the mother of Osiris, the identification of the deceased with Osiris was emphasised. In some texts of the Old Kingdom the chest of a sarcophagus is referred to by the word *mwt* (literally 'mother'), and it is apparent that the mummy deposited inside the sarcophagus or coffin was equated symbolically with a child in the womb of the sky-goddess, a notion which placed the deceased in a situation of potential rebirth. A papyrus in the Louvre alludes to this:

> O you wetnurse, into whom it is good to enter,
> O you, into whom each and every one enters, day after day!
> O Great Mother, whose children are not delivered!

When the mummy was placed inside the coffin, the deceased entered the embrace of the sky-goddess. This idea situates the rebirth of the deceased in the cyclical eternity of the universe. But, although reborn, the deceased is not 'delivered' from the body of the mother-goddess. Instead, the rebirth takes place *inside* the womb (= the coffin = the sky), a concept which is graphically illustrated by the painting or carving of the figure of Nut – sometimes with a star-studded celestial body – on many coffins and sarcophagi.

It was not Nut alone who fulfilled this role. In the texts on some coffins and sarcophagi the position of divine mother of the deceased is taken by the goddess Neith, while Hathor (often in her guise as the Goddess of the West) features prominently in the iconography of post-New Kingdom coffins. The association of the coffin with Nut, however, remained strong for centuries, and the conception of the coffin as a kind of cocoon in which the deceased would be reborn is further revealed through the later use of the word *swht* (literally 'egg') to describe the inner case.

The concept of the coffin as microcosm endured for millennia, and produced a rich and varied use of iconography. It is most clearly recognisable on rectangular coffins, where the lid was equated with the sky, and the base represented the earth or the underworld in which the dead dwelt. The long sides of the coffin could also be equated with the underworld, or with the western and eastern horizons, the physical boundaries of the world. The cosmological role of the coffin also applied to anthropoid coffins, particularly from the New Kingdom onwards.

As mentioned above, the formal, pictorial and textual attributes of coffins, which are the vehicles for these symbolic meanings, also belonged to the tomb. The coffin, therefore, acted as a tomb in miniature. The degree of correspondence between tomb and coffin fluctuated from time to time, becoming closest when (whether for economic, social or religious reasons) the attributes of the tomb were curtailed, and some of its functions were taken over by the coffin. An undecorated chamber tomb without a cult chapel, such as those provided for many minor officials of the Middle Kingdom, often contained a coffin whose interior surfaces mirrored the decoration of walls and ceiling in the chapels of the wealthy. In the Third Intermediate Period, when many burials were placed in communal tombs without decoration, the surfaces of coffins were densely covered with images and short texts to provide for the welfare of the deceased.

There were numerous ways in which the coffin's attributes could be made to activate symbolic associations for the benefit of the occupant. It was common for a body to be placed within a series of coffins, one within the other, each of which might convey different symbolic significance. Thus the outer coffin might be rectangular in shape, imitating the tomb or the shrine in which a divinity was housed, while the inner coffin(s) were anthropoid in shape, representing the deceased with the specific attributes of a transfigured being (*sah*). This multi-level significance in some cases reflected the unity of Osiris and Ra, progressively emphasised in religious texts and iconography after the New Kingdom. On coffins of the later first millennium BC, inner and outer decoration might be complementary without necessarily being unified into a single concept; hence the exterior could identify the deceased with Osiris in the place of embalming, surrounded by protective deities, while the internal space represented the cosmos in which the deceased (i.e. Osiris) lay.

The evolution of the coffin

Early Dynastic Period and Old Kingdom

During much of the Predynastic period, the body was generally placed in a shallow pit, sometimes covered with animal skins or matting. As a rule, coffins were not used, although in some graves of the Badarian culture (*c.* 4400–3800 BC) there is evidence for a framework of reeds, possibly surrounding the body, or as a roofing for the grave pit. In the latter part of the Predynastic period, a more regular type of grave, lined with bricks and roofed with logs, was developed. The body might be wrapped in linen or placed in a wicker basket, and at the same period, in about 3000 BC, primitive coffins of wood, clay or pottery began to be provided. However, it was not until the Early Dynastic Period that a coffin became a regular element of burial equipment. No coffins that were made for

157. The earliest wooden coffins were small rectangular boxes, the components of which had sometimes been recycled after use in domestic structures. The corpse was placed inside in a contracted position, and this custom determined the proportions of the coffin. In this example, part of the lid has been removed to show the skeleton, that of a young adult of uncertain sex. Traces of linen show that the corpse had originally been wrapped. From tomb 1955 at Tarkhan. 1st Dynasty, about 3000 BC. L. 91.2 cm.

kings or persons of high status survive from this period, but people of lower rank were buried in containers made of bundles of reeds, large reused storage jars, simple trays or wooden chests. The chests, the earliest true coffins, were relatively small (approximately 1 metre in length) and held the body in a contracted position with the knees drawn up and the hands in front of the face (see fig. 157). Some examples evoked the architectural forms familiar from the great tombs and funerary 'palaces' of the period, with vaulted lids and recessed panelling on the sides, and provide the first instance of parallelism in the symbolic conception of tomb and coffin – in this case as a 'house' for the use of the deceased.

The development of techniques of mummification during the Old Kingdom had a major impact on the evolution of the coffin. The preparation of bodies with the limbs fully extended necessitated creating a longer type of receptacle. Examples of full-length coffins began to appear in the 3rd Dynasty, though at this stage they seem to have been provided mainly for members of the royal family. In the chambers beneath the Step Pyramid of Djoser (*c.* 2667–2648 BC) at Saqqara were found the remains of a child who had been buried in an elaborate plywood coffin of the 'long' type; it was formed of six thin layers of different types of wood, arranged with the grain running in alternate directions to provide added strength, and gilded on the exterior. This coffin had in turn been placed inside a calcite sarcophagus.

Contracted burials in short coffins remained in use for many years during the Old Kingdom, but were eventually completely superseded by 'long' coffins. Earlier examples of this type generally had panelled decoration on the sides and a vaulted lid, a type created in both stone and wood at the height of the Old Kingdom (see fig. 158). In about the 6th Dynasty, a type with a flat lid and smooth sides was introduced, continuing in use throughout the First Intermediate

158. Red granite sarcophagus made for a high official. The vaulted lid and panelled decoration on the sides are imitated from the iconography of contemporary wooden coffins and are ultimately supposed to derive from the appearance of the royal palace. On the eastern-facing side false doors are added to the pattern of panelling. Traces of an erased hieroglyphic text are discernible along the upper edge of this side; this may have been removed in order to usurp the sarcophagus for a second owner. Probably 5th Dynasty, about 2494–2395 BC. From Giza. L. 2.25 m.

159. Tamarisk-wood coffin of Hetepnebi, Inspector of priests of the *ka*-temple of king Pepy I or II. With its flat lid and plain sides adorned only with offering formulae and a pair of eyes, it represents the earliest version of the standard type of coffin in use from the 6th Dynasty to the Second Intermediate Period. It is constructed of small, irregularly-shaped pieces of wood, dowelled together and originally secured at the corners with leather thongs. Excavated by D.G. Hogarth, 1907, in tomb 56 at Asyut. Late 6th Dynasty or early First Intermediate Period, about 2200–2100 BC. L. 186.5 cm.

Period and the Middle Kingdom (see fig. 157). The religious significance of this type of coffin was reflected in the manner of its positioning in the tomb and in its decoration. The coffin was orientated with the head-end pointing north, and the feet south. The mummy was positioned on its left side, the head supported by a headrest, with the face turned towards the east. This positioning was important for two reasons. Firstly, the deceased looked out from the realm of the dead towards that of the living, ready to take in nourishment from the offerings which – he expected – would be presented to him by relatives or priests entering the tomb chapel from the opposite direction. Secondly, by facing towards the eastern horizon he would see the rising sun each dawn, symbolising the rebirth for which he hoped. The iconography of the eastern wall of the coffin promoted these functions. The most consistent element was a pair of painted or inlaid eyes, through which the deceased could see; care was taken to align the mummy's face with this 'eye-panel' and a headrest was placed under the head to provide the necessary support. To enable the *ka* of the deceased to pass freely in and out, a small-scale image of a false door was often painted on the side of the coffin below the eyes. This functioned in the same way as the stone false-door stelae placed in tomb-chapels. An image of a table of food offerings was regularly painted alongside the false door on the interior. Hence the eastern face of the coffin facilitated the offering-cult.

Hieroglyphic inscriptions began to be added to coffins and sarcophagi in the 4th Dynasty. At first these were standard, offering formulae invoking Osiris and Anubis and other deities to provide the deceased with the basic necessities of existence. These texts were written down the centre of the flat lid of the coffin and along the upper edges of the sides.

A variety of types of stone and wood were used to make coffins and sarcophagi. Timbers such as cedar yielded large straight planks, ideal for the construction of rectangular coffins, but cedar had to be imported from the Lebanon; it was therefore a costly material and its possession was a mark of status. Some high-ranking officials had pairs of coffins made from cedar. Those of individuals of humbler rank were generally made from native timbers, of which the sycomore fig was by far the most extensively used. Since these trees were generally much smaller than the Lebanese cedars, the coffins were usually made from small pieces of irregular shape, ingeniously fitted together in a patchwork fashion, using wooden cramps and dowels and secured at the corners with leather thongs (see fig. 159).

Stone sarcophagi were introduced in the 3rd Dynasty, initially for members of the royal family. Examples were made from limestone, calcite (alabaster) and granite, and in succeeding centuries stone sarcophagi became more widely used for individuals of status, either in place of a wooden coffin or as an outermost container for a series of wooden coffins. As a general rule, the design of stone sarcophagi was adapted from that of wooden coffins, not only in the Old Kingdom but in later periods as well.

160. Exterior of the painted wooden coffin of Ankhef (see fig. 47). The inscriptions contain prayers for offerings and confer the protection of various deities on the deceased. This side of the coffin faced east in the tomb and at the head-end is painted a pair of eyes to enable Ankhef to 'see' the rising sun. Early 12th Dynasty, about 1950 BC. From Asyut. L. 183 cm.

First Intermediate Period and Middle Kingdom

Rectangular wooden coffins remained standard during the First Intermediate Period and Middle Kingdom, but their decoration underwent significant evolution. The horizontal inscriptions on the exterior were augmented by vertical texts arranged at intervals along the sides (see fig. 160). These referred to various deities of the Osirian cycle, whose protection was thereby extended around the deceased. A false door was also added, painted below the 'eye panel' and from the middle of the 12th Dynasty false door motifs were often repeated on all the exterior faces of the coffin. The decoration of the interior became more elaborate than that of the exterior, a reflection of the greater magical importance of the inner surfaces, from the deceased's point of view (see fig. 161). Opposite the mummy's face on the eastern side was a false door, a depiction of an offering

161. Interior of the outer coffin of Seni, showing texts and images painted at the foot end. Below the large band of inscription in which the deceased is named is a frieze of objects (see fig. 162) and extracts from the *Coffin Texts* written in vertical columns. 12th Dynasty, about 1850 BC. From Deir el-Bersha. L. of coffin 256 cm.

162. Interior of the coffin of Seni, showing a section of the 'frieze of objects' – a series of images of commodities and ritual items with which the deceased was equipped for the afterlife. 12th Dynasty, about 1850 BC. From Deir el-Bersha. L. of coffin 256 cm.

table heaped with provisions, and a standardised list of funerary offerings. Around all four sides ran the 'frieze of objects', a narrow band containing images of a wide range of commodities which would both provide for the physical needs of the deceased and assist him in his passage to the afterlife (see fig. 162). The contents of the frieze vary from one coffin to another, but among the items most commonly included are clothing, jewellery, furniture, tools and weapons, as well as amulets and royal insignia – the latter enabling the dead person to be resurrected as Osiris, the ruler of the underworld. These images were often deliberately arranged so that the objects were conveniently positioned for the use of the deceased: headrests appear at the head-end of the coffin, sandals at the foot-end, mirrors and pieces of jewellery close to the upper body, weapons close to the arms.

The interior surfaces of many coffins were inscribed with funerary texts for the benefit of the deceased (see Chapter 6). It is unknown whether or not the inner wooden coffins of kings bore these texts, since no examples have survived from this period, but private coffins were regularly inscribed in this manner. At first, the texts seem to have been copied from those in the 5th–6th Dynasty royal pyramids, and examples of private coffins inscribed with these texts have been found in the Memphite necropolis. The *Pyramid Texts*, however, were soon superseded by the *Coffin Texts*, extracts from which began to appear on coffins in all parts of Egypt. They are first attested in southern Egypt and occurred in non-royal burials as early as the 6th Dynasty. Regional variants occurred, particular texts being favoured in different parts of Egypt. Hence many of the finer coffins from Deir el-Bersha include the text and illustrations from the *Book of Two Ways*, a composition which includes a map to assist the deceased in finding his way through the hereafter. The map is located on the floor of the coffin, a reflection of the conceptual role of this part as a representation of the terrestrial underworld.

The principal changes in the design of coffins were closely related to the growing complexity of their religious function. Thus, the relatively simple exterior decoration of the Old Kingdom coffins was intended mainly to ensure that the deceased obtained material benefits such as a 'good burial in the West' and funerary offerings. On the later coffins the external inscriptions and the more complex internal decoration linked the coffin closely to the rituals performed at the funeral, with the principal aim of ensuring the deceased's resurrection through his association with creator gods, chiefly Osiris and Ra.

Members of the royal family and certain high officials of the Middle Kingdom were provided with stone sarcophagi. Some of these were plain, others carved with panelled decoration. Images were usually avoided, but there are exceptions to this practice. The most notable examples are the sarcophagi made for the wives of Mentuhotep II (*c.* 2055–2004 BC) who were buried within the king's enormous funerary complex at Deir el-Bahri. These unusual sarcophagi were built of stone slabs, instead of being carved from a single block, and their outer surfaces were decorated with scenes of daily life and offering inscriptions.

Early anthropoid coffins

It was during the Middle Kingdom that anthropoid or mummy-shaped coffins were introduced. They were made of wood or cartonnage, usually comprising a lid and a case of approximately equal depth, joined along the sides. These coffins seem to have evolved from the cartonnage masks which were popular in the First Intermediate Period (see pp. 60–3 and 81). Since some masks were extended below the breast, over the front of the body, the full anthropoid covering which

163. Anthropoid coffin of Userhat. This is one of the earliest examples of the mummy-shaped type of coffin. 12th Dynasty, about 1800 BC. From Beni Hasan, tomb 132. H. 182.4 cm.

enveloped the entire mummy can be viewed as a logical development of this trend. The earliest surviving example of a complete anthropoid mummy-case is one found in the tomb of Ashait, wife of Mentuhotep II, at Deir el-Bahri (late 11th Dynasty). Like the earlier masks, it was made of cartonnage. During the 12th Dynasty, anthropoid inner coffins became more widely used in non-royal burials. One of the earliest is that of the court lady Senebtisy, found in her tomb at Lisht.

These early anthropoid coffins reproduced the appearance of the *sah*, the eternal image of the transfigured deceased, of which the mummified body was the prime example (see Chapter 2). In consequence, these coffins represented the body entirely enveloped in a shroud, with only the head emerging, and adorned with only those features which were considered appropriate to a *sah*-image at this period: a *khat* or *nemes* headdress and a bead-collar (see fig. 163). Anthropoid coffins of the later Middle Kingdom had a central column of inscription, usually consisting of the offering formula. On some examples the body had both vertical and lateral bands arranged at intervals. These resemble the outermost binding-tapes placed on mummies of the New Kingdom and later periods to secure the wrappings, but this arrangement is not found on Middle Kingdom mummies, and the bands may have been taken over from the iconography of rectangular coffins. The surface of the coffin was sometimes coloured plain white, in other cases black (a colour associated with Osiris, and hence with resurrection). In a few instances the body was covered with a bead-net pattern, an element not attested on mummies at this period but one which became a feature of the idealised image of the deceased in later periods. Middle Kingdom mummiform cases were always placed inside rectangular coffins, and were distinct from them in significance. The rectangular coffin replicated the architectural form and the conceptual role of the tomb, while the anthropoid coffin evidently acted as a substitute body for the deceased and represented him in the transfigured state to which he aspired, fully equipped with the attributes of a divine being.

Second Intermediate Period

During the 17th Dynasty, a new type of wooden anthropoid coffin was developed. All the examples are made of native timbers, and the majority were hollowed out of tree trunks. These coffins are chiefly distinguished by the decoration of the lid with a feathered pattern, giving the impression that the deceased was enveloped in a large pair of wings (see fig. 164). On account of this decorative design, 19th century diggers dubbed these *rishi* coffins, from an Arabic word meaning 'feather'. The feathered pattern sometimes extended to the headdress, and its use on coffins may have developed from the mummy-masks of the late Middle Kingdom and Second Intermediate Period, many of which were decorated with a similar design. Most *rishi* coffins also had the royal *nemes* headdress, no distinction being made on this basis between the coffins of kings and those of non-royal persons. As mentioned above, the *nemes* had been included in object friezes on non-royal coffins of the Middle Kingdom, and was probably an

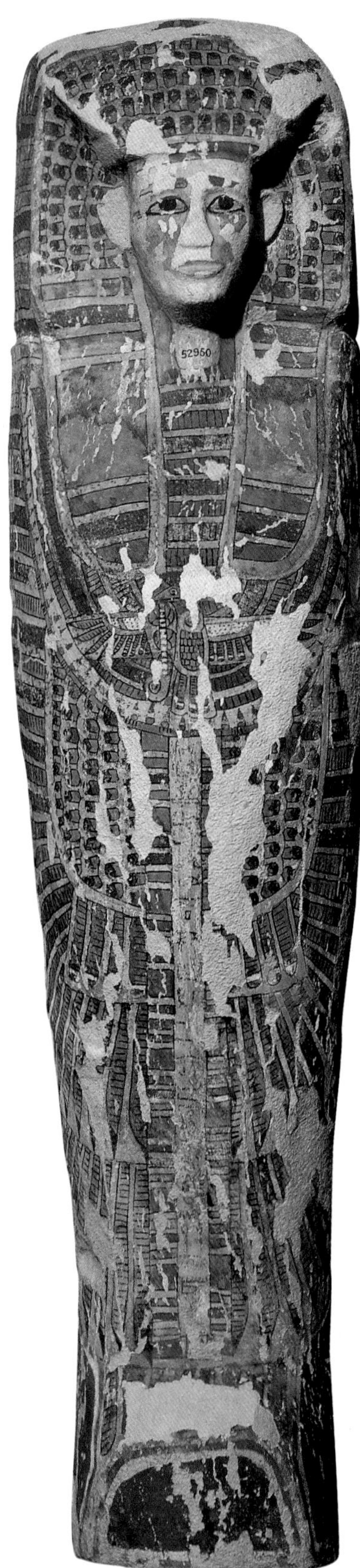

evocation of the deceased's identification with Osiris, rather than a 'usurpation' of kingly prerogatives. Many *rishi* coffins also had a *uraeus* serpent and vulture (or a vulture alone) on the breast and a central inscription. Figures of Isis and Nephthys, carved or painted beneath the feet, would be visible only when the coffin lay recumbent, possibly suggesting that the *rishi* coffin's role was to replicate the environment of the burial chamber. The workmanship of these coffins was generally mediocre, and the faces in particular were often crudely shaped, with only the most rudimentary facial details.

The *rishi* type seems to have originated at Thebes, and it is from the cemeteries there that most of the extant examples come, although a single specimen from Saqqara is known. The finest examples of the type are the coffins made for the kings and queens of the late 17th and early 18th Dynasties, most of which were extensively gilded. Those made for private individuals were usually simply painted.

New Kingdom

At the beginning of the New Kingdom, both rectangular and anthropoid *rishi* coffins were in use at Thebes. The coffin of King Ahmose I (*c.* 1550–1525 BC) and those of several queens of his family show that a modified version of the *rishi* motif continued in use in royal burials, undergoing further developments throughout the 18th Dynasty. Early examples were of gilded wood or cartonnage, and the feathered patterning was more stylised, representing the deceased sheathed in the plumage of a falcon or vulture. This stylised feather design also appears on the royal coffin from tomb 55 in the Valley of the Kings and on those of Tutankhamun (*c.* 1336–1327 BC). His intact tomb shows that by the late 18th Dynasty three anthropoid coffins were required for a king's burial. Each coffin was decorated with a variant of the *rishi* motif but the material and colouring of the coffins differed. Tutankhamun's first and second coffins were of gilded and inlaid

164. Wooden coffin of an unnamed individual. The feathered patterning on the lid is typical of Theban specimens of the 17th and early 18th Dynasties, and gave rise to the modern term *rishi* (Arabic for 'feathered') for these coffins. The majority of *rishi* coffins were roughly carved from hollowed tree-trunks, and were prefabricated rather than made to order. This is apparent in the crudely written offering formula down the centre of the lid, in which the word *men* ('so-and-so') appears in the place usually occupied by the name of the deceased.
17th Dynasty, about 1600 BC. From Thebes. H. 192 cm.

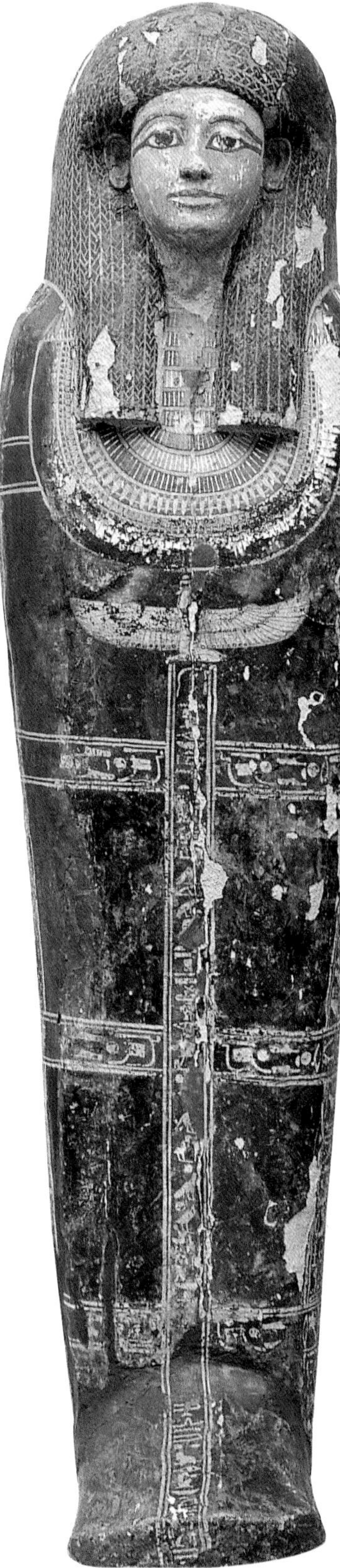

wood, the innermost of solid gold. The multiple anthropoid coffins of kings were placed in stone sarcophagi, which underwent a steady evolution in design from one reign to the next – earlier examples, which resembled the rectangular coffins of the Middle Kingdom being replaced by cartouche-shaped coffers. Following the reign of Akhenaten (*c.* 1352–1336 BC), a new type appeared, the shape reproducing that of a shrine, with cornice-moulding along the top and the carved figures of a protective goddess at each corner. The kings of the 19th and 20th Dynasties arranged for their bodies to be housed in much more elaborate fashion, with multiple sarcophagi of both rectangular and anthropoid types, nested one inside the other. The most grandoise ensemble of this type was that prepared for Merenptah (*c.* 1213–1203 BC), which comprised no fewer than four sarcophagi. The innermost sarcophagi in these assemblages were of calcite and were extensively decorated with texts and representations from the *Books of the Underworld.*

During the reign of Tuthmosis III (*c.* 1479–1425 BC), rectangular coffins and anthropoid *rishi* cases passed out of use, and a different type of mummiform coffin became standard. This type had originated about the reign of Amenhotep I (*c.* 1525–1504 BC) or Tuthmosis I (*c.* 1504–1492 BC). The coffins were usually made from planks of native timber such as the sycomore fig. Their exterior surfaces were divided into compartments by vertical and horizontal bands of inscription meeting at right angles, a feature which had been taken from the earlier rectangular coffins. Wig and floral collar remained standard features, and the space below the collar was usually occupied at first by a vulture with outspread wings (representing the goddess Nut) and subsequently by the figure of Nut as a winged woman, who was requested in the accompanying text to spread herself in protection over the deceased. The spaces between the inscribed bands, at first left vacant, gradually began to be occupied by figures of deities. The sides of the case were sometimes decorated with funeral or offering scenes, or,

165. Lid of the anthropoid wooden coffin of a woman named Tentamentet. During the 18th Dynasty mummiform coffins became the predominant type, and the vertical and lateral inscriptions – originally a feature of rectangular coffins – were incorporated into their design. Below the floral collar is a figure of the winged goddess Nut, who is invoked in the central inscription to protect the deceased. The black background of this example is characteristic of the period from the reign of Tuthmosis III to that of Ramesses II. Mid-18th Dynasty, about 1400 BC. From Thebes. H. 190 cm.

more frequently with figures of the Sons of Horus, Anubis and Thoth. Isis and Nephthys were painted at the foot and the head, and were depicted both lamenting and protecting the deceased as they had done for Osiris on his bier. The motif of the pair of eyes, the most conspicuous feature of earlier rectangular coffins, survived on some 18th Dynasty anthropoid coffins, where they appear on the left upper arm, although they were still sometimes painted on the shoulder-area of the case. These coffins were thus an amalgam of the anthropoid and rectangular types, and the latter in consequence fell out of common use. The basic design elements remained standard throughout most of the 18th Dynasty, but the colour scheme of the coffins changed. Those made from the reign of Tuthmosis I to that of Tuthmosis III usually had polychrome decoration on a white background, to be succeeded by coffins with a black background, on which the texts and images were applied in gold leaf or yellow paint (see fig. 165).

Once the anthropoid coffin had become established as the standard type, its evolution proceeded steadily. Multiple anthropoid coffins, placed one inside the other, began to be provided for private individuals as well as for kings and queens. Features adapted from rectangular coffins became steadily less obtrusive, as the design tended increasingly to reproduce the appearance of the ideal mummy-image of the deceased, and through the attributes of the mummy to emphasise his divine status. In the early 18th Dynasty, the arms began to be depicted on some royal coffins, crossed on the breast, the hands grasping amulets. Arms, or sometimes hands alone, were added to private coffins with increasing frequency from the middle of the Dynasty, the hands sometimes holding *djed* and *tit* amulets. The curled 'divine' beard was also added to the iconography. The conceptual link between coffin and tomb became less overt as iconography emphasised more strongly the coffin's role as a replica of the divine body; to this end, the distinction between the lid and the case was obscured by making the lateral inscriptions continue from lid to case, and by painting the details of the wig on the case as well as the lid. The importance attached to the external appearance is further underlined by the rarity of internal decoration on anthropoid coffins of the New Kingdom. A few exceptions are known, such as the depiction of Nut on the interior of one of the coffins of Tjuiu. This, how-

166. Small painted wooden coffin of the king's scribe Iny, found in the city of Akhetaten (modern el-Amarna). Since its decoration reproduces that of a full-size coffin, it is a valuable indication of the appearance of coffins produced during the religious 'revolution' of Akhenaten. Late 18th Dynasty, about 1352–1336 BC. L. 44.5 cm.

ever, may have been a feature taken from the design repertoire of kings' coffins. Tjuiu was the mother-in-law of Amenhotep III (*c.* 1390–1352 BC), and her coffins were almost certainly made in the royal workshops; indeed, the outer coffin of her husband Yuya is inscribed with the words 'made as a favour from the side of the King' – one of the royal donation formulae also found on *shabtis* such as those of Qenamun (see above, p. 134).

The fragmentary sarcophagi of Akhenaten (*c.* 1352–1336 BC) and other members of his family, recovered from the royal tomb at Amarna, reflect the religious changes promulgated during his reign. The most notable innovations are the suppression of traditional texts and images, redolent of the Osirian afterlife which the king had rejected, and the substitution of figures of Queen Nefertiti for those of the traditional goddesses at the corners of the king's sarcophagus. Few coffins of private individuals survive from this period, but a valuable indication of the likely appearance of the lost specimens is provided by a miniature wooden coffin from Amarna, which was found containing two pairs of ivory clappers. Perhaps originally a *shabti* container, it reproduces the decoration of a full-size coffin (see fig. 166). Traditional texts and figures of gods are replaced by scenes of offering to the deceased, who appears both as a mummy and as a living person.

Immediately after the Amarna Period, many of the traditional features of coffin design returned, but several important innovations are apparent. A new colour scheme was adopted, in which texts and images were painted in polychrome on a yellow background, perhaps to emphasise the idea of the deceased's resurrection through the brilliant rays of the sun. The old black-coloured coffins ceased to be made, finally disappearing in the reign of Ramesses II (*c.* 1279–1213 BC). Features of the mummy-iconography continued, arms and hands crossed on the breast becoming a standard element (fig. 167). The most remarkable innovation at this period was the creation of coffins and sarcophagi which represented the deceased as a living person, dressed in pleated linen garments, wearing a fashionable festal wig, and with the arms arranged in poses associated with the living.

167. Inner coffin of a woman of high status named Henutmehyt (see figs 88, 139 and 149). The iconography is typical of the 19th and 20th Dynasties. The representation of the crossed hands has become a standard feature, and the deceased wears an elaborate wig of the type worn in life on festal occasions. Figures of deities occupy all the compartments formed by the interconnecting bands of inscription. Early 19th Dynasty, about 1250 BC. From Thebes. H. 188 cm.

24789

168. Painted wooden coffin of an unnamed priest of Amun. The surface below the floral collar is densely packed with small figures of gods and symbols of resurrection. At this period, when the decoration of tomb chapels had almost ceased, the surfaces of the coffin were used to accommodate essential funerary imagery. Mid-21st Dynasty, about 1000 BC. From the 'cache of the priests of Amun' at Deir el-Bahri, Thebes. H. 185 cm.

Standardisation of the burial ensemble continued, with two anthropoid coffins becoming the norm for the burial of a high-status person. Mummy-masks, which had remained in use during the 18th Dynasty, were replaced after the Amarna Period by a 'mummy-board', a cover of painted wood or cartonnage which was placed directly over the mummy. Although wooden coffins remained the commonest type, stone sarcophagi were also made for some high-ranking officials. Both rectangular and anthropoid types were used. The earliest are the sarcophagi belonging to the Viceroy of Kush Merymose and Amenhotep son of Hapu (both dating to the reign of Amenhotep III, *c.* 1390–1352 BC). Anthropoid sarcophagi of the 19th Dynasty were made both in mummiform shape and in the image of the living person.

21st Dynasty

The stylistic distinction between royal and private coffins continued in the 21st Dynasty. The intact burial of King Psusennes I (*c.* 1039–991 BC), excavated at Tanis, comprised two reused stone sarcophagi of the New Kingdom and an anthropoid coffin of silver made specifically for Psusennes. The outermost sarcophagus had been made originally for Merenptah (*c.* 1213–1203 BC), and was extracted from his tomb in the Valley of the Kings and reinscribed. The silver mummy-case was strongly traditional in design, with *rishi* decoration and crossed arms grasping royal sceptres, which had been normal for kings' coffins at least since Tutankhamun (*c.*1336–1327 BC). Private individuals were still provided with two wooden anthropoid coffins and a mummy-board. The external surfaces were densely covered with figured scenes and brief texts, while all available spaces were filled with divine figures and symbols (see fig. 168). The colour scheme was normally red, green and blue on a yellow background, and a thick varnish sometimes made from *pistacia* resin intensified the overall yellow/orange colouration.

The scenes on the lid consisted chiefly of symbols of resurrection, notably the scarab beetle and winged sun-disc, and these were juxtaposed with figures of Nut and depictions of the deceased offering to various deities. The sides of the case were painted with a varied selection of scenes, some of which had already appeared in *Book of the Dead* papyri and tomb paintings: the weighing of the heart, the goddess Hathor as a cow emerging from the western mountain of the Theban necropolis (see fig. 169), and the deceased receiving food and drink from Nut, who stands within the branches of a tree. These were augmented with other vignettes belonging to a new repertoire of religious images which also occurred on the funerary papyri at this period, and which included scenes such as the creation of the universe by means of the separation of Geb and Nut. The insides of anthropoid coffins were now also regularly decorated. A large *djed* pillar, enfolded by wings, or a figure of the Goddess of the West (a manifestation of Hathor) was often painted on the floor, while a full-face *ba* bird frequently appeared above the head of the deceased, as though flying down to reunite with the corpse. The inner surfaces of the walls usually had rows of deities, some of

169. Exterior of the case of the outer coffin of the priest of Amun, Amenemope. The pictorial strip contains scenes familiar from tomb decoration of the New Kingdom, such as the goddess Hathor in the form of a cow, emerging from the slopes of the Theban necropolis. Early 22nd Dynasty, about 945–900 BC. L. of coffin 210 cm.

which represented the manifold forms assumed by the sun god during his journey through the night.

Many of these innovations seem to have originated at Thebes, at this time the centre of a virtually independent state controlled by the High Priests of Amun and only nominally under the authority of the kings in Tanis. The intensive use of coffin surfaces to accommodate this rich vein of theological imagery must in part have been a consequence of the decline in the production of decorated tombs (previously the main location of such decoration); the coffins, and the papyri with similar images, may even have taken the place of temple walls as a setting for the visual display of the theology of Amun. The vignettes became progressively complex, and some of the images combined allusions to several different mythological concepts simultaneously, as though to maximise the magical potential of the limited area available for decoration.

Towards the end of the 21st Dynasty the decoration of coffins of the Theban ruling élite began to be distinguished by very large floral collars and representations of red leather straps (*stola*), placed around the neck and crossing on the breast (see fig. 170). This device, originally of protective significance, was often depicted as worn by mummiform deities such as Amun, Min, Ptah and Osiris, and at the end of the New Kingdom the *stola* began to be placed on mummies (see p. 63). Its subsequent appearance among the attributes of mummiform coffins was a further indication that the iconography of the coffin had come to

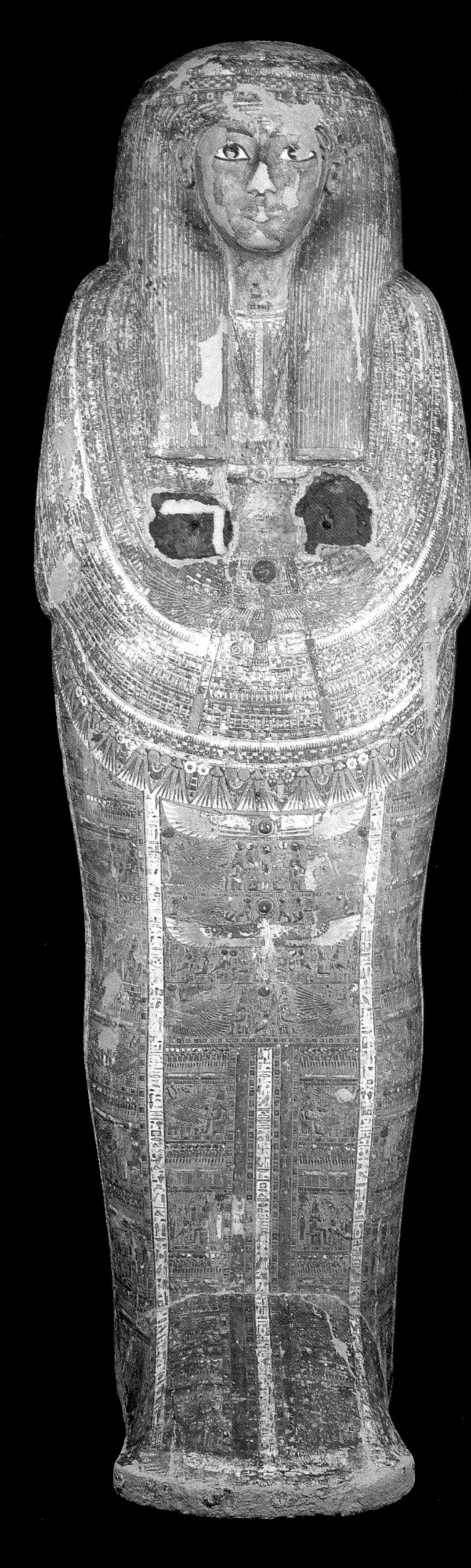

170. Lid of the outer coffin of the priest of Amun Amenemope. The evolution of coffins during the 21st Dynasty culminated in a type distinguished by a very large floral collar and the regular depiction of leather 'mummy braces' on the breast. In addition, there were several scenes and images which had previously been the prerogative of the king – notably the depiction of extracts from the *Book of Amduat* on the sides of the coffins. Early 22nd Dynasty, about 945–900 BC. H. 210 cm.

171. Painted wooden coffin of the priest of Khons in Thebes, Ankhefenkhons. The use of a limited palette on an ungessoed reddish wood background is characteristic of the rather austere style of coffin painting in the 22nd Dynasty. The design on the lid is one commonly found on cartonnage cases of the period. Below the collar is the sun god at dawn in the form of a ram-headed falcon. Other winged deities, including Isis and Nephthys, provide protection for the deceased. 22nd Dynasty, about 850 BC. From Thebes. H. 183 cm.

emphasise more strongly the divine nature of the dead person. The curled divine beard and fillet around the wig had already been added to the repertoire during the New Kingdom, and now, in addition, the deceased was often represented holding in each hand a *mekes*, or container for a rolled document which concerned the status of Osiris as the heir of the god Geb. It is on these same coffins of private individuals that scenes taken from the *royal* funerary repertoire become frequent, notably extracts from the *Amduat* (see pp. 198–9), while in some of the details of the scenes the deceased has royal attributes such as the crook and flail sceptres. This tendency, together with the appearance of the *stola* and *mekes*, points to a closer identification of the dead man with the world of the gods and the divine king. Perhaps the priests of Amun at Thebes enjoyed a relationship with the divine sphere which at other periods was more appropriate to that of the king, and had this manifested in the iconography of their coffins. These same coffins also re-emphasised the connection between coffin and tomb; on some examples, the space above the mummy's head carried patterns traditionally painted on the ceilings of tomb chapels, and the arrangement of scenes on the inner surfaces in horizontal strips recalls the 'picture-strip' style of Ramesside tomb-chapels (see p. 153). It is even possible to recognise in the different decorative elements echoes of the conceptual division which influenced tomb-design in the Ramesside period (see pp. 152–4). Among the most striking images on the interiors of these coffins are figures of the deified kings Amenhotep I (*c.* 1525–1504 BC) and Tuthmosis III (*c.* 1479–1425 BC) and the deceased offering to deities.

22nd Dynasty

The complex and sophisticated coffins of the early 22nd Dynasty were superseded by an alternative style of coffin, which differed strongly from what had gone before. The new types had perhaps been developed in the Delta and their adoption at Thebes may have been imposed by the early 22nd Dynasty kings as a measure to curb the independence of the priesthood there, the design of the priest's coffins having begun to suggest an unprecedented degree of equality between gods and mortals.

Wooden mummiform coffins continued to be made, but they were simplified both in physical form (hands and arms usually being omitted from the lid) and in decoration (see fig. 171). On many coffins the decoration was restricted to a coloured wig, face and collar, with brief inscriptions on the exterior and a figure of the goddess Nut painted full-face inside. On others, a more detailed decorative scheme was applied, but the complex and specific vignettes of the 21st Dynasty were avoided, and replaced by figures of gods arranged in symmetrical groupings, or by a series of apotropaic deities wielding knives, lizards and serpents. These figures belonged to a long-standing tradition (related entities had appeared on ivory wands in the Middle Kingdom and as wooden statues in royal tombs of the New Kingdom; see pp. 211–12). On some 22nd Dynasty coffins their place is taken by deities who guarded the gates to the netherworld, both

172. Painted wooden coffin of Djedkhonsefankh, treasury scribe of the domain of Amun. The colour black was closely associated by the Egyptians with death and resurrection. Djedkhonsefankh's face is covered with gold leaf, and has inlaid eyes, while the remainder of the decoration is executed in cream-coloured paint on black, a colour scheme common in the 22nd Dynasty. On the lid is a winged figure of the goddess Nut. Early 22nd Dynasty, about 945–850 BC. From Thebes. H. 193 cm.

groups having essentially the same function – to form a protective barrier around the deceased.

The innermost case was usually a mummiform envelope of cartonnage, made in one piece to fit closely around the corpse and laced together with string along the back (see fig. 173). The surfaces of these cases were painted in brilliant colours on a white, yellow or blue background. These cartonnages show a mixture of solar and Osirian iconography. A common design shows a large ram-headed falcon with outspread wings over the breast, rising above a second falcon and, below, emblems of Osiris such as the Abydos fetish or the *djed* pillar. The entire image probably represents the emergence of the sun at dawn from the

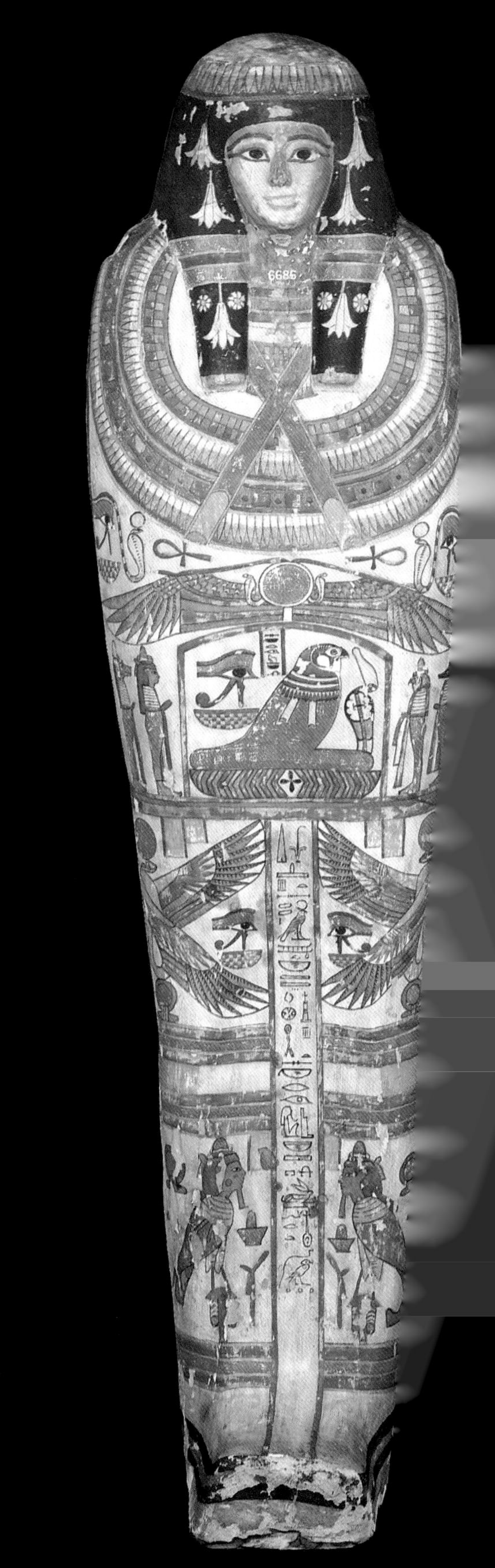

173. Cartonnage mummy-case made for an unidentified woman. The central inscription ends with a blank space for the name of the owner, which was never inserted. A red leather 'stole' (see p. 63) is represented on the breast, below which are depictions of the winged solar disc, Sokar-Osiris as a mummified falcon, the Sons of Horus, winged serpent goddesses and two *ba*-birds. 22nd Dynasty, about 850 BC. From Thebes. H. 170.5 cm.

underworld, a symbolic rebirth in which the deceased was to participate. A further allusion to the sun god at dawn is the scarab beetle, often painted on the top of the head, while the terrestrial realm of Osiris is symbolised again by the frequent depiction of the *djed* pillar on the back of the cartonnage case. Cases of this type have been found at many sites in Upper Egypt, and were even provided for the kings buried at Tanis, as the mummy-case of King Shoshenq II (*c.* 890 BC) demonstrates. This case also exemplifies another remarkable feature of royal coffins of the 22nd Dynasty, the substitution of the head of a falcon for the customary human face-mask. This striking iconography probably represented the deceased as the manifestation of Sokar-Osiris, and appears to have been also a feature of non-royal burials of high status, since an example was excavated in a 22nd Dynasty tomb at Tell Balamun in 1999.

174. Inner coffin of Ankhesnefer, daughter of Khonsmose. This type was very popular in the 25th and 26th Dynasties. The majority of the images and texts relate to the *Stundenwache*, the nocturnal vigil around the corpse of Osiris in the place of embalming, in which various gods and goddesses guarded the mummy from harmful influences. Isis and Nephthys are depicted at the foot and the head, and rows of deities along the sides of the body form a protective cordon around the deceased. 26th Dynasty, about 600–550 BC. From Thebes. H. 190.5 cm.

25th to 26th Dynasties

As with other aspects of the burial assemblage, significant changes in the design of coffins occurred towards the end of the eighth century BC. These changes reflect a different fundamental conception of the role of the coffins, which is most clearly manifested in those made for persons of high status.

A new type of anthropoid case was introduced, one which adopted features from sculptural models. In this iconography, the coffin represents the deceased in mummy form, standing on a rectangular plinth or pedestal, with a pillar supporting the back (see figs 174–5). This was essentially the same image as that adopted for *ushebti* figures and Ptah-Sokar-Osiris statues at the time, and was probably chosen to convey the concept of the resurrection of the deceased. The 'pillar and pedestal' shape was normally used only for the innermost coffin. This was now generally made of wood and, apart from rare survivals, it replaced the cartonnage mummy-cases of the 22nd Dynasty. The faces of these coffins were usually coloured red for men, and yellow or pink for women. Others were painted green to highlight the deceased's identification with Osiris.

As with earlier tombs and coffins, the coffin-ensembles of the 25th to 26th Dynasties fixed the deceased within several different cosmoi simultaneously. Figures on the exterior of the inner coffin recreated the environment of the tomb, with Isis and Nephthys at the foot and head of the bier, and a protective cordon of deities arrayed around the corpse (see fig. 138). This was a realisation of the vignette of the burial chamber, which illustrated spell 151 of the *Book of the Dead*. In mythological terms it represented the *Stundenwache*, a sequence of ritual acts and recitations performed for the protection and transfiguration of the mummified corpse of Osiris at each hour of the night and the day. Other decorative elements located the deceased within the daily cycle of the sun; this was alluded to by depictions of the rising sun on the heads of some coffins, and representations of the winged solar disc on the breast. Once cartonnage cases had been replaced by wooden inner coffins, it became again possible to paint the interior surfaces of the lid and case. The imagery of these inner surfaces frequently relates the deceased to the universe as a whole: the lid above the mummy

175. Rear of the inner coffin of Penamun-nebnesttawy, a priest of Amun. The sculptural morphology of the inner coffins of the 25th to 26th Dynasties is clearly illustrated by the three-dimensional back-pillar and the pedestal which supports the feet. The central area is dominated by a painting of the *djed* pillar, above which rises the sun at dawn. Late 25th Dynasty, about 680 BC. Probably from Thebes. H. 193 cm.

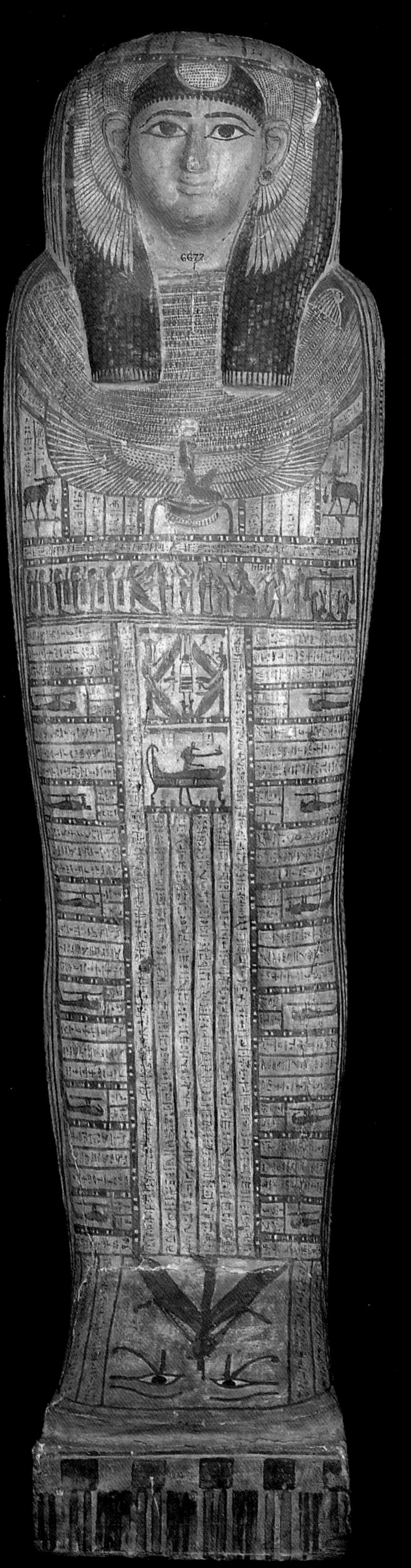

carries the figure of Nut, the sky-goddess, while the base beneath is decorated with the *Djed* pillar, symbolising the terrestrial realm ruled over by Osiris and protected by the Goddess of the West, a form of Hathor. The mummy of the deceased at the centre of this cocoon of potent images takes on the role of creator gods such as Osiris and Ra, who were the chief agents of resurrection. Further allusions to this concept are too numerous to list. One, found on 26th Dynasty inner coffins, is a long snake painted around the edge, its tail grasped in or meeting its mouth; this 'ouroboros' snake has various functions in Egyptian iconography, but here it undoubtedly protected the deceased, as did the 'Encircling Serpent' Mehen in depictions of the sun god in his barque.

The design of these inner coffins allotted much more space to inscriptions than had the cartonnage cases. On coffins made for persons of high status, these inscriptions often included substantial extracts from the *Book of the Dead* and other funerary compositions of earlier eras (see fig. 176). The selection of specific texts and their writing was a task for specialist scribes and would undoubtedly have increased the price of the finished product. Interestingly, even coffins of inferior workmanship (generally prepared for persons of lower status) often had extensive inscriptions, but the content was usually little more than repetitions of the standard offering formula. Alongside these heavily inscribed inner coffins, a simpler type persisted. The decoration of these coffins was predominantly pictorial, and some of the more popular design elements of earlier cartonnage cases were perpetuated in this way.

Just as tombs of earlier periods often contained or represented different structures, sometimes 'hidden' within their masonry, these inner coffins were nested in one, two or even three outer cases. At least one of these was always anthropoid, though of a more traditional shape than the inner coffin, with an undecorated, flat base showing that it was intended to lie horizontally. When functioning as an intermediary coffin, this type usually bore very simple decoration, consisting of little more than the painted face, wig and collar, with brief offering formulae on the lid and sides. In other burials this larger anthropoid case was the outermost coffin of the set, and was then more extensively painted with figures of protective deities and often a scene of the deceased's judgement.

In high status burials the outermost coffin was of rectangular shape, with a barrel-vaulted top and a freestanding post at each corner. This *qersu* type was derived from the shape of coffins and sarcophagi of the Old Kingdom, and ultimately from the traditional iconography of the *per-nu* shrine of Lower Egypt. This shrine never in fact possessed corner 'posts'; they owe their existence to an artistic misinterpretation of earlier two-dimensional images. These coffins provided the vehicle for yet another cosmogram. The vaulted lid represented the arch of heaven, and usually bore two images of the sun god travelling in his barque pulled by a row of deities. The case again symbolised the earthly realm in which Osiris – and by assimilation the deceased – dwelt. The use of a shrine-like form was of course another means of promoting the notion of the divine status of the deceased.

176. Interior of the inner anthropoid coffin of Hor, priest of Montu (see fig. 13). Texts inscribed on the internal surfaces of the coffin – like those on rectangular coffins of the Middle Kingdom – were directly accessible to the deceased, who could thus pronounce them for his benefit. In this example, scribal errors have been corrected and inappropriate signs painted over. 25th Dynasty, about 700–680 BC. From Thebes. H. 180 cm.

177. Painted wooden coffin of a man named Itineb. The green colouring of the face was a frequent feature of coffins made after about 650 BC, and symbolised the identification of the deceased with the god Osiris (see fig. 11). On the breast the goddess Nut, flanked by Isis and Nephthys, spreads her wings in protection, and below this is a scene of the weighing of the dead man's heart before Osiris. Most of the remaining space is occupied by twenty compartments in each of which Itineb is shown adoring a different god or goddess; the associated texts explain that his various bodily members are identified with those of the deity depicted. 26th Dynasty or later, about 600–300 BC. From Saqqara. H. 183 cm.

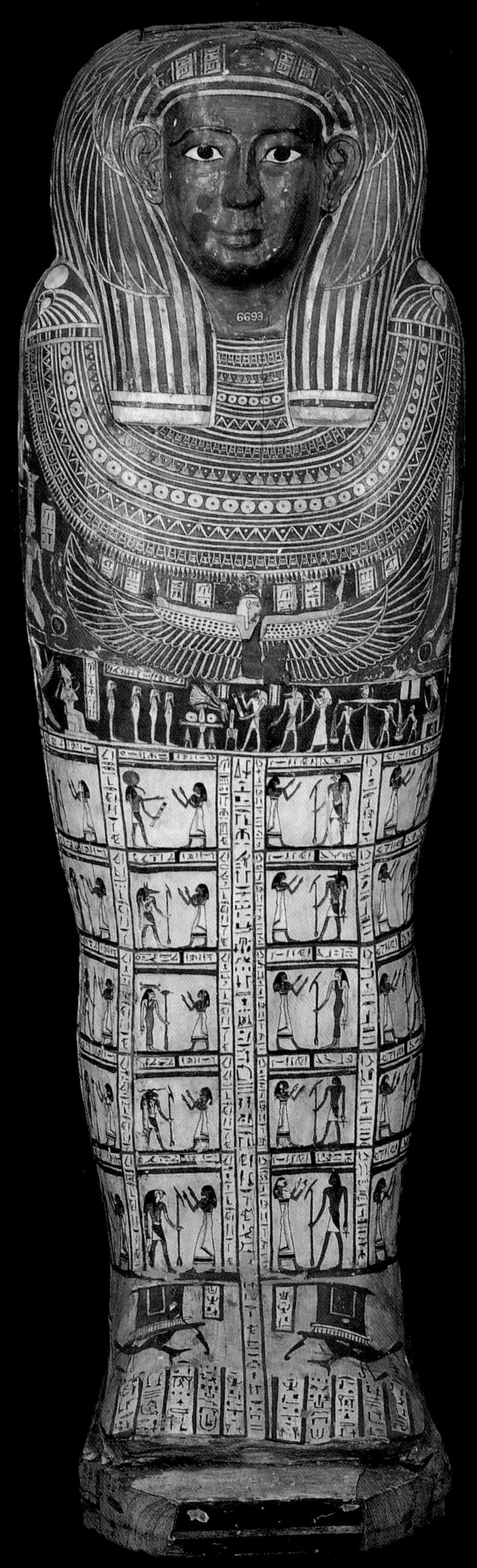

These wooden coffins were extensively used in Upper Egypt: many examples having been found at Thebes and at other sites such as Akhmim. Relatively few burials in the south of Egypt made use of stone sarcophagi in this period, but these became increasingly common in the tombs of high-ranking officials, particularly in the north of the country from the 26th Dynasty to the Ptolemaic Period. Anthropoid sarcophagi once again became fashionable and these closely imitated the appearance of the contemporary wooden coffins. Rectangular or cartouche-shaped sarcophagi also made a reappearance, their surfaces densely covered with images and texts. These include the *Pyramid Texts* and *Book of the Dead*, besides elements of the *Stundenwache*. Particularly full versions of the latter (doubtless taken from Egyptian sources) occur on the massive stone sarcophagi made for the Kushite rulers Anlamani (623–593 BC) and Aspelta (593–568 BC) from Nuri. These exemplify the wholesale adoption by post-25th Dynasty Nubian kings of major elements of Egyptian burial practice.

Post-26th Dynasty

The new types of coffin and sarcophagus introduced in the 25th Dynasty remained in use until the Ptolemaic Period. Among the more significant developments which can be observed in this period is the change in the proportions of anthropoid coffins (see fig. 177). Greater emphasis was given to the head, wig and chest, which became substantially enlarged. The back-pillar and pedestal were retained, and the latter began to appear on outer as well as inner coffins. The reproduction of mummy-trappings again became obtrusive, particularly with regard to the collar, which was extended to cover much of the breast. The range of textual and pictorial matter applied to the surfaces was reduced, and on many coffins of this period the main elements of decoration were a winged scarab, solar disc or figure of Nut, and a scene of the mummy on a lion-headed

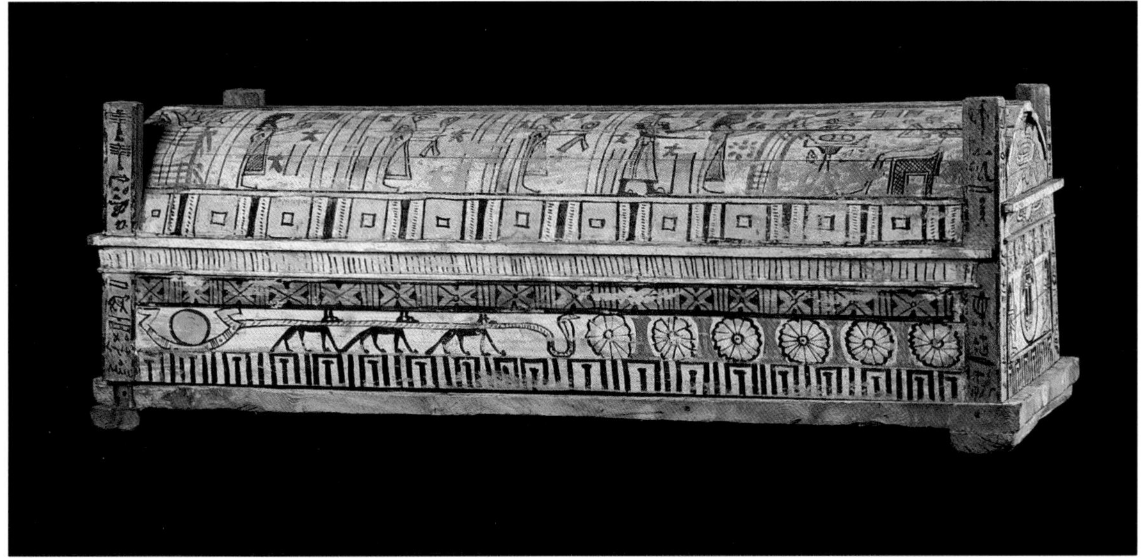

178. Painted wooden coffin of Tphous. The type, with a vaulted top and four corner-posts, became popular in élite burials in the 25th Dynasty and was still used in the Roman Period. The painted scenes include the adoration of Osiris, jackals towing the barque of the sun god, the winged solar disc and the scarab beetle flanked by lamenting goddesses. From the family tomb of the official Soter at Thebes. L. 147 cm.

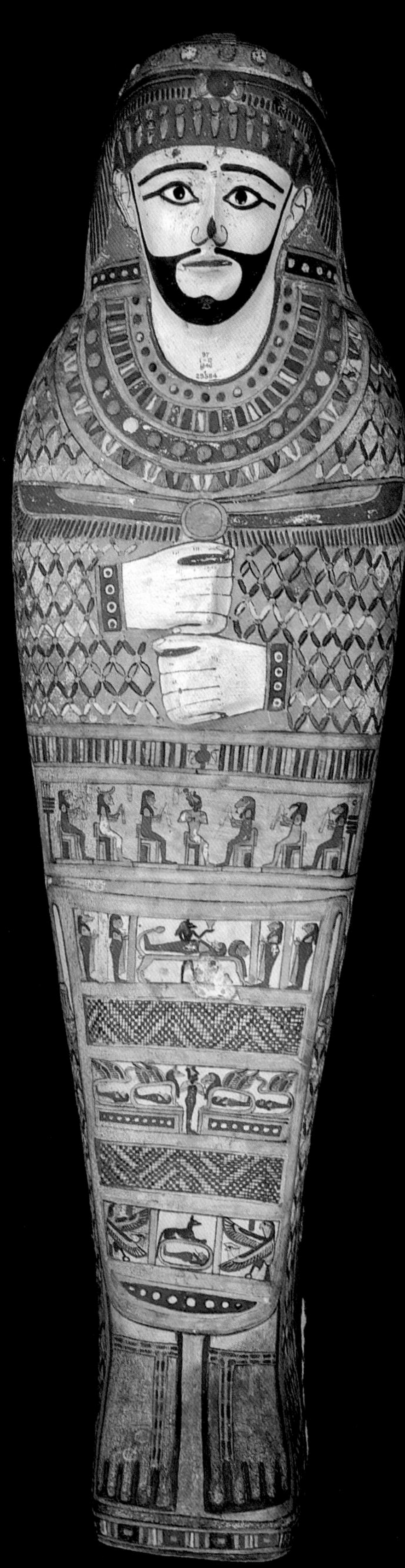

179. This mummy-case is made of mud coated with linen and plaster, with inlaid eyes of glass. It is decorated with a range of traditional Egyptian images, including the winged solar disc, Osiris, Anubis and other deities, and a bead-net design (see fig. 148). The bearded face and the depiction of the exposed feet wearing sandals are, however, more reminiscent of Classical styles. About 50 BC–AD 50. From Akhmim. H. 174 cm.

funerary bier, sometimes attended by Anubis. The texts, while derived from earlier sources, are often ineptly written and contain numerous scribal errors. The mummies were frequently provided with cartonnage coverings, ranging from complete body-cases to ensembles comprising a separate mask, collar, apron and footcase, decorated with short texts and figures of divinities. Bound captives were sometimes painted on the underneath of the footcases, enabling the deceased symbolically to tread his enemies underfoot.

Although anthropoid wooden coffins remained the usual type, some individuals were still buried in a rectangular case with vaulted top and corner posts. This type was being used as late as the second century AD. Among the latest known examples are the coffins of the Theban official Soter and members of his family, which display a mixture of traditional Egyptian motifs (solar barque, judgement scene and full-face Nut figure) and elements from the Hellenistic world, such as the signs of zodiac (see fig. 178). Inner coffins were not provided with these burials, the mummies being instead wrapped in painted shrouds.

The Roman Period witnessed the last manifestations of the long tradition of Egyptian coffin-production. Anthropoid cases of wood were relatively rare, although cartonnage body-cases continued to be produced. These were now increasingly constructed from mud or discarded papyrus, rather than linen, and their iconography – like that of the Soter coffins – blended Egyptian and Hellenistic features (see figs 179–80). Many mummies were buried without coffins, instead being provided with gilded cartonnage masks or plaster heads, while others had portrait-panels in encaustic or tempera inserted into the outer wrappings. In some cases, such as the mummy of Artemidorus from Hawara (see fig. 52), a stucco body-case provided the base for traditional pharaonic funerary images, but the mechanical way in which these were reproduced indicates that much of their original significance had been forgotten.

180. This mummy of a boy (radiography of the body suggests it is that of a young infant) has been wrapped and adorned in a style characteristic of the early Roman Period. The gilded cartonnage headpiece represents an idealised face crowned with stylised curls. The boy wears a mantle, tunic and necklace, and holds a bunch of rosebuds and myrtle, a classical attribute signifiying good fortune. By contrast, the paintings on the torso are drawn from Egyptian traditions. Images which were usually applied to the coffin in earlier periods have thus been transferred to the wrappings of the mummy itself (see fig. 52). A cartonnage footcase, with a depiction of the feet wearing sandals, completes the adornments. About AD 40–60. From Hawara. H. 85.5 cm.

CHAPTER 8

The Burial and Mummification of Animals

Mummification was carried out not only on the bodies of humans, but also on those of animals. In a few cases, these were pets whose companionship their owners perhaps wished to retain in the afterlife, whereas other animals were mummified as food offerings for the dead. However, the vast majority of mummified animals were allotted this treatment for religious reasons. In fact, the number of animals which were mummified far exceeded that of humans, running to several millions.

The role of animals in ancient Egyptian society

The lives of the Egyptians were permeated and influenced by those of animals to a degree almost unprecedented in the ancient world. At all periods the Egyptians maintained an intimate and sensitive relationship with their environment, an important element of which was the exceptionally rich and varied fauna. Moving from a hunting and gathering economy to an agricultural one, they naturally at first perceived animals largely as prey and as a source of food. The domestication and breeding of animals had begun by the fifth millennium BC, and cattle, sheep, goats, pigs and poultry were extensively exploited throughout the historic period. With the beginnings of an agricultural society, involving animal husbandry, a closer relationship with animals was developed. Throughout the pharaonic period, they served as a source of food, as draught animals, and as transport, while their hides were used for clothing and leather, and bones, feathers, sinews, horns, fat and dung were put to other practical uses. Some creatures, however, particularly cats, dogs, monkeys, geese, and gazelles, were also kept as pets. There were few aspects of society and culture in ancient Egypt which remained uninfluenced by animals, but it was in the sphere of religious beliefs and cult practices that they left their deepest imprint.

It was perhaps inevitable that animals would acquire divine associations for the Egyptians. The special qualities of different creatures impressed themselves on human observers: the virility of the bull, the swiftness of the hare, the strength of the lion, the ferocity of the crocodile, the soaring flight and keen eyesight of the falcon. These attributes might inspire admiration, wonder or fear. At an early stage animals became venerated, their worship probably arising out of a desire to either manipulate their positive qualities or avert harmful ones. Out of such attitudes were born animal cults, and these flourished in many different parts of Egypt. The local communities of the prehistoric period which ultimately developed into the provinces, or nomes, of pharaonic Egypt were sometimes identified by emblems or standards in animal shape – the falcon, the oryx, the hare, and others – and these totems may also have played a part in the formation of animal cults. Such cults are often regarded as hallmarks of the religious attitudes of relatively primitive societies, yet even after the evolution of much more sophisticated modes of religious thought among the Egyptians, the association of animals with deities persisted, largely because divine beings were regarded as capable of being manifested in a variety of physical forms, including statues, celestial bodies or animals. The evolution of the supernatural entities which we refer to as 'gods' involved the attribution to many of them of the qualities of particular creatures. Thus the characteristics of the falcon belonged to Horus, those of the lioness or cat to Bastet, and those of the jackal to Anubis. Such relationships were eventually given visible representation in art by depicting the deities either in the form of the animal or in human shape with the head of that animal – a practice which attracted the ridicule of some classical and later observers. By this period, however, it was not the animals themselves that were worshipped; such depictions were not intended to be understood literally, but rather as metaphors, to convey some of the characteristics of particular deities. To refer to Horus as the 'falcon-god', or Anubis as the 'jackal-god' thus is grossly to oversimplify the interpretation of the evidence. The association of various animals with particular deities involved numerous subtle levels of meaning, and is a subject too complex to be considered here. In the following paragraphs we will concentrate on those aspects which led to the mummification and ritual burial of animals.

Sacred animals

The role of animals in Egyptian religion was not limited to graphic portrayals of the gods with animal attributes. Actual specimens of animals both living and dead played a crucial role in cult practices.

181. One of a group of mummified bulls from Thebes. The horns, ears and facial details are imitated in coloured linen, and the frontal wrappings are arranged in an elaborate geometrical pattern. Although this animal was not an Apis bull, its trappings included the triangular patch on the forehead which was one of the distinguishing marks of the Apis. Radiography of this group shows that they died aged between six and twelve months and indicates that the post-cranial remains were prepared on a board, which was incorporated into the wrappings. Roman Period, after 30 BC. H. 45.7 cm.

These sacred animals fell into several categories, of which the most important was the 'temple animal'. This was a creature considered to be a physical incarnation of the god; like a cult statue, it served as a receptacle in which the non-physical essence of the deity could be manifested – more specifically, his *ba*. The animal was thus distinct from the god himself, yet enjoyed a unique relationship with him. The Apis bull was the *ba* of the god Ptah of Memphis; in other words, it was (in the original meaning of the word *ba*, see p. 20) the manifestation of Ptah's power. In the same way, the Buchis bull venerated at Armant was the *ba* of the god Ra, and the sacred ram venerated at the city of Mendes was the *ba* of the god Osiris. These animals had special significance because only a single example of the species was considered to embody the *ba* of the deity at any one time. This unique creature could be recognised by special markings on the body. Once identified by the priests, it was installed in a temple until its death, when it received individual burial with all the formalities accorded to a person of the highest status, including a relatively high standard of mummification.

Other animals were also held to be sacred, but on different terms to those applied to the temple animal (see below, pp. 254–60). No single creature was distinguished as the *ba* or manifestation of the deity, but all examples of the appropriate species were held to be sacred and were in some sense representatives of the deity on earth. They were not, however, the focus of a cult, and were generally buried *en masse*, although they did receive mummification.

The divine associations of animals can be traced as far back as the late Predynastic period. Ritual burials of cattle, baboons, crocodiles, hippopotami and other species have been discovered in Naqada II–III contexts at Hierakonpolis. However, the connections between animals and cult became most emphatically obtrusive in the Late Period and the Ptolemaic-Roman periods, when animal cults became very prominent and their cemeteries expanded enormously. This rise to prominence may have been in part a consequence of an upsurge of popular religious practices. While certain animals had long been associated with major state cults, it is likely that many more animal cults had flourished chiefly among the peasants, leaving relatively little trace in the archaeological record until the mid first millennium BC. The immediately preceding centuries had witnessed political and social changes in Egypt, of which the rule of Libyans, Nubians, Assyrians and Persians had been only the most conspicuous. The changes perhaps brought a move of nationalism, one manifestation being the promoting of peculiarly Egyptian religious practices as a means of asserting national identity. The association of animals with divinity was one of the most conspicuous of these features. Indeed, Greeks and Romans who visited Egypt regarded the animal cults as the most distinctive aspect of the Egyptians' religious practices, although many were clearly puzzled by the contradiction which such 'primitive' practices appeared to offer to the sophistication of other aspects of Egyptian culture. But the late development of animal cults was not purely a popular phenomenon. The huge expansion of cult places and cemeteries associated with sacred animals owed much to active encouragement by the state in the reigns of Ahmose II (570–526 BC), Nectanebo I and II (380–343 BC), and Ptolemy I (305–285 BC). The number of officials serving such cults was greatly increased, and the sale of these offices, together with the taxation of the cult centres doubtless yielded revenue for the crown, in turn.

Did animals have an afterlife?

The majority of the animals mummified in the Late-Roman periods were not assimilated to humans, and for them no afterlife appears to have been envisaged. The situation appears to be different, however, for those animals which were treated to the performance of the full funerary rituals employed for humans, including mummification, the Opening of the Mouth and the offering ritual. This applies to temple animals and favoured pets. The provision of heart scarabs for Apis and Mnevis bulls, and other amulets, together with funerary texts in tombs and on sarcophagi, also suggest that the animal was expected to undergo transfiguration and rebirth. The descriptions of the realm of the dead given in the *Books of the Netherworld* give no hint that it was also inhabited by transfigured animals. Yet, insofar as the hereafter was expected to replicate the environment of the living it is logical to assume that this would also include animals, and indeed the depictions and models of animals found in tombs of many periods were placed there in the expectation that they would be accessible to the tomb-owner in the afterlife. What we lack is any clear explication of the individual fate of animals who had undergone ritual burial and transfiguration.

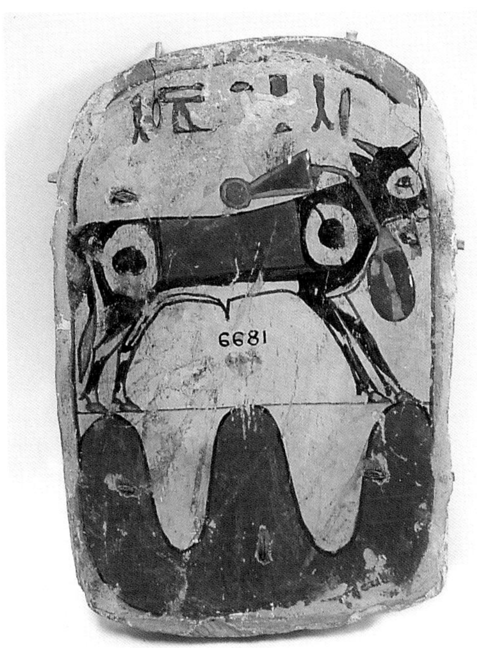

182. The Apis bull, painted on the wooden footboard of the cartonnage mummy-case of an official named Peftjauemawikhons. The bull is depicted as a pied animal wearing a *menyet*-collar with counterpoise. Early 25th Dynasty, about 720–700 BC. Probably from Thebes. L. of case 169 cm.

Sacred Bulls

The most important of the sacred animals was the Apis bull. Apis, originally a god associated with fertility, is mentioned in texts as early as the 1st Dynasty, but his association with the god Ptah of Memphis came later, when he is described as the *ba* or 'herald' (*wehem*) of Ptah. Apis was believed to be incarnate in a bull, born to a virgin cow which was supposed to have been impregnated by Ptah through the agency of fire from heaven (perhaps a bolt of lightning). When an Apis died, a successor was chosen by priests who travelled throughout Egypt searching for the new-born calf which was the next incarnation of Apis. This calf was identified by means of specific body markings. According to Herodotus, the hide of the bull was black, with a white triangle on the forehead, and a mark shaped like an 'eagle' on the back, while 'double hairs' were to be found in the tail and a scarab beetle-shaped mark on the tongue. Bronze figurines of the later first millennium BC show the triangular mark on the forehead, and a vulture and a winged scarab or sun-disc on the back, but paintings of the Apis on coffins

183. Calcite (alabaster) tables for the embalming of the Apis bulls at Memphis. The majority of the tables are carved to represent lion-shaped couches, a type of structure also used for the mummification of humans. Fourth century BC.

from the same general period usually depict it as pied rather than black (see fig. 182). Once identified, the bull was taken in procession to the temple of Ptah at Memphis. Here he was formally inaugurated, and began a life of luxury, pampered by attendants and fed on the richest foods in a special temple of his own, where he received the veneration of worshippers.

The death of the Apis bull was an occasion for national mourning. The practice of giving the bull an elaborate burial seems to date from the reign of Amenhotep III (*c.*1390–1352 BC). At this time there are signs of a strongly increased royal interest in such animal cults and in the special arrangements made for them after death. The burials of the Apis bulls were made at Saqqara, at first in separate chambers, and later in rooms opening off subterranean catacombs. The deceased Apis was identified with Osiris, and was referred to as Osiris-Apis or Osorapis. This name gave rise to the Graecised Serapis, and from this the burial galleries at Saqqara became known as the Serapeum.

Each bull was mummified at death. The rites echoed those of human mummification, beginning with a ritual washing, and proceeding to drying, anointing and wrapping. Indeed, there is evidence that the embalmers who carried out the operation also mummified humans, thus maintaining their skills in the interim between Apis burials, which occurred an average of eighteen years apart. The place of embalming of the Apis bulls has been discovered, south-west of the temple of Ptah at Memphis. This structure dated to the 26th Dynasty, and contained eight large calcite (alabaster) tables carved to imitate the lion-shaped supports used for the mummification of human bodies, and with a receptacle at the foot-end to catch fluids (see fig. 183). The procedure followed is described in a demotic papyrus dating to the Ptolemaic Period, now preserved in Vienna. The body was placed on a layer of clean sand to ensure its ritual purity. According to the papyrus, it was eviscerated via an incision in the left flank, the heart alone being left *in situ*. Some of the Apis burials of the New Kingdom included large canopic jars, though whether these really contained parts of the body or were purely ritual in function cannot be determined. The body cavity was packed with bags of sawdust and natron, to help the corpse retain its shape and – presumably – to absorb moisture, as in human embalming. The wrapping, which occupied sixteen days, took place with the body lying on a board, along the edges of which were fixed metal clamps. The application of the wrappings was a highly ritualised process; the Vienna papyrus records precise instructions for the preparation and application of every piece of cloth. The texts mention that the wrappings were to be secured by passing them through the clamps and beneath the baseboard. This technique has been confirmed through the discoveries of the mummies of Buchis bulls at Armant, which were also prepared on a board, associated with clamps of bronze or iron. The bull was provided with eyes made of glass and stone, and artificial hooves of gold were substituted for the real hooves – corresponding to the application of finger and toe stalls to human corpses.

A stela dated to year 30 of the reign of Ramesses II (*c.* 1279–1213 BC) mentions the mummification of an Apis which had just died, and states that the body was in the embalmer's workshop for seventy days, exactly as would be expected for the mummification of a human body. Other stelae show the funerary rituals performed before the interment of the bull, and here again the acts carried out mirror those in human burial, with an Opening of the Mouth ceremony to restore the use of the bodily faculties.

The mummies of the bulls were taken to the Serapeum at Saqqara for burial. A processional way lined by sphinxes led to the burial place, and the catafalque containing the bull in its coffin was dragged along by soldiers. At the end of the sphinx-avenue stood a temple to Osiris-Apis built early in the reign of Nectanebo II (360–343 BC), the last native-born pharaoh of Egypt. This temple, the 'Place of the Living Apis', served the cult of the deity, though no remains of it survive today.

The Serapeum, with its associated temple and avenue of sphinxes, was well-known to the Greeks and Romans, and was described in the *Geography* of Strabo. Later covered with sand and lost to view, its location was deduced by the English collector Anthony Harris in the mid-nineteenth century and was actually rediscovered by Auguste Mariette in 1851–2. The earliest graves so far discovered were separately constructed. One of them was found undisturbed, and contained the mummies of two bulls who had died in the reign of Ramesses II (*c.*1279–1213 BC). The chamber was faced with limestone on which was a painted depiction of the pharaoh with his son prince Khaemwaset offering to the Apis bull. The mummies lay inside wooden coffins and were adorned with rich jewellery and amulets. They were even provided with bull-headed *shabti* figures. From the later years of the reign of Ramesses II the method of interment changed, each bull being placed in one of a series of chambers which opened from subterranean galleries. The Serapeum remained in use from the New Kingdom to the Ptolemaic Period, although not all the burial places of the bulls from this long time-span have been identified. Each chamber contained a sarcophagus. Those of the 18th to 26th Dynasties were made of gilded wood, while those of the later periods were massive chests hewn from granite blocks, the largest approaching 70 tons in weight. The individual vaults were originally faced with limestone, and many stelae were set up there (see fig. 184). These included formal records of the lives of the bulls, giving the dates of their death and burial, and those of their birth and installation at Memphis. Since the age of the animal at death is often included, these stelae are an important source for the reconstruction of ancient Egyptian chronology. Besides these, there were hundreds of stelae inscribed in hieroglyphic, hieratic and demotic, set up by private individuals to express their piety and devotion to the Apis bull. Many of these stelae were set into the walls of the corridors, where they would be seen by visitors to the Serapeum.

184. Limestone stela dedicated to the Apis bull by a man named Padebehu(en)aset. The devotee is shown kneeling before the bull, behind whom stands a goddess, probably Isis. Probably 26th Dynasty, 664–525 BC. Provenance unrecorded, but probably from the Serapeum at Saqqara. H. 28 cm.

186. Bronze clamps used in the mummification of a Buchis bull. The clamps were located around the edge of the wooden board on which the body was prepared, and served to secure the linen wrappings in place. Ptolemaic or Roman Period, after 305 BC. From the Bucheum at Armant. L. (left) 11.5, (right) 17.5 cm.

The Buchis was closely associated with the sun god Ra and with Montu, an ancient deity of the Theban region who had cult-centres at Medamud, Thebes and Tod as well as at Armant. Like the Apis, the Buchis bull was supposed to have been divinely conceived and born to a virgin cow. The new Buchis, too, was identified by priests on the grounds of physical markings; his body was probably white with a black head. The bull was installed at Thebes and subsequently transported by barge to Armant, his principal residence,where a whole staff of priests and feeders attended to his requirements. The burials of the Buchis bulls were located in a special cemetery now known as the 'Bucheum' at Armant. This seems to have been founded in the reign of Nectanebo II (360–343 BC) of the 30th Dynasty, and the series of burials continued at least until the reign of the emperor Diocletian (AD 284–305). Some of the tombs were individually constructed, with vaulted roofs; in other cases the bulls did not have separate chambers but were laid in the corridors between the tombs of earlier bulls.

The Buchis burials are very informative about the methods used to prepare the bodies and the ritual aspects of the interment. The bodies were placed on

185. Both the Buchis bulls and their mothers were mummified and buried at Armant. The Mothers of Buchis were interred in subterranean vaults at Baqaria, north-east of the Bucheum itself. Their bodies were embalmed in a similar style to those of their offspring, though generally with fewer burial goods. This burial of a cow (Baqaria tomb 16) shows clearly the metal clamps through which the wrappings were passed. First century AD.

187. Reconstruction of the burial of a Buchis bull in the cemetery at Armant. At the rear is the stone sarcophagus in its vault, and in the foreground a stela of the emperor Valerian, an inscribed offering table and pottery offering stands.

boards, into which clamps of bronze and iron had been fixed (see fig. 186). The body was wrapped by passing the wrappings through these clamps which were situated along the edges of the board and flanking the limbs, as described in the Apis embalming ritual in the Vienna papyrus (see fig. 185). In contrast to the treatment of the Apis bulls, there is no evidence that the bodies were eviscerated via an incision; the internal organs may have been treated using an injection of fluid into the anus. The external trappings of the mummies were elaborate, including gilded plaster masks with inlaid eyes set in bronze surrounds, and a headdress of gilded wood with coloured glass inlays. Amulets similar to those made for humans were provided. In the more elaborate burials an offering table with ritual vessels was also supplied (see fig. 187), and stelae were set up, giving details of the life and death of the bull. They bear at the top a scene showing the monarch offering to the bull or burning incense before it (see fig. 188). Whereas many votive stelae were set up at the Serapeum, only a few examples of this type of monument were recovered from the burial place of the Buchis bulls, although there were numerous small votive plaques.

Apart from Apis and Buchis, the most important bovine temple animal was the Mnevis bull, which was the manifestation or 'herald' of Ra; it was venerated at Heliopolis (see fig. 189). The early history of this bull is poorly documented but by the New Kingdom it had acquired great importance. As a manifestation of the sun god, special provision for it was even made in the extreme theological system of Akhenaten (*c.* 1352–1336 BC). Like Apis, the Mnevis bull was distinguished by external signs and had to be searched for at the death of the old bull. The Mnevis also was mummified at death and buried in a special tomb; however, only two of these tombs have been discovered, dating to the reigns of Ramesses II (*c.* 1279–1213 BC) and Ramesses VII (*c.* 1136–1129 BC). Located to the north of Heliopolis, they consisted of roofed chambers constructed of limestone blocks below ground-level. The walls of the tombs were inscribed and covered with reliefs, and the burials were accompanied by offering tables and stelae. The mummies were provided with amulets and canopic jars, the latter perhaps non-functional. Although archaeological traces of later burials have so far not been found, there is documentary evidence that Mnevis burials continued long into the Roman era. A letter written on papyrus by the priests of the temple of Ra and Atum-Mnevis at Heliopolis records the receipt of linen for the burial of a Mnevis bull in AD 210–211.

188. Sandstone stela dated in the 13th year of the reign of Ptolemy II (285–246 BC), recording the death of a Buchis bull who was aged twenty years, eight months and thirteen days. From the Bucheum at Armant. H. 55 cm.

189. Limestone stela showing a sacred bull whose name is damaged, but who is accompanied by the distinctive epithet of Mnevis, 'he who causes truth [*maat*] to ascend to Atum'. The lower register shows the dedicator of the stela, the lector-priest Amenmose. Probably 19th Dynasty, about 1295–1186 BC. Provenance unknown. H. 38 cm.

Towards the end of the first millennium BC the proliferation of animal cults in Egypt led to the establishment of cemeteries for the mothers of sacred bulls, which were themselves considered sacred since they had borne the divine animal. Burial places for the Mothers of Apis and Buchis have been found at Saqqara and Armant respectively.

Sacred rams

In a manner analogous to that of the bulls, sacred rams were also regarded as the sole manifestation of particular deities. The ram Banebdjedet was revered at Mendes in the Delta, and at Elephantine were the burials of rams which were representative of the local god Khnum. They were mummified and adorned with gilded masks incorporating elaborate headdresses, and then placed in stone sarcophagi.

OTHER SACRED ANIMALS

The notion that animals were manifestations or representatives of deities developed steadily during the first millennium BC, with particular emphasis on the idea that *all* examples of a particular species could be regarded as sacred to the deity in question. This led to the keeping of large numbers of animals at the temple of the deity to whom they were sacred, where they were bred and maintained, with a special complement of priests and attendants to take care of their feeding. They acquired their main significance at death, when their bodies were mummified and given ritual burial. This practice was carefully managed by the priests of the temple, and gave pilgrims the opportunity to express their devotion to the god. When visiting the temple a pilgrim could make a donation which would in theory pay for the embalming of a sacred animal. The animals were then ritually buried in special cemeteries by priests on behalf of the dedicators. This expression of devotion was part of a reciprocal arrangement, the balance of which was that the devotee expected some benefit from the god. This might be relief from sickness or the answer to some problem, which might be delivered in the form of an oracle from the god or via a communication in a dream. The temples incorporated special dormitories for pilgrims, in which these dreams might be experienced, besides workshops in which the embalming of the animals took place.

It is clear that royal patronage played a significant role in the promotion of animal cults, which was such a distinctive feature of Egyptian culture in the late first millennium BC. The construction and endowment of large temple complexes, menageries and animal cemeteries required state support, and it is possible that the adoration of sacred animals was closely connected with the worship of the king.

One of the most extensive (and best-documented) complexes devoted to animal cults was excavated at north Saqqara by the Egypt Exploration Society initially under W.B. Emery, then under G.T. Martin and H.S. Smith, between 1964 and 1976. The nucleus of this great complex was the Serapeum, which increasingly with the passage of time came to be a focus for pilgrimage, and required a priesthood to interpret and manage the oracles of the god. The cult of Apis was later augmented (perhaps in the sixth century BC) by that of the Mother of Apis, who became identified with Isis. The mummified bodies of these cows were also allotted a special burial place, initially in a temple dedicated to Hathor, and later in the cliffs north of the Serapeum. Further animal cults were added as the centuries passed. A cult of Thoth, the god of wisdom and writing who was also associated with the moon, was established at Saqqara, where he was venerated as the father of Isis, mother of Apis. Thoth was associated with both the ibis and the baboon, and large numbers of mummies of these animals were deposited there. Horus was also represented by falcon mummies; ideologically the presence of this solar deity provided a harmonious balance to the lunar Thoth, while Horus as son of Osiris, had a manifest relationship with the deceased Apis, himself identified with Osiris.

The steady growth in popularity of these cults owed much to a belief in the oracular powers of the deceased sacred animals, which were believed to be able to reveal future events. To cater for these cults at Saqqara a series of temples and shrines was constructed, stretching northwards along a wadi towards the 'lake of pharaoh'. Pilgrims came to this spot from all over Egypt and from other parts of the eastern Mediterranean. A community grew around the temples and shrines to cater for the needs of these people. In addition to the numerous priests and minor officials who maintained the cults, there were the embalmers who mummified the sacred animals and the labourers who cut the catacombs and stone sarcophagi. There were also other craftsmen who produced bronze statuettes for presentation as votive offerings, astrologers and fortune-tellers, and those who provided lodgings for the many visitors. The life of this society is abundantly documented by many written records on papyri and on ostraca. These include the personal archive of a man named Hor, which reveals details of the day-to-day management of the sacred animal cults, besides throwing light on dishonest practices among the priests.

The range of creatures which was mummified was extensive, including cats, dogs, crocodiles, bulls and cows, rams, baboons, falcons, ibises, lizards, snakes, and even beetles. Some of the deities represented by these animals were worshipped throughout Egypt, while others were 'local' deities, and the attitude to a particular creature varied from place to place. An animal venerated in one province could be reviled in another, and such differences sometimes formed the pretext for clashes between the inhabitants of neighbouring cities.

The mummified animals were buried in mass graves. At some places, such as Thebes and Asyut, rock-cut tombs of earlier periods were reused for this purpose. At the former site, tombs have yielded mummies of bulls, gazelles, ibises, falcons, baboons, cats, rams and crocodiles. A large tomb at Dra Abu el-Naga was reused in the Ptolemaic Period as a necropolis for ibises and falcons, and a series of demotic graffiti on the walls record the names of many of the priests who were connected with the cemetery of these birds. Elsewhere, extensive subterranean galleries were excavated, containing many chambers which were filled to the ceiling with animal mummies. The best-known examples are the Serapeum and the catacombs of other animals at Saqqara; a crocodile cemetery near Manfalut seems to have been installed in caverns of natural origin.

The priests who served the cults and the burial places of sacred animals were organised in groups, and some of the posts were hereditary. One such group, the 'bearers of the gods' (equivalent to the Greek *theagoi*), is often mentioned in papyri and graffiti of the Ptolemaic-Roman periods. Their task was apparently to transport the mummified animals to the cemeteries. They could be carried by hand, or transported on a sledge or wheeled cart. Apart from such creatures as the Apis bull (whose burial was a relatively infrequent event) the numbers of animals mummified and buried all over Egypt at this period was immense. The practice with regard to the majority of animal mummies was to inter them periodically. The ibises and falcons interred at Saqqara were buried on one specific day every year, while at Athribis falcons were buried every month, and at Kom Ombo at irregular intervals.

190. Mummified cat with imitation of the animal's head in linen and plaster. The lozenge-patterning of the interlocking wrappings is a feature which had been adapted from the mummification of humans. Roman Period, after 30 BC. Provenance unknown. H. 53 cm.

Cats

Among the animals most frequently mummified was the cat, which was mainly associated with the goddess Bastet. Although originally associated with the lioness, Bastet later came to be linked with cats, and was regularly depicted as a cat or a cat-headed woman. Herodotus states that dead cats were taken to Bubastis in the Delta, the centre of the cult of Bastet, and there embalmed and buried in sacred receptacles. The remains of a great cat cemetery have indeed been found there, but it had been extensively plundered before archaeologists investigated the site. However, cat cemeteries have been found in many other parts of Egypt (notably at Saqqara and Thebes), perhaps owing their existence to Bastet's association with lion deities such as Sekhmet, worshipped in various places. Radiology of cat mummies in museums has shown that most of them had died within one of two age-ranges: three to four months and one to two years. This uniformity of ages strongly suggests that they had not died natural deaths, and some X-rays provide confirmation of this. The neck-vertebrae of several cats are seen to have been dislocated, while others showed head injuries, suggesting that they had been killed specifically for mummification, perhaps during periodic 'culls' on the temple estates. The majority of cat mummies have a distinctive shape, created by extending the front legs down the body and tucking up the back legs (see fig. 188). This produced an elongated package, which was completed by a stylised image of a cat's head created in dyed linen or drawn in ink on the wrappings, the ears shaped from linen. Occasionally this shape was varied: one famous example in the British Museum was wrapped to resemble a human mummy, with prominent 'shoulders' and a body tapering to the feet (fig. 196). The wrapped mummies were sometimes enclosed in cat-shaped coffins of painted wood, or even inside hollow-cast bronze cat-statues (see fig. 191). Small examples were placed in bronze relic boxes, with figures of cats on the top.

Sacred reptiles and insects

Several classes of reptiles are represented among the mummified fauna. Snakes (sacred to the creator-god Atum) occur, sometimes mummified separately and placed in bronze relic boxes, sometimes in groups wrapped in linen (groups of

191. Just as human mummies were often placed inside coffins shaped like the body, those of animals were sometimes encased in a comparable manner. This wooden coffin made for a cat is almost indistinguishable from a piece of sculpture, but is hollow inside to receive a mummy. Ptolemaic or Roman Period, after 305 BC. Provenance unknown. H. 35.5 cm.

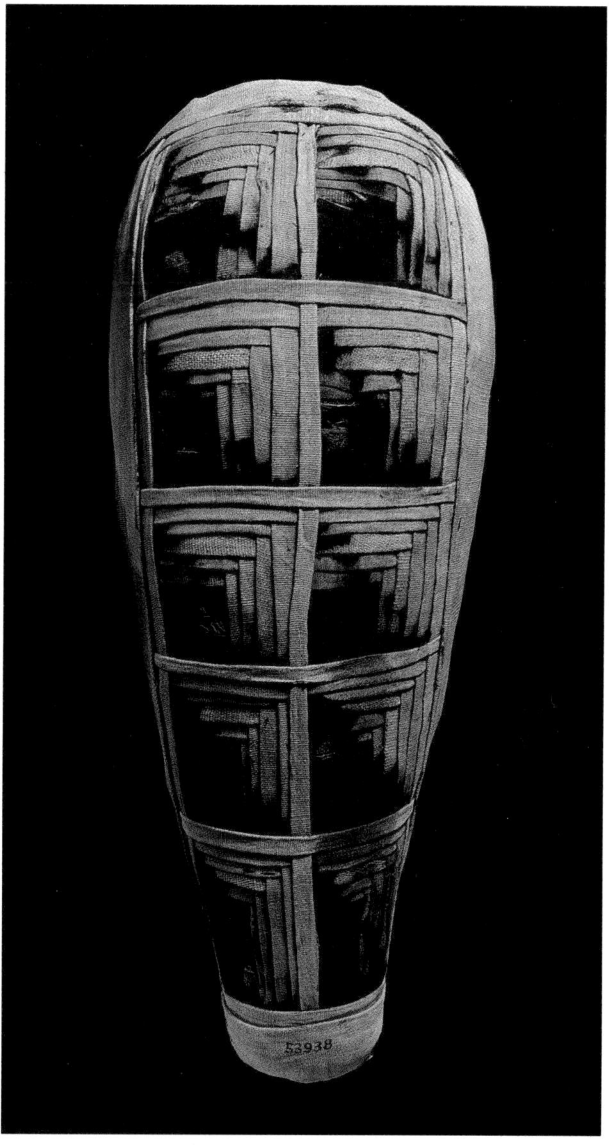

192. Mummy of an ibis wrapped in patterned bandaging. Ptolemaic or Roman Period, after 305 BC. From Abydos. L. 43.2 cm.

vipers were prepared in this way). Mummified lizards also occur, but the most common of the reptile mummies was the crocodile, the sacred animal of the god Sebek. His cult was maintained at various sites, notably Kom Ombo and Shedet (Crocodilopolis). The crocodiles were kept in temple lakes, and force-fed while being physically restrained by holding them down. Large numbers of crocodiles were mummified. One of the biggest crocodile cemeteries was situated east of the temple of Kom Ombo. Another major source was the 'crocodile grottoes' at Maabda, opposite Manfalut in Middle Egypt, visited by many European travellers before they were destroyed in the late nineteenth century. These naturally-formed subterranean galleries were used in the Ptolemaic and Roman periods to house large numbers of mummified crocodiles. These

included very large specimens, some up to 10 m long, individually mummified. There were also small ones (30–50 cm long) made up into bundles, sometimes also including the eggs of the animals. It is supposed that these grottoes – which also contained the mummies of humans as well as of other animals – were related to a local crocodile cult. This seems to have been popular with local Roman garrison troops, for the grottoes also yielded shields and a suit of ceremonial armour made from crocodile-skin (see fig. 193).

A very large crocodile mummy in the British Museum is remarkable because it is really a group, comprising several animals. There are two fully mature animals (perhaps a male and a female), one mounted on the back of the other, and surrounded by numerous baby crocodiles. A comparable 'family group' of crocodiles was found at Lahun in the Faiyum, though here the uppermost adult animal had been cut into pieces. Possibly the arrangement of the two large crocodiles was meant to simulate a mating-position.

Amond the smallest creatures to be mummified were lizards and scarab beetles. The latter, sacred to the sun god, were enclosed in small bronze or stone boxes surmounted by a sculpted image of the beetle.

Sacred birds

Birds were also mummified extensively. Perhaps the most numerous were mummies of the ibis, the bird sacred to the god Thoth. Many ibis mummies have been found at Saqqara, where they were placed in catacombs in conical pottery jars (see fig. 190). An alternative form of container was an ibis-shaped sculpture, comprising a hollow wooden body to contain the mummy, to which a bronze head and feet were fitted. Falcons were also mummified in

193. Ceremonial cuirass and helmet made of crocodile skin, and C14 dated to the third century AD. It was discovered in the grottoes at Maabda, opposite Manfalut. The many mummified crocodiles which were deposited there in the Roman Period probably attest to a local cult, in the rituals of which this armour was perhaps worn.

194. Conical pottery jars containing ibis mummies, stacked in one of the subterranean galleries of the Sacred Animal Necropolis at Saqqara.

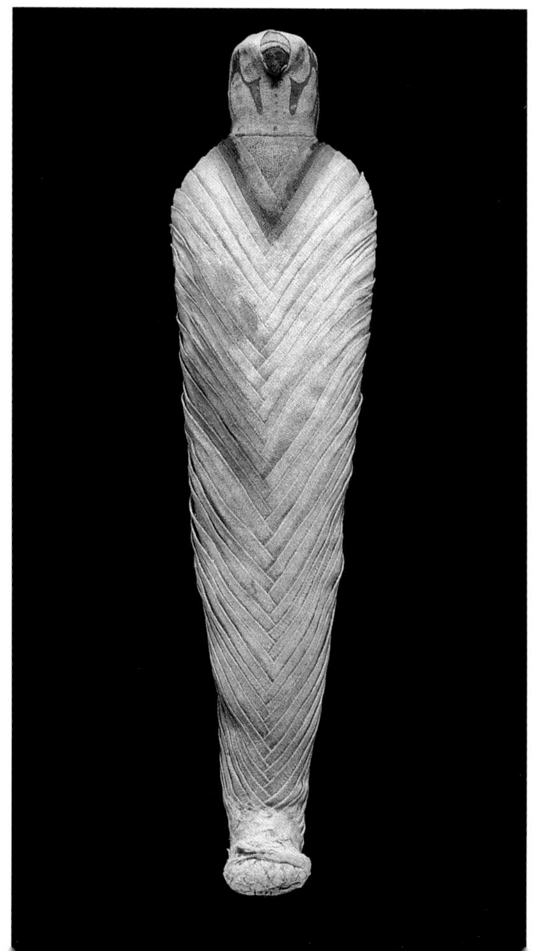

195. Mummified falcon, with elaborately fashioned features, and wrappings arranged in overlapping layers. Ptolemaic or Roman Period, after 305 BC. From Saqqara. H. 39.4 cm.

large numbers (see fig. 191). Most of these were deposited without coffins, although there are exceptions. Examples from Saqqara were placed in wooden coffins, while an example of unknown provenance (Roman Period) had a painted cartonnage mummy-case which was fitted inside a stone shrine-shaped chest.

The process of animal mummification

196. Mummified cat with wrappings dyed in contrasting colours arranged in a geometrical meander pattern. Like other animal mummies, this specimen has a painted headpiece realistically modelled in linen and plaster, but the tapering shape of the body is unusual for a cat, and appears to imitate the form of human mummies. Roman Period, after 30 BC. From Abydos. H. 46 cm.

197. Radiography of the cat mummy shown in fig. 196 reveals that the body inside is not that of a mature animal, as the wrappings suggest. It is actually composed of the skull of an adult cat, attached to the body of a kitten which died at about the age of three or four months. This composite corpse occupies less than half the space within the wrappings, and pieces of wood and scraps of linen were used to help create the desired shape.

In the most elaborate instances of animal burials, such as those of the Apis bulls, the techniques of mummification employed followed those used on human bodies, including evisceration, drying, and wrapping. These operations were carried out in a ritualised context, accompanied by appropriate incantations.

For the millions of ibises, falcons, cats, fish and other animals, embalmed as votive offerings, a much simpler approach was employed. Evisceration was not always performed. When it was, the body cavity would be packed with sand or mud, perhaps mixed with natron. The internal organs do not seem to have been separately preserved; apart from the sacred bulls, no mummified animals are known to have had canopic jars. The bodies were dried or coated with resin, before being wrapped in layers of linen, soaked in resin or natron. Smaller creatures such as ibises might be simply immersed in molten resin, and wrapped. Fish were simply slit open and dried by being covered with a mixture of mud and salt, and buried in sand.

The positioning of the limbs of animal mummies and the method by which they were wrapped led to distinctive forms being created for individual creatures, the shape of the bundle being based on that of the animal's body. For cats, bulls, rams, crocodiles, falcons and gazelles, the head was often modelled in linen, with facial features represented in coloured linen, in paint or ink. The limbs were usually confined within the bundle (as in the majority of human mummies), and for some creatures this meant distorting the body. Hence cats assumed an elongated shape, while bulls, gazelles and rams had their limbs folded underneath their bodies. In some of these packages, substantial parts of the body were omitted, and reeds were used extensively to create the desired shape.

In some cases, the bundle has been made to resemble a human mummy, with prominent shoulders and the body tapering towards a projecting foot. Examples of this type usually contain extensive packing to create the appropriate shape, while the head of the animal may be elaborately modelled in folded linen or may even be covered by a bronze or cartonnage headpiece comparable to the mummy-masks of humans. Wrappings were often dyed in contrasting colours and elaborately arranged in geometric patterns.

Animal mummies often contain an incomplete body, or parts of more than one animal. This state of affairs has been found in bovine mummies (though not those of Apis bulls), as well as in those of birds and crocodiles. In the same way, some cat mummies are found to contain only a head, or the head, forelegs and a few other bones. Some bird mummies contain only a few bones, while gazelle

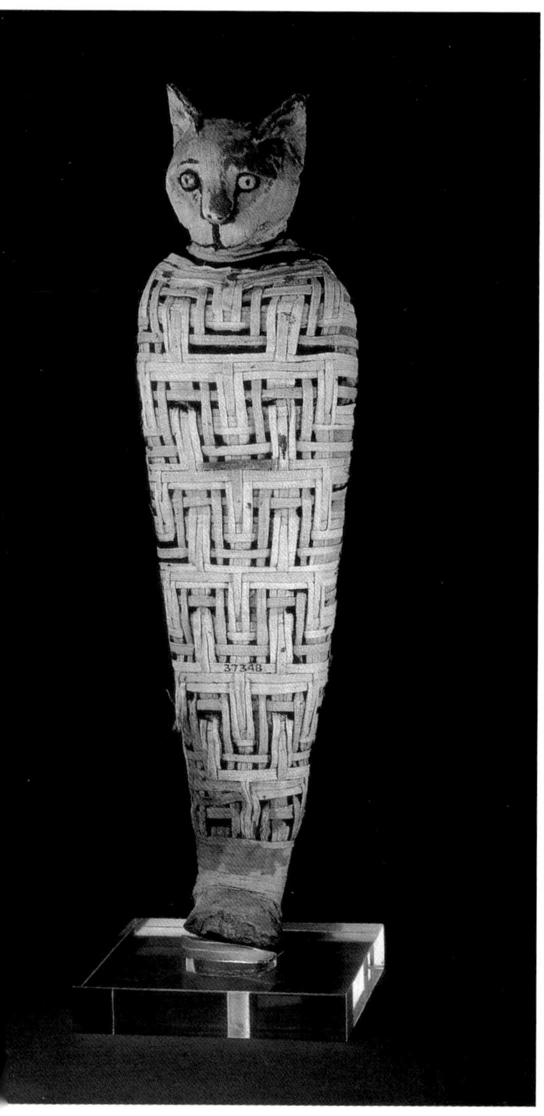

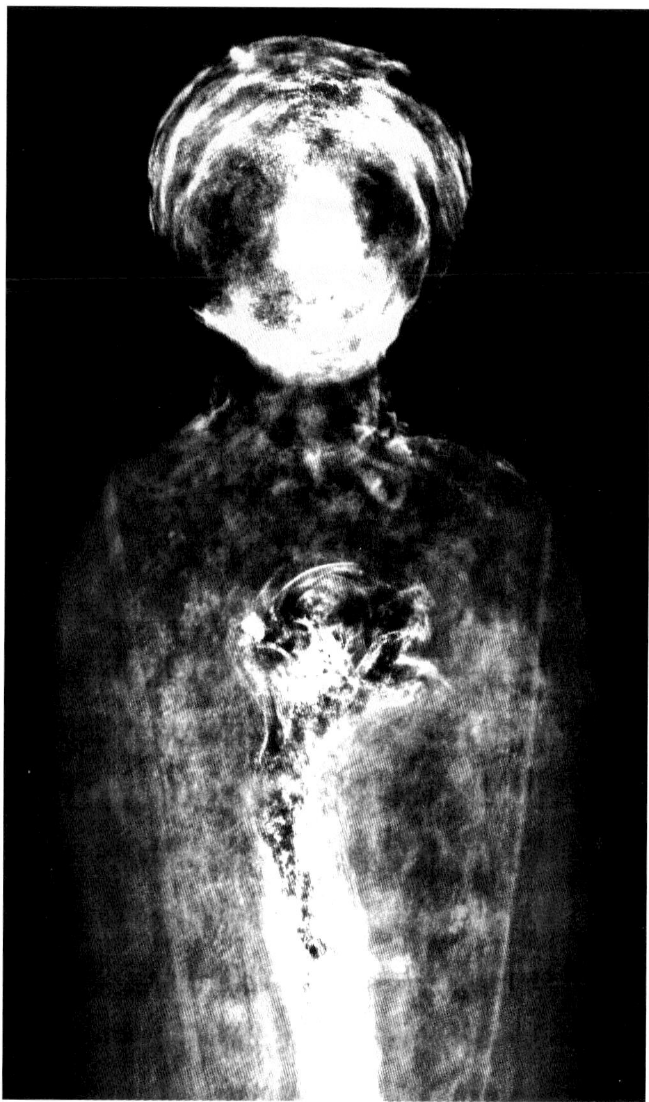

mummies have been found which appear to contain little more than the animal's horns, the shape of the body being represented by bundles of reeds.

The external appearance of an animal mummy may then be deceptive. One of the most imposing mummies in the British Museum (see fig. 196) has been wrapped as though it contains an adult cat, yet X-rays have revealed that it contains the body of a tiny young kitten, probably about 3–4 months old, on to which had been placed the head of an adult animal (see fig. 197).

Some of these cases may represent deliberate attempts by the embalmers to deceive the pilgrim who had paid for an animal to be mummified, or they may have been produced at times when the demand for animals outstripped supply. Yet this may not be the whole story; we cannot be sure that the purchaser expected the mummy-package to contain a complete body. In terms of the cult significance of such votive offerings, a portion of the body may have been sufficient. Perhaps (as was the case with human mummies) the creation of an eternal image using parts of the animal's body was sufficient to fulfill the religious function. The incomplete state of many animal mummies finds a parallel in the often irregular contents of human mummies of the Roman period, and both phenomena may share a common ideological background.

For the most part, only temple animals received elaborate coffins and sarcophagi, but coffins for individual animal mummies are also known. Like the anthropoid coffins of humans, these were sometimes sculpted images of the creature, hollowed out to recieve the mummy. Cat coffins of wood and bronze are known, and ibises were sometimes placed inside the hollow bodies of images of the living bird, although the majority were placed in conical pottery jars. Smaller animals were placed in relic boxes of bronze or wood, with a three-dimensional image of the animal on the top (see fig. 198). Significantly, these coffins do not carry funerary inscriptions or images, indicating that the creatures within were not assimilated to humans, but were simply regarded as offerings to the gods.

198. Bronze reliquary to contain the mummy of an ichneumon, an animal sacred to several deities, including Horus, Atum and Wadjit. Large numbers of smaller creatures were placed inside containers of this kind after mummification. As in this case, a hieroglyphic inscription was often incised around the box, giving the name and parentage of the dedicator. Late Period, 664–305 BC. From Thebes.

Other animal burials

In some cases, the animals interred were clearly beloved pets or companions of their owners. Pets were frequently immortalised in the wall-decoration of tomb-chapels or in scenes on funerary stelae, and were sometimes given a formal burial according to procedures normally reserved for humans. The burial of three donkeys in a grave of the 1st Dynasty at Tarkhan may be an early instance of this practice, although the reason for the animals' presence there is not certain. An Old Kingdom tomb at Giza was prepared at the king's expense for one of his guard-dogs, Abutiu. According to an inscription in the tomb chapel, the king ordered that the dog be provided with a coffin, fine linen and incense – clearly a burial such as a distinguished human might expect. Another example is the burial of a dog named Aya, interred at Thebes during the Middle Kingdom in a wooden coffin which closely reproduced the shape and decoration of coffins made for humans at the same period. The inscriptions included the offering formula, promising funerary offerings for the dog, who is described as 'beloved of her mistress'. The cost of producing such an expensive piece of burial equipment for a dog indicates that the mistress (whose name unfortunately we do not know) belonged to a wealthy family. A later example of even more exalted status is the cat of Prince Tuthmosis, the eldest son of King Amenhotep III (*c.* 1390–1352 BC). This animal, simply named Tamyt ('The [female] cat') was buried in a limestone sarcophagus, which again imitated the shape and decoration of coffins made for human burials. It is inscribed with hieroglyphic texts identifying Tamyt as an Osiris, and invoking the protection of the goddesses Nut, Isis and Nephthys and the Sons of Horus – exactly as would be done for a deceased human. The analogy is carried further by the inclusion of a carved figure of the deceased cat before a heaped offering table. In these cases the animal was assimilated to a human being, rather than being regarded as a representative of a deity. Such instances, however, are rare. Among others are a few mummified gazelles and a baboon found at Thebes – perhaps the pets of the high-ranking women of the 21st to 25th Dynasties – but otherwise, the mummification of animals arose from their association with divinities.

Bibliography

Abbreviations

ASAE — *Annales du Service des Antiquités de l'Égypte*

JEA — *Journal of Egyptian Archaeology*

JESHO — *Journal of the Economic and Social History of the Orient*

JSSEA — *Journal of the Society for the Study of Egyptian Antiquities*

MDAIK — *Mitteilungen des Deutschen Archäologischen Instituts Abteilung Kairo*

OMRO — *Oudheidkundige Mededelingen uit het Rijksmuseum van Oudheden te Leiden*

SAGA — *Studien zur Archäologie und Geschichte Altägyptens*

SAK — *Studien zur Altägyptischen Kultur*

General works

Andrews, C., *Egyptian Mummies* (London, 1984).

D'Auria, S., Lacovara, P. and Roehrig, C., *Mummies and Magic. The Funerary Arts of Ancient Egypt* (Boston, 1988).

Germer, R., *Mummies. Life After Death in Ancient Egypt* (Munich, 1997).

Spencer, A.J., *Death in Ancient Egypt* (Harmondsworth, 1982).

Chapter 1

Assmann, J., 'Death and initiation in the funerary religion of ancient Egypt', in *Religion and Philosophy in Ancient Egypt* (Yale Egyptological Studies 3) (New Haven, 1989), 135–59.

Bolshakov, A.O., *Man and His Double in Egyptian Ideology of the Old Kingdom* (Wiesbaden, 1997).

Englund, G., *Akh – Une Notion Religieuse dans l'Egypte Pharaonique* (Uppsala, 1978).

Gardiner, A.H., *The Attitude of the Ancient Egyptians to Death and the Dead* (Cambridge, 1935).

Gardiner, A.H., and Sethe, K., *Egyptian Letters to the Dead Mainly from the Old and Middle Kingdoms* (London, 1928).

George, B., *Zu den Altägyptischen Vorstellungen vom Schatten als Seele* (Bonn, 1970).

Hornung, E., *Idea into Image. Essays on Ancient Egyptian Thought* (New York, 1992).

Janssen, J.M.A., 'On the ideal lifetime of the Egyptians', *OMRO* 31 (1950), 33–44.

Leahy, A., 'Death by fire in ancient Egypt', *JESHO* 27 (1984), 199–206.

Lloyd, A.B., 'Psychology and society in the ancient Egyptian cult of the dead', in *Religion and Philosophy in Ancient Egypt* (Yale Egyptological Studies 3) (New Haven, 1989), 117–33.

Quirke, S., *Ancient Egyptian Religion* (London, 1992).

Seeber, C., *Untersuchungen zur Darstellung des Totengerichts im Alten Ägypten* (Munich and Berlin, 1976).

Zabkar, L.V., *A Study of the Ba Concept in Ancient Egyptian Texts* (Chicago, 1968).

Zandee, J., *Death as an Enemy According to Ancient Egyptian Conceptions* (Leiden, 1960).

Chapter 2

Bierbrier, M.L. (ed.), *Portraits and Masks. Burial Customs in Roman Egypt* (London, 1997).

Blackman, A.M., 'Some notes on the Ancient Egyptian practice of washing the dead', *JEA* 5 (1918), 117–24, pls XVIII–XIX.

Cockburn, A. and E., and Reyman, T.A. (eds), *Mummies, Disease and Ancient Cultures*, 2nd edition (Cambridge, 1998).

Corcoran, L.H., *Portrait Mummies from Roman Egypt (I–IV centuries AD)* (Chicago, 1995).

Diodorus Siculus, *The Library of History*, Book I, trans C.H. Oldfather (London and New York, 1933).

Dodson, A., *The Canopic Equipment of the Kings of Egypt* (London and New York, 1994).

Doxiadis, E., *The Mysterious Fayum Portraits. Faces from Ancient Egypt* (London, 1995).

Frandsen, P.J., 'On the root *nfr* and a "clever" remark on embalming', in Osing, J. and Nielsen, E. K. (eds), *The Heritage of Ancient Egypt. Studies in Honour of Erik Iversen* (Copenhagen, 1992), 49–62.

Goyon, J.-C., *Rituels Funéraires de l'Ancienne Égypte* (Paris, 1972).

Grimm, G., *Die Römischen Mumienmasken aus Ägypten* (Wiesbaden, 1974).

Harris, J.E., and Wente, E.F. (eds), *An X-ray Atlas of the Royal Mummies* (Chicago and London, 1980).

Ikram, S., and Dodson, A., *The Mummy in Ancient Egypt. Equipping the Dead for Eternity* (London, 1998).

Lipinska, J., 'A note on the problem of false mummies', *Études et Travaux* 5 (1971), 66–9.

Lloyd, A.B., *Herodotus Book II. Commentary 1–98* (Leiden, 1976).

Lüscher, B., *Untersuchungen zu Ägyptischen Kanopenkästen vom Alten Reich bis zum Ende der Zweiten Zwischenzeit* (Hildesheim, 1990).

Nicholson, P.T., and Shaw, I. (eds), *Ancient Egyptian Materials and Technology* (Cambridge, 2000).

Parlasca, K., *Mumienporträts und Verwandte Denkmäler* (Wiesbaden, 1966).

Rogge, E., 'Die Maske eines Königs, Puschkin-Museum I 1 a 4686, und die königlichen Bestattungen des Alten und Mittleren Reiches', in Bietak, M., Holaubek, J., Mukarovsky, H. and Satzinger, H. (eds), *Zwischen den Beiden Ewigkeiten. Festschrift Gertrud Thausing* (Vienna, 1994), 175–90, Taf. VII.

Shore, A.F., 'Human and divine mummification', in A.B. Lloyd (ed.), *Studies in Pharaonic Religion and Society in Honour of J. Gwyn Griffiths* (London, 1992), 226–35.

Taylor, J.H., *Unwrapping a Mummy: the Life, Death and Embalming of Horemkenesi* (London, 1995).

Walker, S., and Bierbrier, M.L. (eds), *Ancient Faces. Mummy Portraits from Roman Egypt* (London, 1997).

Chapter 3

Barta, W., *Die Altägyptische Opferliste von der Frühzeit bis zur Griechisch-Römischen Epoche* (Berlin, 1963).

Barta, W., *Aufbau und Bedeutung der Altägyptischen Opferformel* (Glückstadt, 1968).

Breasted, J.H., Jr, *Egyptian Servant Statues* (Washington, 1948).

Ikram, S., *Choice Cuts: Meat Production in Ancient Egypt* (Orientalia Lovaniensia Analecta 69) (Leuven, 1995).

Tooley, A.M.J., *Egyptian Models and Scenes* (Princes Risborough, 1995).

Chapter 4

Aubert, J.-F. and L., *Statuettes Égyptiennes. Chaouabtis, Ouchebtis* (Paris, 1974).

Chappaz, J.-L., *Les Figurines Funéraires Égyptiennes du Musée d'Art et d'Histoire et de Quelques Collections Privées* (Geneva, 1984).

Haynes, J.L. and Leprohon, R.J., 'Napatan *shawabtis* in the Royal Ontario Museum', *JSSEA* 17, no. 1/2 (Jan/April 1987), 18–32.

Martin, G.T., '*Shabtis* of private persons in the Amarna Period', *MDAIK* 42 (1986), 109–29, Taf 8–19.

Pumpenmeier, F., *Eine Gunstgabe von Seiten des Königs. Ein Extrasepulkrales Schabtidepot Qen-Amuns in Abydos* (SAGA 19) (Heidelberg, 1998).

Schneider, H.D., *Shabtis*, I–III (Leiden, 1977).

Spanel, D., 'Notes on the terminology for funerary figurines', *SAK* 13 (1986), 249–53.

Stewart, H.M., *Egyptian Shabtis* (Princes Risborough, 1995).

Chapter 5

Assmann, J., 'Priorität und interesse: das problem der Ramessidischen Beamtengräber', in Assmann, J., Burkard, G. and Davies, V. (eds), *Problems and Priorities in Egyptian Archaeology* (London and New York, 1987), 31–41.

Černy, J., *A Community of Workmen at Thebes in the Ramesside Period* (Cairo, 1973).

Edwards, I.E.S., *The Pyramids of Egypt*, revised edition (London, 1993).

Eigner, D., *Die Monumentalen Grabbauten der Spätzeit in der Thebanischen Nekropole* (Vienna, 1984).

Garstang, J., *The Burial Customs of Ancient Egypt as Illustrated by Tombs of the Middle Kingdom* (London, 1907).

Hornung, E., *The Valley of the Kings. Horizon of Eternity* (New York, 1990).

Janssen, J.J., and Pestman, P.W., 'Burial and inheritance in the community of the necropolis workmen at Thebes', *JESHO* 11 (1968), 137–70, pls I–II.

Kamrin, J., *The Cosmos of Khnumhotep II at Beni Hasan* (London and New York, 1999).

Lehner, M., *The Complete Pyramids* (London, 1997).

Lesko, L.H. (ed.), *Pharaoh's Workers. The Villagers of Deir el Medina* (Ithaca and London, 1994).

Manniche, L., *City of the Dead. Thebes in Egypt* (London, 1987).

Mostafa, M.M.F., *Untersuchungen zu Opfertafeln im Alten Reich* (Hildesheim, 1982).

Munro, P., *Die Spätägyptischen Totenstelen* (Glückstadt, 1973).

Reeves, C.N., *The Complete Tutankhamun* (London, 1990).

Reeves, C.N., *Valley of the Kings. The Decline of a Royal Necropolis* (London and New York, 1990).

Reeves, N. and Wilkinson, R.H., *The Complete Valley of the Kings. Tombs and Treasures of Egypt's Greatest Pharaohs* (London, 1996).

Reisner, G.A., *The Development of the Egyptian Tomb Down to the Accession of Cheops* (Cambridge, Oxford and London, 1936).

Seidlmayer, S.J., *Gräbfelder aus dem Übergang vom Alten zum Mittleren Reich* (SAGA 1) (Heidelberg, 1990).

Seyfried, K.J., 'Entwicklung in der Grabarchitektur des Neuen Reiches als eine weitere Quelle für Theologische Konzeptionen der Ramessidenzeit', in Assmann, J., Burkard, G. and Davies, V. (eds), *Problems and Priorities in Egyptian Archaeology* (London and New York, 1987), 219–53, pls 20–5.

Stadelmann, R., *Die Ägyptischen Pyramiden. Vom Ziegelbau zum Weltwunder* (Mainz am Rhein, 1985).

Strudwick, N. and H., *Thebes in Egypt. A Guide to the Tombs and Temples of Ancient Luxor* (London, 1999).

Valbelle, D., *Les Ouvriers de la Tombe. Deir el-Médineh a l'Époque Ramesside* (Cairo, 1985).

Chapter 6

Allen, T.G., *The Book of the Dead, or Going Forth by Day* (Chicago, 1974).

Andrews, C., *Amulets of Ancient Egypt* (London, 1994).

Assmann, J., 'Egyptian mortuary liturgies', in S. Israelit-Groll (ed.) *Studies in Egyptology Presented to Miriam Lichtheim*, I (Jerusalem, 1990), 1–45.

Barguet, P., *Le Livre des Morts des Anciens Egyptiens* (Paris, 1967).

Faulkner, R.O., *The Ancient Egyptian Pyramid Texts* (Oxford, 1969).

Faulkner, R.O., *The Ancient Egyptian Coffin Texts*, I–III (Warminster, 1973–8).

Faulkner, R.O., *The Ancient Egyptian Book of the Dead* (edited by C. Andrews), revised edition (London, 1985).

Hornung, E., *The Ancient Egyptian Books of the Afterlife*, trans David Lorton (Ithaca and London, 1999).

Lesko, L.H., *The Ancient Egyptian Book of Two Ways* (Berkeley, Los Angeles and London, 1977).

Niwinski, A., *Studies on the Illustrated Theban Funerary Papyri of the 11th and 10th Centuries BC* (Freiburg and Göttingen, 1989).

Pinch, G., *Magic in Ancient Egypt* (London, 1994).

Quirke, S. and Forman, W., *Hieroglyphs and the Afterlife in Ancient Egypt* (London, 1996).

Raven, M.J., 'Corn-mummies', *OMRO* 63 (1982), 7–38.

Settgast, J., *Untersuchungen zu Altägyptischen Bestattungsdarstellungen* (Glückstadt, Hamburg and New York, 1963).

Silvano, F., 'Le reticelle funerarie nell' Antico Egitto: proposte di interpretazione', in *Egitto e Vicino Oriente* 3 (1980), 83–95, Tav. I–II.

Smith, M., *The Liturgy of Opening the Mouth for Breathing* (Oxford, 1993).

van Walsem, R., 'The PSŠ-KF. An investigation of an ancient Egyptian funerary instrument', *OMRO* 59–60 (1978–9), 193–249, pl. 38.

Werbrouck, M., *Les Pleureuses dans l'Égypte Ancienne* (Brussels, 1938).

Chapter 7

Donadoni Roveri, A.M., *I Sarcofagi Egizi dalle Origini alla Fine dell' Antico Regno* (Rome, 1969).

Hayes, W.C., *Royal Sarcophagi of the XVIII Dynasty* (Princeton, 1935).

Lapp, G., *Typologie der Särge und Sargkammern von der 6 bis 13 Dynastie* (SAGA 7) (Heidelberg, 1993).

Niwinski, A., *21st Dynasty Coffins from Thebes. Chronological and Typological Studies* (Mainz am Rhein, 1988).

Taylor, J.H., *Egyptian Coffins* (Princes Risborough, 1989).

van Walsem, R., *The Coffin of Djedmonthuiufankh in the National Museum of Antiquities at Leiden*, I (Leiden, 1997).

Willems, H., *Chests of Life. A Study of the Typology and Conceptual Development of Middle Kingdom Standard Class Coffins* (Leiden, 1988).

Willems, H., *The Coffin of Heqata (Cairo JdE 36418)* (Orientalia Lovaniensia Analecta 70) (Leuven, 1996).

Chapter 8

Boessneck, J., *Die Tierwelt des Alten Ägypten* (Munich, 1988).

De Gorostarzu, X., 'Lettre sur deux tombeaux de crocodiles decouverts au Fayoum', *ASAE* 2 (1901), 182–4.

Houlihan, P.F., *The Animal World of the Pharaohs* (Cairo, 1996).

Kessler, D., *Die Heiligen Tiere und der König, I: Beiträge zu Organisation, Kult und Theologie der spätzeitlichen Tierfriedhöfe* (Wiesbaden, 1989).

Malek, J., *The Cat in Ancient Egypt* (London, 1993).

Mond, R., Myers, O.H., *et al.*, *The Bucheum*, I–III (London, 1934).

Vos, R.L., *The Apis Embalming Ritual. P. Vindob. 3873* (Orientalia Lovaniensia Analecta 50) (Leuven, 1993).

Chronology

(All dates before 664 BC are approximate.)

Early Dynastic Period

1st Dynasty	*c.* 3100–2890 BC
2nd Dynasty	*c.* 2890–2686 BC

Old Kingdom

3rd Dynasty	*c.* 2686–2613 BC
4th Dynasty	*c.* 2613–2494 BC
5th Dynasty	*c.* 2494–2345 BC
6th Dynasty	*c.* 2345–2181 BC

First Intermediate Period

7th/8th Dynasties	*c.* 2181–2125 BC
9th/10th Dynasties	*c.* 2160–2130 BC, *c.* 2125–2025 BC

Middle Kingdom

11th Dynasty	*c.* 2125–1985 BC
12th Dynasty	*c.* 1985–1795 BC
13th Dynasty	*c.* 1795–1650 BC

Second Intermediate Period

14th Dynasty	*c.* 1750–1650 BC
15th Dynasty (Hyksos)	*c.* 1650–1550 BC
16th Dynasty	*c.* 1650–1550 BC
17th Dynasty	*c.* 1650–1550 BC

New Kingdom

18th Dynasty	*c.* 1550–1295 BC
19th Dynasty	*c.* 1295–1186 BC
20th Dynasty	*c.* 1186–1069 BC

Third Intermediate Period

21st Dynasty	*c.* 1069–945 BC
22nd Dynasty	*c.* 945–715 BC
23rd Dynasty	*c.* 818–715 BC
24th Dynasty	*c.* 727–715 BC
25th Dynasty (Nubian or Kushite)	*c.* 747–656 BC

Late Period

26th Dynasty (Saite)	664–525 BC
27th Dynasty (Persian Kings)	525–404 BC
28th Dynasty	404–399 BC
29th Dynasty	399–380 BC
30th Dynasty	380–343 BC
Persian Kings	343–332 BC
Macedonian Kings	332–305 BC

Ptolemaic Period	305–30 BC
Roman Period	30 BC–AD 395

Illustration References

Front cover EA 6678
Back cover EA 51819
Page 6 EA 22941
Map drawn by Christine Barratt

1. Red-Head: John Williams
2. EA 32751
3. EA 55336
4. EA 9524
5. EA 29554
6. Cairo Museum JE 30948
7. EA 10554/17
8. EA 10470/7
9. EA 8653
10. EA 10471/14
11. EA 9901/3
12. EA 9980
13. EA 69851
14. EA 27735
15. EA 30839
16. EA 9911/2
17. EA 9901/3
18. Left EA 61083, right EA 58783
19. Hierakonpolis Expedition Archives; photographer R. Friedman
20. Roemer-Pelizaeus Museum, Hildesheim
21. From *The Rock Tombs of Meir*, Vol. 5 by A.M. Blackman, pl. 43. By kind permission of the Committee of the Egypt Exploration Society
22. EA 22939
23. EA 22939
24. EA 24957
25. EA 8409, 8410, 58942
26. EA 43218
27. EA 29996
28. EA 6732
29. EA 6516, 6518, 6542
30. EA 29472
31. EA 14438, 23207, 55367, 66417
32. James H. McKerrow, PhD, MD
33. EA 35084
34. EA 58780
35. EA 9535, 9544, 53996
36. EA 36635
37. EA 35808
38. EA 25568
39. From *A Contribution to the Study of Mummification* by G. Elliot Smith, pl. III
40. EA 8389, 8401, 8403,15563-4, 15568, 15569, 15573, 15578
41. EA 59197-59200
42. EA 9562-5
43. EA 36625-8
44. EA 10077
45. EA 6652
46. Rijksmuseum van Oudheden, Leiden
47. EA 46631
48. Katz Pictures
49. EA 6665
50. Metropolitan Museum of Art, New York
51. EA 29776
52. EA 21810
53. EA 6704
54. Hierakonpolis Expedition Archives; photographer R. Friedman
55. EA 5341
56. EA 1450 (1907-10-15,460)
57. EA 1277
58. EA 682
59. EA 1260
60. EA 2378
61. EA 45195
62. EA 41576
63. EA 41573
64. EA 2463
65. EA 30716
66. EA 41574
67. EA 9524
68. EA 21702
69. EA 32613
70. EA 30727
71. EA 41578
72. EA 47570
73. Drawn by Claire Thorne
74. EA 8703
75. EA 8893
76. EA 16672
77. EA 41672
78. EA 24390, 32556, 49343, 50991, 58081
79. EA 16006
80. EA 32191
81. EA 51819
82. EA 65372/53892
83. EA 8522-3, 14423-6
84. EA 8644
85. EA 8894
86. EA 65206
87. EA 22818
88. EA 41549
89. EA 8900, 13808, 33959, 53980, 65205
90. EA 32708
91. EA 30400
92. EA 8724, 67742
93. Left EA 64347, right EA 66822
94. The Illustrated London News Picture Library
95. EA 32692
96. Left EA 56929, right EA 56930
97. Copy by Nina de Garis Davies
98. Red-Head: John Williams
99. Nigel Strudwick
100. Red-Head: John Williams
101. Red-Head: John Williams
102. John Taylor
103. Drawn by Claire Thorne
104. Drawn by Claire Thorne
105. Drawn by Claire Thorne
106. Drawn by Claire Thorne
107. EA 35018
108. EA 1165
109. EA 1242
110. EA 1848
111. EA 1179
112. EA 1783
113. EA 585
114. EA 990
115. EA 289
116. EA 149
117. Left EA 37899, right EA 65354
118. EA 8468
119. From *The Rock Tombs of Meir*, Vol. 5 by A.M. Blackman, pl. 18. By kind permission of the Committee of the Egypt Exploration Society
120. EA 65430
121. EA 29594
122. EA 30715
123. EA 31
124. EA 36
125. Red-Head: John Williams
126. Copy by Nina de Garis Davies
127. EA 718
128. EA 15659
129. EA 461
130. EA 359, 372
131. EA 22941
132. EA 22941
133. EA 9901/5
134. Larger set, left EA 5526, right EA 6123; smaller set EA 58404
135. EA 35273–5
136. EA 30840
137. EA 73807
138. EA 10471/20
139. Courtesy of Reading Museum Service (Reading Borough Council)
140. Copy by Henry Salt
141. EA 9919
142. EA 40928
143. EA 6714
144. Griffith Institute, Ashmolean Museum, Oxford
145. Top row, left to right EA 22991, 8309, 7435; middle row, left to right EA 8327, 8332, 3123, 23123, 14622; bottom row, left to right EA 8088, 59500, 20639
146. Left to right EA 7849, 14653, 24705, 29369
147. EA 24401
148. EA 29593
149. EA 41544-7
150. EA 18175
151. EA 2371
152. Heini Schneebeli, EA 883
153. EA 50702
154. EA 60745
155. Left EA 22913, right EA 23046
156. EA 9737
157. EA 52888
158. EA 71620
159. EA 46629
160. EA 46631
161. EA 30841
162. EA 30841
163. Cambridge, Fitzwilliam Museum
164. EA 52950
165. EA 54521
166. Drawn by A Boyce EA 63635
167. EA 48001
168. EA 24789
169. EA 22941
170. EA 22941
171. EA 30721
172. EA 6662
173. EA 6686
174. EA 6672
175. EA 6676
176. EA 27735
177. EA 6693
178. EA 6708
179. EA 29584
180. EA 22108
181. EA 6773
182. EA 6681
183. Carol A.R. Andrews
184. EA 1491
185. Egypt Exploration Society
186. Left EA 59459, right EA 59460
187. Egypt Exploration Society
188. EA 1694
189. EA 1356
190. EA 6752
191. EA 35853
192. EA 53938
193. EA 5473
194. Photograph by Dr Paul Nicholson, reprinted by kind permission of the Egypt Exploration Society
195. EA 68006
196. EA 37348
197. EA 37348
198. EA 61604

Index

Page numbers in *italics* refer to illustrations